SAMUEL GOLDWYN PRESENTS

Other Books by ALVIN H. MARILL:

The Cinema of Edward G. Robinson
Katharine Hepburn: A Pictorial Study
The Films of Anthony Quinn
The Films of Sidney Poitier
Mitchum's Movies

SAMUEL GOLDWYN PRESENTS

Alvin H. Marill

SOUTH BRUNSWICK AND NEW YORK: A. S. BARNES AND COMPANY
LONDON: THOMAS YOSELOFF LTD

A. S. Barnes and Co., Inc.
Cranbury, New Jersey 08512

Thomas Yoseloff Ltd
Magdalen House
136–148 Tooley Street
London SE1 2TT, England

Library of Congress Cataloging in Publication Data

Marill, Alvin H.
  Samuel Goldwyn presents.

  1. Goldwyn, Samuel, 1882-1974. I. Title.
PN1998.A3G667   791.43'0232'0924 [B]   75-20598
ISBN 0-498-01658-7

PRINTED IN THE UNITED STATES OF AMERICA

CONTENTS

FOREWORD

TERESA WRIGHT
ON SAMUEL GOLDWYN

What I remember most about Goldwyn was the intense personal interest he took in each picture he made, from the earliest stages of creation right through the selling of tickets. He was in a way a parent, and each picture was his baby, which he regarded with paternal love.

Mrs. Eleanor Roosevelt was once asked which of her children was her favorite, and she said, "Always the one who needs me most." The production which Goldwyn felt needed him the most was always his next movie. He set out to make each film the best he had ever made. Though his most famous quote is looked on as funny, I can see how he really meant it. "I don't care if this picture doesn't make a dime as long as every man, woman and child in America sees it."

Naturally he was interested in making money, but I don't really think that was why he made films. He wanted to make them simply to make them good. He made them not necessarily to say something, but to entertain, to create something with warmth and charm, and to do it with style. That was his most important consideration, even more than winning awards. He had to feel he was bringing a picture of quality to the American public, a picture of which he could be proud. He didn't make too many bad ones, and he never wanted to make one simply because somebody else had just had a success with a similar kind of picture.

I feel there really couldn't be another Sam Goldwyn, simply because no producer today would truly care that much about each project. He was a true producer, seeing personally not only to the casting, but also to who would do the sets and who would create the costumes, and even who the hairdresser would be. I found that he would comment on nearly everything I wore in the films I made for him, and he'd come in and sit for a while and tell the hairdresser exactly how my hair should be done. Curiously, he always had my hair lightened, and I thought, "What a crazy man! He hires brunettes and then dyes their hair." He did it with me and with Merle Oberon and, I'm sure, with lots of others. I later found out the reason from the great cameraman, Gregg Toland: dark hair photographs jet black. I don't know how red hair photographs, but Goldwyn made Danny Kaye change his from red to blond.

Goldwyn had a great instinct for what he saw on film, and he seemed to relate to movies much more than to real life. He might not have been able to express in an articulate way what was good or bad about a film, but as a rule he was very right in his judgment, and his innate taste was apparent in everything he did.

Because of the great intensity with which he approached every situation, he created the famed *Goldwynisms* which have become part of his legend and of the lore of Hollywood. I found that these strangely mixed up words and phrases actually made sense and were effective when he spoke them. They only became humorous when one saw them in print.

In addition to being a great producer, Goldwyn could be a great actor. He could put on a marvelous show either to assert his acknowledged powers—not dictatorially, but with an orchestrated routine of cajolery—or to display his paternalism. He guided the young people under contract with some very good advice, and I wish I'd taken some of it: words of wisdom on exercising techniques, weight and posture, even old-fashioned things about brushing your hair one hundred strokes.

Of course there were many well-documented on-set battles with actors, directors and technicians, and continuing confrontations with the press—all, I think, for the sake of publicity. He might threaten to bar from his studio an actor or actress who had displeased him, but all dire warnings and previous rancor evaporated when he found that "exile" perfect for his newest project.

I left Goldwyn, as I assume several before me had done, in a cloud of dust. In my case, I felt that he could be quite difficult in his demands on your time, contending that a contract player should be expected to go out on extended publicity tours or, in the case of some of the studios, preside over supermarket openings. My leaving did not stop him from inviting me to come back for the second "world premiere" of *The Best Years of Our Lives* in 1954, and I had a marvelous time working with him again.

I have an idea that probably Mrs. Goldwyn played a big part in getting her husband to surround himself with all of the great talent—the writers, the editors, the art and set designers—who became an integral part of Goldwyn's productions. I think that as time went on and pictures became more sophisticated, she must have been very helpful in uncovering story material for him.

In the end, though, it was a combination of the intangibles—style, taste, unerring instinct—which came to identify the Goldwyn "touch," and distinguished Samuel Goldwyn in the history of films.

———

Teresa Wright appeared in Samuel Goldwyn's *The Little Foxes, The Pride of the Yankees, The Best Years of Our Lives,* and *Enchantment.*

ACKNOWLEDGMENTS

John E. Allen, Lewis Archibald, Alan Barbour, Dennis Belafonte, John Cocchi, Page Cook, Kirk Crivello, Guy Giampapa, Russ Jamison, Stephen Klain, Miles Kreuger, Leonard Maltin, Judy Marill, Virginia Mayo, Doug McClelland, Joel McCrea, David McGillivray, Leo Pachter, James Robert Parish, Charles Phillips Reilly, Bob Smith, Charles Smith, Lou Valentino, James Watters, Doug Whitney and Teresa Wright

and

Lincoln Center Library of the Performing Arts, Museum of Modern Art, British Film Institute, Academy of Motion Picture Arts and Sciences, American Cinema Editors, Film Favorites, and Samuel Goldwyn Productions.

APPRECIATIONS

Samuel Goldwyn's desire was to bring the ultimate in great entertainment to the public—indeed, to the world. If every producer in motion pictures today had half of his taste and perfection of approach, we would have a better quality product to choose from. Goldwyn's example of giving only the best, needs to be followed more today than ever before in the history of show business.

Virginia Mayo

Goldwyn was, I feel, the finest producer in the business. He was inarticulate, but he possessed a great sense of taste. He wanted everything associated with him to be the very best. Goldwyn was extremely hard to work for, but it was very rewarding to be in his fine films.

Joel McCrea

(Virginia Mayo and Joel McCrea each acted in seven Goldwyn films)

SAMUEL GOLDWYN PRESENTS

PART 1

Goldwyn: Man and Legend

"I make my pictures to please myself."

Samuel Goldwyn

Samuel Goldwyn was born in Warsaw, Poland, 27 August 1882, and died in Beverly Hills, California, 31 January 1974. Between these two dates, one of the screen's truly remarkable characters and careers spanned the epoch that was Hollywood in its Golden Years.

Goldwyn was, during his reign as a "one man gang" (as writer Loudon Wainwright succinctly described him), an absolute monarch and always good "copy" for Hollywood columnists. The ancedotes about Goldwyn are legion and his well-chronicled manglings of the English language—Goldwynisms, as they have come to be known—long since have been established in filmdom's lore. Some have been vouched for and authenticated by contemporaries; others were said to have been invented by publicity agents along the way, like Pete Smith, Howard Dietz, and Jock Lawrence. Nonetheless, they all gave color to Goldwyn, together with his unique status in the industry as THE boss. He took all the risks, made all the decisions, personally cast the films (to the dismay of Central Casting), in many cases directed the directors, supervised all of the publicity, even told the exhibitors how to run the show. Every film he made, in all respects, was his.

"The greatest tribute to him is that the phrase 'the Goldwyn touch' is part of the vocabulary of Hollywood," Alva Johnston, Goldwyn chronicler in the Thirties, wrote,

'The Goldwyn touch' is not brilliance or sensationalism. It is something that manifests itself gradually in a picture; the characters are consistent; the workmanship is honest; there are no tricks and shortcuts; the intelligence of the audience is never insulted.

Goldwyn was a showman by instinct, a producer with taste and artistic conscience, and a salesman par excellence. "Remember Samuel," he once recalled being told as a boy in Warsaw, "a man's most precious possession is his courage. No matter how black things seem, if you have courage, a darkness can be overcome." His courage in going-it-alone in films, of producing films others simply avoided, of believing firmly in motion pictures as family entertainment—this is the legacy he left the American film industry, of which he was the founding father.

Little is known of his childhood, except for the fact that his parents were Abraham and Hannah Goldfisch; that his father died when Sam was quite young; and that, before he was a teenager, the boy who would grow up to be a legend, emigrated to England to live with his aunt, who apprenticed him to a blacksmith in Manchester. At thirteen, Samuel Goldfisch crossed the Atlantic in steerage, arriving in the United States in 1895 with neither friend nor relative to greet him. An agency that located jobs for immigrants found one for him in a factory in the center of American glove-making industry, Gloversville, New York (about forty miles northwest of Albany). He swept floors there and performed other menial tasks for three dollars a week, but propelled by ambition, he became an expert cutter of skins by the time he was fifteen. Less than two years later, he had become foreman to one hundred workers, and at nineteen, he was on the road selling gloves.

His drive made him one of the industry's top salesmen, and his productivity enabled him to begin dictating his own terms and to travel to Europe for a month or two every year. He had learned English (more or less, some intimates and most business rivals later were to admit) in a year at evening school, and in 1902, he had become a U.S. citizen. At twenty-three, young Mr. Goldfisch had become a partner in the glove company and by 1910, he was making more than $15,000 a year, an impressive salary in the pre-World War One days.

Almost by accident, he then entered the movie business—at twenty-eight, a virtual latecomer. A married niece of the owner of the glove factory where Samuel Goldfisch worked, introduced him to her sister-in-law, Blanche Lasky, who, with her brother Jesse, had played cornet duets in vaudeville. Jesse Lasky now was a vaudeville impresario, and at the suggestion of his lawyer, Arthur S. Friend, had begun looking into the idea of film-making. Samuel Goldfish (by this time he had slightly altered the spelling of his name) married Blanche Lasky in 1910 and reportedly already had considered leaving the glove-making industry, believing that Woodrow Wilson's election to the presidency in 1912 would result in the lowering of tariffs on gloves, causing a drastic decline in the American market. His brother-in-law Jesse, convinced him to give up his job in Gloversville and plunge into a daring new venture—motion picture production. Lasky, Goldfish, and Friend each put up $7,500, borrowed an additional $11,000 from the bank, and in December 1913, incorporated the Jesse L. Lasky Feature Play Company. The Goldwyn legend was now born.

In the office at 485 Fifth Avenue in Manhattan, Jesse Lasky was president, Samuel Goldfish became treasurer and sales manager, and Arthur Friend handled legal matters. The next step was to go into production. Appreciative of the work D.W. Griffith had been turning out for Biograph Pictures, Lasky invited the director to make a feature length film for the fledgling Lasky Play Company, but was dismayed when Griffith demanded $250,000. Instead, Lasky turned to a Broadway actor/playwright whom, as an impresario, he had engaged several times to write vaudeville skits. His name was Cecil Blount DeMille. Goldwyn once recalled: "We hired DeMille at $100 a week to direct our first picture, and as he knew nothing about directing, he went out to a studio in Astoria to see how it was done. We had to pay Dustin Farnum $250 a week as the film's hero, and as this was eating into our capital, we offered him a third interest in the firm instead of a salary. He refused. That was his loss."

For the company's first project, Lasky chose *The Squaw Man,* a stage-tested western written by Edwin Milton Royce, and Broadway actor Dustin Farnum was hired to star. Being a western, it was shrewdly decided by the partners that *The Squaw Man* should be filmed in the West, rather than in the Bronx, then the capital of film-making. Legend relates that DeMille and the crew dispatched to Flagstaff, Arizona, to begin shooting, but a raging snowstorm there convinced them to board the train again and continue to the end of the line—a sort of cowpasture on the outskirts of Los Angeles. The original Lasky capitalization of $26,000 was being depleted rapidly, and a sudden demand from Farnum for $5000 in cash failed to encourage Messrs. Lasky, Goldfish, and Friend. To Goldfish, though, the challenge had presented itself, and he took to the road where he sold "states rights" of *The Squaw Man* to veteran film exhibitors all over the country, and collected in advance even before DeMille had begun to roll his cameras at the now fabled old barn he had rented on Selma Avenue in Los Angeles. Although the film was shot at different times by different men with different cameras—even the sprocket holes on the film did not fit the wheels of the conventional projectors—*The Squaw Man* was salvaged by Sig Lubin, a veteran editor, and went on to emerge as a big hit, instantly revolutionizing the industry, and putting Hollywood itself on the map. The film, which had cost $47,000 to make, was released in February 1914, and grossed $244,000, guaranteeing the future of the Lasky Feature Play Company.

"Our next picture was *Brewster's Millions,*" Goldwyn has said,

> Jesse and I saw so much of it while it was being made that when it was finished neither of us could crack a smile. When we showed it to exhibitors at the Carnegie Lyceum in New York, we were so nervous that we walked around the block until it was almost over. Then we went back in and found we had a second success on our hands.

Goldfish was not content to be merely a salesman of movies and soon took a more active interest in the locating and promoting of projects as well as the hiring of players, while Lasky himself pursued his old vaudeville interests.

During the mid-Teens, the Lasky company's only serious competitor in the business, already a giant in American commerce, was Adolph Zukor's, Famous Players Film Company. A merger between the two industry leaders was effected in 1916, creating a combine that was to evolve as Paramount Pictures (the corporation, which at the time had been distributing Famous Players productions and the films of Lasky and others). In the new setup, Zukor was installed as president, Lasky vice-president, Goldfish board chairman, and Cecil B. DeMille director/general. Film historian Herbert G. Luft writes: "Goldfish had become so energetic a movie entrepreneur that Famous Players-Lasky Corporation had been in existence only three months when Zukor told Lasky that there wasn't room in the same corporation for Goldfish and himself (Lasky)." The two agreed to buy Goldfish's stock in the company for $900,000. (The action, it has been noted, not only embittered Goldwyn and affected his marriage, but also caused a rift between Lasky and himself that lasted for forty years. The union with Blanche ended in 1919. They had one daughter, Ruth, who later married McClure Capps, an art director who frequently worked on Goldwyn films in the 1940s. Blanche Lasky subsequently married Hector Turnbull, a writer/director of silent films, discovered by her brother. She died of pneumonia in 1932.)

The $900,000 severance pay was put to good use by Samuel Goldfish. With it, he formed Goldwyn Pictures Corporation with four partners: Broadway producers Edgar and Archibald Selwyn; Edgar's wife, playwright Margaret Mayo; and impresario Arthur Hopkins. The name of the new company, formed in December 1916, combined the first syllable of Goldfish and last syllable of Selwyn. Two years later, Samuel Goldfish legally changed his own last name to Goldwyn, becoming one of the few men named for a corporation. Wags for years have considered the possibilities of the combination of names that might have made the legendary producer, Samuel Selfish.

Nearly overnight, Goldwyn Pictures became a formidable rival for Famous Players-Lasky, with a roster of distinguished players: Maxine Elliot, Geraldine Farrar, Mary Garden, and others (causing Hollywood quipsters of the day to refer to Goldwyn's as the "old ladies home.") The Company's initial production was a cinematization of Margaret Mayo's Broadway comedy, *Polly of the Circus,* starring in the film, Mae Marsh. Following were *Baby Mine* with Madge Kennedy, *Fighting Odds* with Maxine Elliot, and an elaborate version of *Thais* with Mary Garden. As Goldwyn Pictures' prestige increased, its assets diminished, to the financial annoyance of the DuPonts and the Chase National Bank, two of the company's more prominent backers. Goldwyn, it seems, had been concentrating on the stars at the expense of the vehicle. Mary Garden, for instance, had been signed at $15,000 weekly (she was one of Goldwyn's earliest endeavors at bringing culture to the screen), but the public had apparently been confused, thinking they were getting Mary Gardener, a nickelodeon heroine.

By 1918, Goldwyn himself was in trouble. The war had reduced movie attendance, and Goldwyn had invested huge sums in the wrong stars. The government had cut commercial use of electricity to save coal, making it impractical to film at the Fort Lee, New Jersey, site of the Goldwyn Studios, so the company transferred its operations to Thomas Ince's Triangle Studios, at Culver City, California, where it turned out several more unsuccessful films—*The Turn of the Wheel* with Geraldine Farrar; *Jubilo,* one of Will Rogers' earliest movies; Booth Tarkington's *Edgar and the Teacher's Pet;* another Will Rogers starrer, *Doubling for Romeo;* and *The Penalty* with Lon Chaney.

In June 1919, Goldwyn announced the formation within Goldwyn Pictures of a separate unit, Eminent Authors Pictures, Inc. To attempt to achieve a dominant place in the film industry by signing a string of expensive players, it had been noted often in film's earliest days, was to tie up capital to a dangerous extent. Aware of this truism, Goldwyn tried an experiment, intending to place story value above all other elements in moviemaking. He hired a stable of prominent writers, including Rex Beach, Rupert Hughes, Mary Roberts Rinehart, Gouverneur Morris, Gertrude Atherton, Basil King, Leroy Scott and others. Some were brought in merely to make their work available for filming, while others were to adapt existing stories and to write new ones directly for the screen. Already operating under the theory that cost should be no barrier when seeking the very best, Goldwyn put on the payroll at a five figure weekly salary the eminent Belgian poet, Maurice Maeterlinck, who came to Hollywood speaking and writing no English. Goldwyn gave him a suite of offices and commissioned him to write a screenplay from his *Life of a Bee.* It has been reported that Goldwyn was dumbfounded after reading Maeter-

linck's scenario, and ran from his office screaming, "My God, the hero is a bee!" None of Maeterlinck's work for Goldwyn was filmed, and on his departure, he supposedly received a pat on the shoulder from Goldwyn, along with the encouraging words: "Don't worry, Maurice, you'll make good yet." Although the Eminent Authors Pictures plan did not work out to Goldwyn's complete satisfaction (in only one instance was it truly successful in those early days: Rupert Hughes' *The Old Nest* was one of Goldwyn Pictures' few blockbuster hits), the theory was never abandoned, and Goldwyn continued to engage the finest writers that literally money could buy.

Another bold venture for Goldwyn Pictures was importing foreign films, including the German classic, *The Cabinet of Dr. Caligari,* and the Italian-made *Theodora,* both shown first in this country in 1921. Within a year, though, Goldwyn Pictures, Inc. was bankrupt, and a thoroughly disenchanted Edgar Selwyn was said to have told Goldwyn: "Sam, you not only broke us, but took half our good name as well." Herbert G. Luft wrote in *Films in Review*: "As the fortunes of Goldwyn Pictures Corp. declined, an erstwhile swindler and whizbang promoter named Frank Joseph Godsol gained increasing ascendancy in it." Under Godsol's counsel, the company undertook such projects as Erich von Stroheim's *Greed* and the biblical spectacular, *Ben Hur.* Both became Metro-Goldwyn-Mayer's properties under Irving Thalberg within a few months.

Goldwyn himself lost controlling interest of Goldwyn Pictures Corporation in 1922 and was obliged to take an enforced vacation, spending the time writing his autobiography, *Behind the Screen.* Friends were said to have asked him: "Who's going to translate it for you?" Goldwyn Pictures, meanwhile, entered into a merger with Metro Pictures (formed in 1915 and acquired five years later by Loew's, Inc., the distributing company). Soon after the Metro-Goldwyn incorporation, Marcus Loew and Nicholas M. Schenck, of the Loew's, Inc., hierarchy, completed the new corporation's expansion by bringing Louis B. Mayer Productions (formed in 1918) into the fold. Samuel Goldwyn then fought unsuccessfully to have the resulting company known as Metro-Goldwyn-Mayer and Goldwyn, and, rebuffed, left the new organization without having actually worked for it. He withdrew, though, with a substantial financial settlement, but MGM itself had overlooked the fact that Goldwyn had not sold the company his personal right to the use of the Goldwyn name, and a lengthy court battle began when MGM learned that the producer was in the process of forming Samuel Goldwyn, Inc., with Goldwyn owning one hundred percent of the stock. MGM protested that there could not be two studios with the Goldwyn name. Judge Learned Hand's landmark decision on 18 October 1923, allowed Goldwyn to make films under his own name, using first, the phrase "Samuel Goldwyn Presents" above the title, and second, the disclaimer: "Presented by Samuel Goldwyn (not now connected with Goldwyn Pictures)." The judge's comment on the case is nearly as famous in Hollywood history as any verified Goldwynism: "A self-made man may prefer a self-made name." A private agreement with MGM shortly thereafter permitted Goldwyn to use "Samuel Goldwyn Presents" without qualification.

Although Metro-Goldwyn-Mayer was not officially incorporated until 17 April 1924, Goldwyn had been in the business as an independent for nearly a year. Samuel Goldwyn, Inc. Ltd., was formalized in 1924, and space was rented at that now famous Hollywood address: 1041 North Formosa Avenue, Los Angeles (still the home of Samuel Goldwyn Productions, Inc.). In Goldwyn's new operation, there were neither partners, directors, nor outstanding stock. Convinced he could never get along with partners or boards of directors, Goldwyn simply maintained 100% control, sharing power only with ex-actress Frances Howard, who had become the second Mrs. Samuel Goldwyn at a ceremony at City Hall in Jersey City, New Jersey, on 23 April 1925. She abandoned her own career to be merely his wife and lifelong business confidante. One of the countless Goldwynisms aptly fits his decision to go it alone: "It's dog eat dog in this business, and nobody's going to eat me." Less facetious was his explanation given to the press: "I found it took a world of time to explain my plans to associates. Now I can save all that time and energy and put them into making better pictures." In the view of Goldwyn biographer Alva Johnston:

> Samuel Goldwyn could stand no equal or superior in authority. One of Hollywood's foremost autocrats, but a glutton for suggestions, he would not share power or glory, preferring to give money or lavish gifts rather than participation in Goldwyn fame.

At Samuel Goldwyn's wedding, his old partner, Edgar Selwyn, was best man. Selwyn, it has been said, was sworn to secrecy about the nuptials. "No publicity" was the order from publicity-conscious Goldwyn. Curiously, mobs of newsmen and photographers turned up at the ceremony. "I thought you didn't want any publicity," Selwyn later reportedly asked his friend. "Can I control the press?" Goldwyn was heard to have replied. Samuel and Frances Goldwyn had one child: Samuel Goldwyn, Jr., born the following year. He too has become a film producer.*

---

* *Man with a Gun* (1955), *The Sharkfighters* (1956), *The Proud Rebel* (1958), *The Adventures of Huckleberry Finn* (1960), *The Young Lovers* (1964), *Cotton Comes to Harlem* (1970), *Come Back Charleston Blue* (1972).

The initial films to bear the legend "Samuel Goldwyn Presents" were distributed through Associated First National Pictures, which years later would evolve into Warner Bros. Pictures under that now-famous *WB* shield. In this early Goldwyn group were the lavish romantic dramas that were to become the producer's hallmark, together with his three "Potash and Perlmutter" farces. The first Goldwyn production, *The Eternal City,* a spectacular filmed on location in Rome, demonstrated to the industry what could be expected as regular fare from its maverick entrepreneur. Included in the film, along with the conventional stars, were none less than Benito Mussolini and King Victor Emanuel! The earliest screen appearances of Goldwyn's greatest star, Ronald Colman, also were among these Associated First National features, as well as *The Dark Angel,* wherein Goldwyn introduced to American films Vilma Banky, his foremost leading lady of silent movies.

In 1926, Goldwyn was invited to become one of the owner/partners of United Artists, a cooperative that had been formed by Mary Pickford, Douglas Fairbanks and Charles Chaplin to distribute their independent productions, together with those of Joseph M. Schenck, D.W. Griffith, Hal Roach, Gloria Swanson and others. For the next fifteen years, all Goldwyn films were released through U.A., although the producer was soon to decide that he and later member Alexander Korda, the famed British movie impresario, were turning out the bulk of the United Artists product while the other, less active members of the cooperative simply were collecting their percentages of the organization's entire output. Goldwyn finally began trying to make the situation more equitable in 1935, moving to acquire United Artists for himself. He paid $250,000 for the interest held jointly by Schenck and Darryl F. Zanuck, and became sole owner of U.A.'s physical property, equipment, wardrobe, etc. Pickford, Fairbanks and Chaplin, so the story went, owned the real estate itself, while Goldwyn acquired everything sitting on it. Three years later, he installed James Roosevelt, the eldest son of FDR, as vice-president of Samuel Goldwyn, Inc., and shortly thereafter, began in earnest his campaign to buy up the remaining shares in United Artists. Part of his strategy was to have his telephone operators answer calls by responding "Samuel Goldwyn Studios," rather than "United Artists" as they had done for thirteen years. He then mandated his legal staff to bring a court suit asking that either he be freed from his partnership, or be allowed to purchase control of the company from the other members. Since he and Korda, Goldwyn felt, were the only active members, they should have the opportunity to buy up the three-fifths they did not own—and offered six million dollars if Pickford, Fairbanks and Chaplin would vacate the premises. Goldwyn's breach of contract suit against U.A. dragged on for three years, and in February 1941, a settlement was arranged whereby Goldwyn would be, to paraphrase another Goldwynism, "included out." United Artists bought up Goldwyn's stock for $300,000, which the producer claimed was a personal loss of nearly fifty percent. Several months later, he signed a long-term contract for release rights on his pictures with RKO, the least stable of all the major studios and one whose revolving door of studio heads production chiefs made its checkered career one of the industry's question marks. During the 1940s, only the independent films RKO released by Goldwyn and Walt Disney—the two staunchest advocates of family entertainment in Hollywood—guaranteed consistent quality from product sporting the distinctive lightning-flash-in-the-triangle logo.

"From the time he became an independent producer," *The New York Times* wrote,

> Mr. Goldwyn was noted for the reverence in which he held creative talent. He coddled actors, writers and directors, but when he felt they were not producing what he had expected of them, he switched tactics and heaped invectives on them. "I'll take fifty percent efficiency," he once explained, "to get 100 percent loyalty."

Having assembled the cream of the available talent—and some that had not made itself readily available, Mr. Goldwyn would dominate their work and their lives like a benign tyrant, praising them, goading them, encouraging them, browbeating them, as he personally supervised even the tiniest details of each of his productions—each handmade, as it seems, while the rest of the industry operated on an assembly line basis. So zealously did he guard his reputation for quality pictures that he would stop at no expense to make improvements. He scrapped the first version of *Nana* in 1934, for instance, after it had been two-thirds completed because he felt the original director, George Fitzmaurice, had not been capturing the qualities he (Goldwyn) had seen in the lovely Anna Sten and for which he already had paid millions to promote. The cost in this case was a mere $411,000 out of pocket. And in 1947, he halted production on *The Bishop's Wife* after having spent close to one million dollars, simply because he was dissatisfied with the way the film was turning out. After switching directors, Goldwyn started over again.

And in another instance, Goldwyn objected to a single word in a particular scene in one of the pictures he was screening before final release. He then spent $20,000 to reshoot the sequence, recreating torn-down sets and paying actors whose contracts had expired simply to return for a few minutes shooting. Although his quest for excellence continually infuriated his lieutenants and technicians and actors, Goldwyn decreed that each of his films be endowed with a sheen of quality and good taste, two of the many hallmarks that became synonymous with the term "the Goldwyn touch."

During his years of preeminence, Goldwyn became his own best spokesman and was one of the most visible of all the Hollywood moguls as, virtually, the voice of the industry. His byline appeared frequently in *The New York Times Magazine, The Saturday Evening Post, Reader's Digest,* and other national publications, expounding his philosophies and discussing the contemporary movie scene. In 1927, for instance, he announced (in *The New York Times*) that

> the public is being fooled by the combination of vaudeville and films on one bill. It is not getting either good vaudeville or good pictures, and if this practice continues, the film industry will be forced to make poorer pictures because of the heavy vaudeville cost burdens borne by theater owners.

In 1929, he gave his official blessing to talking pictures:

> I believe in the future of "talkies" because the day of the director is over and that of the author and playwright has arrived . . . The future of successful talking pictures will lie in the ability of the producer to make a motion picture with dialogue rather than a so-called talking film in which the lines are all-important. The combination of both, in which pure cinema technique is all important, will make up the great coming sound pictures.

He championed writers' reforms (in 1935):

> At the present time, Hollywood is merely a stop-over place for good writers. They come to work for ten weeks between periods of writing their own plays and stories. They do not realize the possibilities of the screen . . . What Hollywood must do is show writers that they can make as much out of a fine picture as they would from a successful play. That can be done only by letting the writer participate in the profits, getting royalties.

During this period, Goldwyn actively endeavored to revive his old Eminent Authors concept, with a gilt-edged roster of writers that included Dorothy Parker and Alan Campbell, Lillian Hellman, Donald Ogden Stewart, Sidney Howard, Anita Loos, Dudley Nichols, Robert E. Sherwood, Ben Hecht and Charles MacArthur, Moss Hart, Edna Ferber, Sam and Bella Spewack, and Louis Bromfield (whom Goldwyn allegedly promised to make the name "Bloomfield" famous the world over after two or three pictures.)

Goldwyn uncharacteristically inaugurated his own profit sharing plan in 1938 for his upperbracket creative personnel, noting:

> The making of good motion pictures is so personal an endeavor that I feel that better pictures can be accomplished by having my fellow workers feel and have a real interest in the profits of my pictures.

During the war years, Goldwyn took up the battle,

first against double bills in the theaters, and then against "monopolistic practicies" in motion picture exhibition, demanding unsuccessfully that theaters or circuits pay him a percentage of his picture's gross profits. 1945 found Goldwyn forming a new production company, with himself as board chairman of Samuel Goldwyn Productions, Inc., and his long-time assistant, James A. Mulvey, as president. Employees would be permitted to own half the stock, though those offerings were not extended to stars, writers or directors. Among the first to receive Goldwyn stock was Gregg Toland, the producer's chief cinematographer. "Our stockholders," Goldwyn said at the time,

> will consist of executives, creative talents, technicians, and administrative experts—and no one else. Without their combined talents, working together for a common purpose, ownership means little.

Goldwyn stopped making films in 1959, and began renting his studio to independent film and television productions. "He was not pleased with much of the product that emanated from there and other parts of Hollywood, having believed movies and TV had become trashy," *The New York Times* wrote in its obituary of Goldwyn. And *Variety* noted:

> He was a proud, stubborn man, and where clothes were concerned, inordinately vain. Tall, lean and erect as a professional soldier, he had his clothes tailored precisely to his body line. For fear of spoiling the drape, he carried nothing—keys, pencil, etc.—in his pockets other than a handkerchief. When they dined out or traveled, Mrs. Goldwyn always went prepared with folding green to do the tipping.

Toward the end of his life, Goldwyn was seen increasingly less and was made an invalid by a series of strokes in 1969. Among the last public honors tendered him, during a presidential visit to the Goldwyn mansion in Beverly Hills in March 1971, was the presentation of the Freedom Medal, this country's highest award to a civilian.

The countless tales of Goldwyn the autocrat, made his astounding string of superior screen entertainments even more amazing. One of his publicity chiefs said this of his boss: "He'll charm the socks off of you, and then while you're standing there in your bare feet, he'll step on your toes." The legendary battles Goldwyn engaged in, both on and off the set, with his directors and his stars have been well chronicled, and it has been said that few left his employ amicably. Where other departures called for a shaking of hands, with Goldwyn it was a shaking of fists. Often, relationships never got that far. Director George Cukor, for one, refused to allow Louis B. Mayer to let him work for Goldwyn at any price, and so exasperated was the producer, he allegedly created this classic Goldwynism to describe his feelings: "That's

the way with these directors—always biting the hand that laid the golden egg." And he once reportedly rebuked William Wyler for changing a night scene into a daytime shot: "Nobody can change night into day, or vice versa, without asking me first."

Goldwyn, the producer, basked in the glare of publicity, but he left his work at the office. Away from the studio, he could pass for a country squire—loving husband, father and grandfather whose home life was sacred—a man on intimate terms with presidents and prime ministers—a philanthropist whose annual $100,000 donations, for instance, to the United Jewish Appeal were part of the lavish gifts doled out regularly through the Goldwyn Foundation.

It was in the motion picture arena, though, where he thrived as a master showman with his unique flair for publicity and his personal resolve for excellence. He left the American cinema an unmatched legacy of eighty films, each imprinted with his distinctive touch. It is this work that will be discussed in this volume—screen classics studded with memorable cinematic moments—Gary Cooper saying goodbye to his fans in *The Pride of the Yankees;* Mary Astor weathering the spectacular storm in *The Hurricane;* Ronald Colman lighting Helen Hayes' cigarette in *Arrowsmith*; Cary Grant and Loretta Young in the ice-skating sequence in *The Bishop's Wife;* Humphrey Bogart being rebuffed by Marjorie Main, his mother in *Dead End;* Dana Andrews reliving wartime experiences in the nose of a junked bomber in *The Best Years of Our Lives;* Bette Davis coldly watching Herbert Marshall die in *The Little Foxes;* Vilma Banky uncharacteristically flipping pancakes at Childs in *This Is Heaven;* Danny Kaye cavorting in the timeless lobby number of *Up in Arms;* Barbara Stanwyck standing in the rain at her daughter's wedding in *Stella Dallas;* Joel McCrea and Miriam Hopkins engaging in lovers' spat on a tree limb in *Woman Chases Man*; Laurence Olivier's pastoral trysts with Merle Oberon in *Wuthering Heights;* Fredric March joining Anna Sten on the trek to Siberia in *We Live Again*. And the stars whose screen careers Goldwyn made or advanced almost outnumber the catalogue of funny lines attributed to him or spoken about him—unforgettable personalities who lit up the screen for more than forty years: Ronald Colman, Vilma Banky, Anna Sten, Eddie Cantor from the early days; Miriam Hopkins, Joel McCrea, Merle Oberon and Gary Cooper (whose potential Goldwyn had greatly underestimated originally) from the middle years; David Niven, Teresa Wright, Dana Andrews, Danny Kaye, Virginia Mayo and Farley Granger during the 1940s.

Goldwyn, the talent-finder, was a major factor in the film careers of others: Robert Montgomery, whose screen test fell into MGM's hands; Virginia Bruce and Laraine Day, whose very early film work was in Goldwyn movies; Betty Grable, Lucille Ball and Paulette Goddard, among others, who began their screen days as Goldwyn Girls. And it was Goldwyn who made Laurence Olivier a matinee screen idol, reintroducing him to Hollywood moviemaking, on which he (Olivier) previously had soured to the point of nearly forsaking films altogether.

There were, of course, the Goldwyn gaffes, in addition to Vilma Banky, whose inability to master the English language foredoomed her career when sound came to films; Anna Sten, the multimillion dollar (and still inexplicable) mistake whom Goldwyn once called "colossal in a small way," and Sigrid Gurie, Goldwyn's well-publicized Norwegian discovery from Brooklyn. He was said to have turned down Clark Gable because the fledgling actor's ears were too big and he passed over Greta Garbo because she had no potential on the screen. His judgement, on balance, and his keen eye for talent and, as one critic put it, "his instinctive sense of superior rightness" helped reconfirm the Goldwyn legend that has borne out the truisms of the fabled "Great American Dream."

And through the establishment in 1955 of the annual Goldwyn Creative Writing Awards at UCLA, he has been making that dream possible for others. As *Variety* has noted, close to 100% of the neophyte award winners—among them, Francis Ford Coppola—have gone on to professional writing careers as novelists, playwrights and motion picture and television scenarists.

"Dean of independent producers," *Variety* wrote of Goldwyn when he died,

and the only true indie, he began bucking the majors at a time when they dominated the industry. That he succeeded in the rough competition that existed to an even greater degree in the predivorcement days (before film companies were forced by the courts, in 1948, to divest themselves of their distribution arms) and emerged as a dominant personality among giants commanding vast producing/theater-owning combines, he attributed to one factor: having met his competitors with a long string of superior quality pictures.

The industry itself recognized this with its presentation to Goldwyn in 1946 of the Irving G. Thalberg Memorial Award, and in 1957 of the Jean Hersholt Humanitarian Award.

Goldwyn was the first of the great independents in motion pictures. When he died, it was the independent producers who held the future of Hollywood in their hands. As for the Goldwyn career, his own words provide the best summation:

I was a rebel, a lone wolf. My pictures were my own. I financed them myself and answered solely to myself. My mistakes and my successes were my own. My rule was to please myself, and if I did that, there was a good chance I would please others.

Early Goldwyn.

At a Goldwyn party for William Randolph Hearst in 1928. Standing between Goldwyn (left) and Hearst (right) are director Allan Dwan, Charles Chaplin, John Considine Sr., Hans Kraley, Mayor Jimmy Walker, Nate Stein, John Considine Jr., James Warner, director Ernst Lubitsch, Peter Brady and Charles Hand. In the top row; director Henry King and Roland West. Seated, from the left, are: Lupe Velez, Dolores Del Rio, Douglas Fairbanks, Louella Parsons, Marion Davies, Ethel Clark and Nate Free.

Arriving in New York in 1929 with Frances Goldwyn and Ronald Colman for the premiere of Bulldog Drummond.

The United Artists family in 1931: Al Jolson, Mary Pickford, Ronald Colman, Gloria Swanson, Douglas Fairbanks, Joseph Schenck, Charles Chaplin, Goldwyn, and Eddie Cantor.

With Eddie Cantor at the 1934 trial to settle the legal dispute between Samuel Goldwyn Inc. and Warner Bros. over the services of choreographer Busby Berkeley.

The Goldwyn family circa 1934.

With Eleanor Roosevelt, Merle Oberon and James Roosevelt at the Hollywood premiere of Wuthering Heights.

With William Wyler on the set of The Little Foxes.

Flanked by Gary Cooper and William Wyler on the set of The Westerner.

With Mrs. Lou Gehrig and Christy Walsh—Gehrig's former manager—at the contract signing for The Pride of the Yankees.

Overseeing the wardrobe of Danny Kaye and Dana Andrews between scenes of Up in Arms.

With Bob Hope on the set of The Princess and the Pirate.

With Frances in 1946.

With Harold Russell and William Wyler at the Academy Award ceremonies where The Best Years of Our Lives *received seven Oscars, and Goldwyn was given the Irving G. Thalberg Award.*

With Danny Kaye and Jeanmaire on the set of Hans Christian Andersen.

Offering some fatherly advice to Samuel Goldwyn Jr. on the set of Man with a Gun, *the latter's first production. Eavesdropping is Robert Mitchum, the film's star.*

Discussing a production matter with Frank Sinatra on the set of Guys and Dolls.

On the set of Porgy and Bess. *Ira Gershwin is seated in the center, and scenarist N. Richard Nash is on the right.*

Making his last appearance in public at the presentation
in 1971 of the Medal of Freedom from President Nixon.

PART 2
The Films of Samuel Goldwyn

1 THE ETERNAL CITY (1923)

Directed by George Fitzmaurice; scenario, Ouida Bergere; based on the story and play by Sir Hall Caine; photographer, Arthur Miller. Eight reels. Distributed by First National Pictures. Premiere: Mark Strand Theater, New York, 1/20/24

THE CAST:
Donna Roma, Barbara LaMarr; *David Rossi,* Bert Lytell; *Baron Bonelli,* Lionel Barrymore; *Bruno,* Richard Bennett; *Minghelli,* Montagu Love; *Page Boys,* Betty Bronson and Joan Bennett; *Bit Player,* Ronald Colman.

The first of Samuel Goldwyn's personal productions, although the second to be released, *The Eternal City* set the lavish style that through the succeeding years was to be the Goldwyn hallmark. The film was an elaborate, updated remake of the 1915 version wherein silent screen great Pauline Frederick had made her movie debut. Goldwyn's production veered toward the topical, stressing the political upheavals then rumbling through Italy, rather than the human interest of the 1901 Caine novel and the popular play derived from it the following year. The story's hero, for instance, became in the Goldwyn version a Mussolini lieutenant, and long passages dealing with the intrigues of the Communists and the patriotic fervor of the Fascisti imbued the picture with historic rather than romantic coloring. Goldwyn's *The Eternal City,* which was viewed by many of the day's critics as a record of Italian politics since World War One, has remained a subject of controversy over the years as well as a relic, in much the same mold as his *The North Star* of the second World War.

The Eternal City was filmed on location in Rome by Goldwyn's foremost director of silents, George Fitzmaurice (with, subsequently, ten Goldwyn films to his credit). Fitzmaurice, undoubtedly at his boss' insistence, spared no expense, employing thousands of extras to fill the Colosseum as well as utilizing at the film's climax the "services" of none less than Benito Mussolini and King Victor Emanuel—as if cajoled by Goldwyn himself into making guest appearances. The two men are seen standing on the balcony of the royal palace reviewing the entrance of Il Duce's troops into the city.

As pictured in the scenario by Ouida Bergere (then, Mrs. George Fitzmaurice, and later, Mrs. Basil Rathbone), the love story involving childhood sweethearts Donna Roma and David Rossi, the latter having been adopted as a child by the former's wealthy father, rapidly becomes submerged in the much less subtle historical and political aspects that Goldwyn most likely felt was more interesting. In its review, *Variety* felt that all the pageantry and climactic splendor was

> fine spectacle, but it kills Sir Hall Caine's story, and what was designed as a romantic tale with emotional appeal, atmosphere of rich ecclesiastical pomp and glowing warmth has been turned into a rough and tumble "movie," excellent of its type, but far from the spirit of Caine's *The Eternal City.*

In *The Eternal City,* Donna Roma ("the petted darling who inspired all of Rome to vengeance," as Goldwyn's advertising department pictured her) faithfully awaits the return from battle of her true love, David, but is heartbroken at the erroneous news of his death. She accepts an offer of patronage from evil Baron Bonelli, who promises her fame as a sculptress. Bonelli soon reveals himself as the leader of the Communists, seeking the dictatorship for himself, and his relationship with Roma, who becomes known as "the Valonna woman," is the talk of the city. David, meanwhile, has returned home and with his long-time friend, Bruno, begins searching for Roma. David's vagabond life as he wanders aimlessly about the country brings him into contact with widespread political unrest and convinces him to throw in with the Fascisti movement. In Rome, he is introduced at a costume party to "the Valonna woman," whom he at first does not recognize as his beloved Roma because of her masquerade accouterments. Invited to her home, David recognizes himself in a sculpture that Roma had created in his memory, and enraged that Bonelli's "woman" had mocked the fighting men with such a memorial, he smashes it to bits. Learning at last that the sculptress is Roma, David is revolted and plunges even deeper into politics, determined to put her out of his mind forever. David and Bonelli become archenemies, and during a confrontation between the Reds and Mussolini's followers, David kills the evil baron. To protect David from prosecution, Roma assumes the blame for Bonelli's murder, convincing David at last that she has not betrayed him.

In assessing the performances, *The New York Times* felt that

Mr. Lytell plays far better than hitherto in this film, giving a highly satisfactory performance, and Richard Bennett is splendid as Bruno, the old Munchausen. Montagu Love impersonates the active head of the Reds quite well, and Mr. Barrymore has just the part that suits him in Bonelli, for whom, with his well-cut clothes and occasionally a monocle, he causes hate without ever overdoing the acting.

Summing up, the paper's critic decided that "George Fitzmaurice not only tells a story on the screen, but he frames it with commanding and entrancing exteriors" and that "this is a picture which has a gripping story framed in wonderful and beautiful scenes."

Photoplay called *The Eternal City*:

one of the most beautiful pictures ever filmed . . . one that no lover of the best in pictures can afford to miss. It has a charming love story, plenty of melodrama, fine comedy, sets that are exceptional in every way, some of the best acting of the year, and intelligent direction. What more can be asked?

Barbara LaMarr in The Eternal City.

Lionel Barrymore and Barbara LaMarr in The Eternal City.

George Fitzmaurice's

Production of

GEORGE FITZMAURICE

SAMUEL GOLDWYN

The Eternal City

with
Barbara La Marr
Lionel Barrymore
Richard Bennett
Montagu Love
Bert Lytell
and
20,000 others

From the book by
Sir Hall Caine

Adapted by
Ouida Bergere

Produced by
Samuel Goldwyn
not now connected with
Goldwyn Pictures

At Rome, Italy, and
New York, with the
Co-operation of the
Italian Government

*Staged Midst the Historical Beauty
Spots of Rome. A Tense Poignant Romance*

Shown Throughout the World After January First
A First National Picture

The Eternal City

Richard Bennett and Barbara LaMarr in The Eternal City.

Richard Bennett, Lionel Barrymore, Barbara LaMarr,
Bert Lytell and Montagu Love in The Eternal City.

2 POTASH AND PERLMUTTER (1923)

Directed by Clarence Badger; scenario, Frances Marion; based on the play by Montague Glass and Charles Klein; photographer, Rudolph Berquist; art director, William B. Ihnen; titles, Oscar C. Buchheister. Eight reels. Distributed by First National Pictures. Premiere: Rivoli Theater, Baltimore, 9/6/23. New York Premiere: Mark Strand Theater, 9/23/23

THE CAST:
Abe Potash, Barney Bernard*; *Morris Perlmutter*, Alexander Carr*; *Rosie Potash*, Vera Gordon; *Head Model*, Martha Mansfield; *Boris Andrieff*, Ben Lyon; *Henry Feldman*, Edouard Durand; *Irma Potash*, Hope Sutherland; *Ruth Goldman*, DeSacia Mooers; *Office Boy*, Jerry Devine; *Mark Pasinsky*, Lee Kohlmar*; *Wide-Awake Salesman*, Leo Donnelly; *Cabaret Dancers*, Tiller Girls.
* In cast of 1913 Broadway version.

Goldwyn had long hoped to film the "Potash and Perlmutter" stories, probably because his early career as a glove salesman allowed him to closely identify with the characters. His associates at the old Goldwyn company, however, continually had overruled him, but now with his own money and none in his organization to dissent, he put Frances Marion, one of the most prolific scenarists in the business, to work fashioning a script involving the two bickering partners. Films like these, revolving around friendly enemies and ethnic humor, of the "Cohens and Kellys" genre, were popular staples of screen comedy during the Twenties, and Goldwyn was to realize profits from the craze in three cinematizations of *Potash and Perlmutter* Broadway successes.

The play, on which *Potash and Perlmutter* was based, had originally been one of the hits of the 1905 Broadway season, but its subsequent revival in 1913, with Barney Bernard and Alexander Carr in the title roles, had convinced Goldwyn of its screen potential. Bernard and Carr squabbled nightly for 441 performances and later recreated their roles in *Business Before Pleasure* in 1917 (it was to be filmed by Goldwyn as *In Hollywood with Potash and Perlmutter*), and *Partners Again* five years hence. Bernard also starred with Julius Tannen (as Perlmutter) in *Abe and Mawruss* in 1915. Its title was subsequently changed to *Potash and Perlmutter In Society*. One final "P&P" play, *Potash and Perlmutter, Detectives,* turned up on Broadway in 1920 with Ludwig Satz and Robert Leonard in the leads.

In bringing *Potash and Perlmutter* to the screen, Goldwyn naturally sent for Bernard and Carr to recreate their well-established portrayals that had found such success in New York with that city's vast Jewish audience. The trials and tribulations of the clothing business partners created the comic situations that are standard fodder in today's television fare. In the Twenties, however, family-oriented happenings proliferated the screen and, as *Variety* decided,

> *Potash and Perlmutter* has been rounded into a good movie comedy, far better than one would expect. Its humor is founded upon the funny-page humor, usually applied to their (the Jewish) race, and much of it is forced, but all surefire as movie audiences go.

Its simplistic plot: Abe and Morris hire a poor, but honest Russian violinist, Boris Andrieff, as a fitter. Boris immediately falls in love with Abe's daughter, Irma, who happens to be the lady in the life of Henry Feldman, the shyster for Abe and Morris' firm. When a labor agitator is shot, Boris is arrested and accused of his murder, and Abe and Morris mortgage the business to bail out their fitter. Abe urges Boris to flee to Canada, but the young man, learning that the partners have sunk all their savings into his cause, insists on seeing his own troubles through. Boris, of course, is finally vindicated, with the reluctant help of Feldman, and wins Irma's hand with Abe's blessings.

Commenting that the stage play plot was considerably altered, *Harrison's Reports* noted that "There is a mixture of laughs and tears such as is seldom found in one picture." And *The New York Times* raved "Potash and Perlmutter, be it known, are as funny on the screen as they were on the stage, than which there is no higher praise . . . the picture has as many laughs as a Chaplin comedy."

Barney Bernard, Vera Gordon and Alexander Carr in Potash and Perlmutter.

Barney Bernard, Alexander Carr and DeSacia Mooers in Potash and Perlmutter.

3 CYTHEREA (1924)

Directed by George Fitzmaurice; scenario, Frances Marion; based on the novel *Cytherea, Goddess of Love* by Joseph Hergesheimer; photographer, Arthur Miller; editor, Stuart Heisler; art director, Ben Carré. Eight reels. Technicolor sequences. Distributed by First National Pictures. Premiere, Mark Strand Theater, New York, 5/25/24

THE CAST:
Lee Randon, Lewis Stone; *Savina Grove,* Alma Rubens; *Peyton Morris,* Norman Kerry; *Fanny Randon,* Irene Rich; *Annette Sherwin,* Constance Bennett; *William Grove,* Charles Wellesley; *Claire Morris,* Betty Bouton; *Gregory Randon,* Mickey Moore; *Helen Randon,* Peaches Jackson; *Daniel Randon,* Brandon Hurst; *Randon Butler,* Hugh Saxon; *Grove Butler,* Lee Hill; *Laundress,* Lydia Yeamans Titus.

In his elegant production of Joseph Hergesheimer's best-selling novel, *Cytherea,* Goldwyn created box office enthusiasm not only from his highly publicized censorship difficulties, but also several stunning color sequences scattered throughout the film. His troubles with the censors stemmed from his initial plans to graphically picture what most considered a rather bold love story—a middle-aged philanderer who leaves his nagging wife to run off with a lovely lady in whom he sees the image of the porcelain doll he keeps in a niche on his mantle. The color sequences, photographed in Cuba where the couple has fled, helped the shrewd Mr. Goldwyn play off the publicity surrounding another producer's forthcoming all-color film, *Wanderer of the Wasteland,* and be first where it counted—at the box office.

Most critics noted that Goldwyn spent money on *Cytherea* with previously unnoticed lavishness, but with the discrimination and taste with which he rapidly was establishing a trademark. "I was one of the doubting number who could not see how anything good on the screen could come out of Joseph Hergesheimer's book," wrote Louella Parsons in the *New York American.*

I thought that when Samuel Goldwyn saw film material in this hectic love story, he was seeing a mirage. That George Fitzmaurice was able to take Hergesheimer's most daring book, make it so that it passed the censors without a word, and yet keep a semblance of its original theme speaks well not only for him, but for Frances Marion's skill as a scenario writer.

Miss Parsons confessed that the picture was "one of the most colorful dramas of the year."

In casting his "love after forty" drama, Goldwyn chose to play the philanderer Lewis Stone, later to become the ultimate father figure at MGM as Judge Hardy. Frances Marion stacked the deck in his favor, giving him a nagging, punctilious wife, as well as an understanding "other woman," and making him a dreamer who simply feels that youth is slipping away. In addition, Miss Marion altered the story, again in the leading man's favor, by giving it a happy ending. The film's "Cytherea" was Alma Rubens, who played the aunt of the vamp (Constance Bennett in her first Hollywood-made picture) the "misunderstood" husband was trying to warn away from his niece's flirtatious spouse. Irene Rich was the cheated shrew of a wife, and Norman Kerry, the cad who had been running around with the vamp. The Constance Bennett role, incidentally, was that of a beautiful film actress, reputedly patterned after Lillian Gish.

The spicy story revolves itself around the conventional, boring home life of Lee and Fanny Randon and the spark struck when he attempts to break up the budding affair between Peyton Morris, his niece's husband, and calculating actress, Annette Sherwin. Randon meets her aunt, Savina Grove, and sees in her the woman he imagines whenever he gazes at a dream doll he keeps, christened "Cytherea, Goddess of Love." Breaking ties with his family, Randon and Savina begin an intense affair and run off to a new life in Cuba. There, she develops a mysterious tropical illness and dies suddenly. Grief-stricken, Randon returns home, repents, and is reunited with his wife and children.

Critical appraisal of the Goldwyn film, the first of five Goldwyn movies wherein director Fitzmaurice and writer Marion collaborated, was generally favorable. *Variety* straddled the fence, finding that:

> with much of the spice of the novel deleted, *Cytherea* closely resembles the long run of domestic problems the screen has been addicted to . . . It will probably resolve itself into another example of the novel selling the celluloid edition with the readers of the book being the only ones capable of filling in the "naughty" ingredients.

Then, however it credited Stone with "a corking portrayal as the wandering husband" and photographer Arthur Miller with "providing an example of his work that may stand with the best." And while the critic for the *New York Sun* advised his readers to "Add *Cytherea* to the list of the best pictures of the year; it is a powerful and brilliant thing," the anonymous reviewer for *The New York Times* thought that:

> So long as a producer is more or less guided by censorial edicts, it would be almost impossible to make a really good picture of this story. The book was snatched at as a great box office asset, and it is produced with this idea in mind, but the film possesses very little effective drama . . . it is obvious that (George) Fitzmaurice has either been overawed in fear of perpetrating something that would not pass the censors or was handicapped by a stilted scenario.

In contrast, Harriette Underhill, critic for the *New York Herald Tribune,* felt that:

> Frances Marion has done wonders with the script, but Lewis Stone and Constance Bennett are the only players who fit. Alma Rubens can make of Savina nothing but a sloe-eyed and obvious vampire lady . . . where is the pale, icy Savina Grove of Joseph Hergesheimer's dream?

(Miss Underhill compared the casting of Alma Rubens as Savina to the absurdity of having Nita Naldi portray Peter Pan.) "Constance Bennett is intensely interesting as Annette Sherwin," the reviewer continued, "but that is because Miss Bennett is an intensely interesting young person. George Fitzmaurice has done a good piece of work, but we refuse to be comforted, since, in the first place, *Cytherea* was never meant for the screen."

Lewis Stone and Alma Rubens in Cytherea.

Lewis Stone and Constance Bennett in Cytherea.

Lewis Stone and Constance Bennett in Cytherea.

4 IN HOLLYWOOD WITH POTASH AND PERLMUTTER (1924)

Directed by Alfred H. Green; scenario, Frances Marion; based on the play *Business Before Pleasure* by Montague Glass and Jules Eckert Goodman; photographers, Arthur Miller and Harry Hallenberger; editor, Stuart Heisler; art director, Ben Carré; titles, Montague Glass. Seven reels. Distributed by First National Pictures. Premiere: Mark Strand Theater, New York, 9/29/24

THE CAST:
Abe Potash, George Sidney; *Morris Perlmutter,* Alexander Carr*; *Rosie Potash,* Vera Gordon; *Rita Sismondi,* Betty Blythe; *Mrs. Perlmutter,* Belle Bennett; *Blanchard,* Anders Randolf; *Irma Potash,* Peggy Shaw; *Sam Pemberton,* Charles Meredith; *Miss O'Ryan,* Lillian Hackett; *Crabbe,* David Butler; *Film Buyer,* Sidney Franklin; *Film Buyer,* Joseph W. Girard; *Herself,* Norma Talmadge; *Herself,* Constance Talmadge.
* in 1917 Broadway version.

Abe Potash and Morris Perlmutter were brought to the screen for a second time by Goldwyn in his version of the 1917 P&P play, *Business Before Pleasure*. This time, the partners were movie producers in what amounted to a spoof of Goldwyn's early career. Goldwyn, of course, knew exactly what he was doing and was well aware of audience tastes.

Barney Bernard, the original Abe Potash, had died since making the first film in the series, and was replaced by George Sidney (not the director), while Alexander Carr repeated his established stage and screen characterization of the slightly less-excitable Morris Perlmutter. In this outing, the partners foresake their textile business to move into filmmaking, turning out such gems as *The Fatal Murder* with a cast comprised of virtually every member of their respective families. The film-within-a-film is neatly stolen by Abe's wife, Rosie, as a destitute woman, but the initial effort adds up to nil. The boys manage, though, to obtain financial backing from an interested banker named Blanchard, provided they engage his girlfriend, Rita Sismondi, an actress famed for her vamp roles. Rita, however, is forced to audition against several others who have answered an ad by Abe and Morris. Among the applicants are Norma and Constance Talmadge (in gag bits), directed by real life directors David Butler and Sidney Franklin respectively. Abe and Morris, naturally, are unappreciative of the Talmadge Sisters' acting abilities, and the vamp role fall to Rita, who not only devours the picture, but virtually destroys her producers' home lives. Ultimately, though, things straighten themselves out when Rita runs off with the film's director.

The Goldwyn mark is all over this picture, primarily because of its Hollywood setting. Many critics were surprised that the noted producer would satirize so mercilessly the industry he loved—and, to paraphrase one of the well-known Goldwynisms, "bite the hand that laid the golden egg." The joys and woes of movie-making, even in grossly exaggerated form, together with "in" jokes such as the appearances of the Talmadges and spoofs of the ultimate screen epic (a takeoff on *Ben Hur*), made this P&P excursion into one of the better comedies of the day. Even the hoary burlesque routine of inducing a rather timid actor into working with a dog disguised as a lion and then substituting the real beast at the last moment, is reprised here for the expected laughs, as well as age-old gags, such as the introduction of Rita Sismondi as "a real Kipling vampire," with Abe's retort: "For $650 a week, she should kipple some other place."

The New York Times named the film one of the year's ten best, calling it

One of the funniest farces it has been our lot to view on the screen. It is a film in which novel situations have been worked out in a masterful fashion . . . Anyone who wants a good, hearty laugh ought to go and see this pictorial gem.

Writing in the *New York Herald Tribune,* critic Harriette Underhill noted:

We're pleased to report that it is far more amusing on the screen than it was on the stage . . . it's a rollicking comedy with no dull moments and the four stars' performances are flawless. We hadn't known, either, that Al Green was such an excellent director.

Of George Sidney's work in the role of Abe Potash, *Variety* felt that:

(he) is an able choice, replacing the late lamented Barney Bernard. While perhaps missing the degree of pathos in his work that Bernard gives out, nevertheless he gives a performance that is an assured fulfillment of the assignment.

Betty Blythe and George Sidney in In Hollywood with Potash and Perlmutter.

Cyril Ring, Betty Blythe, Alexander Carr and George Sidney in In Hollywood with Potash and Perlmutter.

5 TARNISH (1924)

Directed by George Fitzmaurice; scenario, Frances Marion; based on the play by Gilbert Emery; photographers, William Tuers and Arthur Miller; editor, Stuart Heisler; art director, Ben Carré. Seven reels. Distributed by First National Pictures. Premiere: Mark Strand Theater, New York, 10/12/24

THE CAST:
Letitia Tevis, May McAvoy; *Emmett Carr,* Ronald Colman; *Nettie Dark,* Marie Prevost; *John Graves,* Norman Kerry; *Adolf Tevis,* Albert Gran*; *Josephine Tevis,* Mrs. Russ Whytall*; *Aggie,* Priscilla Bonner; *The Barber,* Harry Myers; *Mrs. Stutts,* Kay Deslys; *Mrs. Healy,* Lydia Yeamans Titus; *Bill,* William Boyd; *Mr. Stutts,* Snitz Edwards.
* in original Broadway version.

Goldwyn's New York people, always looking for commercial properties back East to make points with the boss, convinced him of the values of Gilbert Emery's popular play, *Tarnish,* wherein Ann Harding, Tom Powers and Fania Marinoff were then starring. Goldwyn came to New York, took an admiring look, and bought the screen rights for $75,000. Then he had Frances Marion fashion a screenplay for May McAvoy, the diminutive actress, whose child/woman innocence and large Irish blue eyes augmented her acting talent, and in whom Goldwyn had seen the hard-working Tishy Tevis, the girl who shoulders the family responsibility in place of her spendthrift father. Her leading man, Goldwyn decreed, would be the handsome young actor who had made such an impression playing opposite Lillian Gish in both *The White Sister* and *Romola,* Ronald Colman. In his signing of Colman, Goldwyn would create his first "star" and would cast the dashing Englishman in eighteen films in the next nine years. *The New York Times* commented on Colman in *Tarnish:* "He is a convincing screen actor with a pleasing personality who is just the player for this role."

In his purchase of screen rights to *Tarnish,* Goldwyn continued treading boldly where few other producers were willing to step, and then managed to whip up commercial scripts that would pass the film industry's censor boards. In this case, Goldwyn's censor problems, always carefully publicized for maximum news value, were prompted by suggested vulgarity and a scene showing a woman in a bathtub. Miss Marion, however, was quite sympathetic with Goldwyn, and both knew exactly how to approach the censorable "no-nos" without getting slapped down. Of the producer she has said: "Sam has taste and integrity. There's never any pretense about him. He has always worked harder than anyone he ever hired, and his appreciation for a job well done is always immense and completely genuine." In addition to maintaining the principal situation that initially intrigued Goldwyn—that of having the girl's sweetheart and father both involved with the same calculating woman—Frances Marion kept the action primarily to New Year's Eve, allowing director George Fitzmaurice to alternate and contrast the joy and the sorrow in Tishy Tevis' heart.

Tarnish finds Letitia Tevis working as a stenographer for Emmett Carr to support her once rich family. Her father, an old reprobate, has been squandering every penny on a scheming manicurist, Nettie Dark, and Tishy is determined to get it all back. Emmett not only is in love with Tishy, but previously had been rather closely acquainted with Nettie, who still has some strong feelings toward the upstanding bachelor. Unhappily, Letitia decides to go to Nettie's apartment for a showdown about her father's improprieties—and money—and there, is disillusioned to find Emmett, who had been lured by Nettie's friend, Aggie on the pretense that she (Nettie) was ill and desperate. A dewy-eyed Tishy wanders out and becomes caught up in the midst of a horn-blowing, confetti-throwing New Year's Eve crowd, as Emmett dashes after her, hoping to catch up, striving to explain. Eventually, of course, she realizes his innocence in the affair and tells herself that, if her love for him were great enough, it must include forgiveness of the past moral offenses that he shows he sincerely regrets.

In *Tarnish,* Canadian actress Marie Prevost vamped her way merrily through the role of the gold digging manicurist, while Albert Gran and Mrs. Russ Whytall recreated their original stage roles as Tishy's parents. Norman Kerry's few scenes as a cad were added after principal production had been completed, and William Boyd made one of his early screen appearances in a brief role.

In its appraisal of the film, *The New York Times* found that "the stirring dramatic action and restrained pathos make this production a strong entertainment." *Variety,* on the other hand, thought it "just a good picture of average quality and not nearly so effective on the screen as on the stage . . . the story stood up better when supported with Gilbert Emery's magnificent dialogue than with Goldwyn's flicker cast." In its judgement of the acting, *Variety* said:

May McAvoy has the Tishy role, and despite her pretty face, she doesn't nearly plumb those emotional depths requisite to an adequate portrayal. Marie Prevost as manicurist, however, is excellent, and Ronald Colman, as Emmett Carr, is the best thing in the film.

Harriette Underhill, reflecting in the *New York Herald Tribune* on this film, touted as an exposé on "The fling of youth with the sting of truth!" felt that:

for the first time in her career, May McAvoy seems rather colorless as the upright young heroine. This isn't a fat part, to say the least. But Ronald Colman, that nice man who burst on the screen fan's vision in *The White Sister,* is extremely attractive as the hero, and Marie Prevost is terribly amusing as Nettie Dark, a bad girl but a good manicurist . . . whatever your taste in pictures, you will probably enjoy *Tarnish*—at least mildly.

Ronald Colman and May McAvoy in Tarnish.

Marie Prevost, May McAvoy and Ronald Colman in Tarnish.

William Boyd, Ronald Colman, Marie Prevost and May McAvoy in Tarnish.

6 A THIEF IN PARADISE (1925)

Directed by George Fitzmaurice; scenario, Frances Marion; based on the novel *The Worldlings* by Leonard Merrick; photographer, Arthur Miller; editor, Stuart Heisler; art director, Ben Carré. Eight reels. Distributed by First National Pictures. Premiere: Mark Strand Theater, New York, 1/25/25

THE CAST:
Helen Saville, Doris Kenyon; *Maurice Blake*, Ronald Colman; *Rosa Carmino*, Aileen Pringle; *Noel Jardine*, Claude Gillingwater; *Bishop Saville*, Alec Francis; *Ned Whelan*, John Patrick; *Philip Jardine*, Charles Youree; *Rosa's Maid*, Etta Lee; *Jardine's Secretary*, Lon Poff.

The film version of Leonard Merrick's turn-of-the-century best-seller *The Worldlings,* has established itself as the model of the lavish Goldwyn spectaculars of the silent era and introduced to the screen "a cast of Hollywood's most beautiful peaches" (as the ads boasted), forerunners of the famed Goldwyn Girls. "Indisputably a brilliant entertainment," critic Mordaunt Hall of *The New York Times* wrote, "having been produced with considerable skill and much lavishness."

The drama about a down-and-outer who takes a dead man's indentity to steal his inheritance and marry into society, provided the ideal opportunity for the tasteful Goldwyn opulence to be spread generously over this elegant view of the world of gracious living. Even the mansion that becomes the film's focal point, in one critic's opinion, "at casual glance might be mistaken for the Fifth Avenue Public Library," and boasts an Olympic-sized swimming pool able to contain an underwater extravaganza. Goldwyn lovingly put the responsibility for *A Thief in Paradise* in the hands of his first team: director George Fitzmaurice, scenarist Frances Marion, and photographer Arthur Miller. He then assigned the starring role of the charming rake, the film's "love thief," to Ronald Colman, whose debonair characterization makes him equally at home either as beachcomber or man about town.

To promote the film, Goldwyn had his advertising department come up with such modest enticements as these headlines: "See the big polo match between the blondes and the brunettes in bathing suits! The most original touch to a pageant entertainment has ever conceived!" And as added inducements: "See society splendor! See an aeroplane honeymoon! See a dance pageant at the bottom of the sea!"

In the title role, derelict Maurice Blake has become a beachcomber in Samoa where he earns a precarious living diving for pearls with Philip Jardine, the disinherited son of a San Francisco millionaire. When Philip is killed by a shark after falling from a raft during a fight with Blake, Rosa Carmino, the dead man's half-caste, common law wife, induces Blake to assume Jardine's identity and return to the States to claim his legacy. With Rosa in tow, Blake turns up at the Jardine mansion and rapidly endears himself not only to Philip's grouchy father, but also to Helen Saville, Philip's childhood sweetheart. While Blake dallies with Helen, Rosa tries to pressure him into pushing for the inheritance, and when this fails, she resorts to blackmail. Blake finally manages to shake off the venal Rosa and marries Helen, but the half-caste will not be deterred. Spitefully, she goes to Helen and discloses Blake's charade. The disillusioned Helen leaves Blake and he attempts suicide, but there is the obligatory final reel repentance and reconciliation as Helen nurses Blake back to health, after which the elder Jardine announces his intention of adopting the masquerader so that he (Blake) might legally receive the family inheritance. Rosa, naturally, slinks back to the islands.

Variety considered the picture "a tall and oft-times inconsistent tale, but an entertaining and thrilling film drama (that) shifts from comedy to the depths, from drama to hokum." In its assessment of the performances:

Doris Kenyon as the sweet ingenue is sweeter than usual and Ronald Colman as the imposter does well enough, but fails to reach the heights. But Claude Gillingwater hands forth a character portrayal such as has perhaps not been seen twice since Menjou in *A Woman of Paris*. Tragedy, comedy, story punch all flow from his gifted work.

The *Variety* critic, though, gave thumbs-down to "the other woman":

Aileen Pringle as the Oriental baby is never plausible and gives nothing to the product except hard work and gestures of the sort supposedly obsolete these many years in first-rate films.

Critic Harriette Underhill's opinion was that:

Nothing that ever has been in any other picture has been left out of this one—pearl-diving in the Orient, attacking killer sharks, society revelry at night, women's polo games by day, a daring rescue from a runaway horse, an aeroplane wedding trip, a dashing imposter, a sweet heroine, a dancing vampire, a parting at the altar . . . Now you may not think *A Thief In Paradise* is a good picture. It isn't, but no one could complain that he did not get his money's worth.

Ronald Colman and Doris Kenyon in A Thief in Paradise.

Ronald Colman and Aileen Pringle in A Thief in Paradise.

Doris Kenyon and Ronald Colman in A Thief in Paradise.

7 HIS SUPREME MOMENT (1925)

Directed by George Fitzmaurice; scenario, Frances Marion; based on the novel *World Without End* by May Edington; photographer, Arthur Miller; editor, Stuart Heisler; art director, Ben Carré. Eight reels. Technicolor sequences. Distributed by First National Pictures. Premiere: Mark Strand Theater, New York, 4/12/25

THE CAST:
Carla King, Blanche Sweet; *John Douglas*, Ronald Colman; *Sara Deeping*, Kathleen Myers*; *Carla Light*, Belle Bennett; *Harry Avon*, Cyril Chadwick; *Adrian*, Ned Sparks; *Mueva*, Nick De Ruiz; *Harem Girl in Play*, Anna May Wong; *Pasha in Play*, Kalla Pasha.
* role sometimes credited to Jane Winton.

Following his uncanny ability to read public sentiment where the box office receipts were at stake, Goldwyn selected May Edington's novel *World Without End*, as his next project. He dumped the original title for one more provocative, turned loose (but not too) his peerless creative Fitzmaurice/Miller/Marion team, and assigned Ronald Colman, rapidly becoming the screen's foremost matinee idol, to play opposite Blanche Sweet. The Goldwyn instincts had led him to settle primarily on romantic tales, and *His Supreme Moment* more than filled that bill. A triangle drama, it pitted a lovely actress against a scheming socialite for the affections of a dashing mining engineer—and tossed in several scenes in Technicolor to further entice the moviegoers who, Goldwyn correctly predicted, would flock to enjoy and shed a tear.

His Supreme Moment opens with a spectacular color sequence set in a Moorish harem, with Blanche Sweet as a blonde dancer, Kalla Pasha as a Turkish sultan, and Anna May Wong the latter's evil, number one girl. Director Fitzmaurice then pulls back his cameras to reveal a play in progress, and things get down to business,

with John Douglas, an engineer who has returned from South America hoping to obtain financing for a new venture, attending the theater with socialite Sara Deeping. She introduces him to the play's star, Carla King, with whom he falls madly in love. Jealous over the constant attention John has begun lavishing on Carla, Sara secretly arranges the financing needed for his mine, figuring "out of sight, out of mind." John, however, proposes to Carla and she agrees to marry him only if they first live together simply as brother and sister for a year. Together, they return to the jungles of South America, where Carla, who had been accustomed to glorious shower baths and other luxuries afforded by a salary of $2000 a week, soon becomes depressed by the rough, isolated surroundings where a bath now consists of a jug and a basin. John, meanwhile, is having little luck in his search for gold, causing even more friction between the two. When Sara turns up at the camp, John tries to hide the fact that Carla is living there with him, knowing that the socialite would not hesitate to spread the gossip back home about the couple's relationship. Sara returns to New York with John's promise that he will soon follow, but a labor uprising at the camp, along with malaria, fells John. Carla nurses him back to health, but realizes that their relationship is hopeless.

Returning to the United States, Carla looks up an old acquaintance, millionaire Harry Avon, and promises to marry him if he will back John's venture. The latter, however, learns of her noble sacrifice, prevents the marriage, arranges independent financing, and goes back to South America with Carla as his true wife.

In his review of this impeccably staged melodrama, critic Mordant Hall wrote in *The New York Times*:

Mr. Colman is better in this picture than in any in

which he has appeared since *The White Sister*. He is careful in his makeup and looks every inch a man—rugged and good-looking and thoroughly at ease. Miss Sweet never falters in her work, giving a really remarkable performance.

Of Kathleen Myers' portrayal though, critic Hall noted: "She exaggerates her characterization (and) her acting reminds one of the deep-eyed stage villains of thirty years ago."

Variety felt that:

the women are going to go wild over the lovemaking Ronald Colman does on the screen. He is out for the matinee idol honors and bids fair to receive them. Blanche Sweet has done a comeback in this picture and seemingly the opportunity was all that she wanted. (She) does look wonderfully well, almost startlingly so in the color shots.

That paper's critic also pointed out: "How they ever managed to get by the censors on the Moorish bath scene is going to be a mystery that will remain dark forever."

The following was from the *New York Herald Tribune's* Harriette Underhill:

His Supreme Moment is a large, cheap movie, old style in direction and filled with titles which read like extracts from a primer, but which are not always in good taste nor good English. All along we kept saying (it) is going to be a terrible movie—and it was.

Of the acting, she concluded that "Miss Sweet and Mr. Colman played with a simplicity and sincerity worthy of a better cause (and) are as fine in these two silly roles as any two people can be."

Several reviewers commented on the odd casting of Belle Bennett as Blanche Sweet's mother, noting that she did not look a day older than the heroine and probably was not, and that despite its flyweight, old-fashioned plot, *His Supreme Moment* would be supremely popular (it was) because of the added enticement of the "colored interludes" and the exhortations in the advertising: "A sumptuous romance with love scenes in color! Supreme in everything you can ask!"

Ronald Colman and Blanche Sweet in His Supreme Moment.

Blanche Sweet, Ronald Colman and Kathleen Myers in His Supreme Moment.

His Supreme Moment.

Blanche Sweet, Ronald Colman and player in His Supreme Moment.

8 THE DARK ANGEL (1925)

Directed by George Fitzmaurice; scenario, Frances Marion; based on the play by H.B. Trevelyan (Guy Bolton); photographer, George Barnes; editor, Stuart Heisler; art director, Ben Carré. Eight reels. Distributed by First National Pictures. Premiere: Mark Strand Theater, New York, 10/11/25

THE CAST:

Captain Hilary Trent, Ronald Colman; Kitty Vane, Vilma Banky; Gerald Shannon, Wyndham Standing; Lord Beaumont, Frank Elliott; Sir Hubert Vane, Charles Lane; Miss Bottles, Helen Jerome Eddy; Roma, Florence Turner.

Having successfully turned Ronald Colman into a matinee idol and the silent screen's top leading man, Goldwyn began searching for a female counterpart on whom he could lavish his already famous "touch." He found her in an actress named Vilma Banky, on a visit to Budapest in the summer of 1924. The story goes that he had spotted her photo, summoned her manager, was overwhelmed when she was presented to him as he was about to entrain for home, and immediately signed her to a five-year contract—for $250 a week. Subsequently he tore up the original pact and gave her a new contract calling for $2000 weekly, rising to $5000 in the final year.

Vilma Banky came to America the following spring and was teamed with Colman in the screen version of the then current hit play, The Dark Angel. Overnight, the Colman/Banky combination became the screen's foremost attraction, thanks in no small part to the astute Goldwyn's publicity people who had made certain that Vilma Banky's name was on everybody's lips before reel one of The Dark Angel was ever seen. "Interest naturally centers about Miss Banky, who has been touted to the heavens by Samuel Goldwyn as the greatest ever," noted Variety in its review of the film. "Funniest of all is that (she) is as good as Goldwyn claimed . . . her acting here is as sure and professional as if she had been used to American studios for years."

George Fitzmaurice's creative direction, Frances Marion's exquisite screenplay, and, of course, Goldwyn's distinctive "touch" established The Dark Angel as one of the decade's great romatic dramas. Ronald Colman, in one of his best silent film portrayals ("a bang-up performance" was Variety's appraisal), embodies in Hilary Trent all the dash, sincerity, heroism, gentility and manliness that has become the badge of the stalwart British officer—"the Imperial archetype" as Colman has come to be called. And as Kitty Vane, Vilma Banky radiates warmth, compassion, breeding, and undying love for the handsome captain who had marched from her life to fight for his country, "a young person of rare beauty," wrote The New York Times. "Her acting is sincere and earnest, and her tears seem very real."

"George Fitzmaurice's inspiring masterpiece" (as Goldwyn heralded in his ads) was injected with innumerable directorial touches, adding to the special romanticism of his sentimental drama. In one striking sequence, troops returning from battle come to a halt, and as bereaved parents peer into their depleted ranks, ghosts of dead soldiers slowly rise, resplendent in white uniforms. "This effect is corking," thought Variety,

as is the phantom of the Dark Angel, Death, flying over the battlefields and then into the quiet English home of Kitty . . . in all, a rare, fine, up and outstanding audience picture, produced with taste and care, and in its two leading roles, ideally cast.

The now familiar story centers upon Hilary Trent and Kitty Vane. On the eve of their marriage, he is called up to his regiment, but manages to spend the last few precious hours with his fiancée. When he is subsequently reported killed, Kitty is disconsolate, and finally agrees to marry Hilary's friend, Gerald Shannon, who has been discreetly wooing her. Hilary, meanwhile, had not died in battle, but was blinded, and after being invalided out of the service, he decides that rather than being a burden on Kitty, he will find a new life under a new name in a remote corner of England and devote himself to writing children's stories. On the day she is to be married to Gerald, Kitty learns that Hilary is still alive, and changing from her wedding gown, she goes to the man for whom she had waited for years. Hilary, meanwhile, has been told that Kitty is coming to see him, and to conceal his blindness from her, he memorizes every foot of his room, entertains her while hiding his true feelings, and tries to convince her he no longer cares for her. As she prepares to leave, she extends her hand which he, naturally, does not see. Confused and hurt, she leaves, but is intercepted outside the front door by Hilary's secretary, Miss Bottles, who reveals her boss' blindness. Kitty turns and rushes back into the house and embraces Hilary.

Mordaunt Hall wrote:

Ronald Colman, who acts Trent, is most sympathetic and capable, and a strong man might well be excused for weeping at some of the scenes in this delightful romance . . . This is by all means the best picture George Fitzmaurice has to his credit.

Similarly, Richard Watts, Jr., writing in the *New York Herald Tribune,* thought that:

Ronald Colman plays the blinded hero with suavity and skill, and in that splendid scene at the close, rises to his opportunity fully. Vilma Banky . . . is a handsome young blonde who plays with considerable charm (and) *The Dark Angel* remains George Fitzmaurice's best picture, which in itself insures it long life and prosperity.

In the Broadway production of *The Dark Angel,* which had opened the previous February, Patricia Collinge was Kitty, Reginald Mason played Hilary, and John Williams appeared as Gerald. The Goldwyn remake of this film a decade later would star Merle Oberon, Fredric March and Herbert Marshall in the leads.

Vilma Banky and Ronald Colman in The Dark Angel.

Vilma Banky in The Dark Angel.

Vilma Banky and director George Fitzmaurice on the set
of The Dark Angel.

9 STELLA DALLAS (1925)

Directed by Henry King; scenario, Frances Marion; based on the novel by Olive Higgins Prouty; photographer, Arthur Edeson; editor, Stuart Heisler; art director, Ben Carré. Eleven reels. Released by United Artists. Premiere: Apollo Theater, New York, 11/16/25

THE CAST:
Stephen Dallas, Ronald Colman; *Stella Dallas*, Belle Bennett; *Helen Morrison*, Alice Joyce; *Ed Munn*, Jean Hersholt; *Mrs. Grosvenor*, Beatrix Pryor; *Laurel Dallas*, Lois Moran; *Richard Grosvenor*, Douglas Fairbanks, Jr.; *Miss Tibbets*, Vera Lewis; *Morrison Children*, Maurice Murphy, Jack Murphy, Newton Hall; *Morrison Children, Ten Years Later*, Charles Hatten, Robert Gillette, Winston Miller.

Marking Goldwyn's first association with United Artists was his stunning version of *Stella Dallas,* his finest film during the 1920s and still classic cinema. A superb interpretation by Frances Marion of Olive Higgins Prouty's enduring tale of mother love, *Stella Dallas* is the perfect collaboration of producer, scenarist and director, with a starring portrayal ranking among the screen's unforgettable performances. *Variety* called it "A mother picture . . . not a great picture, but a great mother picture." The connotation was, of course, somewhat different in 1925, but it accurately described this six-handkerchief weeper that became the most popular woman's movie of the era.

Goldwyn, the eternal romantic, hired Henry King, one of the screen's foremost romantic directors, to take charge of the project. King extracted masterful performances from a top-notch cast, headed by Belle Bennett in certainly the performance of her career. She previously had appeared in Goldwyn's *In Hollywood with Potash and Perlmutter* and *His Supreme Moment,* and rose magnificently to the challenge of the title role as the poor, silly, vulgar small-town girl who marries far above herself, and later has a daughter to whom she completely devotes her life. "A memorable performance," is the way *The New York Times* described it, "one which is rarely seen on the screen." And Harriette Underhill wrote in the *New York Herald Tribune* that Miss Bennett's portrayal is "something that probably never will be forgotten in the cinema world. That woman has plucked out the soul of Stella Dallas and presents it as no other actress, we believe, could possibly have done."

The now familiar plot describes how Stephen Dallas leaves his opulent home following the suicide of his father, an accused embezzler, and gravitates to a small town to make a new life. Learning of the engagement of his former sweetheart, socialite Helen Morrison, Stephen consoles himself with Stella, one of the local belles. The two wed in a marriage that is, naturally, doomed from the start, with their daughter, Laurel, the only thing Stephen and Stella have in common. The two soon separate and Stephen returns to his own world in New York, leaving Stella to raise Laurel.

Years pass and Laurel grows to young womanhood, learning to cope with her mother's thoughtlessness, stupidity, and her coarse boyfriends, especially Ed Munn, the foulmouthed, drunken horse trainer. Realizing at last the she cannot properly provide for Laurel, for whom she wants only the best, Stella agrees to divorce Stephen so that he can marry Helen and make a good home for Laurel. The girl, at first, refuses to leave her mother, but Stella marries Ed Munn and cruelly forces Laurel to go to live with her father. As Laurel becomes accustomed to the comfortable surroundings, she grows ashamed of her mother who makes an occasional trip to New York for a visit, turning up on the well-rolled lawns wearing her outlandish ostrich-feathered hats and zebra-striped dresses, and to Laurel's friends, is "that frightful woman."

Stella is overjoyed at the news that Laurel has met and fallen in love with handsome young social lion, Richard Grosvenor, but waits in vain for a wedding invitation. On the day of Laurel's marriage, Stella resists the urge to force herself on the young couple, and not wanting to embarrass her daughter further, simply stands in the rain and watches the wedding ceremony through the window until a policeman orders her to move along.

Stella Dallas brims with heart-tearing sequences. In addition to the famous final scene with Stella in the rain at Laurel's wedding, there are earlier gems, like the birthday party interlude whereat Stella and Laurel sit at the table prepared for the little friends who are never going to show up. Laurel pitifully digs into the ice cream, tears rolling down her face, as the hurt finally explodes. And, at still another age, Laurel entrains for New York as Stella feels the emptiness slowly creeping into her life, walking and then running along the platform, trying to keep gazing at Laurel's window until the train simply outdistances her.

As Stephen Dallas, Ronald Colman plays somewhat against type, portraying a self-centered cad. The role, though, is rather limited. Goldwyn's newest discovery, Lois Moran, is enchanting as Laurel (playing the girl at ten, thirteen and as a young woman). *Variety's* pre-diction, however, that "this picture should do for Miss Moran what *The Birth Of a Nation* did for Mae Marsh" failed to materialize. A youthful Douglas Fairbanks, Jr., shows in his performance as Richard Grosvenor, early promise of the star quality he would attain with talkies.

Critical raves literally swamped *Stella Dallas.* Mordaunt Hall put it on his Ten Best list in *The New York Times;* Louella Parsons, writing in the *New York American* raved: "There has been no picture to surpass *Stella Dallas*—or even to equal it; the *Los Angeles Examiner* found it "marvelous and magnificent"; and the *New Yorker* claimed it "the greatest picture ever made." In the opinion of the *New York Herald Tribune's* critic, Harriette Underhill, *"Stella Dallas* ranks as one of the finest achievements in the history of the screen . . . Henry King has done as fine a piece of work as any director ever did."

Shortly after Samuel Goldwyn remade *Stella Dallas* as a talkie a dozen years later, with Barbara Stanwyck, John Boles and Anne Shirley as Stella, Stephen and Laurel, the long-running (eighteen-plus years) radio serial began charming its way into the hearts of daytime romantics. Anne Elstner portrayed Stella for the entire life of the NBC series.

Belle Bennett, Ronald Colman and Jean Hersholt in Stella Dallas.

Belle Bennett and Lois Moran in Stella Dallas.

Ronald Colman and Lois Moran in Stella Dallas.

Douglas Fairbanks Jr. and Lois Moran in Stella Dallas.

Belle Bennett in the famous climax of Stella Dallas.

10 PARTNERS AGAIN (WITH POTASH AND PERLMUTTER) 1926

Directed by Henry King; scenario, Frances Marion; based on the play *Partners Again* by Montague Glass and Jules Eckert Goodman; photographer, Arthur Edeson; editor, Stuart Heisler; titles, Montague Glass. Six reels. Released by United Artists. Premiere: Mark Strand Theater, New York, 2/14/26.

THE CAST:
Abe Potash, George Sidney; *Morris Perlmutter,* Alexander Carr*; *Hattie Potash,* Betty Jewel; *Dan,* Allan Forrest; *Schenckmann,* Robert Schable; *Rosie Potash,* Lillian Elliott; *Marcus Pazinsky,* Lew Brice; *Pilot,* Earl Metcalf; *Mr. Sammett,* Gilbert Clayton; *Mrs. Sammett,* Anna Gilbert.
* In 1922 Broadway version.

In the midst of the remarkably successful romantic dramas, for which Goldwyn had become renowned in such a short time, the producer's sentimental spot for the comedy antics of Abe Potash and Morris Perlmutter again revealed itself, and the bickering, but always loveable businessmen, made their third and final appearance, dispensing, courtesy of Samuel Goldwyn, gobs of wit, wisdom, laughter and heart. Frances Marion's adaptation of the Broadway smash (the fourth "P&P" play, entitled simply *Partners Again*) was handled with such finesse by director Henry King, whose reputation lay in more serious subjects, that *Variety* was obliged to point out: "Henry King is also responsible for *Stella Dallas* . . . (and) it would be hard to imagine that the two came from the hands of the same director, so different in tempo and styles are the two."

In the last of Goldwyn's silent comedies, the focus is on Abe and Morris' misadventures in the automobile business, where they have obtained the franchise for the redoubtable Schenckmann Six. Introduced into the frantic proceedings are the customary marital squabbles, business disagreements, romantic entanglements between Abe's flighty daughter, Hattie, and the lovesick banker who holds the Potash and Perlmutter mortage, and dubious stock manipulations involving Rosie Potash's good-for-nothing nephew, Marcus Pazinsky. Excitable Abe it appears, never was cut out to be an automobile salesman, a fact made quite obvious when a demonstration given to a hapless prospective buyer gets out of hand, after suffering through the embarrassment of explaining why everything, but the engine makes noise. And finally, after exposing poor Rosie to the luxuries of driving and finding themselves on roller coaster styled roadways—and off the top of a drawbridge—Abe gladly turns the whole business over to Morris and seeks what he hopes will be an easier money-making life. Enter Mark Pazinsky with his grandiose ideas. This time, it's a stock scheme that will put the Potash family on easy street. The less-than-enthusiastic Abe reluctantly becomes involved with his wife's nephew, only to find himself immediately in the midst of a market swindle. Fearing arrest, Abe goes into hiding while Rosie puts in a frantic call to Morris to help bail out his old partner.

Morris arranges for a plane flight to Canada and sneaks Abe aboard before he (Abe) can change from his nightgown to more presentable street clothes. The pair, only a few steps ahead of angry stockholders and the police, take off for Canada, noticing only that they are being trailed by another plane, piloted by a frantically waving figure. In their attempt to lose their pursuer, Abe and Morris have their own pilot engage in various complicated aerial maneuvers, but instead of losing the other plane, they lose Abe, who manages to fall out, saved only when his nightgown does double duty as a parachute. The two planes land nearby, and Morris discovers that the other pilot is Schenkmann, the partners' own banker, who has been trying to tell them that the real stock manipulators have been caught and that Abe is off the hook—and that, as an afterthought, he would like to marry Hattie Potash. With Abe's blessings the pair wed, and with Rosie's blessings, Abe and Morris renew their partnership.

"(It is) a so-so farce with not too many hilarious moments," thought Richard Watts Jr., writing in the *New York Herald Tribune.* "Yet it is given distinction beyond its merits by the admirable comic portrayals of Sidney and Carr. These two comics do marvels with their material." Watts felt, though, that "the trouble with director King's photoplay seems to be that he has relied too heavily for humor on the subtitles." *The New*

York Times' Mordaunt Hall found that: "This production is not as witty as its predecessors, but, as Samuel Goldwyn believes in hearing when it comes to comedy, one might say that there were frequent bits of horseplay that did arouse unexpected mirth." Hall further commented that: "To be true, there are some ludicrous situations, a few calculated to make Buster Keaton stretch his mouth, but a good deal of the comedy is swamped by making Abe more foolish than funny."

Variety decided that this P&P outing was "a screen comedy that combines a measure of thrills at the finish certain to keep the audience on the edge of their seats and at the same time having them scream with laughter." In appraising the acting, *Variety* concluded: "George Sidney pretty much walks away with all the sympathy there is in the picture."

An interesting sidenote is the fact that George Sidney continued his film career in an extension of his Abe Potash characterization, appearing as Jacob Cohen in the more enduring *Cohens and Kellys* ethnic series of the 1920s and early 1930s.

Alexander Carr and George Sidney in Partners Again.

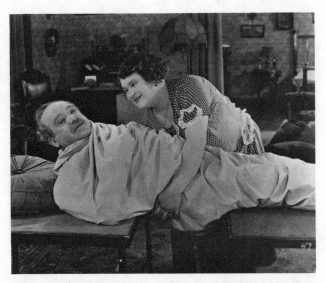

George Sidney and Lillian Elliott in Partners Again.

11 THE WINNING OF BARBARA WORTH (1926)

Directed by Henry King: scenario, Frances Marion; based on the novel by Harold Bell Wright; photographer, George Barnes; associate photographer, Gregg Toland; editor, Viola Lawrence; music score, Ted Henkel; art director, Carl Oscar Borg; titles, Rupert Hughes. Nine reels. Released by United Artists. Premiere: Forum Theater, Los Angeles, 10/14/26. New York premiere: Mark Strand Theater, 11/28/26

THE CAST:
Willard Holmes, Ronald Colman; *Barbara Worth,* Vilma Banky; *Jefferson Worth,* Charles Lane; *The Seer,* Paul McAllister; *James Greenfield,* E.J. Ratcliffe; *Abe Lee,* Gary Cooper*, *Tex,* Clyde Cook; *Pat,* Erwin Connelly; *Blanton,* Sam Blum; *Cowboy,* Ed Brady
* in screen debut

The importance of *The Winning of Barbara Worth* in cinema history lies not in its being Goldwyn's first western as an independent producer, nor its reteaming of Colman and Banky somewhat out of their element in the Old West, nor its status as a "welcome home" gift following the elegant wedding Goldwyn had lavished upon Vilma Banky and Rod LaRoque. It is remembered specifically for marking the debut of Gary Cooper, although he had been doing bits as extras for some time.

Goldwyn had, for several years, been toying with the idea of bringing Harold Bell Wright's popular 1911 epic novel to the screen, and was prompted to reach an immediate decision upon learning that Sol Lesser and Mike Rosenberg were dickering for the property on behalf of Principal Pictures. Outbidding them by more than $125,000, Goldwyn obtained the rights to the book, dealing with the reclamation of desert lands, and handed the story to Frances Marion for a screen adaptation.

Almost at once, she switched the focus of the tale from Jefferson Worth, Barbara's father and the book's hero, to Willard Holmes, the stalwart engineer from the East. Director Henry King, meanwhile, was assembling his cast, in support of Ronald Colman and Vilma Banky (the second of their five Goldwyn movies together). The second male lead, in the role of Abe Lee, was given to cowboy star Harold Goodwin, who, at the time, was completing a film elsewhere. Goodwin's prior commitment kept him from joining the rest of the cast on the Goldwyn lot, and director King recalled a shy actor he had recently signed on as an extra at $50 a week after admiring a screen test the young cowboy had made of himself. The extra, of course, was Gary Cooper, whom King elevated to the role of Abe Lee after obtaining for him an additional $15 weekly stipend from Goldwyn.

On the film's release, virtually all of the attention went, naturally, to Colman and Banky. Said *The New York Times*:

> Miss Banky is essentially a hot-house flower and not the type one would expect to see living in a desert shack. In this picture, her beauty, however, is a delight to gaze upon and she gives a competent performance. Ronald Colman, too, acquits himself competently, and to the casual observer there is no reason why his love for Barbara should not have been reciprocated long before it is.

Columnist Louella Parsons was among the eagle-eyed few who spotted something in the lanky cowboy who plays the other man in Barbara Worth's life, and she called Cooper's portrayal "something one remembers even after the last reel fades from the screen." *Variety* also raved:

An outstanding performance was given by Gary Cooper as Abe Lee, played in a most sympathetic manner, and came near taking the stuff away from Colman. Cooper is a youth who will be heard from on the screen and possibly blossom out as an "ace" lead.

At this point, Goldwyn made one of his few errors in judgement. "It's the only time I ever knew Sam to hesitate too long and offer too little," Frances Marion said many years later. Apparently, through a lack of communication, Goldwyn and Henry King each assumed, so the story goes, that the other had signed Cooper to a contract, and by the time each had realized the error, Cooper had been snatched up by Paramount Pictures for $150 a week. Years later, Goldwyn was obliged to pay dearly for Cooper's services.

The film's lengthy prologue, a creative touch in Frances Marion's altered (from the novel) screenplay, establishes the leading lady's lineage, as a pioneer family struggles to cross the desert, with the mother (also played by Vilma Banky, here doing "her best acting in the film," according to *Variety*) burying her husband and making a cross from the slats of their baby's cradle. The mother subsequently dies in a sandstorm, shortly before the Worth expedition comes onto the scene and finds the infant, allowing Barbara Worth to be transformed ultimately into "the rose of the desert."

Years later, Jefferson Worth, bent on land reclamation, seeks to borrow money from a banker from the east, James Greenfield, who arrives with his foster son, Willard Holmes, an engineer. As development progresses in Worth's irrigation project, a town springs up (it too, is called Barbara Worth, after the owner's lovely adopted daughter), and work begins under Holmes to bring the water of the Colorado River to arid lands. In the midst of this activity, however, Holmes finds time to court Barbara Worth, who is also being wooed by another young engineer, Abe Lee. Trouble arises, though, when

Greenfield decides to double-cross his partners and take the territory for himself, firing all of the engineers involved in reinforcing the dam. Jefferson Worth decides that Holmes is still in league with Greenfield and orders Holmes off his property, choosing to proceed with the project on his own.

Greenfield sees his chance when Worth runs short of cash, and he (Greenfield) incites the workers to riot for their pay. Holmes and Lee offer to go for the money as things get out of hand, realizing a full day's ride by horseback is in store. On the return trip, the two are ambushed by Greenfield's men and Lee is gravely wounded. Lee, understanding that Barbara never really loved him more than as just a brother, urges Holmes to get the money back to Worth and save the town. Holmes arrives in time to appease the mob, which is preparing to lynch Holmes, while Greenfield's own town is wiped out when the weakened dam bursts.

"The film is incomparable in telling on the screen a new angle in the development of the west," wrote *Variety*. "Goldwyn paid heavily for the making of the flood, wiping out the towns he had built in Nevada. The epic had them cheering on opening night." The paper went on: "It should easily repay Goldwyn for his endeavors . . . and the followers of Banky and Colman (also) will not be disappointed."

The spectacularly staged climactic flood (shot in Nevada's Black Rock Desert and in Imperial Valley) was viewed by many of the era's critics as rivalling, if not surpassing, the Red Sea overflow in DeMille's *The Ten Commandments* of a few years earlier. Certainly it overshadowed the romantic portions of the tale and remains an early screen tribute to photographer George Barnes and his assistant, Gregg Toland. The two, between them, captured on film over the years virtually the entire screen legacy that is Samuel Goldwyn's.

Vilma Banky and Ronald Colman in The Winning of Barbara Worth.

Gary Cooper, Vilma Banky and Ronald Colman in The Winning of Barbara Worth.

Vilma Banky and Ed Brady in The Winning of Barbara Worth.

12 THE NIGHT OF LOVE (1927)

Directed by George Fitzmaurice; scenario, Lenore J. Coffee; based on a story by Pedro Calderon de la Barca; photographers, George Barnes and Thomas Brannigan; editor, Viola Lawrence; art director, Carl Oscar Borg. Eight reels. Released by United Artists. Premiere: Mark Strand Theater, New York, 1/24/27

THE CAST:
Montero, Ronald Colman; *Princess Marie,* Vilma Banky; *Duke Bernardo de la Garda,* Montagu Love; *Donna Beatriz,* Natalie Kingston; *Jester,* John George; *Spanish Ambassador,* William Tooker; *Grandee,* Charles Holt; *Gypsy Dancer,* Sally Rand; *Gypsy Bride,* Laska Winter; *Bandit,* Bynunsky Hyman; *Bandit,* Gibson Gowland; *Specialty,* Marion Morgan Dancers.

"While there is nothing startlingly novel so far as screen stories are concerned in having a romance between a handsome gypsy chieftain and a lovely, flaxen-haired princess," wrote critic Mordaunt Hall in his review in the *New York Times,* "the idea is embellished when these characters are impersonated by Ronald Colman and Vilma Banky, and this combination of players is to be seen in Samuel Goldwyn's lustrous production, *The Night of Love.*"

Here are Colman and Banky the way the romantic team is best remembered—elegantly costumed, exotically situated, professing their love on title cards against the sumptuous trappings of bygone eras. Goldwyn the romanticist linked arms with Goldwyn the realist to offer the public the two stars it, Goldwyn was properly convinced, was clamoring to see, teaming the couple in a series of costume dramas, of which *The Night of Love* was the first and most lavish. This after first deciding no longer to make Ronald Colman's services available to other companies—the actor had been doing light comedies with Constance Talmadge and romantic dramas with

Blanche Sweet, as well as scoring his greatest personal triumph in silent films in *Beau Geste,* away from the Goldwyn studios while his boss leisurely considered the right properties for his foremost star.

For *The Night of Love,* Goldwyn assigned George Fitzmaurice, who had directed the pair so successfully in *The Dark Angel,* once again to guide Colman and Banky as they set the screen afire with burning passions in the heart of seventeenth century Spain. Their fans relished every moment of the colorful tale combining the romance of gypsy life—with dashing Ronald Colman perfect as the leader—with the always intriguing *droit de seigneur* plot fillip. The customary good words about the exquisite Goldwyn taste in overall production were tempered somewhat by concern over some rather daring sequences (by 1927 standards), including, in one instance, shots of Miss Banky's nearly bare breast, as well as the quite revealing apparel of many of the young ladies who danced with abandon during the orgy scenes. In addition, there were questions about the church's attitude toward having malevolent Montagu Love posing as a priest to learn of his bride's indiscretions during confession, and of Vilma Banky's donning of the Virgin Mary's robe to frighten her husband and his cohorts long enough to permit captive Colman's followers to attack and free their leader.

"Mr. Fitzmaurice has made a glamorous photoplay," felt Mordaunt Hall.

Except for a persistent desire to make the most of the good looks of his principals and a little straining at shadow effects, (he) has succeeded admirably in making this both an appealing and entertaining effort—Fitzmaurice's mob scenes are singularly cleverly pictured, especially during a scene of a miracle when Montero is saved from the stake . . . (but) the sight of the

Princess running around in a bridal gown before uncouth gypsies and stern soldiers is a little far-fetched even for the period.

In her screenplay, Lenore J. Coffee arranged for Montero, the virile gypsy prince, to lose his bride on their wedding night when the treacherous Duke Bernardo de la Garda demands his right as feudal lord—to bed down with the bride before giving her to her new husband. Rather than acceding to the Duke's advances, the girl hurls herself into the sea. Montero swears to avenge her death and turns outlaw, kidnapping the Duke's own bride, Princess Marie, following a spectacular wedding feast. Montero's men take the Duke to an abandoned castle overlooking the sea and there brand him before releasing him. Despite her protests, meanwhile, Princess Marie, the niece of the King of France, finds herself falling in love with the dashing Montero, but returns to the Duke after leaping out of the castle window. Although she continues to live with her ignoble husband, the Princess cannot forget Montero, and confesses her sin to the royal priest, unaware that it is the Duke in disguise. The Duke's mistress, Donna Beatriz (played by Natalie Kingston, former premier dancer at New York's Winter Garden), in the meantime, is literally waiting in the wings.

The Duke has the princess thrown into the dungeon and then tricks Montero into trying to rescue her.

Capturing the gypsy, the malevolent Duke orders him burned at the stake, but Montero is saved when the princess tricks her husband into believing in a "miracle" by thinking the Virgin Mary has interceded, a diversion allowing Montero's men to storm the Duke's fortress.

In critic Mordaunt Hall's view, "Ronald Colman, with a shock of curly hair, gives a fine performance as the gypsy chieftain, and Miss Banky is as entrancing as she was in *The Dark Angel*." *Variety's* thoughts on this romantic fairy tale were, in part, that

Colman's performance is bound on all sides by the mechanics of pantomiming before the camera. He plays a gypsy Robin Hood and screens as being too well aware of the fact to merge into the role. Miss Banky looks sufficiently gorgeous to demand interest for herself, but cannot make this heavily weighted love story stand up.

In her *New York Herald Tribune* review, Harriette Underhill wrote:

Vilma Banky is sincere, beautiful and believable as the princess and Ronald Colman is sincere, handsome and believable as the gypsy. Their love scenes are charming, the cast is excellent, the settings are beautiful, and so is the photography . . . only in melodrama as mad as *The Night of Love,* sincerity and beautiful love scenes are in a hazardous position, with all the revelry, swordplay and burnings at the stake crowding out the bigger and finer things.

Ronlad Colman and Vilma Banky in The Night of Love.

John George, Ronald Colman and Vilma Banky in The Night of Love.

13 THE MAGIC FLAME (1927)

Directed by Henry King; scenario, Bess Meredyth; based on the play *König Harlekin* by Rudolph Lothar; photographer, George Barnes; editor, Viola Lawrence; assistant director, Robert Florey; art director, Carl Oscar Borg; theme music, Sigmund Spaeth; titles, George Marion Jr. and Nellie Revell. Nine reels. Released by United Artists. Premiere: Mark Strand Theater, New York, 9/18/27

THE CAST:
Tito, the Clown/Count Casati, Ronald Colman; *Bianca,* Vilma Banky; *Ringmaster,* Agostino Borgato; *Chancellor,* Gustav Von Seyffertitz; *De Bono,* Harvey Clark; *Wife,* Shirley Palmer; *Husband,* Cosmo Kyrle Bellew; *Utility Man,* George Davis; *Manager,* Andre Cheron; *Visitor,* Vadim Uranoff; *Manicurist,* David Mir.

While audiences were still starry-eyed from fantasizing over passionate Colman/Banky love scenes in *The Night of Love,* Goldwyn had hustled the pair before the cameras once again, this time under Henry King's creative direction, in a second romantic costume drama. And what could be better than Ronald Colman tenderly seducing Vilma Banky—perhaps *two* Ronald Colmans? *The Magic Flame,* the curious title Goldwyn settled upon in his cinemazation of Rudolph Lothar's 1904 novel and play, *König Harlekin,* provided Colman with the first of several dual role assignments—a sympathetic circus clown and a villainous Crown Prince.

Henry King's imaginative introduction of Colman allowed the actor to make his initial appearance under putty and grease paint, do a circus turn, and then seat himself before a mirror and gradually wipe away the disguise to reveal the well-known Colman face. And later, as the Prince, Colman has altered his appearance with a longer, neatly curled mustache rather than pencil-thin, with which his fans had become so familiar.

George Barnes's superb photography won an Academy Award nomination in the first year of those awards (he also was nominated the same year for his work on Goldwyn's *The Devil Dancer* as well as Gloria Swanson's version of *Sadie Thompson*). And to enhance the proceedings further, a musical score was provided by none less than Sigmund Spaeth, once again confirming Goldwyn's reputation for obtaining only the *creme de la creme* for the films bearing the prestigious "Samuel Goldwyn Presents" legend ahead of the title.

Variety categorized *The Magic Flame* as

a romantic novelty splendidly produced and capitally acted by these two highly satisfactory screen players again in partnership in a graceful story that fits them trimly. All the elements that go to make a class box office picture are here—names, adequate production and interesting story, the trick of a modern tale with modern characters in medieval settings and projected on a background of a traveling circus.

Two members of the circus troupe, working the villages of rural, early Twenties Italy, are Tito the Clown and Bianca the Aerialist—lovers as well as fellow artists. Bianca, however, has caught the eye of the rascally Count Casati, the philandering Crown Prince of Illyria, who is not above seducing local ladies and even killing the husband of one when caught in flagrante. The Count, motoring through the countryside, offers a ride to Bianca, who has just parachuted to earth after being shot from a cannon as part of her act. The count begins paying an increasing amount of attention to Bianca, who resents his advances but allows herself to be lured to his room by a forged letter. When the Count forces himself on her though, she vaults from a window, using her gymnastic skills to escape.

Tito, meanwhile, has followed Bianca and bursts into the Count's room moments after she has fled. In hand-to-hand combat, Tito kills the Count, tossing his body out of the window just as the Count's aide, DeBono, arrives with the news that the King has died and that Casati has ascended to the throne. To avoid being caught, Tito uses his remarkable resemblance to Casati to assume the latter's identity and the forthcoming kingly duties.

Bianca, however, believes that it was Tito, not the Count, who had been killed and plans to assassinate Casati during his coronation, but she is intercepted before she can carry out her vendetta and is tossed into jail. Duke Umberto, the ambitious chancellor, sees in Bianca a chance to get rid of the king and grab the throne for himself. He arranges for Bianca's release and even supplies a murder weapon, but his plan misfires when Bianca discovers that Tito is really alive and posing as the king. Tito and Bianca decide to simply walk away from the masquerade and return to the circus. Umberto, seeking to legitimize his claim to the throne after learning of the impersonation, informs Tito that he must stand trial for Casati's murder. Tito counters with the assertion that Umberto will have difficulty proving that he (Tito) is not the king, and that the king simply chose to leave—with a lovely young lady acrobat from Baretti's Traveling Circus.

Goldwyn's lavish production allowed for generous servings, amid the royal intrigue and the "Prisoner of Zenda" familiarity of the plot, of life in a picturesque European circus, contrasting backgrounds of life in a circus tent with that in the palace of a mythical kingdom. Of course, the brilliantly filmed circus scenes never were allowed to detract from the highly charged romantic interludes between either Ronald Colman (in his various guises) and luscious Vilma Banky. "Mr. Colman fills the dual role with much artistry," wrote critic Mordaunt Hall.

Miss Banky is attractive enough as the circus performer—and delivers a competent performance—but after the Chancellor has bought her one of Illyria's latest creations, she is stunning. Gustav von Seyffertitz is splendid as the Chancellor.

Vilma Banky and Ronald Colman in The Magic Flame.

Ronald Colman and Vilma Banky in The Magic Flame.

14 THE DEVIL DANCER (1927)

Directed by Fred Niblo; scenario, Alice D.G. Miller; based on a story by Harry Hervey; photographers, George Barnes and Thomas Brannigan; editor, Viola Lawrence; assistant director, H.B. Humberstone; art directors, Willy Pogany and Harry Grieve; titles, Edwin Justus Mayer. Eight reels. Released by United Artists. Premiere: Los Angeles, 11/3/27. New York premiere: Rivoli Theater, 12/18/27

THE CAST:
Takla, Gilda Gray; *Stephen Athelson,* Clive Brook; *Sada,* Anna May Wong; *Beppo,* Serge Temoff; *Hassim,* Michael Vavitch; *Sadik Lama,* Sojin; *Tana,* Ura Mita*; *Isabel,* Clarissa Selwynne**; *Arnold Guthrie,* Albert Conti; *Toy,* Kalla Pasha; *Grand Lama,* James B. Leong; *Lathrop,* William H. Tooker; *Audrey,* Claire DuBrey; *Julia,* Nora Cecil; *White Woman,* Barbara Tennant.
 * role sometimes credited to Ann Schaeffer
 ** role sometimes credited to Martha Maddox

Concerning himself briefly with screen matters other than showcasing his and the moviegoers' favorite romantic team, Goldwyn decided to star the famed "Shimmy queen," Gilda Gray, in a tale of mysterious Tibet, complete with Black Lamas, comely virgins, Oriental intrigue, and a great deal of exotic dancing. Miss Gray, who had become one of the entertainment sensations of the era, had made a number of films before Goldwyn hired her for *The Devil Dancer,* and made several afterwards. This one, though, certainly ranked as the highlight of her screen career, and, as *Variety* put it, "If the Gilda Gray fans of the 'Shimmy' still have a desire to see her shake it up, what she does in *The Devil Dancer* is worth the price of admission." The *Los Angeles Record* carried the enthusiasm a step further, noting that "there will be none who will deny that she not only adds to her fame as an exotic dancer, but emerges as an actress who has mastered the techniques of the screen." Goldwyn, in

fact, allowed her the supreme compliment—sole billing above and *twice the size of* the title!

Gilda Gray previously had acted in South Seas adventures, and Goldwyn was determined to give film audiences something different. Always alert to new story situations, he came upon an exciting narrative of the Far East by Harry Hervey, noted authority on tropical and wild tribes, and with the deft hand of scenarist Alice Duer Miller, an imaginative saga that Miss Gray logically fit into, was handed to the boss. The project, however, was hardly a smooth one. The original director, Alfred Raboch, was replaced almost immediately by his assistant, Lynn Shores (the former drifted rapidly into obscurity and the latter had a brief career). Goldwyn decided that Shores was not right either, and he turned the megaphone asd director's chair over to seasoned veteran Fred Niblo—together with a $100,000 stipend. "This production is wonderfully convincing in its atmosphere and rich in scenery," wrote *The New York Times.*

It is evident that Samuel Goldwyn insisted that those working on the film do their utmost to make the background really impress one as being that of the Forbidden City, Lhasa. So it is quite different from the ordinary run of films.

The review went on to state that "few pictures have been filmed with equally faithful modes and moods. Of course the chances are that Mr. Goldwyn will not reap much wealth from Tibet, seeing that the villains are either lamas or their acolytes."

The film, stunningly photographed by George Barnes (he was nominated for an Academy Award for his work) and his assistant Thomas Brannigan, designed by Willy Pogany, and scored by Carli Elinor, tells of Takla, a white girl whose missionary parents had died, leaving her to be raised in a Himalayan monastery. To the Black Lamas, she is a sign from the gods, and they have trained her as a court dancer. When Sada, the head dancer (played by the intrepid Anna May Wong), brings a curse upon the tribe because of a romantic indiscretion, she is ordered killed and Takla is called upon to dance the curse of the devil away. Into the Forbidden City comes Stephen Athelston an English explorer, who is captivated at the very first sight of Takla, and with the help of aged Tana, "rescues" Takla from the grasp of the wily Sadik Lama, ruler of the devil dancers.

Reaching civilization, Athelston introduces Takla to British colonial society, to the embarrassment of his sister, Isabel, who has taken an immediate dislike to her prospective sister-in-law. Isabel arranges to have Takla kidnapped by Hassim, wicked chief of Delhi's infamous nautch house, where Takla will become one of the dancing girls. Athelston eventually traces Takla to the house, where Beppo, the tom-tom boy, has taken it upon himself to protect the lovely dancer from Hassim's continued advances. Beppo helps her escape as Athelston shows up and confronts first Hassim, and then Sadik Lama. He disposes of both, though not before Sadik Lama kills Beppo, mistaking him for the Englishman, and Takla is at last reunited with the handsome explorer who had saved her from the clutches of the Black Lamas.

"Gilda Gray has the best picture of her career," *Variety* decided.

She is handled remarkably in a photographic way, does plenty of dancing and acquits herself capably from the acting end. Mr. Brook gives a sincere performance and struts his stuff right in the tight fight spots; Kala Pasha is great, and Michael Vavitch, as the Nautche chief, gives a typical cruel whip-lashing characterization.

The trade paper further noted: "Direction meant a great deal and, if the majority of the stuff was shot with the megaphone in the hands of Niblo, he should get the certificate of merit. He had a great camera crew who knew angles and how to show Gilda emoting and dramatizing."

Richard Watts, Jr.'s comment in his *New York Herald Tribune* review was that: "Miss Gray's work as the much beset dancer is excellent and Clive Brook is a satisfactory hero," but he saved most of his praise for "the excellent acting of the pleasantly sinister Japanese, Sojin, as the most wicked of the lamas, and the lovely Anna May Wong, perfect in a moving bit. In fact, it is one of the most annoying features of *The Devil Dancer* that Miss Wong should be cruelly confined to an unimportant role." Of the film itself, Watts felt:

The plot is so feeble, so commonplace, so lacking in dramatic value that you are forced to suspect that the author might have used his time in the study of story construction instead of wandering around central Asia. It seems a pity that the film, as a whole, is so emphatically second-rate, and the direction of Fred Niblo helps boost it only upon occasion.

The New York Times figured that

Miss Gray is always interesting, whether whirling around in one of the long skirts or standing quietly, looking affectionately at Clive Brook. She has a charm of her own, and nobody can accuse her of being blase in the love scenes. Mr. Brook does very well with the role of the young Englishman . . . (but) is just a wee bit too careful to have the parting in his hair rather too neat.

To insure "boffo box office," Goldwyn arranged to have Gilda Gray dance on stage during the initial large city engagements of the film—particularly in Los Angeles and New York, where the show cost ticket buyers an incredible $3.00.

Clive Brook and Gilda Gray in The Devil Dancer.

Gilda Gray in The Devil Dancer.

Gilda Gray in The Devil Dancer.

15 TWO LOVERS (1928)

Directed by Fred Niblo; scenario, Alice D.G. Miller; based on the novel *Leatherface: A Tale of Old Flanders* by Baroness Emmuska Orczy; photographer, George Barnes; editor, Viola Lawrence; music score, Hugo Riesenfeld; assistant director, H.B. Humberstone; art director, Carl Oscar Borg; titles, John Colton. Nine reels (silent), 105 minutes (sound). Released by United Artists. Premiere: Embassy Theater, New York, 3/22/28

THE CAST:
Mark Van Rycke, Ronald Colman; *Donna Leonora de Vargas,* Vilma Banky; *Duke of Azar,* Noah Beery; *Prince of Orange,* Nigel de Brulier; *Grete,* Virginia Bradford; *Inez,* Helen Jerome Eddy; *Madame Van Rycke,* Eugenie Besserer; *Ramon de Linea,* Paul Lukas; *Ghent Bailiff Meinherr Van Rycke,* Fred Esmelton; *Jean,* Harry Allen; *Marda,* Marcella Daly; *Dandermonde Innkeeper,* Scotty Mattraw; *Innkeeper's Wife,* Lydia Yeamans Titus.

In his review of *Two Lovers,* critic Mordaunt Hall offered the fateful news in *The New York Times* that "it is sponsored by that Barnum of love, Samuel Goldwyn, who has served notice that this the last picture in which Vilma Banky and Ronald Colman will be seen together." Goldwyn had decreed that the time was now right for each to pursue individual stardom and that Colman's new partner would be Lily Damita, while Banky would next act opposite Goldwyn's latest discovery, British actor Walter Byron.

Using Baroness Orczy's 1916 adventure classic about a masked freedom fighter—story material that hinted strongly of Robin Hood/Zorro style dramatics, Goldwyn coaxed from scenarist Alice Duer Miller an exciting, if occasionally sadistic swashbuckler that he then called *Two Lovers.* Whether the title referred specifically to Colman and Banky, or to the men who fought for Banky's affections (Colman and Paul Lukas, in his American film debut), several critics were undecided, and the reviewer for *Outlook* commented that

Leaving out the consideration that this stimulating title would have eluded Miss Banky, the fact remains that no true film fan would care for a picture called "Leatherface," (except that) the principals respectively hate and distrust each other, unjustly of course, for at least three-fourths of the film.

Fitting snugly into the popular costume drama mold of which moviegoers seemingly never tired, the yarn revolves around the exploits of Mark Van Rycke, also known as "Leatherface, masked avenger of the down-trodden Flems" (as described in Goldwyn's pulse-quickening advertising), and Donna Leonora de Vargas, "the Flower of Spain." Leonora has been forced to forsake her true love, Ramon de Linea, and enter into a marriage of convenience with Mark Van Rycke, son of the burgomaster of Ghent. Leonora's tyrannical uncle, the Duke of Azar, wants inside information on the mysterious figure who has been causing havoc among the Spanish forces on behalf of Azar's arch enemy, William of Orange, and Leonora would make a lovely, quite unsuspecting spy. The girl despises her new husband and yearns for Ramon, commander of the Spanish forces in Ghent, and her hatred is intensified when she learns that her sweetheart has been killed by a man known as Leatherface. What she does not know it that Ramon's death was in retribution for a savage attack on a local barmaid. When she discovers that Leatherface is actually her husband, she is thoroughly revolted and helps her uncle set a trap for the masked man. Leatherface is captured and dragged off to the Duke's castle, where he is viciously beaten about the face with a leather whip.

Leonora, meanwhile, stumbles onto the real reason for Ramon's murder, and slowly becomes convinced that the Dutch cause is just. Following her change of heart, "she does a Paul Revere on a stormy night," in the words of *Variety*, riding through the streets of Ghent calling all the patriots to arms and helping them storm her wicked uncle's fortress, rescuing the man she finally realizes is her true love.

"Ronald Colman proves conclusively," wrote Harriette Underhill in the *New York Tribune*,

> that he is an infallible artist, for in this role, he has no aids to romanticism. (He) uses no make-up and his hair is rumpled, so that when his young wife learned to love him, it was for himself alone. Miss Banky looked exquisite as the bartered bride, but it seemed that the hero's description of her suited the star as well as the character: "If it weren't for your eyes, I should think you were made of marble."

Said *The New York Times'* Mordaunt Hall of the leads:

> Miss Banky is charming, but here she has been told to look as lovely as she possibly can. And she does. Mr. Colman is vigorous in his role, and Noah Beery, discounting what Mr. Niblo has instructed him to do, is still able to prove that he is a master of screen acting.

Critic Hall also noted that

> it might be thought that a girl who rides through a storm, wearing a cape covering her decollete gown, would be slightly fatigued after such a journey, but Banky is a girl of mettle, who only gives in when she hears the voice of Mr. Niblo via his megaphone . . . What suspense!

In spite of the familiarity of the theme, moviegoers once again proved correct the *Variety* prediction that "the Colman/Banky combination in the lights plus the title itself, leave little to guess work as to the box office probabilities, regardless of story and construction." *Two Lovers* marked a tearful (to fans) swan song to the profitable (to Goldwyn) teaming of the two stars. Each went their separate ways with mixed results. Colman soared to greater heights with the coming of sound; Banky failed to survive the end of the silents, making only four more films, two being talkies.

Vilma Banky and Ronald Colman in Two Lovers.

Vilma Banky and Ronald Colman in Two Lovers.

Noah Beery threatening Ronald Colman in Two Lovers.

16 THE AWAKENING (1928)

Directed by Victor Fleming; scenario, Carey Wilson; based on a story by Frances Marion; photographer, George Barnes; editor, Viola Lawrence; art director, William Cameron Menzies; music, Hugo Riesenfeld; song *Marie* by Irving Berlin; titles, Katherine Hilliker and H.H. Caldwell. Nine reels (silent), 100 minutes (sound). Released by United Artists. Premiere: Rivoli Theater, New York, 12/30/28

THE CAST:
Marie Ducrot, Vilma Banky; *Le Bete,* Louis Wolheim; *Count Karl von Hagen,* Walter Byron; *Orderly,* George Davis; *Grandfather Ducrot,* William H. Orlamond; *Lt. Franz Geyer,* Carl von Hartmann; *German Officer,* Ferdinand Schumann-Heink; *Barmaid,* Yola D'Avril.

Samuel Goldwyn's abortive dream of creating twice the interest by separating Vilma Banky and Ronald Colman began with *The Awakening,* when the producer teamed Banky opposite another handsome English actor, Walter Byron, imported supposedly on Colman's recommendation. Banky was given sole billing above the title—and the phrase "of Love" was added following the initial, disappointing engagements. Frances Marion's original story, crafted into a serviceable scenario by Carey Wilson and directed by Victor Fleming, followed the love triangle formula—this time, a French peasant girl, her jealous suitor, and her dashing lover. The film, originally called *The Innocent,* also benefitted from Hugo Reisenfeld's synchronized musical score that interpolated Irving Berlin's subsequent standard, "Marie," written especially for Banky. In his critque in *Outlook,* A.M. Sherwood wrote:

Vilma Banky, as gifted and as physically substantial as ever, is given her first starring vehicle in this story of Alsace-Lorraine in wartime. It is very poignant and *very* Hollywood, with sex rearing its ugly head and promptly being scotched in the approved Will Hays manner . . . A handsome, but not colorful actor

named Walter Byron, from England, woos Miss Banky less entertainingly than Ronald Colman was wont to do it.

Variety went a bit further, seeing in the tale "a pinch of *The White Sister,* a seasoning of *The Scarlet Letter,* a large chunk of all the war pictures since 1918, and several slices of small-time baloney," and then called Goldwyn himself to task, bemoaning that "so gorgeous a creature (as Banky) should not be wasted as a peasant girl and then a novice nun all in one picture."

The romantic entanglements revolve around a local Alsacian beauty, Marie Ducrot, belle of the town of Pre d'Or and fiancee of Le Bete, the wealthiest man around—though hardly the most handsome. On the eve of World War One, a young German officer, Count Karl von Hagen, swaggers into town from his regiment's nearby bivouac area and melts the heart of every local mademoiselle, but his eye, of course, falls immediately on lovely Marie. A torrid romance ensues, despite Le Bete's increasing jealousy, and the night before Karl's unit is to depart for the front, the officer induces Marie to visit him in his quarters—that is, if she *really* cares for him.

When Marie is spotted leaving Karl's quarters, the villagers assume she has surrendered herself to him and gossip-mongers waste no time in getting the news to Le Bete, who flies into a jealous rage. Marie is stoned by an angry mob and the house wherein she lives with her grandfather is smeared with pitch. Fleeing in disgrace, Marie asks for shelter in a nearby convent.

Sometime later, as the battlelines draw near, Marie, now a novitiate on the eve of her final vows, once again meets Karl, who is brought into the convent as a war casualty. As the French army nears, the convent is ordered evacuated, but Marie refuses to leave her beloved Karl, and there, is found by Le Bete, now a sergeant with the

French forces. Seeing the two of them together, Le Bete first tries to vent his jealous rage on the wounded officer, and then realizing that Marie really loves Karl, promises in an act of contrition to help the pair reach the German lines and safety. As the three work their way through no-man's-land, Le Bete is shot, living long enough to see Marie and Karl make the final dash to freedom and a brighter future.

Mordaunt Hall's appraisal of the film noted that:

> (it) may not be all that one could wish for during the dramatic passages, which are at times maudlin, extravagant and strangely coincidental, but it is nevertheless a picture that makes for good entertainment . . . it is a pity that Victor Fleming could not maintain the debonair mood of the early chapters, for, despite the attempts at drama, interest in the narrative slackens when episodes somewhat reminiscent of *The Scarlet Letter* are introduced.

Critic Hall also spoke of the performers, stating that "Mr. Goldwyn is to be congratulated on his selection (of Walter Byron), for Mr. Byron is not only handsome, but he acts the romantic role of an uhlan officer with no little understanding." Of Miss Banky he said: "Some might say that (she) does not resemble an Alsacian country girl, but it should be remembered that she is, after all, that startling exception—a Hungarian blonde."

The *New York Herald Tribune's* Richard Watts Jr. felt that Vilma Banky

> is immeasurably helped by a fine pictorial effectiveness (and) makes a very decent showing in her first lone stardom . . . (She) is excellent as the peasant girl, though we fear that the young lady is a bit too unexciting to be a first-rate cinema star.

Goldwyn's own disappointment with the results manifested itself in (1) his determination to stick with Banky, at least one more time, and (2) his decision to drop his option on Walter Byron, whose unexciting film career in America sauntered through the succeeding decade.

Vilma Banky in The Awakening.

Vilma Banky and Walter Byron in The Awakening.

Vilma Banky and Walter Byron in The Awakening.

17 THE RESCUE (1929)

Directed by Herbert Brenon; scenario, Elizabeth Meehan; based on the novel by Joseph Conrad; photographer, George Barnes; editor, Marie Halvey; assistant director, Ray Lissner; art director, William Cameron Menzies; music, Hugo Riesenfeld; titles, Katherine Hilliker and H.H. Caldwell. Nine reels (silent), 96 minutes (sound). Released by United Artists. Premiere: Rialto Theater, New York, 1/13/29

THE CAST:
Tom Lingard, Ronald Colman; *Lady Edith Travers,* Lily Damita; *Mr. Travers,* Alfred Heckman; *Carter,* Theodore Von Eltz; *Hassim,* John Davidson; *D'Alacer,* Philip Strange; *Jorgensen,* Bernard Siegel; *Daman,* Sojin; *Belarab,* Harry Cording; *Immada,* Laska Winter; *Jaffir,* Duke Kahanamoku; *Shaw,* Louis Morrison; *Wasub,* George Regas; *Tenga,* Christopher Martin.

While awaiting the public's response to Vilma Banky's first starring role alone, Goldwyn began production on Ronald Colman's first film with exclusive star billing, and his last silent role. The canny producer again correctly judged the moviegoers' tastes with their unflagging acceptance of Ronald Colman alone—or with any actress Goldwyn chose to have the gallant "Mr. C" make cinematic love to. In the screen adaptation of Joseph Conrad's *The Rescue,* it was Lily Damita, the French actress who was to be Goldwyn's latest "gift" to the American screen.

In spite of the casting of Colman as Tom Lingard (who also turns up in Conrad's *Outcast of the Islands*), Goldwyn was to discover that Conrad's novels, like Jack London's, might be adventure-packed literary successes, but were somewhat lacking as screen material, regardless of the merits of the scenarists. *Time Magazine,* in its review of the film, commented that:

Scenarists do not discover until too late that Conrad's tales of adventure, seemingly straightforward enough,

are complicated struggles about honour (and) even superb photography cannot make more than a routine film out of his brooding, but somehow unreal and tormented story.

With the exception of the telescoping of certain episodes and characters, and making Jorgensen, so vital to the Conrad original, merely part of the scenery, the Goldwyn production followed the novel faithfully enough. The critical consensus, noting that there is enough action in Conrad's novel for at least two movies, was that *The Rescue* was merely a skeleton of the book, with little suggestion of Conrad's mood, manner, or even characterizations, resulting simply in a nicely photographed, competently acted, South Seas melodrama.

In his production of *The Rescue,* billed on the ads as Samuel Goldwyn's SOUND Presentation, Goldwyn put Colman in the competent hands of director Herbert Brenon, who had guided the actor through his greatest triumph to that time, *Beau Geste.* Brenon, noted *Variety* in its review, "has erected a pictorial construction radiating almost every known variety of human emotion with a burning force which satisfied every desire in motion picture entertainment." (Goldwyn's own publicity people might well have written that statement.) The director filled the screen with all manner of heroics, framed in picturesque and atmospheric settings and color costuming, paced by Colman's vigorous performance as "King Tom," fighting to restore his faithful friend, Rajah Hassim, to the throne of the jungle kingdom of Wajo, and indulging in a glamorous, if illicit, romance with Edith Travers, wife of an English M.P. whose yacht is stranded in an exotic Java Sea bay.

"King Tom" is forced to choose between love and duty— between the charms of Lady Travers and the ill-fated promise made to the Rajah, caught in the crossfire of his own people on one side and the followers of pirate chief Daman on the other. "Add to all of this," wrote Richard Watts in his review in the *New York Herald Tribune,*

> excellent photography, an attractive star, competent direction and proper titling, and you would expect an extremely effective and exciting photoplay. Unfortunately, though, it isn't, and you are likely to find *The Rescue* a disappointment . . . Ronald Colman is attractive and believable, if a bit monotonous, but among the things in the picture to be grateful for. Lily Damita is a great disappointment, and the cool, enigmatic Mrs. Travers of the book is turned into a professional, conventional seductress.

An entirely different view came from Mordaunt Hall in *The New York Times,* who thought that

> Herbert Brenon has done valiant work in his pictorial transcription of *The Rescue,* and has skillfully preserved the essence of the narrative . . . the most exacting of Conrad enthusiasts will find in this picture a number of inspiring passages that are filmed with a high degree of artistic taste.

Of the acting, critic Hall said:

> Even though Ronald Colman may not answer Conrad's description of Tom Lingard, his performance is so earnest and sensitive that in spite of his coal black hair, his clean-shaven chin and small mustache he is not only far from disappointing but he reflects the spirit of King Tom . . . Lily Damita is fascinatingly handsome and gives an intelligent performance of the difficult role allotted to her (although) Mr. Brenon might have insisted upon less makeup on her eyes, as it hardly seems natural for even such a character to spend so much time on her appearance in view of the somewhat disturbing events.

Goldwyn apparently decided that Miss Damita failed to exhibit star potential and he neglected to pick up her option after this one film. She subsequently drifted into a so-so career in American films, capped by her tempestuous marriage (1935–1942) to Errol Flynn. Her son, Sean, actor turned news photographer, disappeared in Vietnam while covering the war in 1972.

Lily Damita and Ronald Colman in The Rescue.

Lily Damita, Theodore Von Eltz and Ronald Colman in
The Rescue.

Lily Damita and Bernard Siegel in The Rescue.

18 BULLDOG DRUMMOND (1929)

Directed by F. Richard Jones; screenplay, Wallace Smith and Sidney Howard; based on the novel by Herman Cyril "Sapper" McNeile and the play by McNeile and Gerald DuMaurier; photographers, George Barnes and Gregg Toland; editors, Viola and Frank Lawrence; assistant director, Paul Jones; art director, William Cameron Menzies; song "(I Says To Myself Says I) There's the One for Me" by Jack Yellen and Harry Akst. Running time, 80 minutes. Released by United Artists. Premiere: Apollo Theater, New York, 5/2/29

THE CAST:
Hugh "Bulldog" Drummond, Ronald Colman; Phyllis Benton, Joan Bennett; Erma, Lilyan Tashman; Peterson, Montagu Love; Dr. Lakington, Lawrence Grant; Danny, Wilson Benge; Algy, Claud Allister; Marcovitch, Adolph Milar; Hiram J. Travers, Charles Sellon; Chong, Tetsu Komai; Singer, Donald Novis.

Ronald Colman made the transition to talking pictures effortlessly when Samuel Goldwyn cast him in the title role of Bulldog Drummond, and the actor's magnificent voice and impeccable diction, together with his polished accent, became one of the great joys of the screen. Like many of the early film stars, Colman brought with him extensive stage experience, although few today remember him other than as a fine motion picture actor. Unlike many of the early stars though, Colman retained his silent film celebrity and was among the very few male stars who remained stars when the movies began to talk. In Colman, Goldwyn could have found no better "Bulldog Drummond."

The suave, intrepid detective of fiction, created by former army officer turned author, Herman Cyril "Sapper" McNeile had become established as an appealing hero in books, as well as on the London and Broadway stage before being adopted by films. On screen, in the company of Sherlock Holmes, Captain Hugh Drummond (known henceforth as Bulldog) became the world's best known,

and most serviceable, private eye. The Drummond character has been used in two dozen films, beginning in 1922, and was a major figure on radio in the forties, as well as a television hero in the fifties. In addition, several successful Drummond novels have been published since the detective was first introduced in 1920, and of course, there was the hit play in 1921 with Sir Gerald DuMaurier in the lead on London's West End and A.E. Matthews playing the role on Broadway. It was to be Ronald Colman, though, whose name would be synonymous with that of Bulldog Drummond.

The Goldwyn production, an action-packed adventure laced with humor and romance, scrupulously followed the McNeile novel about a former army officer who finds civilian life a bore, and yearning for excitement, advertises in the Times of London. He is hired by an American girl to free her uncle from a sanatarium where a sadistic physician is trying to induce him into signing away his fortune. With his friend and confidante, Algy Longworth (comparable to Holmes' Dr. Watson), Drummond mixes deduction with seduction while deftly outmaneuvering the evil Dr. Larkington and his dastardly associates, Carl Peterson and the treacherous Erma. With Bulldog Drummond, cinema progressed to its next logical step. Previous talkies were static and stagey—the Goldwyn production moved, thanks to speedy action and creative direction by F. Richard Jones, the deft performance of Colman, and the witty screenplay by noted author, Sidney Howard. Colman received an Academy Award nomination for his portrayal of Drummond, and William Cameron Menzies was given one for Best Art and Set Decoration.

To play Colman's leading lady in Bulldog Drummond, Goldwyn hired Joan Bennett, also making her "talkie" debut (she previously had acted in only one film, although she and Colman had been seen briefly several years earlier in bits in Goldwyn's *The Eternal City*). Claud Allister was engaged to supply the comedy as the faithful, mono-cled Algy, a part he again played in two later Drummond films.

Reviewing *Bulldog Drummond* in *The New York Times*, Mordaunt Hall wrote: "It is the happiest and most enjoyable entertainment of its kind that has so far reached the screen." Even more extravagant praise came from A.M. Sherwood, critic for *Outlook*, who thought "Nothing better in the way of Simon-pure entertainment than *Bulldog Drummond* has come this reviewer's way since Douglas Fairbanks put on *The Mark of Zorro*, and no better performance of its kind than Ronald Colman's in *Bulldog Drummond* has ever been seen in the history of filmdom." Richard Watts, in his *New York Herald Tribune* critique, observed that

> an entirely preposterous concoction which neither took itself with intense seriousness nor indulged in comic self-deprecation, it proved to be, thanks to a brilliant and imaginative production and an admirable perform-ance by Mr. Ronald Colman . . . the fortunate man whose stature increases about 300 times by the coming of speech (on film). The possessor of a pleasant, cul-tured voice and an easy manner, he plays with such charm, gaiety, ease and resource, that his portrayal is one of the distinct achievements of his talking photoplay.

Of Colman's leading lady, Watts wrote: "The heroine is the exquisite Miss Joan Bennett, who is not only un-believably beautiful but who plays her ingenue role with a slight undercurrent of humor that is completely en-gaging." *Variety* complained about the wisdom of sched-uling *Bulldog Drummond* on a twice daily reserved seat policy (at least in its New York engagement) at $2 a ticket, but conceded that "Samuel Goldwyn gave the story a good production in all ways, with F. Richard Jones expertly handling the direction and Colman de-livering a surprisingly good performance."

After concluding his contract with Goldwyn in 1933 when they exchanged several caustic comments, duly reported in the press, Colman once again played the famed detective in *Bulldog Drummond Strikes Back*. In addition to Colman's interpretations of Captain Hugh Drummond, screen annals make note of eleven others who have played the role. Carlyle Blackwell (in 1922) and Jack Buchanan (1925) starred as Bulldog Drum-mond in silent films, and Kenneth Mackenna imper-sonated the intrepid folk hero in 1930, Ralph Richardson in 1934, Atholl Fleming in 1935, John Lodge (later Connecticut's governor) in 1937, and Ray Milland also did a version in 1937. Between 1937 and 1939, John Howard was Drummond in seven movies before the detective "retired" from the screen for the duration of the war. The detective next appeared in films when Ron Randall took up the impersonation twice in 1947 and Tom Conway twice in 1948. In 1951, Walter Pidgeon assumed the guise of Bulldog Drummond, and most recently, Richard Johnson offered his interpretation in 1967 and 1969. On radio, Drummond was played, suc-cessively, by George Coulouris, Santos Ortega and Ned Weaver, and on the television series, Robert Beatty enacted the role.

Ronald Colman and Joan Bennett in Bulldog Drummond.

Ronald Colman and Joan Bennett in Bulldog Drummond.

Ronald Colman in Bulldog Drummond.

19 THIS IS HEAVEN (1929)

Directed by Alfred Santell; scenario, Hope Loring; based on a story by Arthur Mantell; photographers, George Barnes and Gregg Toland; editor, Viola Lawrence; music, Hugo Riesenfeld; title song, Jack Yellen and Harry Akst; titles and dialogue, George Marion Jr. Nine reels (silent), 90 minutes (sound). Released by United Artists. Premiere: Rivoli Theater, New York, 5/26/29

THE CAST:

Eva Petrie, Vilma Banky; *James Stackpoole,* James Hall; *Mamie Chase,* Fritzie Ridgeway; *Frank Chase,* Lucien Little-field; *E.D. Wallace,* Richard Tucker

"The screen's most beautiful actress as Manhattan's prettiest waitress—in a mad, merry romance of New York," proclaimed the ads for Goldwyn's newest comedy. "VILMA BANKY," they trumpeted, "whose voice is heard for the first time in *THIS IS HEAVEN*!" And Goldwyn, coming to New York to help promote Banky's newest film, was quoted as declaring that in casting the actress in her first dialogue picture, he discovered that "her slight continental accent was a decided asset to the dramatic effect of *This Is Heaven.*" The consensus of the critics, however, was that Banky's "slight continental accent" made her virtually unintelligible. Like John Gilbert and his thin, high-pitched voice, Banky and her guttural, garbled English saw their film careers disintegrate with the coming of sound. "Miss Banky is heard to talk in several places," wrote *Harrison's Reports* in its review of *This Is Heaven.* "She has a decided accent and her punctuation is not very good. It might have been better to have left the talk out entirely."

At the time of his choice of this frothy, rather silly, little tale for his foremost leading lady, Goldwyn seemingly had been convinced to abandon his attempts to mold her into his Garbo, and try instead to turn her into Mary

Pickford. The ploy, rather than simply being dismissed as ill-advised, was instead a financial gamble, and Banky was woefully miscast in this Cinderella story of a young immigrant girl who gets a job making flapjacks at Child's on Fifth Avenue and falls in love with a millionaire who has passed himself off as a chauffeur. The usual laughs and tears follow, after which the standard silver lining glistens a few feet ahead of the end titles.

A young Hungarian immigrant, Eva Petrie (at least Banky was perfectly cast for the initial premise), is met at Ellis Island by her uncle, Frank Chase, a subway conductor, and his daughter Mamie, who has lined up a waitress job for her cousin. On her way to work by subway one morning, Eva spots a good-looking young man, Jimmy Stackpoole, who is wearing a chauffeur's cap, though actually he is a society playboy. Later, sent to the Stackpoole estate to preside over the griddle at a charity bazaar, she again runs into Jimmy, but this time, she passes herself off as an exiled Russian princess. He sees through the deception, though, and decides that he will play the game as a chauffeur, while courting her and telling her that he is hoping to go into the taxi business. Eva promises to advance Jimmy the money out of the wages she has been squirreling away.

Uncle Frank, however, has located Eva's money and gambled it away, forcing Eva, in desperation, to borrow $300 from cousin Mamie's wealthy lover E.D. Wallace. Wallace then insists on driving Eva back to her Bronx flat, where, by coincidence, Jimmy sees her alighting from Wallace's car. In a fit of jealousy, Jimmy drops the pretense, reveals his true self, learns of Eva's desperate attempt to get financing for his taxi business, and proposes marriage immediately. Eva at last realizes "This *ees* heaven!"

"As with all the Goldwyn productions, "said *Variety,*

"the photography is splendid. Alfred Sawtell tells the story simply and humanly, accomplishing with quiet competence the transition of Banky from a lady of royalty to the flapjack queen of Child's." That paper's critic concluded, though, that "grooming Miss Banky for permanency as a star is going to tax Goldwyn's smartness (although) *This Is Heaven* is much better stuff toward that end than *The Awakening.*" In her review in the *New York Herald Tribune,* Marguerite Tazelaar found that:

Vilma Banky, looking lovelier than ever, contributes an excellent performance to its earlier reels, and the whole picture, in fact, in spite of a thin, padded little story, manages to be entertaining much of the time.

This came from *The New York Times,* which noted that Banky "like Olga Baclanova, has a charming accent," speaks for the first time: "Whether she is silent or talking, Miss Banky is always radiant."

Actually, *This Is Heaven* was not a sound movie, but one with talking sequences and a musical score (by Hugo Riesenfeld). Only about fifteen percent of the film's ninety minutes contained dialogue, and Banky spoke only briefly during the final reel—enough, though, to seal her fate in films. The picture opened in New York, unfortunately, three weeks *after* Goldwyn's first "all dialogue" venture, *Bulldog Drummond.*

Despite Goldwyn's urgings that Banky improve her English diction and comprehension of the language, the actress, either because of difficulty or simple laziness, exhausted the producer's patience and he gave up on her, allowing her to merely sit out the remainder of her contract at $5000 a week. She subsequently made one other American movie, and later, one in France. Otherwise, Vilma Banky resigned herself to being plain old Mrs. Rod LaRoque.

James Hall and Vilma Banky in This Is Heaven.

Vilma Banky and Fritzie Ridgeway in This Is Heaven.

James Hall, Vilma Banky and Lucien Littlefield in This Is Heaven.

Vilma Banky and James Hall in This Is Heaven.

20 CONDEMNED (1929)

Directed by Wesley Ruggles; screenplay by Sidney Howard; based on the novel *Condemned to Devil's Island* by Blair Niles; photographers, George Barnes and Gregg Toland; editor, Stuart Heisler; dialogue director, Dudley Digges; art director, William Cameron Menzies; song "Song of the Condemned" by Jack Meskill and Pete Wendling. Running time, 93 minutes. Released by United Artists. Premiere: Selwyn Theater, New York, 11/3/29 (Reissued in 1944 as *Condemned to Devil's Island*)

THE CAST:
Michel Oban, Ronald Colman; *Madame Vidal,* Ann Harding; *Jean Vidal,* Dudley Digges; *Jacques Duval,* Louis Wolheim; *Pierre,* William Elmer; *Felix,* Albert Kingsley; *Vidal's Orderly,* William Vaughn; *Brute Convict,* Constantine Romanoff; *Inmates,* Henry Ginsberg, Bud Somers, Stephen Selznick, Baldy Biddle, John George, Arturo Kobe, Emil Schwartz, John Schwartz.

For his screen version of Blair Niles' *Condemned to Devil's Island,* Goldwyn engaged Sidney Howard once again to write the screenplay for Ronald Colman, whom Goldwyn's publicity people were now billing as "The King of Romance." Colman headed, so the ads led audiences to believe, "The greatest talking cast in the greatest of talking pictures," in this strangely carefree tale of a French thief, serving time on Devil's Island, who becomes butler to the lovely wife of the pompous warden. Devil's Island, in this screenplay, though, is seen as a lush, tropical paradise, enhanced by lovely, soft-focus photography and artistic seetings—and looking surprisingly like Malibu on a clear June night. In addition, the prisoners chant the film's theme song at regular intervals with a gaiety normally found in a Romberg operetta, as the hero, immaculately groomed and clean-shaven, except for the mandatory pencil-thin Colman mustache, melts the heart of the warden's wife and

even manages to swim through jungle waters to meet her boat at Paramaibo.

Colman, who won his second Academy Award nomination of the year for his performance as Michel Oban (in addition to the one for *Bulldog Drummond*), carried *Condemned* with his now patented *joie de vivre* and romantic heroics. "He plays well," wrote *Variety,*

> and at times is outstanding in his pantomime [*mocking the warden and his wife as the two engage in an off-camera spat*]. He has already established his ability to handle lines, and if ever given a chance, will probably scintillate in a light comedy theme.

Critic Julia Shawtell, writing in the *New York Graphic,* commented that "Not only is *Condemned* the best work which Colman has contributed to the screen, silent or talkie, but it surpasses in caliber of story, direction and characterization anything which producer Samuel Goldwyn has ever put on celluloid." In *The New York Times,* Mordaunt Hall described the film as

> another capital piece of work, in which Mr. Colman, as a good-looking, agreeably impudent thief, attacks his role in a facile manner . . . Seldom has any motion picture proved as stirring as this offering (and) it would be difficult to think of another film of its kind that has been produced anything like as well.

John S. Cohen, Jr., critic for the *New York Sun,* called it simply "an overwhelming talking picture . . . quite real, quite powerful."

Michel Oban, a convicted thief, is assigned by the dictatorial warden as servant to the warden's wife, who is repelled by the island. "No good will come of this," Madame Vidal tells her husband when introduced to her new houseboy. "You'll see . . . you'll be sorry."

Madame Vidal does nothing to encourage Oban, although she finds herself immediately attracted to him. Gossipers and eavesdroppers soon arouse the warden's suspicions, however, and he realizes his mistake in throwing the two of them together. Vidal confronts Oban and goads the prisoner into punching him in the mouth. The warden slaps Oban into solitary for six months, replacing him with a new servant, Jacques Duval, Oban's ugly friend and a convicted murderer.

Madame Vidal finally admits to her husband that she never loved him and now plans to leave him, after secretly communicating with Oban through Jacques. Oban manages to break out of solitary and meet with Madame Vidal before her departure, conspiring to join her aboard a steamer at Paramaibo. Jacques joins his fellow prisoner on the escape attempt through the jungle, while the warden decides to trail his wife, catching her finally with Oban in her shipboard stateroom. As the warden orders Oban arrested once again, Jacques jumps him from behind and plunges with him into the water.

Vidal is drowned and Jacques fatally shot, as Oban surrenders after exchanging an oath of eternal fidelity with Madame Vidal. She promises to meet him in Paris after he has served his sentence (which they do at the film's fadeout, neither looking a day older).

All goes to demonstrate, as one writer put it, what happens when the stuffy, egotistical husband of a pretty blonde wife hires Ronald Colman for a kitchen boy. "If *Condemned* adhered throughout," noted A.M. Sherwood in his critique in *Outlook*

to the excellent light romantic comedy at which Colman is so adept, it would have been far better entertainment, and if it led up to an amusing, exciting climax, its improbable portions, labored plot and far-fetched situations could have been more easily forgiven . . . and *Condemned*, well played, well directed, and, in parts, well written, suffers heavily and ends on a flat note. The distinction and rare ability of its star alone make it worth seeing.

Ronald Colman, Ann Harding and Dudley Digges in
Condemned.

Ronald Colman, Ann Harding and Louis Wolheim in Condemned.

Ronald Colman and Louis Wolheim in Condemned.

21 RAFFLES (1930)

Directed by Harry D'Arrast and George Fitzmaurice; screenplay, Sidney Howard; based on the novel *The Amateur Cracksman* by Ernest William Hornung and the play *Raffles, The Amateur Cracksman* by Hornung and Eugene Wiley Presbrey; photographers, George Barnes and Gregg Toland; editor, Stuart Heisler; assistant director, H.B. Humberstone; art directors, William Cameron Menzies and Park French. Running time, 70 minutes. Released by United Artists. Premiere: Rialto Theater, New York, 7/24/30

THE CAST:
A.J. Raffles, Ronald Colman; *Lady Gwen*, Kay Francis; *Bunny Manders*, Bramwell Fletcher*; *Ethel Crowley*, Frances Dade*; *McKenzie*, David Torrence; *Lady Kitty Melrose*, Alison Skipworth; *Lord Harry Melrose*, Frederick Kerr; *Cranshaw*, John Rogers; *Barraclough*, Wilson Benge; *Blonde*, Virginia Bruce.
* in screen debut

Ronald Colman's next (thirteenth) starring role for Samuel Goldwyn was as the roguish, devil-may-care A.J. Raffles, debonair cricket star by day and clever safecracker by night. For the third screen version of the best-selling (1899) novel and smash (1903) play, Goldwyn ordered up a breezy script for his comedy/thriller from his prestigious author turned scenarist, Sidney Howard. Howard, who previously had written screenplays to Goldwyn/Colman films, *Bulldog Drummond* and *Condemned,* had been in the vanguard of leading novelists and playwrights being lured to Goldwyn's growing stable, soon to evolve as Eminent Authors Pictures. Following Howard to Hollywood were Louis Bromfield, Elmer Rice, Charles MacArthur, Ben Hecht, Maxwell Anderson, Lillian Hellman, Edna Ferber, along with several who never did work for Goldwyn: Rex Beach, Rupert Hughes, Mary Roberts Rinehart, et al. Goldwyn even attempted to cajole George Bernard Shaw into grinding out screenplays, but Shaw

was said to have told Goldwyn: "We can never agree, because your ideals are those of an artist and mine are those of a businessman." And it has been said that if Shakespeare had been alive when Hollywood found its voice, he would have been working for Goldwyn.

Goldwyn had convinced himself sooner than did his contemporaries that talkies were here to stay. "I believe in the future of the talking film," he was quoted in the spring of 1929. "The day of the director is over and that of the author and playwright has arrived." (Goldwyn was at least half-right, as such luminaries as William Wyler, John Ford, Mervyn LeRoy, King Vidor and Howard Hawks certainly must have concurred.) From writer Howard, Goldwyn received in *Raffles* the tale of a thoroughly charming romantic rascal, so completely captivating that, though guilty, he has no trouble winning audience sympathy and approval at each triumphant encounter with the law. From Colman, Goldwyn received in *Raffles* the engaging, affable performance that the actor had by now been able to toss off to his fans' delight as if by second nature, leading critic Richard Watts to the conclusion (in his review of the film) that Colman's "ironic bantering nonchalance has become one of the most satisfying institutions of the talking cinema," and that the actor's portrayal is "as deft and attractive a light comedy characterization as the pictures have yet offered."

Raffles had become a familiar plot through its various stage and screen incarnations. Sir Gerald DuMaurier had played the role on the London stage during the century's early days, and Kyle Bellew had recreated it on Broadway. In 1914 John Barrymore first impersonated Raffles on the screen, and House Peters took the part in the 1925 remake. Samuel Goldwyn's 1939 remake, almost scene for scene from the Colman version, starred David Niven, and a Spanish language version, called

El Raffles Mexicano, starred Mexican actor, Rafael Bertrand in 1960. All indulged in the delicious cat-and-mouse game between the gentlemanly crook, who steals to pay off a friend's debt, and the intrepid Scotland Yard inspector, who comes to admire his suave adversary's civilized manner.

A.J. Raffles is a rakish sportsman who moonlights as a thief, relishing the sport of eluding the law rather than stealing for profit. When he meets and falls in love with Lady Gwen, darling of English society, he decides to go straight. She, of course, has no idea that he is the much discussed and greatly publicized "Amateur Cracksman," so-labelled by Scotland Yard. When his close friend, Bunny Manders, attempts suicide in desperation over a debt, Raffles offers to help acquire the needed money and through Gwen, manages an invitation to the gala weekend party being given by Lord and Lady Melrose. There he plans to steal the hostess' necklace, but learns that Inspector McKenzie of Scotland Yard is there on a tip that a robbery might be imminent. After an enjoyable evening of parrying with McKenzie, each knowing why the other is there, Raffles announces his intention of retiring for the night. McKenzie, however, decides to keep an eye on Raffles, who manages to elude the detective long enough to make his move for the necklace. Raffles discovers Crawshaw, a petty thief just about to pocket the jewelry though, and proceeds to surprise the robber and take the necklace himself. Then he "captures" the crook and turns him over to the Inspector. As Crawshaw is being led away, he denounces Raffles, who naturally, claims the man is lying.

McKenzie's suspicions are aroused when he learns that Lady Melrose's necklace has disappeared and nothing was found on Crawshaw. Suspecting Raffles, he tells his men to allow the famed sportsman to leave the house and then to release Crawshaw, so that the police may use a thief to catch a thief. Raffles returns home, stuffs the necklace in his tobacco humidor, and has his valet, Barraclough, book passage for Amsterdam. Then Gwen appears at his flat and learns of his masquerade. She is followed by Inspector McKenzie, who has trailed Crawshaw. McKenzie is invited to search Raffles' place, and finding nothing, he leaves. Crawshaw then breaks in, but Raffles overpowers him, slips him a five pound note and induces him to flee before the police return.

When Bunny Manders arrives, following a call from Raffles, he is given the necklace to return to Lord Melrose, who has offered a generous reward. Then Raffles eludes McKenzie by disappearing through a secret opening in the grandfather clock standing in the corner, and wearing the inspector's cape, casually strolls by the police who are waiting by the front door. With a promise from Gwen that she will meet him, Raffles departs for Paris, and a new life.

"Mr. Colman offers one of his most engaging performances," said Richard Watts in the *New York Herald Tribune,* "and Miss Francis demonstrates once more that she is one of the most interesting, as she is one of the handsomest, actresses in Hollywood." Critic Watts decided that "the picture is so splendidly acted and so tastefully directed that it emerges as an entirely superior motion picture entertainment."

The New York Times, on the other hand, felt that "*Raffles* is not the picture by which Sidney Howard, Samuel Goldwyn or Mr. Colman will be longest remembered. It is a film of which even the most ardent admirer of any one of the above trio would say only 'good—but.' "

Raffles was the last film that Goldwyn made both in sound and silent versions. Nevertheless, the Motion Picture Academy gave an Oscar nomination to Oscar Lagerstrom for Best Sound (1929–30), the first year of that award.

Ronald Colman in Raffles.

Kay Francis and Ronald Colman in Raffles.

Wilson Benge, Ronald Colman and Bramwell Fletcher in
Raffles.

22 WHOOPEE! (1930)

Directed by Thornton Freeland; coproducer, Florenz Ziegfeld; screenplay, William Conselman; based on the musical by William Anthony McGuire, Walter Donaldson and Gus Kahn, the play *The Nervous Wreck* by Owen Davis, and the story *The Wreck* by E.J. Rath; music director, Alfred Newman; songs, Walter Donaldson and Gus Kahn, except "I'll Still Belong To you" by Nacio Herb Brown and Edward Eliscu; dance director, Busby Berkeley; photographers, Lee Garmes, Ray Rennahan and Gregg Toland; editor, Stuart Heisler; assistant director, H.B. Humberstone; art director, Captain Richard Day; costumes, John Harkrider. Running time, 85 minutes. Technicolor. Released by United Artists. Premiere: Rivoli Theater, New York, 10/1/30

THE CAST:
Henry Williams, Eddie Cantor*; *Sally Morgan*, Eleanor Hunt#; *Wanenis*, Paul Gregory*; *Sheriff Bob Wells*, John Rutherford*; *Mary Custer*, Ethel Shutta*; *Jerome Underwood*, Spencer Charters*; *Black Eagle*, Chief Caupolican*; *Chester Undewood*, Albert Hackett*; *Andy McNabb*, William H. Philbrick*; *Judd Morgan*, Walter Law; *Harriet Underwood*, Marilyn Morgan (Marian Marsh); *Deputy*, Dean Jagger; *Specialty*, George Morgan and his Orchestra*; *The Goldwyn Girls*, Joyzelle Jacques Cartier, Betty Grable, Virginia Bruce, Muriel Finley*, Jeanne Morgan, Ruth Eddings, Ernestine Mahoney, Christine Maple, Dorothy Knapp, Claire Dodd, Jane Keithley, Mary Ashcraft, Betty Stockton, Georgia Lerch; and Theodore Lorch, Budd Fine, Gene Alsace, Frank Rice, Edmund Cobb, Martin Faust, Arthur Dewey, William J. Begg, John Ray, Frank Lanning, Paul Panze
* in original Broadway production
# in original production as chorus girl

Musical numbers: (sung by)
"Cowboy Number" (Betty Grable, Goldwyn Girls and chorus)
"I'll Still Belong to You" (Paul Gregory)
"Makin' Whoopee" (Eddie Cantor)
"Mission Number" (Chorus)
"A Girl Friend of a Boy Friend of Mine" (Eddie Cantor)
Reprise: "Makin' Waffles" (Eddie Cantor)
"My Baby Just Cares For Me" (Eddie Cantor)
"Stetson" (Ethel Shutta and chorus)
Reprise: "I'll Still Belong to You" (Paul Gregory)
"The Song of the Setting Sun" (Chief Caupolican and chorus)
Reprise: "My Baby Just Cares for Me" (Eddie Cantor)

Samuel Goldwyn's screen version of *Whoopee!*, the smash musical of the 1928–29 Broadway season, is significant for many reasons, not the least being its position among the pioneer motion picture musical spectaculars. *Whoopee!* marked the first and only time since becoming an independent producer in 1923, that Goldwyn worked with a partner, joining forces, more or less, with Florenz Ziegfeld, who had brought *Whoopee!* to the stage. The film made a Goldwyn star of Eddie Cantor, who recreated his original stage role, with the musical comedy favorite joining Ronald Colman as the producer's reigning superstar—Cantor previously had appeared in several silent films, but his unique brand of humor and ebullient personality were born for talkies. *Whoopee!* confirmed Busby Berkeley's status as the foremost choreographer and dance innovator then working in films—he, too, had had screen experience, creating the routines for *The Cocoanuts,* the Marx Brothers' debut movie the previous year, among others. The Goldwyn/Ziegfeld musical remains the best example of two-color Technicolor of this period of filmmaking. And because it was a judiciously pruned restaging of the live production, the film of *Whoopee!* is, in the opinion of Miles Kreuger, the movie/musical authority and author of *The American Musical Film,* "an ideal time capsule, preserving better than any other screen musical the flavor and style of Broadway musicals during the late 1920s."

Whoopee! is regarded as the high point of Eddie Cantor's career—stage and screen. In addition to dispensing his distinctive style of comedy, Cantor sang his trademark song, "Making Whoopee," as well as

"My Baby Just Cares For Me," did one of his patented blackface routines (there is one in every Cantor movie), established his screen image as the nervous, timid little mirror of everyman, and proved himself as much at home in films as on the stage. Cantor's stay with Goldwyn lasted for six years, and for six Goldwyn movies, the comedian was said to have been making an astronomical (for the day) $150,000 per picture against ten percent of the gross, or an average of $250,000 for each film.

Whoopee!, the musical adventures of a hypochondriac in the wide open spaces, came to the screen with a convoluted history. It began life as *The Wreck,* a serial by Edith R. Rath and Robert W. Davis, which began running in *Argosy/All Story Magazine* in December 1921. In October 1923, Owen Davis turned it into a play entitled *The Nervous Wreck,* starring Otto Kruger, June Walker and Albert Hackett. From that, producer Al Christie came up with a screen comedy in 1926, starring Harrison Ford, Phyllis Haver and Chester Conklin. Next, Florenz Ziegfeld mounted an elaborate stage spectacular with a score by Gus Kahn and Walter Donaldson, especially for Ziegfeld's foremost star, Eddie Cantor, who had refused to appear in any more Ziegfeld Follies, demanding instead the starring role in a book show. Goldwyn then filmed it both as *Whoopee!,* and fourteen years later as *Up In Arms,* refashioned for his other famous musical comedy star, Danny Kaye.

For his screen version of *Whoopee!,* Goldwyn wisely imported from Broadway most of the other stage principals to recreate their roles in support of Cantor. Only the leading lady was different—Eleanor Hunt, who had graduated from the chorus line of the Broadway production to become the film's ingenue lead, Sally Morgan (played on the stage by Frances Upton). Then Goldwyn engaged Busby Berkeley to create a series of distinctive routines for the first crop of Goldwyn Girls—a fixture in virtually all of the producer's subsequent musicals. Among the examples of the Berkeley work that was to become legendary are the famed overhead dance shots and the familiar introduction of the chorus girls, face by shining face. Also to be found in *Whoopee!,* leading the chorus, is Betty Grable, spotted prominently in the opening "Cowboy Number" as well as several later routines.

Since *Whoopee!* had been constructed primarily as a vehicle for Cantor's comic routines and sketches, and on stage at least, Ziegfeld's latest tribute to American womanhood, much was to be desired in the way of plot complications. Basically, it concerns itself with the adventures of Henry Williams, a pill-popping nervous wreck from the east, taking the sun on an Arizona ranch with his nurse/companion, Mary Custer (played by Ethel Shutta, in her only film role). While there, he takes an interest in the plight of Sally Morgan, engaged to Sheriff Bob Wells, but in love with Wanenis, an Indian lad living nearby. Henry manages, amid elaborate production numbers by gorgeously gowned, smiling girls, to orchestrate Sally's flight from the Sheriff's clutches to Wanenis' arms, while along the way discovering the happy news that Wanenis actually a paleface, abandoned at birth and raised by Indians.

After opening his film in New York at a $5 per seat premiere, Goldwyn was comforted by basically glowing reports of his $1,000,000-plus Technicolor opus. Mordaunt Hall wrote:

Mr. Cantor's clowning transcends even Mr. Ziegfeld's shining beauties, the clever direction and the tuneful melodies, and this is saying a great deal, for there is much for the eyes to feast on . . . this results in the film being a swift and wonderfully entertaining offering, a feature that should prove to motion picture chieftains that such attractions are well worth all the trouble taken in production, despite the subordinating of the popular romantic theme.

Variety felt that "Cantor has never been funnier on the stage than in this talker," and called the film "dandiest of all screen musicals" and the "best musical comedy to date."

In his review, Richard Watts spoke of *Whoopee!* as "a loyal and handsome picturization of the talents of Cantor, Goldwyn, Ziegfeld and American womanhood." He tempered his praise, however, by pointing to

the unfortunate fact that screen musicals, even when done by Ziegfeld, have come to seem a trifle outmoded. Then there is the familiarity of the Cantor comedy plus the sullen truth that the cliches of a familiar romantic operatic story of the usual Broadway school stand out more embarrassingly on the screen.

Regardless, Goldwyn and Ziegfeld undoubtedly repeated the show's title during innumerable sojourns to the bank with the film's receipts. In addition to appreciative audiences, the motion picture academy also took note of *Whoopee!,* giving an Oscar nomination to Captain Richard Day for his art direction.

Eleanor Hunt and Paul Gregory in Whoopee!

Ethel Shutta and Eddie Cantor in Whoopee!

Muriel Finley, Eddie Cantor and Ruth Eddings in
Whoopee!

23 THE DEVIL TO PAY (1930)

Directed by George Fitzmaurice; screenplay, Frederick Lonsdale; music, Alfred Newman; photographers, George Barnes and Gregg Toland; editor, Grant Whytock; assistant director, H.B. Humberstone; art director, Captain Richard Day; dialogue coach, Ivan Simpson. Running time, 72 minutes. Released by United Artists. Premiere: Gaiety Theater, New York, 12/18/30

THE CAST:
Willie Leeland, Ronald Colman; *Dorothy Hope,* Loretta Young; *Susan Leeland,* Florence Britton*; *Lord Leeland,* Frederick Kerr; *Mr. Hope,* David Torrence; *Mrs. Hope,* Mary Forbes; *Grand Duke Paul,* Paul Cavanagh; *Arthur Leeland,* Crauford Kent; *Mary Crayle,* Myrna Loy
* in screen debut

Goldwyn's next assignment for Ronald Colman was as the aristocratic ne'er-do-well in Frederick Lonsdale's sophisticated drawing room comedy, brimming with witty dialogue, grace and polish. "The smartest of all modern comedy romances," exhorted the ads, "a departure in picture ideas." Richard Watts classified it in his *New York Herald Tribune* review as "six reels of Mr. Colman being charming," which in itself was enough to do brisk business when the film opened on reserved seats in New York and lingered for a very profitable two-a-day run. Under the capable direction of George Fitzmaurice, long familiar with his leading man's effortless portrayals, Ronald Colman breezed through the role of Willie Leeland, the family blacksheep, who loves dogs and romantic challenges.

Samuel Goldwyn was said to have scrapped around $75,000 worth of production after being dissatisfied with the rushes, and started again. Whatever the problems, nothing but class was evident in the final product, from the clever opening sequence in Kenya with Willie Leeland auctioning off his house and every bit of furniture his wealthy father had given him, to the wry wink and exquisite lover's pout at the fadeout. Returning home to England with twenty pounds in his pocket, happy-go-lucky Willie proceeds to invest fifteen of them in a charming wire-haired terrier named George, and the other five on dinner with an old girlfriend, actress Mary Crayle.

Turning up at "good old dad's place," Willie accepts a fatherly tongue-lashing about his shiftless manner, and then talks the irascible old man into advancing him 100 pounds. Once again solvent, Willie strolls into the drawing room where his sister Susan, introduces him to Dorothy Hope, fianceé of insufferable Grand Duke Paul. Convincing her to break a date with Paul, Willie captivates Dorothy at an amusement park, with sister Susan chaperoning. By coincidence, Paul spots Dorothy with Willie and becomes furious, breaking off his engagement to the girl. As Willie continues romancing Dorothy and using his dog George as a confidante, the girl's father tries to convince her that Willie is only after her money. Scoffing at the suggestion, Dorothy becomes engaged to Willie after suggesting to her carefree fiancé that he stop seeing his other lady friends.

Dorothy's father, though, learns that Willie had gone to Mary Crayle—to tell her that he could not see her again. Being informed of this rendezvous, but not waiting for an explanation, Dorothy breaks off with Willie after giving him a check for 500 pounds, thinking, as her father had warned, that her audacious boyfriend really was only after her money. To her surprise, however, Willie takes the check and sends it to the impoverished Grand Duke, her ex-intended. Dorothy, ashamed, pleads with Willie to forgive her, and the pair is reconciled.

"Rarely has Hollywood issued so thoroughly civilized a picture as *The Devil to Pay,*" wrote the critic for

Theatre. "It is a superfine comedy, distinguished in plot, acting, photography, direction, and what is most pleasant to record, in dialogue." The *New York Herald Tribune's* Richard Watts found it "a polished, tasteful and entirely likeable screen comedy . . . in the manner of most of Mr. Goldwyn's films, the production is smooth and filled with a pleasant air of debonair good breeding."

Variety thought that "Ronald Colman impresses as having a good time, sailing through this naughty boy part, and no one has a chance to catch up with him on performance, with his role written so far above the rest."

The New York Times critic, Mordaunt Hall, included *The Devil to Pay* among his Ten Best Movies of the Year, and hailed Ronald Colman's "excellent acting," while commenting that

this latest Samuel Goldwyn production is a wholesome, carefree picture with bright lines and one in which a cheery mood is sustained from the opening scene to the final fadeout. It has been admirably directed by George Fitzmaurice . . . (and) gives Mr.

Colman even better opportunity than he had in *Bulldog Drummond,* and he takes full advantage of his witty lines.

Hall also decided that the film was "a light, but charming affair with a really clever denouement" that he thought "is worked out with a far greater degree of originality and intelligence than one is apt to observe in motion pictures."

When *The Devil to Pay* first was released, Ronald Colman rightly received sole billing above the title, with Loretta Young's name in letters one-quarter the size below the film's title, and that of blonde-wigged Myrna Loy (listed ninth in the cast) nowhere to be found on the ads. When the movie was reissued in the 1940s, Miss Loy's name was prominently displayed just under Colman's but ahead of now third-billed Miss Young's above the title—an interesting example of the vagaries of screen popularity during cinema's Golden Days.

Ronald Colman in The Devil To Pay.

Loretta Young and Ronald Colman in The Devil To Pay.

Loretta Young and Ronald Colman in The Devil To Pay.

24 ONE HEAVENLY NIGHT (1930)

Directed by George Fitzmaurice; screenplay, Sidney Howard; based on a story by Louis Bromfield; music director, Frank Tours; photographers, George Barnes and Gregg Toland; editor, Stuart Heisler; art director, Richard Day. Running time, 82 minutes. Released by United Artists. Premiere: Rialto Theater, New York, 1/9/31

THE CAST:
Lilli, Evelyn Laye; *Count Mirko Tibor,* John Boles; *Otto,* Leon Errol; *Fritzi Vyez,* Lilyan Tashman; *Janos,* Hugh Cameron; *Liska,* Marion Lord; *Zagen,* Lionel Belmore; *Papa Lorenc,* George Bickel; *Egon,* Vincent Barnett; *Almady,* Henry Victor; *Violinist,* Luis Alberni; *Police Chief,* Henry Kolker.

Musical Numbers: songs by Nacio Herb Brown and Bruno Granichstadten; lyrics by Edward Eliscu and Clifford Grey (sung by)
"I Belong to Everybody" (Lilyan Tashman)
"Along the Road of Dreams" (Evelyn Laye)
Reprise: "Along the Road of Dreams" (Evelyn Laye)
"My Heart Is Beating" (Evelyn Laye, John Boles)
"Goodnight Serenade" (John Boles, Evelyn Laye, men's chorus)
"Heavenly Night (When Evening Is Near)" (John Boles, Evelyn Laye)

During one of Goldwyn's annual pilgrimages to Europe in search of talent while drumbeating current product, the producer became enchanted with the darling of the British musical comedy stage, Evelyn Laye, and induced her to become his next star. On her way to Hollywood, she stoped off in New York to entrance Broadway in the initial American production of Noel Coward's *Bitter Sweet,* while Goldwyn was preparing not only a royal welcome, but a captivating screen operetta by none less than *two* Pulitzer Prize winners, Louis Bromfield (story) and Sidney Howard (screenplay).

Originally entitled *Lilli,* after the leading character, the plots revolves around a charming, flaxen-haired flower girl in Budapest who masquerades as a racy cabaret performer, falls in love with a handsome prince, sings duets with him to avoid being lured into his bed, and eventually gets to marry him despite a last minute bit of competition from the gold digging star she had been impersonating.

Evelyn Laye's film debut was a personal triumph. Surrounded by a top drawer cast, appearing opposite a dashing leading man, singing several solos and a couple of duets, the lovely actress drew nothing but praise. Unfortunately, Goldwyn had failed to see the vehicle itself for what it was: an elaborate, but decidedly second rate slice of baloney, with music. Only *Variety* "loved" it calling *One Heavenly Night* "a charming film composite of the Brothers Grimm, a typical American musical comedy, and a trace of vaudeville knockabout," while labelling its star "probably the world's most captivating blonde actress on screen or stage." More to the point was *The New York Times* opinion that

why it should be necessary to have Mr. Bromfield and Mr. Howard go to Hollywood to write such a story is another of those mysteries of the film capital . . . it certainly would not tax a youngster's mentality to concoct what is beheld here, and almost anybody could suggest more propitious moments for singing than occur in this picture.

Of the acting:

Nobody can deny Miss Laye's beauty and she does her best to add glamour and life to the episodes . . . (her) singing is pleasing and Mr. Boles also tempers his none-too-convincing performance with some fairly good singing.

And from Richard Watts in the *New York Herald Tribune:*

It becomes particularly upleasant to report that *One Heavenly Night* is a routine and unskillful screen operetta. The production, of course, is good, and Miss Laye, although not photographed flatteringly, is a pleasant and charming, if emotionally unconvincing, heroine . . . the photoplay, in a phrase, is not one of the masterpieces of the Goldwyn studio.

The film opens with Lilyan Tashman, playing Fritzi Vyez, the "Toast of Budapest," singing rather effervescently "I Belong to Everybody," and apparently the Prefect of Police takes her at her word and suggests that she might enjoy an extended vacation in the quiet town of Zuppa. Fritzi is averse to leaving with all of those high rollers in town, and prevails, without much difficulty, upon Lilli to go in her stead. In Zuppa, with musician friend and guardian Otto, Lilli is immediately taken for the tempestuous Fritzi and treated accordingly by roguish Count Mirko, who romances her with song as he tries to maneuver her into his bedroom, and even chases her through a downpour to her own door, where both pause to serenade each other through sheets of rain. Mirko, of course, realizes he is truly in love with the stunning young lady when the real Fritzi shows up ready for the pursuit, and discovering Lilli's whereabouts in the final reel, Mirko bounds up to her flat three steps at a time, sweeps her into his arms, and breaks into the title song.

One of the joys of *One Heavenly Night* remains the work of Leon Errol, offering hilarious samples of his varied repertoire, highlighted by his rubber legs routine, wherein he staggers through the Count's gallery of china and glassware; his definitive drunk, as he tries in vain to paste a postage stamp on an envelope; and the famed double and triple takes. Riding a bicycle throughout the proceedings while all others are on horseback, Errol offers yet another distinctive touch to the several set pieces director George Fitzmaurice allowed the popular Ziegfeld star.

One Heavenly Night was, Goldwyn probably decided reluctantly, a mistake. Never again did he attempt an operetta, nor did he again use Miss Laye, Boles, Errol or Lilyan Tashman. Evelyn Laye made only a handful of films in America before deciding that she would be more at home on the British stage, where for more than three decades she remained a popular star.

John Boles and Evelyn Laye in One Heavenly Night.

Leon Errol and Evelyn Laye in One Heavenly Night.

Leon Errol and Evelyn Laye in One Heavenly Night.

Lilyan Tashman and John Boles in One Heavenly Night.

25 STREET SCENE (1931)

Directed by King Vidor; screenplay, Elmer Rice; based on his Pulitzer Prize play; music, Alfred Newman; photographer, George Barnes; editor, Hugh Bennett; assistant director, H.B. Humberstone; art director, Richard Day. Running time, 80 minutes. Released by United Artists. Premiere: Rivoli Theater, New York, 8/26/31

THE CAST:

Rose Maurrant, Sylvia Sidney; *Sam Kaplan,* William Collier, Jr.; *Anna Maurant,* Estelle Taylor; *Emma Jones,* Beulah Bondi*#; *Abe Kaplan,* Max Montor; *Frank Maurrant,* David Landau; *Vincent Jones,* Matt McHugh*; *Steve Sankey,* Russell Hopton; *Mae Jones,* Greta Grandstedt; *George Jones,* Tom H. Manning*; *Olga Olsen,* Adele Watson; *Karl Olsen,* John Qualen*; *Shirley Kaplan,* Anna Konstant*; *Filippo Fiorentino,* George Humbert*; *Dick McGann,* Allan Fox; *Greta Fiorentino,* Eleanor Wesselhoeft*; *Alice Simpson,* Nora Cecil; *Harry Easter,* Louis Natheaux; *Willie Maurrant,* Lambert Rogers; *Mary Hildebrand,* Virginia Davis; *Laura Hildebrand,* Helen Lovett; *Charlie Hildebrand,* Kenneth Selling; *Dan Buchanan,* Conway Washburne*; *Dr. John Wilson,* Howard Russell; *Off. Harry Murphy,* Richard Powell; *Marshal James Henry,* Walter James; *Fred Cullen,* Harry Wallace; and Monti Carter, Jane Mercer, Margaret Robertson, Walter Miller.

in screen debut

* in original Broadway production

Demonstrating again his continuing efforts to bring culture to the screen, Goldwyn bought the rights to Elmer Rice's Pulitzer Prize-winning drama *Street Scene,* one of the hits of the 1928–29 Broadway season, and then brought the author to Hollywood to adapt to films his incisive look at big city tenement life. To direct, Goldwyn engaged King Vidor, knowing that the latter's technical virtuosity could easily overcome the built-in problems inherent in a single-set production. (Like the Broadway play, the movie of *Street Scene* limited the action to the front of a dingy brownstone in Manhattan's West Forties.) Vidor confirmed Goldwyn's confidence by creating, with a particularly fluid camera, striking pictorial effects resulting in a remarkable illusion of movement that the play itself sorely lacked.

To people his *Street Scene,* Goldwyn wisely chose several key members of the Broadway cast to recreate their roles, Among them: Beulah Bondi (in her screen debut) as the local gossip, Matt McHugh as the cabbie, and Anna Konstant as the school teacher sister of the Jewish hero. Next, Goldwyn negotiated with Paramount for the services of Nancy Carroll to play Rose Maurrant (Erin O'Brien-Moore enacted the role on Broadway) and prematurely took out full page trade paper ads announcing the signing. Miss Carroll, however, was suddenly made unavailable after having some difficulty with her home studio. To assuage Goldwyn, B.P. Schulberg, Paramount's head of production, offered to loan Sylvia Sidney, in whose career he (Schulberg) was then quite interested. He convinced Goldwyn that Miss Sidney already had established herself portraying put-upon young ladies from the lower class, and would be an ideal Rose Maurrant.

In his assessment of Sylvia Sidney's work, critic Richard Watts thought that "she is honestly moving and entirely simple and credible as the girl of the story, giving one of the most satisfying characterizations of the year." Similar reviews came from *Variety,* which noted that:

(she) gives an even, persuasive performance in a role for which she is particularly fitted, typifying, as she somehow does here, the tragedy of budding girlhood cramped by sordid surroundings. Even her lack of formal beauty intensifies the pathos of her character.

Street Scene is a painting of gregarious, urban life,

passed on the front steps of a tenement, where loves and hates flourish publicly in the street. Over the harsh metallic noises of the city, the grating of the nearby elevated, the fumes of the asphalt on a mid-July day, little knots of people gather to discuss the current neighborhood scandal—Anna Maurrant and her milk collector paramour, the amorous Sankey. The affair is a rather open secret, although Anna's husband Frank, a hard, unsentimental man, can only rely on his suspicions. As the tenants pour from the building to face another day—daughter Rose going to her job, Frank leaving for Stamford, he says to work—life begins again on the front stoop. Sam Kaplan, Rose's boyfriend, watches Sankey sneak up to the Maurrant flat, and then notices, as the shades are being pulled down, the lurching figure of Frank Maurrant making for the doorway. Hysterical screams—a thud—a shot. Neighbors, startled, look up at the drawn blind. Suddenly the shade opens and Sankey appears. Then there is a hand on his shoulder and another shot. As neighbors begin emptying from surrounding buildings, Frank, disheveled, lunges from the doorway, gun in hand.

He orders them out of his way as he dashes down an alley, as pandemonium breaks loose. Ambulances and police signal more crowds and hysteria seizes the curiosity-mad crowd. Now they have new gossip, a new scandal—double murder. Rose reaches the scene of the turmoil in time to see her mother being brought out on a stretcher, and Sam's sister, Shirley, tries to console her. They talk of the tragedy—of her mother's death, of the impossible situation with Sam. Suddenly, between two policemen, Frank stumbles into view. He has returned to say goodbye to Rose, to tell her that he did not mean it, that he was drunk, crazy.

Now come the sightseers, the tabloid reporters, the photographers. Rose prepares to leave with her brother, Willie, refusing Sam's offer to go with her. Following a last look at their callous neighbors, Rose and Willie leave the tragic street to find new lives.

Creighton Peet, critic for *Outlook* found that "King Vidor's first important film since *Hallelujah* is a skillfully directed edition of the Rice drama." Richard Watts wrote in the *New York Herald Tribune*: "Faithfully adapted, admirably directed, and quite brilliantly acted, the photoplay emerges (from its handicaps) as the fine, honest, genuinely stirring drama which it seemed on the stage . . . and is a brilliant motion picture." Mordaunt Hall's opinion, expressed in *The New York Times,* was that

It is a swiftly moving production, this shadow version of *Street Scene,* but one that in comparison with the play always seems to be more than slightly exaggerated. It is a good picture, but the acting lacks the naturalness of the original work and the lines are invariably overstressed . . . while this film lacks the finesse of the stage production, Mr. Vidor has maintained a good deal of its human quality. Those who have not seen the play undoubtedly will be satisfied with this screen interpretation sponsored by Samuel Goldwyn.

Surviving the film somewhat better than most elements is the familiar main theme by Alfred Newman. It has stood the years as classic film music, and for more than four decades, has been incorporated into other (usually Newman) scores for films dealing with the teeming life-style embodied by New York City.

William Collier Jr. and Sylvia Sidney in Street Scene.

David Landau (in felt hat), George Humbert (straw hat), Estelle Taylor (in white) and Beulah Bondi in Street Scene.

Nancy Carroll, the star who never was, in a premature advertisement for Street Scene.

Greta Grandstedt and Allan Fox in Street Scene.

26 PALMY DAYS (1931)

Directed by A. Edward Sutherland; screenplay by Eddie Cantor, Morrie Ryskind and David Freedman from their original story; music director, Alfred Newman; photographer, Gregg Toland; editor, Sherman Todd; dances staged by Busby Berkeley; art director, Richard Day; sets, Willy Pogany; costumes, Chanel. Running time, 80 minutes. Released by United Artists. Premiere: Rialto Theater, New York, 9/23/31

THE CAST:
Eddie Simpson, Eddie Cantor; *Helen Martin,* Charlotte Greenwood; *A.B. Clark,* Spencer Charters; *Joan Clark,* Barbara Weeks; *Joe the Frog,* George Raft; *Steve Clayton,* Paul Page; *Plug Moynihan,* Harry Woods; *Yolando,* Charles B. Middleton; and *The Goldwyn Girls,* Loretta Andrews, Edna Callahan, Nadine Dore, Ruth Edding, Betty Grable, Amo Ingraham, Jean Lenivick, Betty Lorraise, Fay Pierre, Hylah Slocum, Betty Stockton, Nita Pike, Nancy Nash, Neva Lynn, Hazel Witter.

Musical numbers: (performed by)
"Bend Down Sister" *by Ballard MacDonald and Con Conrad* (Charlotte Greenwood and The Goldwyn Girls)
"Goose Pimples" (Charlotte Greenwood)
"Dunk Dunk Dunk" (The Goldwyn Girls)
"There's Nothing Too Good For My Baby" *by Eddie Cantor, Benny Davis and Harry Akst* (Eddie Cantor in backface)
"My Honey Said Yes, Yes" *by Cliff Friend* (Eddie Cantor and The Goldwyn Girls)
"My Honey Said Yes, Yes" *finale reprise* (Charlotte Greenwood, preacher, and Eddie Cantor)

Goldwyn's second annual Eddie Cantor frolic was no *Whoopee!* in spectacle, but the production values remained at the producer's high standards and the original story allowed *Palmy Days* to be more a movie than the filmed stage play atmosphere of its Cantor predecessor. "A surging Niagara of entertainment with more girls, more fun, more story and more CANTOR than you've ever seen before!" The promise of the Goldwyn ad campaign, together with dance routines by Busby Berkeley and gowns by Chanel, plus of course, the curvacious Goldwyn Girls (Betty Grable once again quite prominent among them)—all combined to bring moviegoers flocking to theatres to relish the multifaceted, happily satisfying, Goldwyn/Cantor extravaganza. Berkeley's work, much of it borrowed from his Broadway days, had yet to show the legendary technique and panache displayed in his later Warner Bros. spectaculars, but it did offer 1931 audiences generous samples of the kaleidoscopic routines that were to become synonymous with his name. Also offered was Berkeley's "cheerful eroticism" (as one writer terms it), with his, now familiar long-tracking shots displaying the legs of the high-kicking Goldwyn Girls, and in the "Bend Down Sister" number, a good deal of cleavage.

Director A. Edward Sutherland's rapid-fire pacing balanced Cantor's buffoonery and audacious, frantic manner, with the professional work of the rest of the cast, and in particular, delightfully funny Charlotte Greenwood as the athletic gym instructor, while allowing enough footage for Cantor's obligatory songs, as well as his standard blackface production number.

In *Palmy Days,* Cantor is the timid assistant to a phony spiritualist who lives in the downstairs apartment. Cantor, as Eddie Simpson, a nervous little man who sings when excited, is mistakenly hired as efficiency expert at the gigantic bakery run by A.B. Clark, whom, by chance, Yolando, the crooked medium, has been preparing to swindle. Eddie, though, bumbles his way into the bakery operation and thinks he has fallen in love with the boss' daughter Joan, while he has really captured the eye of physical culturist, Helen Martin. Yolando cons Eddie into obtaining the combination to the safe containing the company payroll, but Eddie then refuses to turn over the papers with the numbers. Yolando then dispatches two of his hoods, Plug Moynihan and Joe the Frog (the latter played by George Raft in one of his early screen roles), to persuade Eddie to reveal the combination. Spotting his pursuers, Eddie ducks into the company gym while the girls are taking their daily swim (and performing the "Bend Down Sister" number). Disguising himself as a girl, he almost manages to slip past the hoods, but is stopped by Helen Martin who, not recognizing Eddie, orders him into the shower with the other girls.

When he finally eludes Plug and Joe the Frog, Eddie makes his way to Clark's office, removes the payroll and hides it in a lump of dough, which unfortunately, becomes baked into a loaf of bread. Eddie is then accused by Yolando of stealing the money, and Clark is urged to have his efficiency expert arrested, but Eddie, with Helen Martin, dash off to locate the correct loaf among all that are being stored next to the oven. The frantic search—in a Keystone Kops-style finale—keeps the two just out of the grasp of Yolando and his accomplices, as well as the police, until the panting Eddie can at last deliver the missing $24,000 to Clark, who then orders Yolando taken into police custody. Learning that pretty Barbara Clark plans to marry Steve Clayton, Eddie decides that his "physical torturist," Helen Martin will make a nice substitute for the girl of his dreams. After all, Eddie reveals (among the many incongruous *bon mots* he finds time to utter), "There is a Minneapolis in heaven, just as there is a St. Paul."

Cantor manages a big production number during a party sequence so that he may work with and further ogle the nubile Goldwyn Girls, singing to "My Baby said Yes, Yes," which is reprised with Charlotte Greenwood at the wedding finale. The Cantor blackface number, "There's Nothing Too Good for My Baby," and Charlotte Greenwood's solo, "Goose Pimples," are included among the fairly unmemorable *Palmy Days* score.

Variety found the film "Another Eddie Cantor laugh picture, heavily hoked but made funny throughout. *Palmy Days* is not a *Whoopee!*, but it's a laugh—and that's what Cantor in a theatre guarantees." *The New York Times'* Mordaunt Hall called it

a cleverly staged screen potpourri of songs, dances, buffoonery and pulchritude . . . quite good entertainment, with Eddie Cantor's nimble and indefatigable shadow very much in evidence . . . the wit may not be as nimble as Mr. Cantor's image, but it is good enough to make one laugh heartily.

Richard Watts, critic for the *New York Herald Tribune,* felt that although "Mr. Goldwyn's musical comedy film belongs to a rather outmoded photoplay form," Eddie Cantor is "so earnestly hilarious and some of his comic inventions so shrewdly devised that *Palmy Days* becomes a genuinely entertaining picture . . . and (in it), Mr. Cantor proves pretty conclusively what a fine comedian he is."

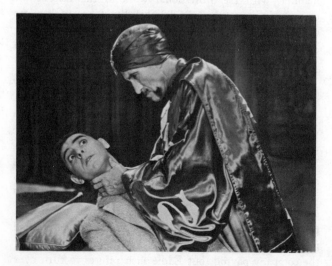

Eddie Cantor and Charles B. Middleton in Palmy Days.

The Goldwyn Girls in Palmy Days.

Eddie Cantor and friends in Palmy Days.

27 THE UNHOLY GARDEN (1931)

Directed by George Fitzmaurice; original screenplay, Ben Hecht and Charles MacArthur; music, Alfred Newman; photographers, George Barnes and Gregg Toland; editor, Grant Whytock; art directors, Richard Day and Willy Pogany. Running time, 75 minutes. Released by United Artists. Premiere: Rialto Theater, New York, 10/28/31

THE CAST:
Barrington Hunt, Ronald Colman; *Camille de Jonghe,* Fay Wray; *Elise Mowbry,* Estelle Taylor; *Baron de Jonghe,* Tully Marshall; *Smiley Corbin,* Warren Hymer; *Colonel von Axt,* Ulrich Haupt; *Prince Nicolai Poliakoff,* Mischa Auer; *Nick the Goose,* Henry Armetta; *Dr. Shayne,* Lawrence Grant; *Captain Kruger,* Morgan Wallace; *Kid Twist,* Kit Guard; *Lucie Villars,* Lucille LaVerne; *Louis Lautrec,* Arnold Korff; *Alfred de Jonghe,* Charles Mailes; *Native Dancer,* Nadja; and Henry Kolker, William Von Brincken.

Considering the talent associated with this incredulous seventy-five minutes worth of hokum, wherein a gentleman thief hides out and falls in love in a North African den of misfits, it remains a mystery as to how Goldwyn ever convinced himself of its worth. Equally intriguing is whether Ben Hecht and Charles MacArthur purposely set out to write this confection in complete dedication or simply for the generous salary Goldwyn had promised them. All of Ronald Colman's considerable charm was required to give even the slightest believability to the debonair scoundrel he portrays in *The Unholy Garden,* playing, as the ads claimed, "in the role you love in a headstrong story of desperate deeds and quick love."

The story tells semiseriously about how Barrington Hunt, a dashing thief who, through boredom, has drifted into bank robbery, eludes the police on the Continent and turns up in Algeria, hoping to lose himself for a while in a desert hideout on the edge of the Sahara with an underworld buddy, Smiley Corbin. Hunt and Smiley find sanctuary and make themselves at home in a run-down hotel occupied primarily by murderers and thieves on the lam. Local authorities, though, are warned of Hunt's presence and send Elise Mowbry, an undercover agent, to smoke him out. Hunt, however, already is occupying his time with another of the hotel's residents, Camille de Jonghe, granddaughter of an elderly, blind embezzler who has stashed his ill-gotten money somewhere on the premises. Hunt's ongoing romance with Camille finds him falling in love with the girl and ignoring the pleas of Colonel Von Axt and Kid Twist, leaders of the gang trying to get its hands on the old Baron's cache of stolen francs.

Not one to let work get in the way of romance, Hunt continues to dally with Camille, while Prince Nicolai Poliakoff, one of the gang, decides to hurry things along by shooting the Baron. Enter Mrs. Mowbry to work her wiles on Hunt who, in his usual carefree manner, accepts an invitation to join her for a spin in her car and soon discovers that it belongs to Louis Lautrec, the local police commandant. Spotting a romantic trap, Hunt nonchalantly plays along with Elise and even reveals his plan to double-cross his compatriates. When Hunt returns to Camille, however, hoping to turn her and the stolen money over to her uncle, for whom he had sent, Elise flies into a jealous rage and allows herself to get drunk with the mob and tell Von Axt of Hunt's noble scheme. Von Axt, Nick the Goose, Prince Poliakoff and Kid Twist frantically try to stop Hunt from carrying out his plan, but with the able assistantance of Smiley Corbin, Hunt manages to fend off the gang's attacks and sends Camille to her uncle with the money after turning down her offer to join him in his constant flight from justice.

Following the tearful departure, Hunt waves his

friend Smiley into the commandant's car, conveniently parked nearby, for their getaway. "But what did you do with the millions?" Smiley asks Hunt. "I'm sorry," the hero replies, "I just met a dame."

Variety commended Goldwyn on "a splendid presentation of an ordinary story" and noted that

> George Barnes' camera work is outstanding and (George) Fitzmaurice's achievement is that he has taken an all-too-familiar script and made it interesting. Like most Goldwyn pictures . . . the footage speaks the excellent workmanship and care throughout.

Its conclusion: "Few features have been better made than this, and not so many as well."

The New York Times had these favorable words for Goldwyn's airy desert drama:

> Shooting and spoofing take their turns in this packet of excitement and fun . . . this jocular melodrama was written by Ben Hecht and Charles MacArthur and directed in the desirable mood by George Fitzmaurice. It is quite a clever piece of work in which Mr. Colman is kept on the *qui vive* from the moment he appears

on the screen . . . (and) performs with his usual *savoir faire.*

A thumbs-down opinion came from Richard Watts, who found the film

> a confused and ineffective romantic photoplay which never manages to be successful as either melodrama or comedy . . . Mr. Colman, of course, is an effective actor who can look romantically bored in the best English drawing room manner, and here he is as suave and debonair as usual, though a bit too smug. Otherwise his performance is reasonably effective. That excellent actress, Miss Estelle Taylor, is provided with the character of an old-time villainess of the early Owen Davis days, and the result is not altogether happy. Miss Fay Wray does as well as possible, I suppose, as the incredible heroine . . . (although) it is difficult to figure out how she suddenly appeared in this curious melodrama.

The Unholy Garden marked the eighth and final collaboration between Ronald Colman and director George Fitzmaurice.

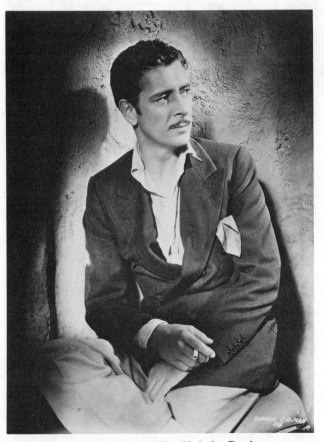

Ronald Colman in The Unholy Garden.

Fay Wray and Ronald Colman in The Unholy Garden.

Estelle Taylor and Ronald Colman in The Unholy Garden.

Tully Marshall, Fay Wray, Ronald Colman, Warren Hymer, Henry Armetta and Ullrich Haupt in The Unholy Garden.

28 ARROWSMITH (1931)

Directed by John Ford; screenplay by Sidney Howard; based on the novel by Sinclair Lewis; music, Alfred Newman; photographer, Ray June; editor, Hugh Bennett; art director, Richard Day. Running time, 112 minutes. Released by United Artists. Premiere: Gaiety Theater, New York, 12/7/31

THE CAST:
Martin Arrowsmith, Ronald Colman; *Leora Tozer*, Helen Hayes; *Dr. Gustav Sondelius*, Richard Bennett; *Prof. Max Gottlieb*, A.E. Anson; *Doctor Tubbs*, Claude King; *Terry Wickett*, Russell Hopton; *Joyce Lanyon*, Myrna Loy; *Bert Tozer*, Bert Roach; *Mrs. Tozer*, Beulah Bondi; *Mr. Tozer*, DeWitt Jennings; *Henry Novak*, John Qualen; *Mrs. Novak*, Adele Watson; *Sir Robert Fairland*, Lumsden Hare; *Miss Twyford*, Florence Britton; *Twyford*, Alec B. Francis; *Doctor Hesselink*, Sidney DeGrey; *Oliver Marchand*, Clarence Brooks; *Pioneer Girl*, Charlotte Henry; *The Old Doctor*, James Marcus; *Veterinarian*, David Landau; *City Clerk*, Walter Downing; and Ward Bond, Raymond Hatton, Pat Somerset, Eric Wilton, Erville Anderson, George Humbert, Theresa Harris, Bobby Watson.

Arrowsmith, somewhat more than *Street Scene,* is the first of the producer's talkies that can be rightly called "a Goldwyn picture." Persuaded by his senior screenwriter, Sidney Howard, to make a film of Sinclair Lewis' episodic 1926 best seller, Goldwyn put his remarkable and quite uncanny touch on one of the decade's earliest and most forceful "message pictures." He borrowed John Ford from Fox—Ford was quoted in 1968 by Peter Bogdanovich as saying simply, "It was a good story and I think it's still a very modern picture"—to direct Ronald Colman in the title role of the idealistic young research doctor and Helen Hayes, in only the second of her astonishingly few screen performances, as his self-effacing wife.

The Sidney Howard adaptation telescoped a great deal of the novel's early expository action, skipping over Martin Arrowsmith's college days, as well as sloughing much surrounding his later affair with vampy Joyce Lanyon (played quite strikingly by Myrna Loy, whose photo accompanied the film's review in the *New York Herald Tribune*). The Howard script concentrated on the more melodramatic passages of Lewis' story at the expense of the author's generalized comments on American life, and Ford's eloquent stamp fleshed out through his deft camera movements countless classic scenes, such as the soft focus, shadowy, plague-induced death of Leora as she smokes that fatal cigarette, in addition to the impersonalization of the staff of the McGurk Institute by dwarfing the people under the cold splendor of the dominating modern architecture.

In the review in *Outlook,* the comment was made that

another of Hollywood's rare accidents has occurred— a fine, honest film has slipped by the boys on the Coast who spend their lives garbling every serious effort and who pride themselves on their God-given mediocrity.

Several negative comments were voiced toward the casting of Colman in the title role. Richard Watts, for one, suggested that "he is too definitely British for the part and perhaps a bit too dashing and romantic-looking for the role of an eager-eyed zealot with a religious passion for scientific research," while Margaret Marshall, writing in *Nation,* felt that

the character presented by Colman is hardly Martin Arrowsmith, small-town grandson of an American pioneer. His is a richer, more sophisticated character who has neither the unmodulated voice nor the awkward eagerness of the Martin of the book.

Most vocal was the critic for *Variety* who found it

hard to believe Colman in the title role . . . (he) either

lacks the depth to portray such a part or has been permitted by his superiors to seem to be in over his head. At no time does he impart the unquenchable thirst for research, the sense of humility, or the idolatry for the older scientist which the author wrote into the characterization . . . (his) performance is all on one plane and quite colorless,

(Curiously, this was the first of a succession of downbeat *Variety* critiques about Colman's work.)

Arrowsmith details the life of the young medical school graduate from his first practice in a small North Dakota town to his installation in a magnificent research laboratory in New York, and on to his dedicated work in the West Indies fighting bubonic plague, and following the death of his wife, his decision to shun his status as a great scientist to return to an out-of-the-way country practice.

"Samuel Goldwyn, that pioneer picture producer who has quite often shown a desire to lear the public rather than follow it, is responsible for the intelligent and forceful film version," Mordaunt Hall wrote in *The New York Times.*

No pains or expense have been spared in bringing this narrative to the screen. Sidney Howard was employed to write the adaptation, which he has accomplished with a full appreciation of the limitations of a film. John Ford was entrusted with the direction, and he, too, has done his task with a good understanding of the author's writing. It is an impressively staged production.

The *Times* placed *Arrowsmith* on its list of the Ten Best Films of 1931.

Among the superb cast of *Arrowsmith* were many of the players seen in Goldwyn's earlier *Street Scene,* including Beulah Bondi, Russell Hopton, John Qualen, Adele Watson, David Landau and George Humbert. Richard Bennett, one of the stars of Goldwyn's *The Eternal City,* etches in *Arrowsmith* a memorable portrait as Martin's fellow microbe hunter; A.E. Anson is unforgettable as Arrowsmith's mentor and medical school professor; and Miss Bondi and DeWitt Jennings are splendid as lovely Leora's narrow-minded parents.

Despite its status as an American classic, both as a novel and a film, and its Academy Award nominations notwithstanding—Best Picture of 1931, Best Screen Adaptation (Sidney Howard), Best Art/Set Decoration (Richard Day), Best Cinematography (Ray June)—*Arrowsmith* never has been remade, nor is the original Goldwyn version readily accessible on television. The first (of at least four) TV adaptations of Sinclair Lewis' creation was a live production on "Robert Montgomery Presents" in October 1950, with Van Heflin making his TV debut in the role of Martin Arrowsmith. Ten years later, Farley Granger, the last of the Goldwyn stars, gave his TV interpretation of the role which Ronald Colman, the first of the Goldwyn stars, had created in the definitive screen version.

Richard Bennett, Raymond Hatton and Ronald Colman in Arrowsmith.

Richard Bennett and Ronald Colman in Arrowsmith.

Myrna Loy and Ronald Colman in Arrowsmith.

29 TONIGHT OR NEVER (1931)

Directed by Mervyn LeRoy; screenplay, Ernest Vajda; based on the play by Lili Hatvany; adapted by Frederic and Fanny Hatton; music, Alfred Newman; photographer, Gregg Toland; editor, Grant Wytock; art director, Willy Pogany; costumes, Chanel. Running time, 66 minutes. Released by United Artists. Premiere: Rialto Theater, New York, 12/17/31

THE CAST:
Nella Vago, Gloria Swanson; *The Unknown Gentleman (Jim),* Melvyn Douglas*#; *Rudig,* Ferdinand Gottschalk*; *The Butler,* Robert Grieg*; *The Maid,* Greta Meyer*; *Count Albert von Gronac,* Warburton Gamble*; *The Marchesa,* Alison Skipworth; *The Waiter,* Boris Karloff
in screen debut
* in original Broadway production

Goldwyn's *Tonight or Never* was an expensive, lavishly mounted bauble designed to reverse the downward trend of Gloria Swanson's rapidly faltering career. At the urging of his United Artists partners (Mary Pickford, Douglas Fairbanks and Charles Chaplin), Samuel Goldwyn found a property in the still-running Broadway version of a popular Hungarian play to justify the exorbitant salary being shelled out week after week to the famed silent star who had come to the studio several years earlier through a complicated business arrangement with Joseph P. Kennedy. Goldwyn purchased the Frederic and Fanny Hatton adaptation of the Lili Hatvany play, wherein Helen Gahagan was costarring with her husband Melvyn Douglas and Ferdinand Gottschalk, and assigned Ernest Vadja the task of turning a credible screenplay with Miss Swanson as a volatile European *prima donna.*

Mervyn LeRoy was then engaged by Goldwyn as director, and several members of the original Broadway company, including Douglas (here making his film debut) and Gottschalk, were brought to Hollywood to recreate

their roles. Also among the film cast of *Tonight or Never* was Boris Karloff, fresh from his work in *Frankenstein* (which premiered in New York thirteen days before the Goldwyn film), in a rare comedy performance.

Gloria Swanson, swathed in Chanel gowns, framed in Willy Pogany's sumptuous settings, photographed lovingly by Gregg Toland, plays Nella Vago, a tempermental diva who becomes irate when her music teacher/fiance, Rudig, tells her that unless she goes out to experience life, she will never become a great singer. When she falls for a handsome gigolo, however, she determines to know more about him and goes to his apartment, pretending to be there by mistake. After spending the night with him, she sings at the next day's recital like a new woman, with remarkable new color to her voice. The love affair her own fiance had prescribed has done the trick, but backfires when Nella breaks her engagement shortly after receiving her long-desired contract with the Metropolitan Opera. Ignoring warnings about running around with a gigolo, always seen in the company of the Marchesa, who is introduced to all as his aunt, Nella continues to throw herself at him and offers to tear up her prized contract if he will have her. Only then does he tell her that he actually is an impresario traveling incognito while studying foreign talent, and it was he who arranged her Met contract, and yes, the Marchesa *is* his aunt. Relieved to learn the refreshing truth, Nella sings with a glowing warmth reflecting her new love and career.

"An unusually striking production," is the way Mordaunt Hall described the film, and of the acting, he found that "it is for the most part of a far higher order than in the average picture. It is an amusing if implausible tale, which to carry out the plot, calls for the characters to be more than slightly credulous." Critic Hall thought that "Miss Swanson's portrayal of the opera singer falls short of Helen Gahagan's performance (on stage) . . . and Melvyn Douglas' bright interpretation rather puts Miss Swanson in the shade."

Variety decided that Miss Swanson gave "a capital performance" and that Melvyn Douglas "now under long-term contract to Goldwyn, looks good, and he seems the perfect leading man." (Actually, Douglas never made another film for Goldwyn.) Of the picture itself, *Variety* wrote simply that "the telling is graceful and charming, the details are exquisitely polished and engagingly wrought—and that's all."

In the opinion of critic Richard Watts, *Tonight or Never* was

attractively acted by Gloria Swanson and Melvyn Douglas and produced with taste and good sense, emerging in the cinema as decidedly pleasant, if slightly reminiscent, romantic drama . . . (Miss Swanson's) is a genuinely attractive portrayal, light and humorous and pleasantly lacking in the suggestion of coyness which has sometimes overwhelmed her in her earlier comedies. Mr. Douglas is excellent as the hero, investing a possibly irritating role with an earnest and knowing skill which keeps it from being disagreeable.

Summing up, he thought that *"Tonight or Never* is, as a result, an invariably likeable carnival for its gallant star."

Unfortunately *Tonight or Never* failed to rally the Swanson fans, and after two more films, the actress' film career went into a hiatus lasting, except for one movie in the early forties, until her stunning comeback in *Sunset Boulevard* in 1950. Her leading man, however, went on to become one of the screen's most debonair light comedy stars (and subsequently a distinguished character actor) in a career spanning more than four decades of sound and more than sixty films. And of course, as the Swanson star faded, Karloff's skyrocketed on the success of his simultaneously released *Frankenstein.*

Gloria Swanson in Tonight or Never.

Melvyn Douglas and Gloria Swanson in Tonight or Never.

Robert Grieg and Gloria Swanson in Tonight or Never.

30 THE GREEKS HAD A WORD FOR THEM (1932)

Directed by Lowell Sherman; screenplay, Sidney Howard; based on the play *The Greeks Had a Word for It* by Zoë Akins; music, Alfred Newman; photographer, George Barnes; editor, Stuart Heisler; art director, Richard Day; costumes, Chanel. Running time, 77 minutes. Released by United Artists. Premiere: Rialto Theater, New York, 2/3/32 (TV title: *Three Broadway Girls*)

THE CAST:
Polaire, Madge Evans; *Schatze,* Joan Blondell; *Jean Lawrence,* Ina Claire; *Dey Emery,* David Manners; *Boris Feldman,* Lowell Sherman; *Justin Emery,* Phillips Smalley; *Waiter,* Sidney Bracey; *Showgirl,* Betty Grable.

Samuel Goldwyn, attempting to get Norma Talmadge to change her mind about calling it a career after unfavorable reviews were heaped on her two talkies, purchased the rights to Zoë Akins' uproarious Broadway smash, *The Greeks Had a Word for It,* and sent forth the word in late 1930 that he had found exactly the property for Miss Talmadge. The actress, though, remained true to her word about never again acting in films, and Goldwyn was obliged to put his Zoë Akins acquisition on the shelf.

As a change of pace, however, from his carousel movie activities involving Colman and Cantor productions, as well as an occasional serving of "serious art" (in the form of *Street Scene* and *Arrowsmith*), Goldwyn revived his plans to film the raucous tale about the predatory trio known as the "Three Musketeers of Riverside Drive." Sidney Howard handed him a literate adaptation that retained the wit, sophistication and biting satire (within the limits of the censors) that had captured New York's playgoers. Goldwyn then signed Ina Claire, Joan Blondell

and Madge Evans to the roles played on Broadway by Verree Teasdale, Dorothy Hall and Muriel Kirkland, respectively, and next saw personally to the elegant trappings that continued to distinguish his films. In this case, they included eye-popping Chanel creations, the lavish settings everyone had come to expect from Richard Day, and exceptionally loving photography by George Barnes, who fell for one of the leading ladies, Miss Blondell, and married her.

Censor problems forced Goldwyn to marshall his lieutenants for a high-level session on an acceptable title. Zoë Akins' "It" connotation—with apologies to Clara Bow, the "It" girl herself—could not, ridiculously, be remotely connected with a Samuel Goldwyn movie, always the epitome of good taste. The *New York Herald Tribune* critic, Richard Watts, declared in his review:

It was a proud moment for Hollywood ingenuity when Mr. Goldwyn and his cohorts emerged from earnest executive session proudly holding aloft their official decision on the proper title. How mortified Miss Akins must have been that she had never thought of it. After performing miracles of imagination, the cabinet decided upon a new name. Unfortunately, there is no scene in the picture as funny as that.

The bouncy little tale revolves around the ongoing series of squabbles of three dyed-in-the-wool gold diggers and their constant search for more and better millionaires to keep them in the delightful luxury to which they long had become accustomed. Jean, the wildest of the trio, relishes the challenge of stealing her friends' boyfriend(s) of the moment, and when Polaire snares wealthy playboy Dey Emery, Jean wangles her way into the Emery mansion, using a bit of petty thievery, to get her clutches on Dey's filthy rich father. Schatze, meanwhile, reveals that she is having an affair with an old moneybags known to all as Pops (he is never seen), who happens to have been Jean's former sugar daddy.

Jean's almost-wedding to millionaire Justin Emery never comes off when she learns that Polaire and Schatze are off to Paris, and following several "little drinkies" while the old bridegroom-to-be waits at the altar and the orchestra practices the wedding march, Jean decides that there are still several dozen fat cats she has not batted her big blue eyes at, and figures that she might just as well join the girls—taking with her of course, the expensive baubles Justin had lavished upon her. Dey persues Polaire to the ship and persuades her to become his wife, while Schatze is busy lining up some male companionship on deck and Jean is already planning her tactics for stealing Schatze's new admirer.

Lowell Sherman, the actor and sometimes director, both acted in and directed *The Greeks Had a Word for Them,* portraying an egotistical concert pianist who manages to entice Jean and her two cohorts, dragged along for protection, up to his apartment where he bets her $5,000 that he can make her fall in love with him merely by playing to her, but only succeeds in putting her to sleep.

"The picture is an example of inspired casting," wrote *Variety,*

and the dialogue crackles with swift comedy. It is a direct reversal from the feminine side of the McLaglen-Lowe love 'em-and-leave-'em technique, and from the first to the last an opulent spoof at the male gender on the make. The wit of the dialogue may be a bit

polished for the proletariat, but the basic human humor of the situations of these three lilies of the field in rivalry, in battle and in comradeship will register universally.

The New York Times felt that:

a riot of fun emanates from the screen shadows. There is beauty, too, lavish settings and good acting . . . Miss Evans is pretty and quite capable, Miss Blondell and Miss Claire keep the merriment bright, and Mr. Sherman gives a smooth performance.

The negative reports were best represented by Richard Watts. "The film version, as adapted by Sidney Howard, does straighten out the formlessness of the original," Watts commented,

but in the effort to supply a properly sentimental touch, the adapter has been forced to omit a great part of what humor there was, including the excellent comedy of the final episode. The picture emerges as noisy and unfunny farce.

The Greeks Had a Word for Them was the first of several screen variations on the gold digger plot. 20th Century-Fox later made a number of films using the theme that it adapted from Stephen Powys's play, *Three Blind Mice.* Among them, the actual screen version of the play (Loretta Young, Binnie Barnes and Marjorie Weaver were the girls), *Moon Over Miami* (Betty Grable, Carole Landis, Cobina Wright Jr.), *Three Little Girls in Blue* (June Haver, Vivian Blaine, Vera-Ellen), and finally *How to Marry a Millionaire* (Grable, Marilyn Monroe, Lauren Bacall), which was an amalgam of the plays by both Zoë Akins and Mr. Powys.

Madge Evans, Joan Blondell and Ina Claire in The Greeks Had a Word for Them.

Ina Claire, Joan Blondell and Madge Evans in The Greeks Had a Word for Them.

31 THE KID FROM SPAIN (1932)

Directed by Leo McCarey; original screenplay, William Anthony McGuire, Bert Kalmar and Harry Ruby; music director, Alfred Newman; songs, Bert Kalmar and Harry Ruby; dances staged by Busby Berkeley; photographer, Gregg Toland; editor, Stuart Heisler; art director, Richard Day; costumes, Milo Anderson. Running time, 118 minutes. Released by United Artists. Premiere: Palace Theater, New York, 11/17/32

THE CAST:
Eddie Williams, Eddie Cantor; *Rosalie,* Lyda Roberti; *Ricardo,* Robert Young; *Anita Gomez,* Ruth Hall; *Pancho,* John Miljan; *Alonzo Gomez,* Noah Beery; *Pedro,* J. Carrol Naish; *Crawford,* Robert Emmet O'Connor; *Jose,* Stanley Fields; *Border Guard,* Paul Porcasi; *American Matador,* Sidney Franklin; *Dalmores,* Julian Rivero; *Martha Oliver,* Theresa Maxwell Conover; *The Dean,* Walter Walker; *Red,* Ben Hendricks Jr.; *Specialty Dancer,* Grace Poggi; *Bull Handler,* Edgar Connor; *Thief,* Leo Willis; *Traffic Cop,* Harry Gribbon; *Patron,* Eddie Foster; *Man on Line at Border,* Harry C. Bradley; *The 1932 Goldwyn Girls,* Jean Allen, Loretta Andrews, Consuelo Baker, Betty Bassett, Lynn Browning, Maxie Cantway, Hazel Craven, Dorothy Rae Coonan, Shirley Chambers, Patricia Farnum, Betty Grable, Paulette Goddard, Jeannie Gray, Ruth Hale, Pat Harper, Margaret La Marr, Adele Lacey, Bernice Lorimer, Nancy Lynn, Vivian Mathison, Nancy Nash, Edith Roark, Marian Sayers, Renne Whitney, Diana Winslow, Toby Wing.

Musical numbers: (performed by)
"The College Song (Opening Number)" (Betty Grable, Goldwyn Girls)
"In the Moonlight" (Eddie Cantor, Goldwyn Girls)
"Look What You've Done" (Lyda Roberti, Eddie Cantor)
Untitled Dance (Grace Poggi)
"What a Perfect Combination" (Cantor in blackface, Goldwyn Girls)
Finale: "What a Perfect Combination" (Eddie Cantor, Lyda Roberti)

"It is the ambition of Samuel Goldwyn," wrote *Time Magazine,* to make his cinema comedies resemble in opulence the musical shows of the late Florenz Ziegfeld. *The Kid from Spain* cost about $1,400,000, and a chorus which is probably the handsomest ever assembled for the cinema appears exactly twice.

Here again is Goldwyn's familiar and very successful formula musical built around the visual talents of Eddie Cantor; Busby Berkeley to stage the dances; a practically all-new batch of Goldwyn Girls (this time, in addition to Betty Grable—a Goldwyn Girl for the third time—Paulette Goddard and Toby Wing were to be glimpsed briefly); a bouncy score by Bert Kalmar and Harry Ruby; and a competent supporting cast, including an incredibly young Robert Young (completely miscast as a Mexican); and the daffy musical comedienne, Lyda Roberti, here billed as "The Hotcha Blonde." The plot, this time, manages to get Cantor into a Mexican bull-ring as the wild finale to the proceedings that include a bumbled bank robbery, several cases of mistaken identity, two intricate Berkeley routines, three Cantor songs and the now standard Cantor blackface number.

To direct this lavishly produced melange, Goldwyn chose Leo McCarey, who was elevated to the big time with his work on the Cantor film. His notable climax sequence, in which a reluctant Cantor and an equally reluctant bull face each other in the ring, prompted the Marx Brothers to ask for McCarey for their next film, *Duck Soup.* In *The Kid From Spain,* Eddie Williams and his roomate Ricardo, are expelled from college after being found in the girls' dormitory—an opening Busby Berkeley ballet in the dorm is led by Betty Grable. Ricardo induces Eddie join him at his home in Mexico and suggests that they first stop off at the local bank where he (Ricardo) has to withdraw his savings. Eddie, waiting outside, is mistaken for the driver by a gang that has just knocked over the bank, and is forced to flee to Mexico when the robbers fear he might testify against them. At the border, however, Eddie has difficulty getting past the guard, but finally succeeds after posing as a Mexican. On the other side of the border though, Eddie is immediately mistaken for the bullfighter son of the famed matador, Don Sebastian, and is unable to reveal his true identity because an American detective, Crawford, is tailing him on the assumption that Eddie is one of the bank robbers.

Making his way, finally, to Ricardo's home, Eddie discovers his friend preoccupied with Anita Gomez and has as his rival, Pancho, the noted matador, whom Anita's father would rather see as his son-in-law. While trying to help Ricardo straighten out his romance, Eddie becomes involved with Anita's flighty friend, Rosalie, who pleads with Eddie to "kees me like a hawk . . . like a heagle." Unfortunately for Eddie, Rosalie also has captured the eye of Pancho's sinister accomplice, Pedro, who, along with the American detective, keeps Eddie hopping.

At the Sunday bullfight, whereat Eddie has been badgered into performing, Pedro switches a vicious bull for the tame one Ricardo had promised—one that stops dead when it hears the word "Popocatepetl," which, naturally, Eddie promptly forgets. After nearly running the substitute bull into the ground, both in the ring and along the gangways, Eddie manages the vanquish the beast with chloroform, win Rosalie, set things right between Ricardo and Anita, and reprise the film's biggest number, "What a Perfect Combination," this time with Rosalie. (Previously, he had done it in blackface and then in a Berkeley routine with the Goldwyn lovelies.)

Cantor, of course, carried the film on his stock characterization with facial expressions mirroring bewilderment, despair and false assurance. "The picture," agreed *Variety,* "is all Cantor's and almost every scene, save the opening coed stuff with Berkeley's water ballet, has Cantor in it. To his credit, he more than sustains the tempo." The *Los Angeles Express,* similarly enthused, called it "One of the funniest, most exciting, most eye-filling comedies yet offered on the screen." *Time Magazine's* comment: "If you like Eddie Cantor, you'll probably like this picture in which, surrounded by prettier girls than usual, he per-

forms thoroughly typical Cantor antics while rolling his popeyes and giving exaggerated gulps."

In his review, Richard Watts said:

Before its entertaining finish, (the film) is a spectacular and lavish screen musical comedy that suffers considerably from stage musical comedy defects as a routine book, much antique comedy and a score that is no better that it should be. Mr. Cantor is probably as funny as his material permits; the engaging Miss Roberti [*her picture rather than Cantor's accompanied the Watts review*] is rather buried in the proceedings, which is a shame; and the other members of the cast (except for Brooklyn's matador, Sidney Franklin), are, for one reason or another, negative.

Mordaunt Hall, on the other hand, had these observations:

The Kid from Spain is an astutely arranged combination of fun and beauty, with such effective groupings of dancing girls that these scenes themselves aroused applause. This film keeps that nimble little comedian, Eddie Cantor, busy most of the time, and there is no objection to this . . . On several occasions, director Leo McCarey takes advantage of the graceful girls in this film to give it a musical comedy angle. These scenes are always directed in an imaginative fashion so that they are invariably compelling."

This was the third film for Polish born Lyda Roberti, daughter of the celebrated European clown, Roberti. Her rapidly ascending star and her growing reputation as a comedienne flickered out tragically when she died of a heart attack in 1938 at the age of thirty-two. She had made eleven movies and starred on Broadway opposite newcomer Bob Hope in Jerome Kern's *Roberta.* Goldwyn, for reasons unexplained, failed to use her again after *The Kid from Spain.*

When the Goldwyn film opened in New York, it was given a road show run at the Palace Theater, playing twice daily with tickets scaled at $2.20. *Variety,* in its review, complained about the exorbitant ticket price, and even Cantor himself, already renowned for his business acumen, chided Goldwyn, noting in a letter to *Variety*: "I'd be much happier if *The Kid from Spain* were playing the Rivoli at 75¢."

Eddie Cantor and Paul Porcasi in The Kid from Spain.

Eddie Cantor in The Kid from Spain.

Robert Young and Lyda Roberti in The Kid from Spain.

Theresa Maxwell Conover, Eddie Cantor and The Gold-wyn Girls in The Kid from Spain.

32 CYNARA (1932)

Directed by King Vidor; screenplay, Frances Marion and Lynn Starling; based on the play by H.M. Harwood and Robert Gore-Brown and the novel *An Imperfect Lover* by Gore-Brown; music, Alfred Newman; photographer, Ray June; editor, Hugh Bennett; art director, Richard Day. Running time, 78 minutes. Released by United Artists. Premiere: Rivoli Theater, New York, 12/26/32. (Reissued in 1945 as *I Was Faithful*)

THE CAST:

Jim Warlock, Ronald Colman; *Clemency Warlock*, Kay Francis; *Doris Lea*, Phyllis Barry; *Sir John Tring*, Henry Stephenson*; *Milly Miles*, Viva Tattersall; *Gorla*, Florine McKinney; *Onslow*, Clarissa Selwynne; *Mr. Boots*, George Kirby; *Joseph*, Paul Porcasi; *Henry*, Donald Stuart; *Merton*, Wilson Benge; *Constable*, C. Montague Shaw
* in original Broadway production

For his second film using King Vidor as director and his *seventeenth* using Colman as his star, Goldwyn chose the popular drama about marital infidelity that had been "wowing" them on the London and Broadway stages for two years, *Cynara* (pronounced, as Goldwyn's advertising department insisted, "SIN-ara"). The play in turn had been taken from the Robert Gore-Brown novel, *An Imperfect Lover,* while the title itself comes from the famed line by poet Ernest Dowson, "I have been faithful to thee, Cynara, in my fashion."

Cynara is a good old-fashioned weeper wherein a happily married, middle-aged barrister reluctantly becomes involved with a pretty shopgirl in a casual affair that ends in tragedy. Colman, at his most debonair, followed in the role Sir Gerald DuMaurier (playing Jim Warlock on London's West End with Gladys Cooper and Celia Johnson) and Philip Merivale (on Broadway with Phoebe Foster and Adrianne Allen). His Warlock is the epitome of respectability among the day's ruling class, perfectly described by his wife Clemency in her

admiration: "There are two things in the world you can trust—The Church of England and Jim Warlock." This, however, is just before Clemency decides to accompany her sister Gorla, on a trip to Venice. Clemency is certain that Jim will not mind her leaving on the eve of their wedding anniversary because, after all, Gorla needs help in forgetting a just-ended romantic entanglement.

After seeing Clemency off, Jim joins his good friend, the Honorable John Tring, for an early dinner at a charming out-of-the-way restaurant in Soho. There they encounter Doris Lea and Milly Miles, her roommate, and soon the four are at the same table. That evening soon might have been forgotten, but the philandering Tring paves the way for a second meeting between Jim and Doris, resulting in a serious affair. Aware that Jim is a married man, Doris nevertheless pleads with him to stay with her, and Jim manages to keep the whole business quite discreet. Gossip does seep out and Doris loses her job, just as Clemency returns from Venice and Jim is obliged to move back into his own home.

Jim continues to meet Doris secretly, giving her money to live, but the girl, desperately in love with him, refuses his checks. Milly, alarmed at Doris' growing dispondency, goes to Jim's home and unbraids him for the cad that he is. While she is there, a policeman turns up at Warlock's house with word that Doris has killed herself and Jim's letter had been found at her side. A scandal follows, but Jim refuses to besmirch Doris' reputation by telling the truth at the inquest. He and Clemency leave London in disgrace, going to Naples where they agree to part after Jim tries to explain his actions to his wife. After Jim boards his ship for South Africa in search of a new career, Tring turns up in time to convince Clemency how much her husband really needs her, and manages to reunite the two on the deck of the ship as it prepares to sail.

the simplicity of the story, the fact that its elements have been used in the cinema a thousand times before, make it easy to overlook the truth that *Cynara* is a most unusual picture . . . because it presents, with somber thoughtfulness, a situation which the cinema almost always handles blatantly, and because the values which it involves, while not particularly subtle, are wholly unlike those which U.S. cinema audiences are usually called upon to comprehend.

The review concluded that "*Cynara* possesses the surface excellences—sensitive direction by King Vidor and more than competent acting—with which shrewd old Samuel Goldwyn quite often equips his productions." *Variety*, too, found that "Goldwyn this time comes through with a class production—in all respects worthy of the quality of the play itself. It finds Ronald Colman in probably the best bit of clean-cut acting."

Critic Richard Watts thought the film

is honest and straightforward drama. Mr. Colman is quite good as the disturbed barrister, even if he is less moving in the role than was Philip Merivale. Portrayed by Miss Phyllis Barry, the British musical star making her American film debut, the shopgirl is to be seen for what she was—a very bad sport, and the result is more honest and less tragic effectiveness. Miss Kay Francis is good in the colorless role of the wife, and that perfect actor, Mr. Henry Stephen-son, who has never given a bad performance, repeats his brilliant stage role of the amiably satanic friend.

Mordaunt Hall observed that *Cynara*

is faithful to the parent work and King Vidor, the director, gives to his scenes effective and restrained guidance. Mr. Colman gives an ingratiating protrayal . . . and there is a pleasing sincerity about his acting, which evidently has been helped by Mr. Vidor's imaginative direction.

Shortly before the end of production on *Cynara*, Goldwyn and Colman had their celebrated row, when the outspoken producer asserted publicly that "Colman feels he looks better for pictures when moderately dissipated than when completely fit," and that Colman was drunk on the set. Colman sued for $2,000,000 and vowed he would never again work for Goldwyn. Goldwyn countered with an injunction prohibiting Colman from working anywhere else until his contract expired. While the suit was working its way through the legal processes (it finally was settled out of court), Colman cooled his heels by embarking on an around-the-world voyage. The impasse between Goldwyn and Colman was broken when the actor agreed to honor his contract for one more film and the producer allowed him to sign with 20th Century, then being formed by Darryl F. Zanuck and Joseph M. Schenck.

Kay Francis and Ronald Colman in Cynara.

Ronald Colman and Phyllis Barry in Cynara.

Florine McKinney and Ronald Colman in Cynara.

33 THE MASQUERADER (1933)

Directed by Richard Wallace; screenplay, Howard Estabrook; based on the play by John Hunter Booth and the novel by Katherine Cecil Thurston; music, Alfred Newman; photographer, Gregg Toland; editor, Stuart Heisler; art director, Richard Day. Running time, 78 minutes. Released by United Artists. Premiere: Rivoli Theater, New York, 9/3/33

THE CAST:

Sir John Chilcote/John Loder, Ronald Colman; Eve Chilcote, Elissa Landi; Lady Joyce, Juliette Compton; Brock, Halliwell Hobbes; Fraser, David Torrence; Lakely, Claude King; Robbins, Helen Jerome Eddy; Alston, Eric Wilton; Speaker of the House, C. Montague Shaw.

Fulfilling his commitment to Goldwyn, Ronald Colman brought to an end the lengthy producer/actor epoch with his eighteenth Goldwyn film, The Masquerader, and once again played a dual role. Not one to permit personal feelings to interfere with business—or art—Goldwyn poured his characteristic good taste and handsome production values into this absorbing if somewhat implausible melodrama about a drug-addicted Member of Parliament who switches places with his amiable, look-alike, distant cousin at a time of national crisis. Goldwyn also gave Colman his customary sole, above-the-title billing for the role(s) of Sir John Chilcote and John Loder, played in the 1922 silent version by Guy Bates Post who had also created the part(s) on Broadway and ran with the play for six years. Colman once again is involved in a theme of honor, duty and self-sacrifice, and assuming the role of the imposter, finds himself falling for the wife of the man he is impersonating and later facing the agonizing choice during the final reel.

As a best-seller in 1905 and maintaining its popularity over an entire generation, Katherine Cecil Thurston's novel was a natural choice for a dramatization, first in

John Hunter Booth's successful play and then in two films. Goldwyn hired Moss Hart to write the screen dialogue (although Howard Estabrook receives screenplay credit), undoubtedly accounting for the witty lines and literate observations the suave "Mr. C" bounces off his fellow players, including Elissa Landi as the estranged wife, Juliette Compton as the mistress, and wonderful Halliwell Hobbes as the man Friday/confidante. Gregg Toland's superb photographic effects during the confrontations between the two Ronald Colmans—one disheveled, dissipated and wildeyed, the other well groomed, affable and easygoing, remain interesting early examples of the artistry that came to be standard with Toland during his lengthy stay at the Goldwyn Studios.

The Masquerader opens during a stormy session of Parliament with an obviously ill Sir John Chilcoate having difficulty concentrating on the delivery of an important speech. Rebuffing several of his friends as well as his mistress Lady Joyce, who had been seated in the gallery, Chilcoate staggers into the foggy London night where he bumps into his distant cousin, John Loder. Sneering at Loder, a remarkable look-alike, the lightheaded Chilcoate passes a few disdainful remarks, and as he is about to stumble on, hears Loder remind him: "Anytime you need a double for a dull dinner, I'm available. Very nominal fee. Day or night service." Chilcoate makes his way to Lady Joyce's flat, Loder's words still playing against his brain.

Returning home, later, Chilcoate runs into estranged wife Eve, who still shares his house. She has just returned from Paris, and he snaps sarcastically, "Why did you come back? Did the gigolos run out?" He then retires to his room where his valet, Brock, who alone knows of Chilcoate's drug problems, gets him into bed. The next day, fed up with the hounding of his fellow MPs and other party members, Chilcoate, still in a stupor, vows to disappear, and makes his way to Loder's house where he collapses. Brock, who had followed him urges Loder to take Chilcoate's place in Parliament just long enough to give the rousing speech all had been expecting.

After Brock coaches him on Chilcoate's gestures and mannerisms, Loder undertakes the masquerade and delivers a brilliant off-the-cuff address, then reluctantly returns to Chilcoate's home with party leaders Fraser and Lakely, and "learns" his way around the house. At a party that night, Loder mistakes Chilcoate's mistress for his wife, until being straightened out by Brock, who tells Loder he must continue the masquerade for awhile. Brock then confides that Chilcoate treats his own wife formally as she knows about Lady Joyce, but Loder finds himself falling in love with Eve, who, after seven years, suddenly discovers that she loves her husband. Joyce, meanwhile, has become suspicious and, hiring a detective, stumbles onto the possibility of a double.

Chilcoate, during one of his gradually more infrequent lucid moments, complains to Brock, from the confines of Loder's flat, that: "Not only does Loder want to fill my shoes, but my slippers as well." Determined to end the charade, despite Brock's pleadings, Chilcoate manages to clean himself up enough to attend a long-planned party and arrives through the garden entrance just in time to save Loder from being exposed as a fraud by Lady Joyce, who had noticed a scar on Loder's wrist that she knew Chilcoate did not have. Chilcoate is then hustled quickly back to Loder's flat, while Loder repairs to the Chilcoate home and is about to disclose the masquerade to Eve when Brock takes him aside, telling him that Chilcoate has died and that he (Loder) must carry on the deception permanently.

Time thought that

Colman succeeds (in giving two characters definite and different personalities) most brilliantly when, as Loder, he is imitating Chilcoate's mannerisms just badly enough to make the audience feel the imitation might have fooled Chilcoate's intimates.

In *The New York Times,* Mordaunt Hall wrote of Colman's dual portrayal: "He accomplishes his task with such thoroughness that improbable as is the tale, it affords genuinely pleasing entertainment." Of the other performances, Hall felt:

Miss Landi gives an ingratiating portrayal and Juliette Compton handles the unsympathetic role efficiently. Mr. Hobbes, who, whether cast as a butler, lawyer, judge or banker, always does well by his part, is especially good as Brock. The production itself is effectively staged with an excellent suggestion of the atmosphere of the British metropolis.

Newsweek's critic commented that Goldwyn's people

have turned out a believable and dignified screenplay, and all traces of the hamminess of the original have been eliminated . . . (it is) the first amusing and believable film of English politics and society—made of all places in Hollywood.

Variety, on the other hand, felt that "Colman can be relied on to do as well as can be done with a part that suits his style, but here his best is not enough."

Colman never again worked for Samuel Goldwyn.

Elissa Landi and Ronald Colman in The Masquerader.

Ronald Colman and Elissa Landi in The Masquerader.

Elissa Landi in The Masquerader.

34 ROMAN SCANDALS (1933)

Directed by Frank Tuttle; screenplay, William Anthony McGuire, George Oppenheimer, Arthur Sheekman and Nat Perrin; based on a story by George S. Kaufman and Robert E. Sherwood; music director, Alfred Newman; songs by Al Dubin, Harry Warren and L. Wolfe Gilbert; dances staged by Busby Berkeley; photographer, Gregg Toland; editor, Stuart Heisler; art director, Richard Day; costumes, John Harkrider. Running time, 93 minutes. Released by United Artists. Premiere: Rivoli Theater, New York, 12/25/33

THE CAST:

Eddie, Eddie Cantor; *Olga,* Ruth Etting; *Princess Sylvia,* Gloria Stuart; *Emperor Valerius,* Edward Arnold; *Josephus,* David Manners; *Empress Agrippa,* Verree Teasdale; *Major-domo,* Alan Mowbray; *Manius,* John Rutherford; *Slave Dancer,* Grace Poggi; *Warren F. Cooper,* Willard Robertson; *Mayor,* Harry Holman; *Police Chief Charles R. Pratt,* Charles C. Wilson; *Beauty Salon Manager,* Jane Darwell; *The 1933 Goldwyn Girls*: Katherine Mauk, Rosalie Fromson, Mary Lange, Lucille Ball, Vivan Keiffer, Barbara Pepper, Theo Plane, Iris Shunn (Iris Meredith), Jane Hamilton, Gigi Parrish, Bonnie Bannon, Dolores Casey; and Lee Kohlmar, Stanley Fields, Charles Arnt, Clarence Wilson, Stanley Andrews, Stanley Blystone, Harry Cording, Lane Chandler, William Wagner, Louise Carver, Francis Ford, Leo Willis, Duke York, Frank Hagney, Michael Mark, Dick Alexander, Paul Porcasi, John Ince, Billy Barty, Aileen Riggin, The Abbottiers (Florence Wilson, Rose Kirsner, Genevieve Irwin, Dolly Bell).

Musical numbers: (performed by)
"Build a Little Home" (Eddie Cantor, Goldwyn Girls)
"No More Love" (Ruth Etting, Goldwyn Girls, danced by Grace Poggi)
"Keep Young and Beautiful" (Eddie Cantor, Goldwyn Girls, Billy Barty)
"Tax on Love" (Eddie Cantor)
Finale: "Build a Little Home" (Eddie Cantor, chorus)

Goldwyn had planned, as Eddie Cantor's fourth movie, a musical version of Shaw's *Androcles and the Lion.* He found it less expensive though, to hire luminaries such as George S. Kaufman and Robert E. Sherwood to come up with an original script that would allow Cantor to be found in old Rome, clad in a toga, facing the lions—well, anyway, crocodiles—in Rome? After Kaufman and Sherwood worked out their idea (and subsequently sued Goldwyn for $25,000 when he refused to pay them, contending they had supplied only a rough draft that they declined to work into acceptable shape), Goldwyn brought in three high-priced gag writers to punch up the story that was then turned over to screenwriter William Anthony McGuire, who, having done *The Kid from Spain,* fashioned this new scenario to Cantor's particular talents.

Despite Goldwyn's inability in the long run to get G.B. Shaw to whip *Androcles* into shape for Cantor, the resultant *Roman Scandals* somehow emerged as lively, colorful, lavish Goldwyn entertainment, fitting nicely into the well established and ever-successful style of the other Cantor pictures, with the star playing an eccentric delivery boy who gets involved in local politics in a midwestern town called West Rome and dreams himself back to the real Rome of the evil Emperor Valerius. There he is sold into slavery and becomes the Emperor's foodtaster, a seemingly short-lived position because of Empress Agrippa's continuing efforts to poison her spouse. All ends, in the customary manner dictated by musical comedy, with Cantor stealing vital documents proving the Emperor guilty of fraud, escaping in a runaway chariot after seeing to the well-being of the two young lovers he had befriended, and riding back into his own time, where he then stumbles on incriminating papers proving that the mayor of West Rome is also a thief.

"The subject matter," *Variety* felt, "is the hokiest

kind of hoke, but it has the virture of being vigorous low comedy conveyed in terms of travesty, and the device is almost foolproof."

The 1933 Goldwyn Girls, here given, astonishingly, second billing (Lucille Ball is included among this comely batch), turn up in an inventive Busby Berkeley Harem-situated routine, elaborately devised with hundreds of floor-to-ceiling mirrors, performing with Cantor a spectacular number to the Al Dubin-Harry Warren song, "Keep Young and Beautiful." The girls also drape themselves decorously, this time as slaves, for Ruth Etting's big number, "No More Love," and in modern dress, fill the scenery nicely as a contemporary Cantor cheers his Depression-crushed West Rome neighbors with "Build a Little House," also reprised at the finale.

Cantor's usual, self-deprecating character ("I'm a failure," he bemoans when the Emperor fires him. "I can't even keep a job as a slave."), provides the crux of this, and all Cantor films. Lengthy set pieces, designed especially for the star, become the well-spotted highlights. In *Roman Scandals,* whatever plot there is builds to a crescendo wherein Cantor, cautioned that the Emperor was to be poisoned, is told his own life would be spared if he reaches for the chicken without the deadly parsley dressing and then is faced with two chickens, each garnished with parsley. (A variation on this routine was used by Danny Kaye in *The Court Jester* two decades later.) The closing sequence with the wild chariot race copies in structure the bullfight finale in *The Kid from*

Spain, and with slight variations, was incorporated more than three decades later into Zero Mostel's *A Funny Thing Happened on the Way to the Forum.*

Of the screenplay-by-committee, critic Mordaunt Hall felt that "any of them might have written a more effective story alone . . . some of the fun is effective without being especially keen wit, such as one might expect from either Mr. Kaufman or Mr. Sherwood." Judging the work of the stars, Hall noted that

Cantor does as well as possible in his role and is exceptionally good in the episodes in which he sings . . . Gloria Stuart has little opportunity to do more than look beautiful. Edward Arnold as the Emperor is splendid and Ruth Etting sings in her usual fashion.

Time Magazine stated that

several thousand showgirls received tests for the chorus. The picture cost $1,100,000. The result is an extraordinary rigamarole containing everything from chariot races to a torch song by Ruth Etting . . . and Cantor himself in a slave market (with) females of all useful shapes, sizes and colors.

Marguerite Tazelaar's view, expressed in the *New York Herald Tribune,* was that *"Roman Scandals'* lively tunes, its rapid pace, and Mr. Cantor's characteristic comedy give it its real entertainment . . . however, as the end product of a succession of talent, the piece is disappointing."

Eddie Cantor in Roman Scandals.

The Goldwyn Girls in Roman Scandals.

Eddie Cantor in Roman Scandals.

35 NANA (1934)

Directed by Dorothy Arzner; screenplay, Willard Mack and Harry Wagstaff Gribble; suggested by the novel by Emile Zola; music, Alfred Newman; song "That's Love" by Richard Rodgers and Lorenz Hart; photographer, Gregg Toland; editor, Frank Lawrence; art director, Richard Day; costumes, Travis Banton, John W. Harkrider and Adrian. Running time, 87 minutes. Released by United Artists. Premiere: Radio City Music Hall, New York, 2/1/34

THE CAST:

Nana, Anna Sten; *Col. Andre Muffat,* Lionel Atwill; *Satin,* Mae Clarke; *Gaston Greiner,* Richard Bennett; *Lt. George Muffat,* Phillips Holmes; *Mimi,* Muriel Kirkland; *Bordenave,* Reginald Owen; *Grand Duke Alexis,* Lawrence Grant; *Sabine Muffat,* Helen Freeman; *Zoe,* Jessie Ralph; *Finot,* Ferdinand Gottschalk; *Lt. Gregory,* Hardie Albright; *Leon,* Branch Stevens; *Louis,* Barry Norton; *Estelle Muffat,* Lauri Beatty; and Eily Malyon, Clarence Wilson, Albert Conti, Gino Corrado, Bramwell Fletcher, Wilson Benge, Tom Ricketts, Charles Middleton, Lucille Ball.

The long association Goldwyn had with Ronald Colman was followed by the Anna Sten affair, which wags have always referred to as "Goldwyn's folly." The producer long had harbored the dream of creating his own Garbo, since Louis B. Mayer rightly refused to give the great Greta to Goldwyn. On a trip to Poland in 1932, Goldwyn convinced himself that he had found his Garbo when he saw her in a German film version of *The Brothers Karamazov.* Excited with his find, Goldwyn tracked down the actress, Anjuschka Stenski of Kiev; brought her and her husband, Dr. Eugene Frenke (who had directed her in *Karamazov*), to Hollywood; and began the arduous process of "Americanizing" the lady while paying her $1500 a week. During the two years Miss Sten was taking English lessons, the Goldwyn Studios worked ceaselessly issuing press releases, announcing that the actress' American debut would be opposite Ronald Colman in Goldwyn's version of *Karamazov.* The Colman/Goldwyn rift aborted this plan. Instead, he introduced Anna Sten in a lavish production of *Nana,* "suggested," as the credits read, by the Emile Zola novel.

Goldwyn tapped his old reliable George Fitzmaurice to direct the Sten debut, which would be the first sound adaptation of the Zola tragedy. Previously, there had been a Danish version in 1912 with Ellen Lumbye in the title role, and Jean Renoir's French production in 1926 starring Catherine Hessling. After Fitzmaurice had finished nearly two-thirds of the film, at a cost of nearly $411,000, Goldwyn chose to scrap what was done, replace Fitzmaurice with the screen's most famous female director, Dorothy Arzner, and begin again. It is speculated that Fitzmaurice's never publicly seen footage captured the sordidness of Zola's novel too well, and that Goldwyn instead opted for Miss Arzner's somewhat rose-colored treatment, resulting in a handsomely staged production burdened by an artificial story. (Screenwriters Willard Mack and Harry Wagstaff Gribble chose to give their Nana a shred of decency by having her take her own life during the film's final minutes so that the Muffat brothers might be brought together again. In Zola's novel, an unrepentent Nana dies a lingering death from smallpox.) Goldwyn, too, managed to entice Richard Rodgers and Lorenz Hart to write a torch song, "That's Love," with which Nana could captivate Paris in her stage debut. And, with his sanitized *Nana,* Goldwyn was able to attain his first Radio City Music Hall booking. (Of Goldwyn's eighty personally produced films, only thirteen were exhibited at the world's largest indoor theatre.)

Nana's well-known story concerns a lovely young street girl who is skyrocketed to fame by an eminent impresario; abandoned when she falls for a dashing officer in Napoleon III's army; coveted by the soldier's respectably married brother; depressed when her true love is reassigned to a distant post by the brother; elated when the latter agrees to reestablish her in the luxury that she had become accustomed to as a star; and remorseful when her young officer returns to discover the truth. Knowing that she could not bring happiness to either brother, she kills herself.

A top-notch cast acted in support of Miss Sten, Mae Clarke and Muriel Kirkland portray Nana's friends, Satin and Mimi; old reliable Richard Bennett (in his third Goldwyn film) is the egotistical producer, Gaston Greiner; Phillips Holmes is George Muffat, in some respects, the romantic lead; Lionel Atwill is the stuffy older brother, Andre, who leaves home for his "gilded fly"; delightful Lawrence Grant is Grand Duke Alexis, the old roué whose unrestrained admiration for Nana helps her become the toast of Paris; and Reginald Owen as Greiner's shadowlike aide, Bordenave.

"Samuel Goldwyn brilliantly launched a new star in a not so brilliant vehicle," wrote *Variety*.

The satellite eclipsed her setting. Miss Sten has beauty, glamour, charm, histrionic ability (although there are a couple of moments which seemed a bit beyond her) and vivid sex appeal. That's the difference between just a good leading woman and a potent gate-getting star.

Literary Digest suggested that:

Miss Sten is worthy of serious attention as a performer, but it is the suspicion of some observers, though, that Mr. Goldwyn is making a great mistake in presenting his young Ukranian actress as one of those lyric, mysterious and studiously "glamorous" screen personages that strive so desperately for the laurels of the great Garbo. The evidence supplied by *Nana* indicates that Miss Sten belongs to the earthy, realistic, zestful school, rather than that of the wistful dream.

The critic for *Time Magazine* felt:

Producer Goldwyn's extravagance was misplaced. *Nana* is sad but spurious and stodgy. All that saves it from complete mediocrity is Anna Sten who, although her accent is still outlandish, is a cheery, wise and personable importation from Russia. (Otherwise) Zola's story is about a Parisian gutter-lily, gilded by Goldwyn.

Richard Watts' observations were that

Anna Sten . . . proves to be an interesting actress (and) a splendid example of the strikingly vigorous peasant type that, in its lusty beauty, may end by being far superior to the effete Glamour Girl of the current school of picture-going in dramatic qualities.

He also thought that

the picture, in which Miss Sten begins to celebrate the emergence of the gorgeous peasant type as screen heroine, is hardly worthy of her. Mr. Goldwyn, who is—despite the things that are frequently said about him—one of the most conscientious and idealistic of producers, has obviously attempted so carefully to provide for his star a vehicle that would establish her among the film fans that he had ended by overdoing the plot requirements of her vehicle (and) the result is a labored sort of amalgamation of *Camille* and *Rain*.

Watts concluded, though, that "(Anna Sten) reveals every sign of developing into a distinguished screen personage as soon as she gets over that inevitable glamour period."

Mordaunt Hall found Goldwyn's new star

a flighty and vivacious Nana, if not the woman one visualizes while reading the Zola book. She wears the costumes of yesteryear with much grace and her fascinating delivery of English is apt to remind the onlooker of Marlene Dietrich's speech in her Hollywood films.

The critic decided that "Through Miss Sten's efficiency and charm and the splendid portrayals by Mr. Bennett, Mr. Owen and Mr. Grant, (*Nana*) offers a fair measure of entertainment, even though it wanders far from Zola's work."

Nana was brought to the screen several times subsequently. A Mexican version in 1944, directed by Celestino Gorostiza, starred Lupe Velez in her last role. Christian-Jacque's French version in 1955 costarred Martine Carol and Charles Boyer. And in 1970, a semi-porno adaptation, subtitled *Take Me, Love Me,* was filmed in Sweden by Mac Ahlberg and featured Anna Gael as Nana. The definitive *Nana*, it is agreed, is the nearly five hour television production made by BBC in 1973, with Katherine Scofield in the title role.

Anna Sten in Nana.

Anna Sten and Lionel Atwill in Nana.

Anna Sten and Phillips Holmes in Nana.

*Anna Sten, George Baxter, Jessie Ralph and Richard
Bennett in* Nana.

36 WE LIVE AGAIN (1934)

Directed by Rouben Mamoulian; screenplay by Maxwell Anderson, Leonard Praskins and Preston Sturges; based on the novel *Resurrection* by Leo Tolstoy; music, Alfred Newman; photographer, Gregg Toland; editor, Otho Lovering; assistant director, Robert Lee; art director, Richard Day and Sergei Sordeikin; costumes, Omar Kiam. Running time, 85 minutes. Released by United Artists. Premiere: Radio City Music Hall, New York, 11/1/34

THE CAST:

Katusha Maslova, Anna Sten; *Prince Dmitri Nekhlyudov,* Fredric March; *Missy Kortchagin,* Jane Baxter; *Prince Kortchagin,* C. Aubrey Smith; *Gregory Simonson,* Sam Jaffe; *Aunt Maria,* Ethel Griffies; *Aunt Sophia,* Gwendolen Logan; *Mrs. Kortchagin,* Mary Forbes; *Matrona Pavlovna,* Jessie Ralph; *Simon Kartinkin,* Leonid Kinsky; *Yaphemia Batchkova,* Dale Fuller; *Colonel,* Morgan Wallace; *Tikhon,* Davison Clark; *Lt. Schonbock,* Crauford Kent; *Kortchagin's Butler,* Barron Hesse; *Theodosia,* Cecil Cunningham; *Korbalova,* Jessie Arnold; *Judge,* Edgar Norton; *Judge,* Michael S. Visaroff; *Redhead,* Fritzi Ridgeway; *Aunt's Footman,* Newton House; *Aunt's Coachman,* Akin Dobrynin; *Specialty Dancer,* Serge Temoff; and Halliwell Hobbes, James Marcus, Gilbert Clayton, Alex Kandyba, Harry Cording, John Ince, George Burr MacAnnan, Jack Kenny, Theodore Lorch, Stanley Blystone, Bud Fine, Gordon DeMain, Harry Myers, Edwin Mordant, Dick Alexander, Anders van Haden, Tom Wilson, Edward Gargan, Roger Gray, Agnes Steele.

More heartened by critical acceptance of Anna Sten in her debut than by the generally negative response to his interpretation of Zola, Goldwyn decided that perhaps a drama of her native Russia would be more apt for Miss Sten. And as the Hollywood axiom of the day suggested, when in doubt, turn to Tolstoy's *Resurrection*. Reminded that Dolores Del Rio and Lupe Velez already had played Katusha in recent screen versions, Goldwyn was said to have retorted: "It has not been made until I make it."

To direct his *Resurrection,* which he called *We Live Again,* after having the screenwriting talents of such disparate people as Maxwell Anderson, Leonard Praskins and Preston Sturges (most likely working independently of each other) reduce the Tolstoy novel to a fast eighty-five minutes, Goldwyn hired Rouben Mamoulian, fresh from his work with Dietrich in *Song of Songs* and Garbo in *Queen Christina*. With immense care and impeccable taste, Tolstoy's theme of sin and regeneration was polished to a high veneer and emerged under Goldwyn's guidance and Mamoulian's artistry as a stunning, atmospheric tale of tragedy and human suffering, with, at the beginning, a dash of happiness, while all of the novel's revolutionary implications linger only in the dim shadows.

Under the glow of Gregg Toland's camera, Anna Sten radiates the type of electricity that should have elevated her to the highest plateau alongside the great ladies of the era's screen. Why she failed to catch on with the American moviegoer remains one of the imponderables of film history. In any event, she once again received fine notices, best exemplified by these words from *Time Magazine*:

That producer Samuel Goldwyn's version seems sincere is due mainly to his leading lady, (since) *We Live Again* exhibits her where she belongs, in Russia, and should cause her to be classed with Garbo and Dietrich as an importation who deserves all the attention she can get.

Her Katusha had a strong Dmitri in Fredric March, giving a wonderful interpretation of the idealistic young nobleman who declines into a jaded, heartless aristocrat, but in the end, finds his resurrection in rebellion against the brutalities of the Russian caste system and his love for the peasant girl he long ago had seduced and abandoned.

137

The famed seduction scene, as staged by Mamoulian, remains one of the film's highlights. Dmitri has returned to the manor of his maiden aunts (played by Ethel Griffies and Gwendolyn Logan) after two years of army service and again gazes upon the lovely face of Katusha, the peasant girl who lives with them and who he innocently had romanced. He invites her to stroll with him into the garden after the others have retired for the night, passing the private tree where they long before had pursued their idyll, and leading her into the greenhouse where she yields to him.

Equally as vivid is the stunning Easter service that precedes the seduction sequence. For nearly ten screen minutes, the magnificent pagentry of a Russian Orthodox mass unfolds, with its spectacular processions of ikons and haunting Gregorian chants—in addition naturally, to a veritable sea of patriarchal beards. (Somewhat later, the story was circulated that the music for the mass was recorded onto the soundtrack backwards, but discovering that Goldwyn was enthralled with the sequence, none on the lot would agree to tell the boss, and the entire service actually was performed in reverse.)

The plot of *We Live Again* was familiar to the day's moviegoers, particularly after its several earlier screen incarnations (D.W. Griffith first filmed it in 1909 with Marion Leonard and Arthur Johnson in the leads; Pauline Frederick portrayed Katusha in the 1918 version; Dolores Del Rio and Rod LaRocque were the ill-starred lovers in the 1927 interpretation; and Lupez Velez played opposite John Boles, and in the Spanish version made simultaneously, Gilbert Roland in the 1931 adaptation.) The well-worn saga deals with a dashing, happy-go-lucky royalist officer who romances and finally seduces the young servant girl living at the home of his aunts. He leaves for his regiment, promptly forgetting her, while she has his baby. When the infant dies, she goes to Moscow where she falls into a life of prostitution and is brought to trial on charges of having murdered one of her customers. There the girl and the hardened officer, now a bearded patrician about to marry into one of Moscow's wealthiest families, once again meet when he is selected to sit as a juryman. Through an error in the wording of the verdict, the girl is sentenced to a term in Siberia.

The Prince, at first shocked into silence when seeing her, tries to obtain her freedom, but is only scorned. Instead, he goes to her prison cell to plead in vain for forgiveness. (The jail sequence, typical of a grade-B women's prison movie, is one of Mamoulian's lapses in judgement in *We Live Again*.) Feeling he must atone for the suffering he had caused her, he gives to his retainers all of his possessions and lands, realizing that he and his class have been wronging her class all along. "All I ask is to live again with your forgiveness and your help and your love," he tells her, as he joins her and the other prisoners on their long trek to Siberia.

Shortly before *We Live Again*, like *Nana* eight months earlier, opened at Radio City Music Hall, *Variety* reported in its review:

(It) is a fine, artistic production which further impresses Anna Sten as a celluloid satellite, vividly displaying her histrionic talents, with Fredric March equally effective. It's Tolstoy's novel beautifully recreated in dialog and endowed with lavish Goldwynesque artistry.

Noted critic Otis Ferguson observed that:

In *We Live Again*, Anna Sten is actually brought back to life as a person, partly by casting, no doubt. She still seems incompetent in the higher ranges of acting, but is a good, healthy peasant type and capable of the reactions you might expect.

Norbert Lusk, reviewing in *Picture Play*, meanwhile, spoke of Miss Sten as an actress "whose beauty seems to have sprung from the soil and whose intelligence is that of the instinctive artist and earnest student of life." *Literary Digest* thought that the picture

offers an excellent role for the attractive and skillful Miss Sten, and there is also good work by Mr. March, who invariably is at his best in this florid type of costume role. Rouben Mamoulian's direction is rich and atmospheric, and the picture itself is visually striking, although there are times when the drama seems lacking in credibility and power and when its action does seems a trifle stagey.

Mordaunt Hall, a staunch supporter of Anna Sten, wrote in *The New York Times*:

For a time, Mr. Goldwyn's kindly efforts to publicize the electric Muscovite had the unhappy effect of making her look like the screen impresario's private discovery. Miss Sten, of course, it not simply a young woman of extraordinary charm and unusual talent, but an experienced actress with a distinguished background in the Russian and German cinema and in the Soviet State Theatre. In *We Live Again*, she gives an enormously attractive performance in what is surely the most faithful of the screen editions of Tolstoy's novel . . . and it is (her) vitality, loveliness and dramatic skill which impress the spectator.

Of the film's direction, critic Hall felt: "The occasionally eccentric Rouben Mamoulian has thoughtfully submerged his stylized manner in the material of the drama, and he achieves a photoplay which is both visually and dramatically stirring."

In the years since Goldwyn proved of Tolstoy's classic that, "it has not been made until I make it," there have been several further cinemazations. A Mexican version was made in 1943 by Gilberto Martinez Solares, with Lupita Tovar and Emilio Tuero in the leads. Fifteen years later, a French/German production, entitled *Auferstehung,* costarred Horst Buchholz and Lea Massari. It was codirected by Rolf Hansen and Gabrielle Dorziat. The sole Russian screen adaptation of the Tolstoy novel was made by director Mikhail Shveitzer in 1961, with Tamara Semina as Katusha and Eugenii Matreev as Dmitri.

Goldwyn's ads for *We Live Again,* incidentally, gushed: "The directorial genius of Mamoulian, the beauty of Sten, and the producing genius of Goldwyn have combined to make the world's greatest entertainment." Of which, Goldwyn allegedly said: "That's the kind of ad I like. Facts. No exaggeration."

Fredric March and Anna Sten in We Live Again.

Ethel Griffies, Gwendolyn Logan and Fredric March in We Live again.

Anna Sten in We Live Again.

Fredric March and Morgan Wallace in We Live Again.

140

37 KID MILLIONS (1934)

Directed by Roy Del Ruth; original screenplay, Arthur Sheekman, Nat Perrin and Nunnally Johnson; music director, Alfred Newman; dances staged by Seymour Felix; songs by Walter Donaldson and Gus Kahn, Burton Lane and Harold Adamson, and Irving Berlin; photographer, Ray June; editor, Stuart Heisler; assistant director, Walter Mayo; art director, Richard Day; costumes, Omar Kiam. Technicolor sequence directed by Willy Pogany; photographed by Ray Rennahan. Running time, 90 minutes. Released by United Artists. Premiere: Rivoli Theater, New York, 11/11/34

THE CAST:

Eddie Wilson, Jr., Eddie Cantor; *Joan Larrabee,* Ann Sothern; *Dot Clark,* Ethel Merman; *Gerald Lane,* George Murphy; *Ben Ali,* Jesse Block; *Fanya,* Eve Sully; *Colonel Larrabee,* Burton Churchill; *Louis the Lug,* Warren Hymer; *Sheik Mulhulla,* Paul Harvey; *Khoot,* Otto Hoffman; *Toots,* Doris Davenport; *Herman,* Edgar Kennedy; *Oscar,* Stanley Fields; *Adolph,* John Kelly; *Pop,* Jack Kennedy; *William Slade,* Guy Usher; *Stymie,* Mathew Beard; *Pianists,* Jacques Fray and Mario Braggiotti; *Specialty,* Nicholas Brothers; *Attorney,* Henry Kolker; *Tommy,* Tommy Bond; Leonard Kibrick; *Steward,* William Arnold; *Ship's Bartender,* Harry C. Bradley; *Colonel Witherspoon,* Clarence Muse; *Announcer,* Sam Hayes; and *the 1934 Goldwyn Girls,* Lucille Ball, Irene Bentley, Dudone Blumier, Mary-Jane Carey, Lynne Carver, Doris Davenport*, Mary Lou Dix, Bonnie Bannon, Helen Ferguson, Gail Goodson, Jane Hamilton, Betty-Joy Howard, Vivian Keiffer, Caryl Lincoln, Mary Lange, Janice Jarratt, Ruth Moody, Barbara Pepper, Wanda Perry, Charlotte Russell, Virginia Reed, Gwen Seager, Helen Wood; and Fred Warren, Edward Peil Sr., Harry Ernst, Eddie Arden, Ed Mortimer, Zack Williams, Everett Brown, Harrison Greene, Noble Johnson, George Regas, Lon Poff, Constantine Romanoff, Ivan Linlow, Lalo Encinas, Bud Fine, Leo Willis, Larry Fisher, Bob Teeves, Malcolm Waite, Steve Clemento, Art Mix, Silver Harr, Bob Kortman, Robert Ellis, Bobby Jordan, Theodore Lorch, Bobbie LaManche, John Dowd, Charles Hall, John Collum, Wally Albright, Mickey Rentschler, Jacqueline Taylor, Carmencita Johnson, Patricia Ann Rambeau, Ada Mae Bender, Billy Seay.

* in one number as a Goldwyn Girl before being elevated to ingenue lead opposite Cantor.

Musical numbers: (performed by)
"An Earful of Music" (Ethel Merman, Goldwyn Girls, Fray and Braggiotti)
"When My Ship Comes In" (Eddie Cantor)
"Your Head on My Shoulder" (Ann Sothern, George Murphy)
Reprise: "An Earful of Music" (Ethel Merman, Goldwyn Girls)
"I Want To Be a Minstrel Man" (Harold Nicholas, Goldwyn Girls)
"Mandy" (Eddie Cantor in blackface, Ethel Merman, Ann Sothern, George Murphy, Goldwyn Girls, Nicholas Brothers)
Reprise: "Your Head on My Shoulder" (George Murphy, Ann Sothern)
Reprise: "Mandy" (Eddie Cantor, Ann Sothern, Ethel Merman)
Untitled dance (George Murphy, Eddie Cantor, Nicholas Brothers, Goldwyn Girls)
"Okay Toots" (Eddie Cantor, Goldwyn Girls)
"Ice Cream Fantasy" (Ethel Merman, children, Goldwyn Girls, Eddie Cantor, Warren Hymer)
Finale: "When My Ship Comes In" (Eddie Cantor)

By the time Goldwyn had come up with an acceptable new vehicle for Eddie Cantor in *Kid Millions,* a serious deterioration had begun in their producer/star relationship, not helped in the least by the fact that Busby Berkeley had left the Goldwyn Studios to sign on with Warner Bros. (instigating a lengthy legal dispute between Goldwyn and Jack L. Warner). The crux of the problem(s) with both Cantor and Berkeley was Goldwyn's infrequent productions of musicals. The ambitious Cantor had moved into radio and had become a major star in the medium, which unfortunately, was based on the East coast. Goldwyn, of course, was unaccustomed to dealing with anyone, let alone the stars he created, as equals, and blithely ignored Cantor's burgeoning radio popularity. And besides, Goldwyn invariably countered, Cantor should be happy with the $270,000 yearly salary he was then making (Cantor in 1934 was the highest paid actor in films; Mae West, the highest paid actress).

Kid Millions temporarily assuaged Cantor. The film, expensively produced, unsparingly cast, unstintingly appointed, and lavishly topped with an opulent Technicolor fantasy at its climax, was among the most extravagant of the Goldwyn/Cantor musicals and received excellent reviews. Unfortunately, Cantor found himself virtually upstaged by one of the supporting players—a vibrant musical comedy star from Broadway named Ethel Merman (she also gave Cantor a run for his money in his next film, *Strike Me Pink*).

In *Kid Millions,* Cantor pleased audiences as Eddie Wilson, Jr., a simpleton who falls heir to $77 million plundered from Egyptain tombs by the archeologist father he never knew. Sailing for Egypt with his lawyer friend, Gerald Lane, Eddie is forced to dodge a series of obstacles set up by others anxious to get their hands on his fortune. First there are Dot Clark, a brash Broadway songplugger, and her cohort, Louie the Lug. Dot nearly succeeds in convincing Eddie that she is his long lost mother. Then there is Colonel Larrabee, a Southern gentleman who would like his cut because he had financed the original expedition for Eddie's father. And as a diversion, Larrabee has brought along his niece Joan, to keep Eddie's lawyer buddy occupied. Evading all the hazards though, including the obvious diversions supplied by the 1934 Goldwyn Girls (among whom is a scantily-clad Lucille Ball), Eddie finds other problems on his arrival in Egypt, not the least, becoming involved with the daffy daughter of a villainous sheik (the girl and her jealous boyfriend are played by vaudeville stars, Eve Sully and Jesse Block, in their screen debuts). Eddie commits the unpardonable crime of *Tramofatch,* translating roughly to "kissing a sheik's daughter while riding a camel." And this before Eddie learns that the sheik has sworn to exterminate the infidel who proves his right to the treasure, boiling the culprit in oil with a dash of salt and pepper. The final outcome of Eddie's tribulations never is in doubt, and ten production numbers later, he is back in Brooklyn with his girlfriend Toots, presiding over the spectacular opening (in Technicolor) of a monumental ice cream factory.

Interestingly, it is not Cantor, but Ethel Merman who is given the film's opening number, "An Earful of Music," performed with the Goldwyn Girls and duo-pianists, Jacques Fray and Mario Braggiotti. Cantor's first song, sung to Doris Davenport, is "When My Ship Comes In," reprised at the finale as part of the "Ice Cream Fantasy." The movie's big love song, "Your Head On My Shoulder," is introduced by the romantic leads, Ann Sothern and George Murphy, who get to perform it twice during the film.

A shipboard minstrel show provides the setting for Cantor's obligatory blackface routine, as he and virtually everybody else (Merman, Sothern, Murphy, the Nicholas Brothers, and the Goldwyn Girls) become involved in "I Want To Be a Minstrel Man," with Cantor as the end man and Murphy the interlocutor. Without pausing for a breath, Cantor then launches into one of his trademark songs, "Mandy," which Irving Berlin originally had written for the World War I revue, *Yip Yip Yaphank* in 1918, and which had become popularized the following year after being inserted into the *Ziegfeld Follies of 1919* (Cantor was in that version, but Marilyn Miller sang the song).

"Samuel Goldwyn, the Ziegfeld of the Pacific, has mounted the million dollar orbs of his favorite comedian in a rich and merry setting for the annual Eddie Cantor show," wrote *The New York Times'* Andre Sennwald, calling it "a superior screen comedy in which the generous Mr. Goldwyn has poured almost everything that seemed helpful to the cause of pleasure." Slightly less enthusiastic was *Variety,* which reported that "the plot is musical comedy, strictly carried along by Cantor's breeze and the Goldwynesque showmanship."

Richard Watts' review, accompanied by a photo not of Cantor, but of Ethel Merman, made the point that

Mr. Goldwyn's latest vehicle for his male Anna Sten, Mr. Cantor, is a brisk, lively and reasonably tuneful musical extravaganza that boasts the presence of Miss Merman and an elaborate sequence in Technicolor . . . it is on the whole a pleasant and harmlessly entertaining work (with) some modestly lunatic comedy in Mr. Cantor's most characteristic vein.

Ethel Merman, Eddie Cantor and Warren Hymer in
Kid Millions.

*Eddie Cantor is nuzzled by a blonde Lucille Ball as the
other Goldwyn Girls look on in* Kid Millions.

Eddie Cantor in Kid Millions.

The Goldwyn Girls in the Ice Cream Fantasy of Kid
Millions.

38 THE WEDDING NIGHT (1935)

Directed by King Vidor; screenplay, Edith Fitzgerald; based on a story by Edwin Knopf; music, Alfred Newman; photographer, Gregg Toland; editor, Stuart Heisler; assistant director, Walter Mayo; art director, Richard Day; costumes, Omar Kiam. Running time, 81 minutes. Released by United Artists. Premiere; Rivoli Theater, New York, 3/16/35

THE CAST:
Tony Barrett, Gary Cooper; *Manya Nowak,* Anna Sten; *Fredrik Sobieski,* Ralph Bellamy; *Dora Barrett,* Helen Vinson; *Jan Nowak,* Siegfried (Sig) Rumann; *Kaise Nowak,* Esther Dale; *Mr. Sobieski,* Leonid Snegoff; *Mrs. Sobieski,* Eleanor Wesselhoeft; *Grandmother,* Milla Davenport; *Helena,* Agnes Anderson; *Hezzie Jones,* Hilda Vaughn; *Bill Jenkins,* Walter Brennan; *Heywood,* Douglas Wood; *Gilly,* George Meeker; *Anna,* Hedi Shope; *Taka,* Otto Yamaoka; *Frederica Sobieski,* Violet Axelle; *Uncle,* Ed Eberle; *Doctor,* Robert Bolder; *Waiter,* Alphonse Martell; *Man at Party,* Robert Louis Stevenson 2nd; *Truck Driver,* Richard Powell; *Men at Wedding,* Auguste Tollaire, Dave Wengren, George Magrill, Bernard Siegel, Harry Semels; *Party Guests,* Miami Alvarez, Constance Howard, Jay Eaton, Jay Belasco

The public's continued indifference to Anna Sten now called for drastic measures, and a series of high-level conferences were called in Goldwyn's offices. If the actress apparently was unacceptable in classic period pieces, with which audiences could not identify, perhaps contemporary drama would be the solution. Goldwyn called in his friend, Edwin Knopf, to write an original screenstory for Miss Sten, one guaranteed to arouse audience sympathies. And to star opposite her, Gary Cooper would be cast. Cooper—the same actor Goldwyn short-sightedly had let slip by years before, seeing limited screen potential in the gangly performer, and now had just spent a small fortune to lure away from Paramount where he had become a major star. (In 1936, Paramount slapped Goldwyn with a $5 million actor-alienation suit

for influencing Cooper not to re-sign with the company that had molded him into stardom.)

Writer Knopf came up with the somehow unexciting little soap opera of a penthouse novelist, a member of the lost generation who, suffering from a dissipating talent and a grasping wife, returns to the soil and finds renewed inspiration with the young daughter of a neighboring Polish farmer. His still viable marriage and her unhappy engagement to a man chosen by her father, naturally makes the romance impossible and the denouement inevitably tragic. King Vidor, once more Goldwyn's choice to direct, staged the proceedings in the distinctive style that made him one of America's most vital behind-the-camera talents, injecting genuine human emotions, credible characterizations and authentic feeling for the soil into the story to create a mature and poignant film. Especially interesting are his celluloid observations of Polish customs, viewed through Gary Cooper's eyes.

The film's title refers to the climactic episode of the impossible love affair when the girl dies in a fall down a flight of stairs during a battle between the loutish farmer she had just wed and the married writer she had grown to love. It provided a convenient out for the intolerable situation between the two lovers from disparate worlds.

Praise, though, for Goldwyn's production and Vidor's direction, and the acting of Sten, Cooper and Helen Vinson, was unstinting, while curious indifference from the moviegoing public was profound. Few reviewers were more generous with accolades than was Richard Watts, who wrote in the *New York Herald tribune*:

Miss Sten ceases to be a great publicity stunt and becomes a fine actress in the new Goldwyn film. Certainly never before has the passionate peasant been so real and vividly moving in her portrayal . . . Mr. Goldwyn, one of the shrewdest men in cinema history, never makes the same mistake for any length of time, and so he has wisely given up his stubborn determination to make his Ukranian peasant star into a Glamour Girl, and sagely presents her in just the sort of role for which she is handsomely equipped.

Watts further noted: "Thanks to (Vidor's) gift for persuasive detail, *The Wedding Night*, despite minor lapses in its story, becomes a believable and touching motion picture . . . convincing and curiously powerful."

Newsweek decided that "Miss Sten, who in her first two pictures was just a Hollywood Glamour Girl, at last has a chance to act, and for the first time, critics felt that the Ukranian actress might someday live up to Goldwyn's opinion of her."

Time observed that the film "is written with honesty and humor, acted with understanding, and made exciting by King Vidor's intelligent direction." In its appraisal of the leading lady, *Time* said:

Since Anna Sten has been introduced to the American public as a glamorous composite of Greta Garbo and Mae West, a picture in which her physical charms are concealed by a mackinaw and a woolen stocking cap obviously constitutes a daring innovation.

Andre Sennwald, writing in *The New York Times*, called the film "a decided credit both to Mr. Goldwyn and Mr. Vidor," noting that, told in "an uncommonly adult style," *The Wedding Night*

displays an unusual regard for the truth and it is courageous enough to allow an affair which is obviously doomed to end logically in tragedy . . . and it represents a satisfying compromise between Mr. Vidor, the realist, and Mr. Goldwyn, the romantic.

Sennwald viewed that

led by the handsome and highly talented Russian star, the performances are uniformly evcellent. Mr. Cooper continues to reveal a refreshing sense of humor in his work. Helen Vinson is excellently right as the wife, playing the part with such intelligence and sympathy that she contributes definitely to the power of the climax.

The major review came from William Troy, critic for *The Nation*.

Mr. Vidor's task has not been lightened by a cast which includes Anna Sten and Gary Cooper in the principal roles. Mr. Cooper continues to be one of those players who can endow even the most casual remark with a preternatural phoniness. And it is now clear that it is a mistaken kindness to regard Anna Sten's frozen makeup as an outward sign of an inward Chekhovian restraint . . . For those who cherish the notion that King Vidor is to be taken seriously as a director—one of the few really serious Hollywood directors—*The Wedding Night* is going to be a hard case to defend.

The failure of *The Wedding Night* to establish Anna Sten at last as one of the great screen luminaries, in addition to the fact that the story, despite having been written especially for her, allowed her to be eclipsed not only by her costar, but also by the second female lead, was a devastating blow to the man who had lavished fortunes attempting to make her a favorite with movie-goers. Goldwyn reluctantly let Anna Sten go, and she drifted through a rag-tag film career in several minor British films and lesser roles in an occasional American movie through the early 1960s.

Goldwyn's chief consolations from his experience with *The Wedding Night* were in acquiring Gary Cooper, who would star in six subsequent Goldwyn films, including two all-time screen classics, and in finally appreciating the talents of Walter Brennan, here doing comedy relief in a small role as a rustic cabdriver. Although never under exclusive contract to Goldwyn, Brennan worked in nine later Goldwyn films, including a pair that won him the first two of his three Best Supporting Actor Oscars.

An interesting glimpse of how the star system worked in Hollywood's golden days can be seen by the altered ad billing on *The Wedding Night* during the film's re-issue in the mid-1940s. Anna Sten was dropped to *fourth,* in type half the size of Gary Cooper, Ralph Bellamy, and even Walter Brennan! All proving one wag's latter day description of Miss Sten as "the Edsel of the movie industry."

Gary Cooper and Anna Sten in The Wedding Night.

Anna Sten and Gary Cooper in The Wedding Night.

Helen Vinson and Gary Cooper in The Wedding Night.

Anna Sten and Ralph Bellamy in The Wedding Night.

39 THE DARK ANGEL (1935)

Directed by Sidney Franklin; screenplay, Lillian Hellman and Mordaunt Shairp; based on the play by H.B. Trevelyan (Guy Bolton); music, Alfred Newman; photographer, Gregg Toland; editor, Sherman Todd; assistant director, Hugh Boswell; art director, Richard Day; costumes. Omar Kiam. Running time, 105 minutes. Released by United Artists. Premiere: Rivoli Theater, New York, 9/5/35

THE CAST:
Alan Trent, Fredric March; *Kitty Vane,* Merle Oberon; *Gerald Shannon,* Herbert Marshall; *Sheila Shannon,* Janet Beecher; *Sir George Barton,* John Halliday; *Granny Vane,* Henrietta Crosman; *Ann West,* Frieda Inescort; *Lawrence Bidley,* Claud Allister; *Kitty as a child,* Cora Sue Collins; *Alan as a child,* Jimmy Baxter; *Gerald as a child,* Jimmie Butler; *Lawrence as a child,* Randolph Connolly; *Joe Gallop,* George Breakston; *Betty Gallop,* Fay Chaldecott; *Ginger Gallop,* Dennis Chaldecott; *Roulston,* Douglas Walton; *Josephine Bidley,* Sarah Edwards; *Henry Vane,* John Miltern; *Mills,* Olaf Hytten; *Mr. Tanner,* Lawrence Grant; *Hannah,* Helena Byrne-Grant; *Mr. Shannon,* David Torrence; *Shannon's Butler (Martin),* Edward Cooper; *Mr. Gallop,* Andy Arbuckle; *Mrs. Gallop,* Ann Fiedler; *Vicar,* Colin Campbell; *Major in Dugout,* Holmes Herbert; *Station Attendant (Jarvis),* Harold Howard; *Innkeeper,* Albert Russell; *Sir Mordaunt,* Claude King; *Shannon's Maid,* Phyllis Coghlan; *Chauffeur,* Francis Palmer Tilton; *Guests at Hunt,* Tom Moore, Major Sam Harris, Doris Stone, Louise Bates, Audrey Scott

Having failed to develop his own leading lady, first with Banky and later with Sten, Goldwyn finally succeeded in his quest when he turned a glamorous young actress from Tasmania (the island off the southeast coast of Australia that also gave the movie world Errol Flynn) from a sloe-eyed exotic type into an international celebrity through a series of impeccably produced films. His new star, Merle Oberon, had been a discovery, and longtime girlfriend, of Alexander Korda, the nearest thing the English cinema had to Samuel Goldwyn. For her,

Goldwyn dusted off his Colman/Banky silent of 1925, *The Dark Angel,* engaged Fredric March, then next to Colman, the screen's most popular leading man (hoping, undoubtedly, that March's box office attraction would help Oberon where it unfortunately failed Sten). To direct, Goldwyn selected perceptive Sidney Franklin, whose sensitive, tasteful work throughout a long career made many wonder why he of all the craftsmen was not Goldwyn's leading director, so simpatico were their views.

If the earlier version of *The Dark Angel* could have been called a four-hankerchief weeper, this elegant, literate production was a six-handkerchief job. Adapted from the Guy Boulton play by Lillian Hellman and Mordaunt Shairp (after Goldwyn originally announced Thorton Wilder for the assignment), and strikingly photographed by Gregg Toland, *The Dark Angel* emerged as outstanding screen drama, combining deep emotional appeal, tender pathos, suspense, romance, and most importantly, gratifying entertainment. Merle Oberon's performance as Kitty Vane not only established her as a major star (in only her second American movie, after ten in Great Britain), but also earned her an Academy Award nomination as Best Actress. Fredric March's intelligent protrayal of Alan Trent ranks among his best work of the Thirties, and Herbert Marshall is gallant and upperclass as always in his superb delineation of Gerald Shannon (in this version, Trent's cousin as well as his commanding officer and gracious rival for Kitty's affections).

Without deteriorating into a mawkish tear-jerker, this production differed only slightly in interpretation from Goldwyn's sentimental 1925 version. The heart of *The Dark Angel* remains the love story of Kitty Vane and Alan Trent, childhood sweethearts, and the tragedy that overtakes them when she presumes that he has been killed in battle, although he was only blinded and has removed himself from her life in order not to become a burden on her. The tearful climax still comes in the scene when Kitty discovers, as she is about to marry Gerald, that Alan is still alive and goes to visit him. Alan, meanwhile, has learned of Kitty's imminent arrival and memorizes every detail of his drawing room in order to hide the fact that he is blind. Kitty and Gerald are at first deceived, but soon realize what Alan has done, and, as Gerald steps aside, the lovers are reunited.

The New York Times' Andre Sennwald had these thoughts about Goldwyn's new drama: "The impresario's first photoplay of the season is a happy adventure in sentimental romance . . . in the handsome Goldwyn tradition of visual excellence . . . a highly literate screen adaptation telling the story with feeling and good taste." Sennwald also felt that "both Mr. March and Mr. Marshall contribute their best performances in months, and Miss Oberon, abandoning the Javanese slant of the eyes for the occasion, plays with skill and feeling."

Other views ranged from Richard Watts' rave: "The most honest and effective sentimental drama of the season . . . a masterpiece," to the notice from Edwin Shallert in the *Los Angeles Times* calling the film "one of the finest romantic studies yet given to the screen," while *Variety* used its colorful jargon to exclaim simply: "A sockeroo woman's picture."

In *The Literary Digest* there was this opinion:

In *The Dark Angel,* Fredric March is minus doublets, sword, Russian blouses, wigs, beards, or Jekyll-and-Hyde grimaces; Miss Oberon has abandoned her tiresome Oriental sleekness; but Herbert Marshall returns to uniform. (The film) has followed the now traditional path of a talkie . . . skillfully adapted by Miss Hellman and Mr. Shairp, it is a more mature and satisfying work than its predecessor (and) a sincerely moving screenplay.

Buoyed by the success of this remake, Goldwyn would later film new versions of two other profitable productions that earlier had starred Ronald Colman: *Stella Dallas* and *Raffles.* Both, he hoped, would become as popular in new dress as *The Dark Angel,* which, in addition to finding a place among the great films of 1935, won two Academy Awards—Best Art and Set Decoration (Richard Day) and Best Sound (Thomas T. Moulton). Merle Oberon, as observed above, was nominated for her performance, but lost to Bette Davis who starred in *Dangerous.*

Fredric March and Merle Oberon in The Dark Angel.

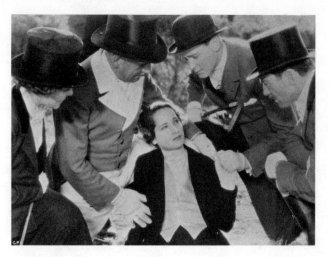

Doris Stone, Claude King, Merle Oberon, Herbert Marshall and Tom Moore in The Dark Angel.

Merle Oberon and Fredric March in The Dark Angel.

40 BARBARY COAST (1935)

Directed by Howard Hawks; original screenplay, Ben Hecht and Charles MacArthur; music, Alfred Newman; photographer, Ray June; editor, Edward Curtiss; assistant director, Walter Mayo; art director, Richard Day; costumes, Omar Kiam. Running time, 97 minutes. Released by United Artists. Premiere: Grauman's Chinese Theater, Los Angeles, 10/5/35. New York premiere: Rivoli Theater, 10/13/35 (Reissued in 1960 as *Port of Wickedness*)

THE CAST:

Mary 'Swan' Rutledge, Miriam Hopkins; *Louis Chamalis,* Edward G. Robinson; *Jim Carmichael,* Joel McCrea; *Old Atrocity,* Walter Brennan; *Col. Marcus Aurelius Cobb,* Frank Craven; *Knuckles Jacoby,* Brian Donlevy; *Oakie,* Clyde Cook; *Jed Slocum,* Harry Carey; *Peebles,* Otto Hoffman; *Joseph Wigham,* Rollo Lloyd; *Sawbuck McTavish,* Donald Meek; *Sandy Ferguson,* Roger Gray; *Judge Harper,* J. M. Kerrigan; *Bronco,* Matt McHugh; *Ah Wing,* Wong Chung; *Sheriff,* Russ Powell; *Ship's Captain,* Fredrik Vogeding; *McCready,* Anders Van Haden; *Ship's Pilot,* Jules Cowles; *Steward,* Cyril Thornton; *Man Tossed from Saloon,* David Niven; and Dave Wengren, Clarence Wertz, Harry Semels, Theodore Lorch, George Magrill, Jack Pennick, Nina Campana, Constantine Romanoff, George Lloyd, Jimmie Dime, Leo Willis, John Ince, Frank Rice, Patricia Farley, Hank Mann, Blackie Whiteford, Edward Gargan, Monte Montague, Harry Holman, Ethel Wales, Kit Guard, Herman Bing, Heinie Conklin, Tom London, Jim Thorpe.

While Samuel Goldwyn was planning the stardom of Merle Oberon, he also had elaborate blueprints for Miriam Hopkins, whom he had just picked up on the rebound from Paramount Pictures. Although Miriam Hopkins made only four films for Goldwyn, she nevertheless was his foremost leading lady of the thirties, and was constantly being lent to other studios at princely sums. And probably no actress was announced for as many unrealized projects by one producer as was she. Her four Goldwyn films (all, interestingly, opposite Joel McCrea) included one costume drama, one contemporary soap opera, one classic triangle story, and Goldwyn's sole, ill-advised venture into the screwball comedy genre. First, after a couple of loan outs following acceptance of Goldwyn's lucrative, long-term contract, Miss Hopkins starred in *Barbary Coast*.

The history of the film itself spanned several years. Goldwyn long had considered making a spectacular about the rip-roaring gold rush era, and learning of a novel by Herbert Asbury entitled *Barbary Coast,* purchased it without, apparently, first reading it. The book, however, turned out to be simply a record of the history of the San Francisco underworld, and according to *Harrison's Reports,* was "one of the filthiest, vilest, most degrading books that has ever been chosen for the screen." Goldwyn, never one to be scared off, simply chose to retain the title, discard the story, and hire Ben Hecht and Charles MacArthur (who previously had sneaked *The Unholy Garden* by Goldwyn) to write a colorful, action-filled romantic drama wherein Gary Cooper and Anna Sten could star. Under director William Wyler, filming began in late May, 1934, but was halted several weeks later when a dissatisfied Goldwyn, unable to spot exactly what was wrong, sent forth a cease-and-desist decree. He returned *Barbary Coast* to the Hecht/MacArthur drawing boards, shifted Cooper and Sten to *The Wedding Night,* and moved to other projects.

Encouraged by the new *Barbary Coast* script, Goldwyn then began recasting. Howard Hawks was brought in to direct; Edward G. Robinson was borrowed from Warner Bros.; Joel McCrea, who was to become Goldwyn's most serviceable leading man of the era, was given the romantic lead; and Miriam Hopkins would star as the gambling hall hostess, the infamous "Swan." Suddenly, Goldwyn changed his mind and settled on Gloria

Swanson for the role as a comeback attempt, but in the end, he returned the part to Miss Hopkins.

"Swan" is a proper girl who came from the East as Mary Rutledge to marry her fiancé, Dan Morgan, who has struck it rich. On her arrival though, she learns that he had been killed over a gambling loss. Refusing the protection of newspaper publisher Col. Marcus Aurelius Cobb, who urges her to return to New York, Mary decides to remain, and at the Bella Donna Club, the town's leading gambling palace, she meets San Francisco's underworld leader, Louis Chamalis. She accepts his offer to become the club's hostess, and as Swan, bedecked in diamonds, she presides at Chamalis' roulette wheel. When Sandy Ferguson, a Scotch miner, loses his year's diggings at the table and is killed protesting the game's crookedness, Cobb prepares to print the true story of the murder. Chamalis gives orders to have Cobb's plant demolished, but Swan intervenes in the publisher's behalf, infuriating Chamalis, who threatens to toss her back onto the streets.

While riding in the goldfields one day, Swan meets Jim Carmichael, an idealistic young prospector who takes her for a lady. The next night, when Carmichael wanders into the Bella Donna, he is shocked to find Swan handling the roulette wheel, and completely disillusioned, he recklessly gambles, and because the games are crooked, loses everything. He has fallen in love with Swan though, and is unable to give her up. When she continues to see Carmichael, Chamalis becomes suspicious and, learning of their meetings, orders the miner killed.

Chamalis, however, is distracted when violence breaks loose following the death of Sandy Ferguson's partner, Sawbuck McTavish, who had tried to avenge his friend's murder, and the subsequent killing of Cobb, who had printed an expose of Chamalis. The local community forms a vigilante committee to clean up Frisco and close down Chamalis who, meanwhile, has learned that Swan has doublecrossed him by letting Carmichael win back his money at the Bella Donna. When Chamalis' chief henchman, Knuckles Jacoby, is hanged by the vigilantes, the gambler is forced to take charge of Carmichael's disposal personally, chasing the young prospector and Swan out into the bay, where one of Chamalis' men shoots Carmichael. Swan promises to return to Chamalis in return for Carmichael's life, but the gambler, with a sudden change of heart, decides to let the two go off together. As the lovers are reunited, Chamalis turns to find himself facing the vigilantes with drawn guns.

"A gaudy, gripping melodrama of guns and gold," wrote Regina Crewe in the *New York American,*

made colorful by the histrionics of Edward G. Robinson (who) dominates every instant of the drama with a superlative conception of the sinister spoilsman. The film blazes with action and romance through every sequence, is studded with color and bespangled with the scintillance of a half dozen stirring performances. . . . Howard Hawks has directed with brilliance.

Equally as enthusiastic were the other New York critics: Andre Sennwald called it "one of Samuel Goldwyn's visually striking productions (with) a jovial virility that makes it one of the show pieces of the season"; Richard Watts found it "a thumping melodrama of the Gold Rush days, filled with gusto and gaudy colorfulness . . . a typically excellent Goldwyn production"; Rose Pelswick, in her *New York Evening Journal* review, labeled it "grand entertainment . . . a vivid and absorbing melodrama produced with Samuel Goldwyn's customary, painstaking care"; and Thornton Delahanty, in the *New York Post,* viewed it as "a thumpingly good picture which runs for an hour and a half and is worth every minute of it." Delahanty also concluded that the Hopkins role is "the only sanely written part in the picture, and her performance is a steadying point against the footlight savagery of Edward G. Robinson and the troubadour excesses of Joel McCrea."

Variety balanced its comments by noting first that *Barbary Coast* "has all it takes to get along in thoroughbred company. The atmosphere of the period has been richly caught, and production excellence is one of its charms." Then the paper's critic harped on the fact that Edward G. Robinson's Chamalis had too rapid a change of heart at the end by graciously allowing Swan to leave, after being developed throughout the film as too jealous and too mean. All in all, Robinson got the best notices for the film, although there were enough kind words for Miriam Hopkins to satisfy Goldwyn. Joel McCrea was merely there, but Walter Brennan, as Old Atrocity, the treacherous barfly, easily walked off with the film and, in all likelihood, would have won an Academy Award had they been giving them out in 1935 for supporting roles. (He won the following year, though, as well as in 1938 *and* 1940.) The Motion Picture Academy did not completely overlook *Barbary Coast.* Ray June's outstanding photography won him an Oscar nomination.

Seen very briefly in *Barbary Coast* in what is probably his first role in an American film is David Niven, who was to go on to become a major Goldwyn star, appearing in nine Goldwyn movies. Niven, then a $75-a-day extra, is a cockney sailor with a drooping mustache, and has described his single scene: "I was thrown out of the window of a brothel in San Francisco and into the mud, where Miriam Hopkins, Joel McCrea, Walter Brennan, thirty vigilantes and some donkeys walked over the top of me."

Miriam Hopkins and Edward G. Robinson in Barbary Coast.

Walter Brennan, Miriam Hopkins and Harry Carey in Barbary Coast.

Joel McCrea and Miriam Hopkins in Barbary Coast.

Joel McCrea and Walter Brennan in Barbary Coast.

41 SPLENDOR (1935)

Directed by Elliott Nugent; screenplay by Rachel Crothers; based on her own story; music, Alfred Newman; photographer, Gregg Toland; editor, Margaret Clancey; assistant director, Hugh Boswell; art director, Richard Day; costumes, Omar Kiam. Running time, 77 minutes. Released by United Artists. Premiere: Rivoli Theater, New York, 11/22/35

THE CAST:
Phyllis Manning Lorrimore, Miriam Hopkins; *Brighton Lorrimore*, Joel McCrea; *Martin Deering*, Paul Cavanagh; *Mrs. Lorrimore*, Helen Westley; *Clarissa*, Billie Burke; *Martha Lorrimore*, Katharine Alexander; *Edith Gilbert*, Ruth Weston; *Clancey Lorrimore*, David Niven; *Major Ballinger*, Arthur Treacher; *Fletcher*, Ivan F. Simpson; *Baron von Hoffstatter*, Torben Meyer; *Billy Grimes*, Reginald Sheffield; *Jake*, William R. (Billy) Arnold; *Mrs. Hicks*, Maidel Turner; *Process Server*, Clarence H. Wilson; *Lena Limering*, Lois January; and Frederick Lee, Violet Axelle, Nina Penn, Eddie Craven, Cosmo Kyrle Bellew, Connie Howard, William Cartledge, John Van Eyck, Frank H. Hammond, William O'Brien, George Bruggeman, Henry Hall, Dick Allen, Bob Beasley, Clinton Lyle, Betty Blair, Phyllis Crane, Jeanie Roberts, Mildred Booth, Georgette Rhodes.

In contrast to the time he had taken putting Miriam Hopkins into one of his films after signing her, Goldwyn hustled her, along with Joel McCrea and even David Niven (now elevated to featured player status), virtually overnight from the set of *Barbary Coast* to that of *Splendor*. The well-appointed soap opera had been written more than fifteen years earlier by Rachel Crothers who, unable to develop it for the Broadway stage, finally sold it to Goldwyn, whose films displayed with increasing regularity in the 1930s the elegant life-styles of upper-class America and the activities of the idle rich—excepting, of course, *Street Scene* at one end of the decade and *Dead End* at the other. Goldwyn then hired Miss Crothers to write the screenplay from her story and Elliott Nugent,

the actor/playwright who also directed on the stage and in films, to lead Goldwyn's stock company through its stylish paces in *Splendor*. The title, it turns out, did not necessarily refer to the film's quality, but certainly justified the Goldwyn gloss lavished on the physical accouterments.

Steeped in Thirties-style social criticism, Miss Crothers' sentimental opus deals with a country girl who marries the sincere, but rather irresponsible heir of a once prominent family of Park Avenue aristocrats, the dowager of which having expected him to marry the nice rich girl down the block to drag the clan out of poverty. Among the unpleasantries dropped into the saga is dear old mom's suggestion that her daughter-in-law give herself to another man, the mother's filthy rich nephew, in order that her idealistic son might latch onto a career, allowing the other leeches in the family, the young man's social butterfly sister and wastrel brother, to again live in the grandeur to which they had become accustomed. These rather depressing proceedings crept along through Nugent's lethargic direction and the competent, if not especially exciting work by Miriam Hopkins (billed alone above the title) and Joel McCrea (billed below it).

Bringing his charming young wife into the family townhouse for the first time, Brighton Lorrimore is greeted with frosty stares from his domineering mother, his sister Martha and his brother Clancey, all of whom had expected him to marry heiress Edith Gilbert. Brighton's wife Phyllis, is installed in the upstairs guest room and treated with cold correctness while the family resentfully lets Brighton know that he has failed its great expectations and asks him how he expects the Lorrimores to keep up appearances. Angered by his suggestions that they sell the place and move into smaller quarters, and perhaps even go to work, his embittered mother determines to break up her son's marriage. When her nephew, Martin Deering, becomes attracted to Phyllis during a family get-together, though, Mrs. Lorrimore decides to use her daughter-in-law to advance Brighton's stagnant career. Aware that Deering has grown fond of Phyllis, Mrs. Lorrimore suggests that the girl be extra nice to the wealthy playboy industrialist, who offers to sponsor Brighton in business—especially as his company's travelling representative.

During Brighton's increasingly frequent business trips, Phyllis, naively thinking she is helping her husband's career, allows Deering to escort her to all of the town's leading social functions, including several aboard his yacht. She soon realizes the gossip in the circles she is now travelling is destroying her marriage and tries to convince Brighton to give up his job and get into writing. He insists, however, that money is what he wants and enraged, Phyllis arranges with Deering to send Brighton to Mexico on an important assignment. In return, she offers herself to Deering, and then confesses to Brighton on his return. Leaving him, Phyllis finds a job in a fashionable boutique and begins divorce proceedings. Brighton at last comes to his senses and, telling his family that he has sold their house, tosses them into the street and suggests they look for work. Then he obtains a position as a newspaper reporter and finally goes to see Phyllis, offering to start over like most married couples—in a small apartment. "Darling," she tells him, "that would be such splendor!"

The critic for *Variety* wrote: "Here is a rare combination of a well-written story, interpreted in skilled and sympathetic action under able and understanding direction." The New York *Daily News* found *Splendor* "richly set, smoothly directed, expertly acted . . . made with the lavishness that is becoming a synonym for Goldwyn."

Not as enthusiastic was *The New York Times'* Andre Sennwald, who said:

The film is managed with impeccable intelligence and good taste, but it is to be feared that Miss Crothers and Mr. Goldwyn are sacrificing their heavy artillery in a cause that is not worth the trouble . . . it suffers from inaction and its theme is too commonplace to hold an audience when the pace is slow and the conversation merely careful.

Critic Sennwald's view of the acting:

Mr. McCrea and Miss Hopkins are excellent in the roles (and) the unpleasant Lorrimores are acted with poisonous effectiveness by Helen Westley as the embittered dowager, Katharine Alexander as the scornful daughter, and David Niven as the useless son.

Splendor's best moments were contributed by the comedy relief supplied delightfully by a pair of ever-reliables, Billie Burke, as charming as always in one of her frothy bits as a social gadfly, and Arthur Treacher, offering another of his patented snooty fops who is a friend of the family.

During the production of *Splendor,* Goldwyn kept his publicity people busy handing out releases about Miriam Hopkins' future roles. Next she was slated to costar once again with Joel McCrea in *Navy Born,* a slapstick comedy based on Mildred Cram's *Cosmopolitan Magazine* stories. Then this project was withdrawn and Goldwyn announced that Miss Hopkins would act opposite Gary Cooper and Merle Oberon in a historical spectacular entitled *Maximilian of Mexico.* Neither production materialized. Nor did a property called *Perfectly Good Woman,* in which, Goldwyn had planned to star David Niven.

Miriam Hopkins and Joel McCrea in Splendor.

Joel McCrea, Arthur Treacher, Miriam Hopkins and Billie Burke in Splendor.

Miriam Hopkins and Joel McCrea in Splendor.

42 STRIKE ME PINK (1936)

Directed by Norman Taurog; screenplay, Frank Butler, Francis Martin and Philip Rapp; based on the story *Dreamland* by Clarence Budington Kelland; music director, Alfred Newman; songs by Harold Arlen and Lew Brown; dances staged by Robert Alton; photographer, Gregg Toland; editor, Sherman Todd; assistant director, Walter Mayo; "High and Low" number photographed by Merritt Gerstad; art director, Richard Day; costumes, Omar Kiam. Running time, 99 minutes. Released by United Artists. Premiere: Radio City Music Hall, New York, 1/17/36

THE CAST:
Eddie Pink, Eddie Cantor; *Joyce Lenox,* Ethel Merman; *Claribel Hayes,* Sally Eilers; *Harry Park,* Parkyakarkus (Harry Einstein); *Copple,* William Frawley; *Ma Carson,* Helen Lowell; *Butch Carson,* Gordon Jones; *Vance,* Brian Donlevy; *Thrust,* Jack LaRue; *Sunnie,* Sunnie O'Dea; *Rita,* Rita Rio (Dona Drake); *Killer,* Edward Brophy; *Chorley,* Sidney H. Fields; *Marsh,* Don Brodie; *Selby,* Charles McAvoy; *Miller,* Stanley Blystone; *Smiley,* Duke York; *Hardin,* Charles Wilson; *Pitchman,* Clyde Hagar; and *The 1936 Goldwyn Girls,* Gail Sheridan, Vicki Vann, Kay Hughes, Elaine Johnson, Eugenia (Jinx) Falkenberg, Gail Goodson, Eleanor Huntley, Dorothy Dugan, Marcia Sweet, Mary Gwynne, Charlotte Russell, Blanca Vischer, Geraine Greer (Joan Barclay), Anya Taranda; and Monte Vandergift, Fred Kohler Jr., Nick Lukats, Howard Christie, Wade Boteler, Tammany Young, Lee Phelps, Robert Homans, Harry C. Bradley, The Flying Kitchens.

Musical numbers: (performed by)
"First You Leave Me High, Then You Leave Me Low" (Ethel Merman, chorus)
"The Lady Dances" (Eddie Cantor, danced by Rita Rio, Goldwyn Girls)
"Calabash Pipe" (Eddie Cantor, Ethel Merman)
"Shake It Off with Rhythm" (Ethel Merman, Goldwyn Girls, danced by Sunnie O'Dea and dancers)

The sixth and final Goldwyn/Cantor musical originally was to have been called *Shoot the Chutes* and was filmed over a four month period beginning in September 1935, but not completed in time to cash in on the lucrative Christmas trade. Harold Lloyd had first laid claim to Clarence Buddington Kelland's story, *Dreamland,* but Goldwyn came up with cash and walked off with the property, altering it to fit the Cantor style, allowing four writers liberal use of shears, and bringing Harold Arlen and Lew Brown to write a handful of songs—most of which, incredibly, went to Ethel Merman! Shortly before the film's release, the title was changed to *Strike Me Pink,* after Lew Brown's musical of recent vintage, the rights to which Goldwyn shrewdly secured.

In this romp, somewhat less lavish than Cantor fans had come to expect, the star turns up as a shy tailor who has inured himself to the unmerciful heckling of the local college students—until he purchases a book called *Man or Mouse: What Are You?* With the help of his girlfriend Claribel, Eddie Pink somehow becomes a big man around campus by taking on the job of amusement park manager, unaware that others have declined it because of gangster interests who have been eying the slot machine concession. With Claribel as his secretary and Parkyakarkus (Cantor's radio sidekick as his G-man bodyguard—the *G* stands for Greek—Eddie continues to somehow outwit mobsters Copple, Vance and Thrust, and to fend off the advances somewhat weakly, of Joyce Lenox, the brassy torch singer they have sent in to soften him up. In addition to ogling the 1936 Goldwyn Girls, Eddie finds time for two production numbers—singing the tuneful *The Lady Dances,* while Rita Rio (later known in films as Dona Drake) does a breathtaking tap routine on a mirror stage, and later performing *Calabash Pipe* with Ethel Merman, while the two are stuck on a ferris wheel.

A slam-bang Keystone Kops finale takes advantage of every corner of the amusement park Eddie is running, as he is chased by the hoods disguised as policemen, up the framework of the park's roller coaster and through its chutes (hence the film's original title). Soon he is careening around the scenic railway, after which he and Parkyakarkus are trapped in a runaway balloon, falling at last into the arms of a troupe of acrobats (The Flying Kitchens), who offer him a spot in their act—as Ethel Merman belts home "Shake It Off with Rhythm," ably accompanied by the Goldwyn Girls and Sunnie O'Dea, the latter shaking it off nobly. Of course, the real cops turn up to nab the mobsters as Eddie falls into Claribel's waiting arms.

"Cantor is aces all the way," is the way *Variety* summed up the proceedings, as hectic as they were. Frank S. Nugent, though, found in his review in *The New York Times* that the film contained

> considerably less hilarity than we have come to expect of the annual Goldwyn/Cantor shows. (It) appears to lack some of Goldwyn's customary expansiveness and much of the comic invention that has made the well-known father of five one of the screen's most likable funny men. Perhaps this is an ungrateful way of summing up a lavish cinema entertainment which does, after all, present several extended moments of low comedy, some handsomely executed dance spectacles and the always enjoyable singing of Ethel Merman and of Mr. Cantor himself.

In Richard Watts' review, the critic had his usual nice words for Eddie Cantor, took note of "a splendid finale in the best tradition of the immortal Keystone comedies . . . celebrated with admirable pictorial abandon," and then devoted space to Ethel Merman, observing:

> The lavishness of the handsomely staged song and dance episodes rather tends to dimisish the value of Miss Merman, who is such a gay, direct, infectious person, that all of these camera complexities tend to obscure rather than emphasize her superb merits as singer and comedienne.

Said *Time Magazine*:

> In the process of establishing himself as a Hollywood incarnation of Ziegfeld, producer Samuel Goldwyn, who says he does not care how much a picture costs so long as it pleases Mrs. Goldwyn, expended more than the usual pains on *Strike Me Pink*.

(*Time* reported that the original script was worked over by fourteen writers in teams of two, and that later, Goldwyn dropped a $100,000 dance sequence because the picture was running long and then reversed himself by substituting a $75,000 episode to the plot because it made the story more exciting.) *Time* also judged that Cantor gives "a fair imitation of Chaplin's famed characterization of a peewee battling gaily against overwhelming destiny," and then concluded that:

> what makes *Strike Me Pink* slightly superior to its more recent predecessors in the series of pictures made by Cantor and Goldwyn is not so much the elaborate production numbers . . . but the activities of an animated young woman named Ethel Merman.

Miss Merman, it seems, had been included among Goldwyn's prominent feature players in a two page ad in *Variety's* first-of-the-year anniversary issue. Named as Goldwyn stars: Eddie Cantor, Gary Cooper, Miriam Hopkins, Joel McCrea, Merle Oberon and Anna Sten (since departed). The feature players, in addition to Miss Merman: Billie Burke, Walter Brennan, David Niven, Douglas Walton and Frank Shields (the tennis pro who turned actor and later in 1936, made his debut in Goldwyn's *Come and Get It*).

Goldwyn announced, shortly after *Strike Me Pink* premiered at Radio City Music Hall, that Cantor would next star in Sam and Bella Spewack's *Pony Boy*, to be directed (like *Strike Me Pink*) by Norman Taurog. Cantor, however, was holding out for the George Abbott-John Cecil Holm knockabout farce, *Three Men on a Horse*, that he tried to cajole Goldwyn into buying for him as the last film in his original Goldwyn contract. Annoyed upon learning that Warner Bros. had bought the rights to the play, Cantor urged Goldwyn to loan him out for the role of Patsy. Goldwyn stubbornly refused and Cantor just as stubbornly balked when handed alternate properties. The impasse between the two ended when Goldwyn simply gave Cantor his release—*after* Warner Bros. had begun production on *Three Men on a Horse*, with Sam Levene recreating the stage role that Cantor had wanted.

Although Cantor's radio and later TV career flourished, his days as a major film star dwindled rapidly. He starred in only four more movies and did guests bits in two others, plus a walkon with his wife Ida in the 1953 film biography of his life.

Brian Donlevy, Eddie Cantor, Duke York and Ethel Merman in Strike Me Pink.

Sally Eilers, Eddie Cantor, William Frawley, Jack LaRue, Charles McAvoy and Don Brodie in Strike Me Pink.

Eddie Cantor in Strike Me Pink. *The extra arm belongs to Parkyakarkus.*

43 THESE THREE (1936)

Directed by William Wyler; screenplay, Lillian Hellman; based on her play *The Children's Hour**; music, Alfred Newman; photographer, Gregg Toland; editor, Daniel Mandell; assistant director, Walter Mayo; art director, Richard Day; costumes, Omar Kiam. Running time, 93 minutes. Released by United Artists. Premiere: Rivoli Theater, New York 3/18/36
* screen credit read "original story and screenplay by Lillian Hellman".

THE CAST:
Martha Dobie, Miriam Hopkins; *Karen Wright,* Merle Oberon; *Dr. Joseph Cardin,* Joel McCrea; *Mrs. Lily Mortar,* Catherine Doucet; *Mrs. Tilford,* Alma Kruger; *Mary Tilford,* Bonita Granville; *Rosalie Wells,* Marcia Mae Jones; *Evelyn,* Carmencita Johnson; *Joyce Walton,* Mary Ann Durkin; *Agatha,* Margaret Hamilton; *Helen Burton,* Mary Louise Cooper; *Taxi Driver,* Walter Brennan: and Frank McGlynn, Anya Taranda, Jerry Larkin

In a masterful stroke of Goldwyn genius, combining his astute acumen, extraordinary showmanship, acute aesthetic sense, and publicity awareness for the controversial, the producer confidently purchased the screen rights to Lillian Hellman's bold 1934 Broadway success, *The Children's Hour.* Success or no, the property was considered by the film industry as a dead horse because of its theme: *lesbianism.* This subject the Hays Office, the industry's censor body, would never permit as the premise of a film. Forewarned, Goldwyn knew he could use neither the title nor the plot, and was prohibited from even publicizing the fact that he had acquired this hot property, but he remained, as always, undaunted. As Frank Nugent, film critic for *The New York Times,* later wrote: "Mr. Goldwyn, much to everyone's amusement (in Hollywood), donated $50,000 for the privilege of carting it [*the dead horse*] away under the cover of night." That dead horse, it soon was agreed nearly unanimously, came to life as

one of the classics of American cinema, under the title, *These Three.*

Goldwyn contracted Miss Hellman to write the screenplay to the skeletal outlines of her stage drama, creating in this virtual redrafting a work that surpassed the original. In *The Children's Hour,* two young lady schoolteachers find their lives ruined when one of their malcontent pupils maliciously spreads a rumor intimating an unnatural relationship between them. In fashioning the screen scenario, Miss Hellman deftly skirted the lesbian theme and focused on the perfectly sound relationship wherein the teachers are each in love with the same man, a young doctor. The screenplay still managed to remain faithful to the concept of the stage version by retaining the underlying evil of the pubescent gossip monger's insidious hatefulness, and because of her rumors, one of the teachers is accused of having a clandestine affair with the doctor, spotted one night leaving her room. The weakness of the premise, both in the play and in the film, was the faith placed in the word of the young brat who was known to be a compulsive liar and the loss of the teachers' libel suit and livelihood in the waspish community, despite the minimal effort to unsuccessfully locate a vital witness, the evil-minded aunt whom the girls had employed as an elocution teacher and whose loose tongue had been the direct cause of the trouble. Her testimony would have easily cleared "these three" of their "unnatural affair."

Goldwyn's cast for *These Three* was headed by his A team, with Miriam Hopkins and Merle Oberon sharing star billing as the teachers who had been college classmates before opening a private school for girls in the stately old New England home one of them inherited. Hopkins is the cold, rather aloof Martha Dobie; Oberon plays the warm, ladylike Karen Wright; and both are in love with Joel McCrea (once again below the title), the upstanding Doctor Joe, who is a good friend to both girls, but hoping to marry Karen, sacrificing his career in the process. To portray Lily Mortar, Martha's aunt, Goldwyn had announced Alice Brady, but her schedule prevented her from doing the role, and it went to Catherine Doucet. *These Three* marked the start of an extraordinary and consistently stormy producer/director relationship between Goldwyn and William Wyler, resulting in eight screen classics. In 1962, when Wyler remade the film, reinstating both the lesbian theme and the original title, he brought Miriam Hopkins out of screen retirement to play the overbearing Lily Mortar, in support of Audrey Hepburn, Shirley MacLaine and James Garner.

In *These Three,* the pivotal role of Mary Tilford, the spoiled, insidious little brat, was given to precocious, twelve-year-old Bonita Granville, chosen by director Wyler (who had come to the project with the script already written and the three leads cast). Miss Granville proved herself to be a thoroughly obnoxious and expert young tantrum-thrower. Her astonishing performance is rather excessive by contemporary acting standards, but for it, she received an Academy Award nomination as Best Actress in a Supporting Role (in the first year of that category). Nearly matching the Granville portrayal is that given by nine-year-old Marcia Mae Jones as Rosalie Wells, the fellow student Mary terrifies into substantiating the devastating lie about the teachers and Doctor Joe. Equally superb is Alma Kruger, as young Mary's snooty grandmother, a pillar of the community, whose very word is virtual law among the social elite. Her self-serving offer to finance the teachers after learning the truth when the damage has been done, provides another of the countless stirring scenes studded throughout the film.

Providing comedy relief were Margaret Hamilton (who appears never to have aged in the four subsequent decades) as the Tilford housekeeper with a bravura scene wherein she delivers a well-deserved slap across Mary's face, and Walter Brennan in a running bit as a cantankerous "taxy" (sic) driver. Later in 1936, Brennan had his (first) Oscar role in another Goldwyn film, *Come and Get It.*

More than the acting, however, William Wyler's masterful direction gave *These Three* its distinction. Alistair Cooke wrote in *Sights and Sound:*

> William Wyler's directing used the distance between us and the characters for the most effective and bloodless Aristotelian purpose, tracking the camera relentlessly up to their faces when we would rather have escaped from the problem, scuttling pitifully away from them when we ached to give them a warm embrace.

More succinct was Richard Watts' comment in the *New York Herald Tribune* (his review was accompanied by Bonita Granville's photo): "William Wyler's direction is exceptional." Wyler had been hired by Goldwyn— with Lillian Hellman's blessings—after the producer had seen Wyler's work on the comedy, *The Gay Deception,* his first film after leaving Universal where he had spent the previous decade as a journeyman director.

Like most Goldwyn doubters, Wyler too was taken back when the producer, after giving him a five year contract calling for $2500 a week to start, told him his first assignment would be the cinemazation of the Hellman play. Wyler though, approached the project keeping in mind what Miss Hellman tried to explain to Goldwyn—that the story is the struggle of three adults to sift out the single piece of truth from a fabric of lies, and did not matter whether its focus was on an "unnatural relationship" (i.e., lesbianism), or simply a romantic triangle. Wyler, in fact, cleverly hinted at both by filming the crucial scene wherein Martha confesses to Karen of her love for Dr. Joe with Miriam Hopkins standing with her back to the camera. She might well have been exposing her desire for Karen herself.

These Three also marked the first association between Wyler and cameraman Gregg Toland, who had joined the Goldwyn organization in 1929 and was there until his death twenty years later at age forty-four. Toland photographed thirty-seven of Goldwyn's eighty films (some of the earlier ones with George Barnes), and worked on seven of the eight Wyler movies made for Goldwyn.

In his review of the film in *The New York Times,* Frank S. Nugent said: "From story, through William Wyler's direction and Gregg Toland's photography, to performances, *These Three* is capital. You can be reasonably certain that it will find its way into the ranks of the year's Ten Best." (It made that paper's Best Eleven of the Year.) Nugent also felt that "Miss Hellman's job of literary carpentry is little short of brilliant" and that "a gifted cast has contributed lavishly of its talents (so that) in its totality the picture emerges as one of the finest screen dramas in recent years." Richard Watts, agreeing, found *These Three* "a stirring, mature and powerful motion picture that is in every way worthy of its celebrated original, and perhaps, in one or two ways, surpasses it."

When *These Three* premiered on Broadway in the spring of 1936, Lillian Hellman's *The Children's Hour* (with Katherine Emery, Anne Revere and Robert Keith as Karen, Martha and Joe, and Florence McGee as Mary Tilford) was in its seventy-first week at Maxine Elliott's Theatre just around the corner.

Miriam Hopkins and Merle Oberon in These Three.   *Miriam Hopkins and Catherine Doucet in* These Three.

Joel McCrea and Merle Oberon in These Three.

44 DODSWORTH (1936)

Directed by William Wyler; screenplay, Sidney Howard; based on the novel by Sinclair Lewis; music, Alfred Newman; photographer, Rudolph Maté; editor, Daniel Mandell; assistant director, Eddie Bernoudy; art director, Richard Day; costumes, Omar Kiam. Running time, 101 minutes. Released by United Artists. Premiere: Rivoli Theater, New York, 9/23/36

THE CAST:
Sam Dodsworth, Walter Huston*; *Fran Dodsworth,* Ruth Chatterton; *Arnold Iselin,* Paul Lukas; *Edith Cortwright,* Mary Astor; *Capt. Clyde Lockert,* David Niven; *Baron Kurt von Obersdorf,* Gregory Gaye; *Baroness von Obersdorf,* Maria Ouspenskaya*; *Madame Renee de Penable,* Odette Myrtil; *Matey Pearson,* Spring Byington; *Tubby Pearson,* Harlan Briggs; *Emily McKee,* Kathryn Marlowe; *Harry,* John Howard Payne (later John Payne)**; *Hazzard,* Charles Halton; *Dodsworth Maid (Mary),* Beatrice Maud; *Steward,* Wilson Benge; *Orchestra Leader,* Jac George; *American Express Clerk in Naples,* Gino Corrado; *Edith's Housekeeper (Teresa),* Ines Palange; *Ship's Waiter,* Fred Malatesta; *Guests in Ship Salon,* Dale Van Sickel and Joan Barclay.
* in original Broadway production
** in screen debut

Dodsworth has rightly been called by cinema historians, "the epitome of the Goldwyn pictures," and ranks at the very top of the list of classics bearing the legend *Samuel Goldwyn Presents.* The screen adaptation by Sidney Howard of his own successful play and Sinclair Lewis' 1929 novel was further confirmation of Goldwyn's efforts to shape classic literary material to cinematic form and deliver class to the masses, while proving that stories about middle-aged people, in this case, two woolly Americans abroad, need not be boxoffice poison.

Goldwyn, it is said, had been told of Sinclair Lewis' book and its screen possibilities in 1932 by Sidney Howard himself, and that Goldwyn could have the property for only $20,000. When Goldwyn decided that Howard had

been right, the price had soared to $165,000 due to the success of the Broadway play. "I told you I could get it back in 1932 for twenty thousand," Howard told Goldwyn, to which Goldwyn countered: "I don't care. This way, I buy a successful play, something already in dramatic form. With this, I have more assurance of success and its worth the extra money I pay."

Dodsworth on Broadway starred Walter Huston, whose screen career, begun in 1929, never quite approached the one he had had on the stage. The role of Sam Dodsworth, however, was tailor-made for Huston, and for his performance came nothing but critical accolades. He played the part throughout the Broadway run and then went on the road with the production before returning to Hollywood to recreate Sam Dodsworth for Sam Goldwyn. The role brought Huston his first Academy Award nomination, and he was selected Best Actor of the Year by the New York Film Critics.

William Wyler also received an Oscar nomination for his masterful direction, which not only amplified the details of the narrative that followed the novel almost to the letter, but also expanded (with Sidney Howard's okay) the original narrative by inventing new details of the Dodsworth's Grand Tour, incorporating them into the fourteen scenes required to tell the story. Film historian Richard Griffith observed that, despite the staging virtually scene for scene, *Dodsworth* was not simply a photographed play because the play itself was nearer to screen form than orthodox dramaturgy.

Huston and costar Ruth Chatterton, in the part that Fay Bainter had created on the stage, had the best roles of their careers, although Wyler and his leading lady frequently differed as to how Fran Dodsworth should be interpreted. Huston's effortless performance made it easy to sympathize with the small-town, homespun businessman whose efforts to indulge his spoiled, shallow wife bring him nothing but unhappiness, although his deep love for her makes it difficult to leave her despite her romantic philanderings among Europe's idle rich.

Dodsworth began production on the first of May 1936, shortly before the breaking of l'affaire Mary Astor, who plays Edith Cortright, the understanding other woman. The actress, on loan from Warner Bros., embroiled the Goldwyn company and the whole industry in a front page marital scandal that dragged on for months. Involved were her husband, Dr. Franklyn Thorpe, and playwright George S. Kaufman, with whom she had had a rather open affair the previous year. And interwoven: a divorce suit, custody of the actress' daughter, and a diary of her amorous encounters with Kaufman. The sensational trial dragged on concurrently with the filming of *Dodsworth,* with Miss Astor working on the set days and turning up in court at night. Reporters, hungry for more juicy tidbits, kept the Goldwyn Studios under constant surveillance, and the boss relished the publicity.

Dodsworth's now classic story revolves around the retirement of millionaire automobile manufacturer, Sam Dodsworth of Zenith, Ohio. Succumbing to his wife Fran's, urgings, Sam agrees to a European jaunt. Fran always had hated Zenith and yearned for a more sophisticated cosmopolitan existence. And their daughter's marriage and forthcoming child reminded her of her fear of oncoming age. They embark on a continental tour with different purposes: Sam to see something of the world, Fran to win admiration. While Sam is wandering around, soaking up culture, Fran drifts into a series of affairs, first with a worldly English playboy, Capt. Clyde Lockert, then with a charming banker, Arnold Iselin, with whom she dallies in Biarritz, and finally with impoverished Baron Kurt von Obersdorf. When Sam and Fran receive word that they had become grandparents, she warns him not to speak of it to anyone, and then announces that she wants a divorce in order to marry the Baron. Sam reluctantly consents, and then begins traveling around Europe by himself. In Italy, he meets Edith Cortwright, a shipboard acquaintance, and accepts her invitation to stop at her villa. Their companionship ripens into love and Sam recovers his old-time enthusiasm.

Fran, meanwhile, has been invited to meet the Baron's iron-willed mother (played superbly by Maria Ouspenskaya, recreating her stage role and garnering an Oscar nomination as Best Supporting Actress). The Baroness, in a brittle tongue-lashing, forbids Fran from marrying her son, and Fran mortified, wires Sam and asks to be taken back to Zenith. He goes to her and returns home, only to learn that instead of being sorry what her actions abroad she is still the same posturing woman.

"You're rushing at old age," she tells Sam. "I'm not ready for that yet!" Realizing at last that twenty years of his life have been ruined, Sam responds: "Love has got to stop someplace short of suicide." Leaving Fran for good, Sam goes back to Edith for a happier future.

Virtually all critical opinions of *Dodsworth* were raves. and most started with hosannahs for Huston. Frank S. Nugent felt that

> Mr. Huston still is foremost, lending a driving energy and a splendid vitality to the character . . . It must be a studied characterization, but we are never permitted to feel that, for Mr. Huston so snugly fits the part we cannot tell where the garment ends and he begins.

Critic Nugent decided, however, that "For all the skill of the Lewis-Howard writing and the deftness of Miss Chatterton's portrayal (one of her best, by the way), Fran is just convincing fiction against Sam Dodsworth's unquestionable fact." Of the screen translation by Sidney Howard, Nugent wrote:

> Mr. Goldwyn has had the wisdom to accept his judgement; William Wyler the director, has had the skill to execute it in cinematic terms, and a gifted cast has been able to bring the whole alive to our complete satisfaction.

Howard Barnes found *Dodsworth* "handsome, provocative and sometimes emotionally compelling," noting that

> Samuel Goldwyn has lavished his traditional largess on the production, William Wyler has directed with considerable cunning, and it is singularly blessed by having Walter Huston once more in the title role . . . (his) is not only a brilliant characterization but it is so beautifully integrated and modulated that it makes those sequences in which he does not appear seem superfluous.

Barnes further said: "Miss Chatterton's portrayal is that she makes the wife so contemptible that her hold over him, even after infidelities, appears ridiculous." His conclusion: "An excellent screen entertainment which falters because its brilliance is neither evenly distributed nor sustained."

Variety simply called *Dodsworth* "a superb motion picture . . . one of the best of this or any year and a golden borealis over the producer's name."

Curiously, *Dodsworth* was not included among *The New York Times'* Ten Best Films of 1936 (although *These Three* was). It did receive, though, eight Academy Award nominations: Best Picture, Best Director, Best Actor, Best Supporting Actress, Best Screenplay, Best Art/Set Decoration (Richard Day) and Best Sound (Oscar Lagerstrom). Only Day won an Oscar.

Ruth Chatterton's screen career was virtually over

when Goldwyn asked her to play Fran Dodsworth. He even offered her the title role in the remake of *Stella Dallas,* his next production, but the actress turned him down, refusing to play another mother. She appeared in only two more films, both produced in England, and then made her television debut (1950), recreating her role as Fran Dodsworth in a "live" production of the Goldwyn classic, opposite Walter Abel. By the time *Dodsworth* was reissued in the mid-1940s, she was all but forgotten as a major star and was billed fifth. David Niven, Paul Lukas and her rival, Mary Astor, all were jumped over her. Even John Payne, who made his film debut in *Dodsworth* as Sam and Fran's son-in-law, received more prominent billing.

Walter Huston and Ruth Chatterton in Dodsworth.

David Niven and Ruth Chatterton in Dodsworth.

Ruth Chatterton and Walter Huston in Dodsworth.

Paul Lukas, Ruth Chatterton, Mary Astor and Walter Huston in Dodsworth.

45 COME AND GET IT (1936)

Directed by Howard Hawks and William Wyler; screenplay, Jules Furthman and Jane Murfin; based on the novel by Edna Ferber; music, Alfred Newman; photographers, Gregg Toland and Rudolph Maté; editor, Edward Curtiss; assistant director, Walter Mayo; logging sequences directed by Richard Rosson; special effects, Ray Binger; art director, Richard Day; costumes, Omar Kiam. Running time, 99 minutes. Released by United Artists. Premiere: Rivoli Theater, New York, 11/11/36 (Reissued in 1960 as *Roaring Timber*.)

THE CAST:
Barney Glasgow, Edward Arnold; *Richard Glasgow,* Joel McCrea; *Lotta Morgan/Lotta Bostrom,* Frances Farmer; *Swan Bostrom,* Walter Brennan; *Evvie Glasgow,* Andea Leeds; *Tony Schwerke,* Frank Shields*; *Karie Linbeck,* Mady Christians; *Emma Louise Glasgow,* Mary Nash; *Gunnar Gallagher,* Clem Bevans; *Sid LeMaire,* Edwin Maxwell; *Josie,* Cecil Cunningham; *Gubbins,* Harry Bradley; *Steward,* Rollo Lloyd; *Jed Hewitt,* Charles Halton; *Goodnow,* Al K. Hall; *Chore Boy,* Phillip Cooper; *Young Man,* Robert Lowery*; *Lumberjacks,* Stanley Blystone, Constantine Romanoff, Harry Tenbrook; *Scalded Lumberjack,* Max Wagner; *Foreman,* Jack Pennick; *Hewitt's Secretary,* Russell Simpson; *Shell Game Operator (Earle),* Earle Hodgins; *Diner,* Lee Shumway; *Headwaiter,* George Humbert; *Porter,* Snowflake; *Waiter,* Gino Corrado; *Schwerke,* Egon Brecher; *Wine Steward,* William Wagner; *Man in Saloon,* Bud Jamison; *Pianist,* Fred Warren; *Restaurant Patron,* Frances Dee.
* in screen debut

Goldwyn's robust *Come and Get It,* based on Edna Ferber's sweeping fifty year history of a Wisconsin lumber dynasty, is a perfect example of the logistics involved in the revolving door production policy that has become part of the Goldwyn legend. First the producer paid $100,000 for the rights to the novel and then he hired Edna Ferber as script consultant, paying her $30,000 while Jules Furthman and Jane Murfin fleshed out a screenplay. Next he tried to talk Louis B. Mayer

into lending him Spencer Tracy for the part of Barney Glasgow opposite Miriam Hopkins in the dual role of Lotta, mother and daughter (in the Ferber novel, it was mother and *grand*daughter), while issuing one of his many premature press releases announcing his casting. Tracy, it is said, told his boss he would rather not do the part because the character dies at the end (in the book, Barney is killed off, while the film simply leaves him a broken old man who had tried to recapture his youth with the daughter of the woman he had once loved, only to have the younger woman taken from him by his own son). At the same time, the name of Miriam Hopkins suddenly disappeared from Goldwyn's casting notices to be replaced by that of Virginia Bruce; then Miss Bruce gave way to Paramount starlet, Frances Farmer, who finally got the role Goldwyn should have given in the first place to his own starlet, Andrea Leeds (who turned up as Barney's daughter).

Unable to get Tracy for the lead, Goldwyn turned to veteran character actor Edward Arnold (previously seen menacing Eddie Cantor in Goldwyn's *Roman Scandals*) and gave him star billing in letters twice the size of anyone else (except Goldwyn). Goldwyn's perceptive, somewhat belated matching of star and role was rewarded with a brilliant portrayal by Edward Arnold, probably his very best, as the ruthless paper mill baron who fights and schemes his way to the top. Goldwyn's choice to direct was Howard Hawks (his second for Goldwyn), who left the project during the final week of shooting in a dispute of story angles and the film's ending. Goldwyn then dragged William Wyler, virtually kicking and screaming, from the adjoining *Dodsworth* set to shoot the remaining scenes (about 800 feet worth) after reading Wyler the riot act and the small print in his contract. Reluctantly, Wyler acceded to Goldwyn's urging and just as reluctantly took codirector billing.

The screen *Come and Get It* is less the sweeping panorama of the American scene that Ferber's book had offered and more the portrait of the lusty, brawling Barney Glasgow and his rise from overseer of a lumber camp *circa* 1884 to timber tycoon. With his lumberjack pal, Swan Bostrom, known to all as "that crazy Swede," ambitious Barney swaggers around, subduing rebellious jacks, charming local dancehall girls, craving barroom brawls, and conniving his way into the boss' business. During one night on the town with Swan, Barney spots singer Lotta Morgan in Sid Le Maire's saloon. When he goes on a winning streak at the roulette table with Lotta by his side, she is ordered by her boss to get the money back. Instead, she helps Barney and Swan fight their way out of the saloon by scaling metal serving trays at Le Maire's men, reducing the place to kindling. Lotta becomes Barney's girl until he unceremoniously drops her when she gets in the way of his ambition—which means marrying the boss' dour daughter, Emma Louise. Swan is the bearer of the bad tidings to Lotta, who on the rebound, agrees to Swan's spur-of-the-moment proposal.

Barney's unhappy marriage to Emma is not allowed to stand between him and success as a lumber baron. His idealistic son has been installed as his assistant at the plant, and his social butterfly daughter has already softened him up enough to accept the bohunk who works at the mill as his future son-in-law. Through the years, however, he has kept in touch with Swan and finally decides to visit his old pal who had been suggesting they get together for a hunting trip. At Swan's place back in the old lumber town, Barney learns that Lotta had died, but that Swan has a lovely daughter, named for her mother. When Barney is introduced to young Lotta, all of the memories of his first love are brought back.

Seeing the chance once again for the ideal romance he had tossed aside in his youth. Barney offers to bring Swan, young Lotta and Lotta's spinster Cousin, Karie Linbeck, to the big city where he installs them in a comfortable cottage and gives Swan a nonexistent job at the mill while pursuing his infatuation for the girl, not too discreetly. Soon, Barney's son Richard, discovers Lotta and becomes a rival for the girl's attention. Angered, Barney tries to get rid of Richard by opening another mill for his son to operate back East. Richard refuses to leave though, deciding that he has fallen in love with Lotta. Not accepting the opinion of his friends that he is simply a foolish old man, Barney chooses to fight Richard for Lotta, but the outcome is inevitable, particularly after Lotta herself calls Barney an old man.

In his review in the *New York Herald Tribune*, Howard Barnes saw the film as "vivid and exciting" and found it "robustly acted and staged in sweeping cinematic strokes." Barnes' comments on the acting:

Essentially it is the brilliant portrayal of the leading role by Edward Arnold that gives the photoplay power and distinction . . . all of the handsome mounting of the film would go for little without (his) splendid realization of Barney. Walter Brennan is splendid as the devoted Swan Bostrom, while Frances Farmer is attractive and sings pleasantly, but she rarely rises to the emotional exigencies of either characterization (mother or daughter).

The New York Times' Frank Nugent wrote:

Chalk up another hit for Samuel Goldwyn, one of the few producers in Hollywood who refuses to be content with mediocrity . . . (he) has been the butt of many Broadway and Hollywood wits, but he has acquired the habit of laughing last, and best, when his pictures have come to town. *Come and Get It* has the same richness of production, the same excellence of performance, the same shrewdness of direction (as the year's earlier Goldwyn successes).

Critic Nugent felt that

Edward Arnold gives a virile and full-blooded characterization; Walter Brennan is faultless as that honest Swede; and Frances Farmer, first as Lotta Morgan, the cabaret singer, and then as her daughter, is not merely a delight to the masculine eye, but an actress of more than usual merit.

The *Variety* critic wrote:

The meticulous care as to detail which Samuel Goldwyn takes with all his pictures is evident in this one, along with the customary luxuriant mounting and faithful adherence to technical facts, regardless of cost . . . from a production standpoint, Goldwyn, as usual, shoots the works. It's regrettable that the story isn't worthy of it all.

For his performance as Swan Bostrom, Walter Brennan won the first of his three Academy Awards. Editor Edward Curtiss also was honored with a nomination for his work on the film.

Frances Farmer and Edward Arnold in Come and Get It.

Edward Arnold, Frances Farmer and Walter Brennan in Come and Get It.

Walter Brennan, Frances Farmer and Edward Arnold in Come and Get It.

Frances Farmer and Joel McCrea in Come and Get It.

46 BELOVED ENEMY (1936)

Directed by H.C. Potter; screenplay, John Balderston, Rose Franken and William Brown Meloney; additional dialogue, David Hertz; based on a story by John Balderston; music, Alfred Newman; photographer, Gregg Toland; editor, Sherman Todd; assistant director, Eddie Bernoudy; art director, Richard Day; costumes, Omar Kiam. Running time, 90 minutes. Released by United Artists. Premiere: Rivoli Theater, New York, 12/25/36

THE CAST:
Lady Helen Drummond, Merle Oberon; *Dennis Riordan,* Brian Aherne; *Cathleen O'Brien,* Karen Morley; *Tim O'Rourke,* Jerome Cowan*; *Gerald Preston,* David Niven; *Lord Athleigh,* Henry Stephenson; *Liam Burke,* Donald Crisp; *Jerry O'Brien,* Ra Hould; *Ryan,* Granville Bates; *Rooney,* P.J. Kelly; *Connor,* Leo McCabe; *Patrick Callahan,* Pat O'Malley; *Casey,* Jack Mulhall; *Colonel Loder,* Claude King; *Thornton,* Wyndham Standing; *Perrins,* Robert Strange; *Crump,* Lionel Pape; *Hall,* John Burton; *Hawkins,* Leyland Hodgson; *Airoyd,* David Torrence; *O'Brien,* Theodore von Eltz; *Murphy,* Frank Roan.
* in screen debut

After delivering three 1936 classics, Goldwyn capped the year with his handsome, if slightly incredible tale of the Irish troubles, *Beloved Enemy.* Based on a story by John Balderston, author of *Berkeley Square,* and called during production *Love Under Fire* (a more apt title), it is a romantic tragedy between the leader of the Black and Tan insurgents and the titled daughter of the British conciliator. Robert Garland, critic for the *New York American,* correctly tagged it "*The Informer* in evening clothes," mainly because of the admirable performances of the two stunning stars, Merle Oberon and Brian Aherne, she working on her British accent, he struggling with an Irish brogue.

Beloved Enemy, marking the directorial debut of thirty-one-year-old H.C. Potter, is based loosely on the exploits of Michael Collins, one of the "cause" leaders who was assassinated by his own men for making peace with the British during the 1921 Irish Rebellion. Tacked onto these incidents is a romanticized yarn, subordinating the real issues to background filler for the melodramatic love story that ends with the hero dying in his sweetheart's arms in a Dublin drugstore. (A happy ending also was filmed and is the one seen on the television prints of *Beloved Enemy.*) Far more compelling would have been a story centering on the Damon and Pythias relationship of Dennis Riordan (the character patterned on Michael Collins) and his loyal friend and bodyguard, O'Rourke, whose utter devotion is shattered when he suspects that his leader has sold out to the enemy.

Instead we have Riordan, a patriot with a price on his head, riding around Dublin on a bicycle, flaunting his defiance of the British, and falling in love with the "beloved enemy," the English friend of one of the "cause" widows. Ignoring the warnings of his fellow rebels, led by diehard Liam Burke, Riordan continues to romance Lady Helen Drummond, whose father, Lord Athleigh, has come from London to investigate the troubles. When their trysts are discovered, Lady Helen unwittingly sets up Riordan for capture, but he manages to escape, and realizing Helen was unaware that he had been walking into a trap, forgives her, but vows not to see her again. After she sails for home with her father, contact is made with Riordan to come to London with a delegation to attempt to work things out peaceably. Outside the council hall, Riordan runs into Lady Helen, along with Gerald Preston, her father's aide. It is obvious to Riordan that Preston is in love with Lady Helen, but he asks for a few minutes alone with her. Spotted ducking into an empty room with her by Burke and O'Rourke, Riordan is once again suspected of being a traitor, and at the end of the council, when Riordan announces to his compatriots an "accomodation" with the English, Burke accuses him of having sold out.

Returning to Dublin, Riordan begins campaigning for the peace referendum, while those irrevocably dedicated to "the cause" make plans to get rid of him. An assassination council is set up and O'Rourke is given the job of executioner, shooting his old friend and then turning the gun on himself.

"It is one of the most incredible yarns which has been shown in many a day," decried *Variety*. "And one of the most remarkable things about it is that it is done with such consummate histrionic and directorial finesse that one almost believes it."

Frank Nugent is one who did believe. He loved it in fact, calling it, in his review in *The New York Times,*

a fine and mature drama (with) the stamp of quality on each of its departments—story, direction, performance and production—and it tempts us mightily to revise our tentative list of the year's ten best to make a fitting place for it . . . It is a story that required prose touched with poetry and has it from its writers. It demanded the most convincing performances and it received them from Brian Aherne, Merle Oberon (and the cast). It cried out for an understanding director (and) H.C. Potter, with his former Broadway partner,

George Haight, as associate producer, has matched his drama's moods perfectly.

Critic Nugent concluded that "giving it its final luster is Gregg Toland's photography which has almost a golden patina, and the usual—so usual that we accept it as a matter of course—handsome Goldwyn production."

Time Magazine determined that "the incidents on which *Beloved Enemy* are based are so exciting that it would be hard for them to inspire a really dull picture" and then called the film "strenuously romantic, magnificently acted and produced." Howard Barnes agreed, adding that:

produced by Samuel Goldwyn with all his accustomed flair for cinematic urgency and beauty, it is performed with great skill by an assured company, and H.C. Potter has staged it with a keen sense of camera values . . . The production itself is handsomely mounted and full of pictorial splendor. The difficulty with *Beloved Enemy* is that its boy-meets-girl theme is so dwarfed by its powerful Irish revolutionary background.

Barnes also singled out for comment actor Jerome Cowan who made his debut as O'Rourke and went on to a long career in character work, including roles in several other Goldwyn films, such as *The Hurricane, The Goldwyn Follies* and *The Kid From Brooklyn.*

Merle Oberon and Brian Aherne in Beloved Enemy.

Brian Aherne in Beloved Enemy.

173

Merle Oberon and Henry Stephenson (in car), Claude King (in officer uniform), Brian Aherne (in raincoat) and David Niven in Beloved Enemy.

Donald Crisp, Brian Aherne and Patrick J. Kelly in Beloved Enemy.

47 WOMAN CHASES MAN (1937)

Directed by John Blystone; screenplay, Joseph Anthony, Mannie Seff and David Hertz; based on a story by Lynn Root and Frank Fenton; music, Alfred Newman; photographer, Gregg Toland; editor, Daniel Mandell; assistant director, Eddie Bernoudy; art director, Richard Day; costumes, Omar Kiam. Running time, 71 minutes. Released by United Artists. Premiere: Radio City Music Hall, New York 6/10/37

THE CAST:
Virginia Travis, Miriam Hopkins; *Kenneth Nolan,* Joel McCrea; *B.J. Nolan,* Charles Winninger; *Henri Saffron,* Erik Rhodes; *Judy Williams,* Ella Logan; *Nina Tennyson,* Leona Maricle; *Hunk Williams,* Broderick Crawford*; *Mr. Judd,* Charles Halton; *Doctor,* William Jaffrey; *Taxi Driver,* George Chandler; *Process Servers,* Alan Bridge, Monte Vandergrift, Jack Baxley, Walter Soderling; *First Man on Subway,* Al K. Hall; *Second Man on Subway,* Dick Cramer.
* in screen debut

Few of Goldwyn's productions had a more tortuous route from typewriter to screen than his sole venture into the realm of screwball comedy that was finally called *Woman Chases Man.* For Goldwyn, the effort to make this one bordered on being a personal crusade. Its genealogy and accompanying problems themselves would have made a deliciously wacky screenplay.

Once upon a time, way back in 1935, Ben Hecht it seems, was summoned by Goldwyn once again, hired as the highest paid writer in Hollywood at that time, and implored to turn out a comedy for Miriam Hopkins. Several weeks later came something entitled *The Duchess of Broadway,* and back to New York went Mr. Hecht. Goldwyn then ushered into his office Sam and Bella Spewack to punch up the script that apparently had fallen below the producer's expectations. *The Duchess of Broadway* proved to be unsalvageable and the Spewacks instead went about extracting a screenplay from a story called

The Princess and the Pauper, that Goldwyn had purchased from Lynn Root and Frank Fenton. The Spewacks soon departed after working on the tale and coming up with a new title, *The Woman's Touch.* That team was succeeded by Dorothy Parker and her husband Alan Campbell, together with *Variety* writer, Joe Bigelow. Their rewrite of the previous rewite was finally half-heartedly accepted by Goldwyn who set a November 1936 production start with Edward Ludwig directing. The cameras never rolled.

The Woman's Touch went back to the typewriters where a battalion of studio writers began slaving in shifts over the project that rapidly was becoming a "cause" for Goldwyn.

Dozens of drafts later, Goldwyn appeared to have been sufficiently satisfied to cable vacationing William Wyler back to the lot to look at the script. Wyler found it hopeless and paid Goldwyn not only the two weeks salary he had drawn, but also the $25,000 bonus Goldwyn had given him for *Dodsworth* and *Come and Get It*—just to be left off the project. Then Miriam Hopkins asked to be relieved of the starring role, but reconsidered when Goldwyn made allusions to her upcoming option, and finally consented only if Gregory LaCava (late of *My Man Godfrey*) were hired to direct. LaCava, like his parade of predecessors, refused after reading the script. This prompted an executive committee to be formed to argue *en masse* that Goldwyn write off the $100,000 he had already invested and junk the whole idea. The unwelcomed suggestion made Goldwyn only more determined to realize the production. Goldwyn eventually settled on John Blystone, who had worked on several Will Rogers films, as director, and production began anew in February 1937. Goldwyn was then stunned when another of his contract players, Andrea Leeds, whose only other credit had been a minor role in his *Come and Get It,* marched into his office and told the boss that she could not feel her part. She undoubtedly impressed Goldwyn with her courageous act. He, of course, suspended her and borrowed Leona Maricle from Columbia, where she was specializing in "other woman" roles, to play the other woman in *The Woman's Touch.*

The casting was now complete: Joel McCrea, naturally, was Hopkins's costar (for the fifth and last time); Charles Winninger would play another of his delightful old codger characters; Broderick Crawford would make his screen debut; Ella Logan would be another comedy foil; and many of the Goldwyn stock players would round out the company. Most, though, were extraneous to the plot: a fortune hunter adventuress and her punctilious boyfriend (Leona Maricle and Erik Rhodes); a movie doorman and usherette transformed into phony butler and maid (Crawford and Logan); a hard-hearted banker (Charles Halton).

The Woman's Touch, or, as it soon became, *Woman Chases Man,* uses as its premise a reversal of position of a wealthy father and ne'er-do-well son into a relationship between a practical son and an erratic father. Virginia Travis, an aggressive lady architect who has found obstacles in her way because of her sex, brings to land developer, B.J. Nolan, a set of blueprints that she is certain will turn his suburban development project into a success. She is told that he needs a $100,000 loan to hold off creditors, and volunteers to persuade his millionaire, ultra-conservative son Kenneth, to invest, although he wants no part of his father's scheme. This means setting up the old man with servants to simulate wealth and coming between Kenneth and the gold digger who wants to become Mrs. Nolan. Learning finally of Kenneth's weakness for the bubbly, Virginia plies him with enough drinks to get his signature on a contract—and, of course, falls in love with him while bringing son and father together for the fadeout.

"*Woman Chases Man* is spun out of the sheerest nonsense," wrote critic Howard Barnes.

It throws daffy characters together in daffy situations and gives them glib, amusing speech. Unfortunately, farcical invention runs thin before the ending and the show goes over into rather strained slapstick. Even with the comparative letdown, though, *Woman Chases Man* is to be credited with gay characterizations, smooth direction and the smart production that Samuel Goldwyn has a way of giving to his offerings . . . Miss Hopkins breezes through the complications of the plot with uplifted face (and) McCrea is properly dull as

the young man until he loses his sobriety and common sense simultaneously.

Variety reported that

laughs ceased after three-quarters of the picture when action on screen became so insanely illogical and dull that amazed disappointment in Radio City Music Hall expressed itself in chilly silence . . . Three top-flight players simply run out of material, and, towards the end, Hopkins and McCrea literally find themselves, somewhat inebriated, up a tree. There they are, out on a limb, so to speak, bereft of business or dialogue. It's the meanest trick scenario writers have played on actors for a long time.

The journal, though, concluded: "Fine settings, splendid photography, and general production excellence are as expected in a Goldwyn picture, and John Blystone, the director, has really performed legerdemain with scanty material."

In Frank S. Nugent's opinion: "The members of the cast are up on their assignments and if the same could have been said for the writers, *Woman Chases Man* would have been a first-rate comedy instead of one that needs the courtesy of a Summer-season appraisal." In his review, Nugent felt that

straining the quality of mercy, we might call it a pleasant warm weather fabrication—lightweight, porous, attractively tailored and not meant to withstand the rigors of wear or the chill blasts of the critics. One real huff and puff would blow it away.

Miriam Hopkins made no more films for Goldwyn. He had planned to star her in a story called *Honeymoon in Reno* (with, as usual, Joel McCrea), a comedy by Virginia Kellogg. The actress though, talked Goldwyn into allowing her to return to the stage in S.N. Behrman's *Wine of Choice.* She left the production in Pittsburgh and the show itself closed shortly after its New York opening. Returning to Goldwyn, she immediately was loaned to RKO for *Wise Girl* with Ray Milland, with which she concluded her Goldwyn contract. Her then-husband, director Anatole Litvak, obtained a Warner Bros. contract for her, but her days as a powerhouse figure in film were numbered, and her star faded after just five more screen appearances.

Joel McCrea, post-Hopkins, came into his own as a first-string Goldwyn leading man and valuable trading property before altering the direction of his career to major stardom in westerns.

Joel McCrea, Leona Maricle and Erik Rhodes in Woman Chases Man.

Joel McCrea, Leona Maricle and Miriam Hopkins in Woman Chases Man.

Joel McCrea and Miriam Hopkins in Woman Chases Man.

48 STELLA DALLAS (1937)

Directed by King Vidor; screenplay, Sarah Y. Mason and Victor Heerman; based on the adaptation by Harry Wagstaff Gribble and Gertrude Purcell of the novel by Olive Wiggins Prouty; music, Alfred Newman; photographer, Rudolph Maté; editor, Sherman Todd; assistant director, Walter Mayo; art director, Richard Day; costumes, Omar Kiam. Running time, 104 minutes. Released by United Artists. Premiere: Radio City Music Hall, New York, 8/5/37

THE CAST:
Stella Dallas, Barbara Stanwyck; *Stephen Dallas*, John Boles; *Laurel Dallas*, Anne Shirley; *Helen Morrison*, Barbara O'Neil; *Ed Munn*, Alan Hale; *Mrs. Martin*, Marjorie Main; *Mr. Martin*, Edmund Elton; *Charlie Martin*, George Walcott; *Carrie Jenkins*, Gertrude Short; *Miss Phillibrown*, Ann Shoemaker; *Richard Grosvenor 3rd*, Tim Holt; *Mrs. Grosvenor*, Nella Walker; *Con*, Jimmy Butler; *Con as a child*, Bruce Satterlee; *Lee*, Jack Egger; *John*, Dickie Jones.

"Say what they may about Samuel Goldwyn," the *Variety* critic wrote in his review of the remake of *Stella Dallas*, "one thing all must admit—he has his finger on the audience pulse at all times and here is the proof . . . a tear-jerker of A ranking."

And this from *Time Magazine*:

If for producer Samuel Goldwyn *Stella Dallas* does not capture Warner Bros.' laurels as Hollywood's top investigator of the social scene, he is not likely to feel aggrieved . . . (he) was less interested in the class implications of (the film) than in recreating a story which made him a fortune in 1925 because cinemaddicts of all classes like to weep . . . and they, as they did twelve years ago, will find *Stella Dallas* dolefully delicious.

The new Goldwyn version of *Stella Dallas,* the first by one King (Henry King), the second by another King (King Vidor), is, except for slight updating, a scene for

scene recreation of the silent production while providing its stars the opportunity for characterizations suited to their particular styles. Ruth Chatterton had been Goldwyn's original choice for the lead this time. Following her rebuff, the producer turned to Gladys George, whose impressive performance in *Valiant Is the Word for Carrie* the previous year had earned her an Oscar nomination. For reasons unexplained, the role was still open when Barbara Stanwyck's name was offered to Goldwyn by Joel McCrea (her frequent costar who worked with her in six films—although none for Goldwyn). In her book on Barbara Stanwyck, author Ella Smith has Joel McCrea say:

King Vidor wanted Stanwyck from the start, but Goldwyn wanted to test three or four other good actresses to be sure. Barbara didn't want to test, and I got Vidor to promise to hold out for her if she made the test. He agreed. Then I talked her into taking it. She was far and away the best, but she shouldn't have had to test—any more than you would test Gable for a part. There is no better actress than Stanwyck if she is cast correctly. Goldwyn was a peculiar man, but he made fine pictures.

The test, of course, would seem unnecessary for an actress who already was a major star with twenty-nine films to her credit. In any event, as Stanwyck later related to the *New York World Telegram*:

Goldwyn had flatly refused to consider me because he told me quite frankly that first, he didn't believe I was capable of doing it; second, he thought I was too young; and third, I hadn't enough experience around children. When he finally agreed to give me a test, Anne Shirley and I did the birthday scene. We shot the scene for a whole day with King Vidor instead of in the customary few hours. When Goldwyn saw it, he gave me the part.

Stella Dallas is Stanwyck's favorite Stanwyck role, as it is the favorite Stanwyck role of most knowledgeable film critics.

More pertinent to the Thirties than to the Twenties, *Stella Dallas* works as a social comment along with its parallel theme of mother love and devoted sacrifice. Stella is seen for much of the early part of the story as a social climber. Daughter of one mill worker, sister of another, she sees in the eccentric young socialite who comes to Millhampton and goes to work in his shirt sleeves, the opportunity to advance herself. She tries desperately to be seen as a lady, but lacks the capacity to become one. She may have married socially prominent Stephen Dallas, but she was more at home with racetrack tout Ed Munn.

The same outstanding sequences that had made the original *Stella Dallas* memorable are as powerful in the talking version: the small tragedy of the unattended birthday party; the humiliation before Laurel's friends when Stella appears in all her ostentatious bad taste; the renunciation scene wherein she tells Laurel she wants her to leave; and of course, the unforgettable wedding scene with Stella standing outside in the rain.

Howard Barnes viewed *Stella Dallas* as

a surprisingly fine motion picture . . . Samuel Goldwyn has cloaked it in a handsome and restrained production, marked by beautiful photography and excellent scoring. What is more important and more surprising is the performing of a none-too-promising company under King Vidor's consummate staging. It is a notable personal triumph for one of the few really great directors.

In discussing the acting, Barnes wrote:

The portrayal of the title role by Barbara Stanwyck is something I would not have believed possible . . . her Stella is more restrained and credible than Belle Bennett's in the silent version. John Boles is comparatively wooden, but the role is so bad that it doesn't really matter. The outstanding performance is

that of Anne Shirley, as Laurel, acting of distinction and great promise.

Douglas Gilbert, writing in the *New York World Telegram,* thought that *Stella Dallas* "is the sort of film that . . . could have been ruined by a less sensitive and understanding director than Mr. Vidor." The critic also said:

Having always felt that Miss Stanwyck would prove herself one of the screen's finest actresses if given half a chance, this department is happy to report that in *Stella Dallas* she turns in a sensitive, beautifully shaded charaterization and that there are monents of uncommon beauty in her acting . . . No less superb is little Anne Shirley.

And in *The New York Times,* Frank Nugent reported, after viewing the premiere performance, that

there were muted audiences that shed a communal tear and cleared their communal throat as Stella made the gallant gesture and abandoned her daughter to the proper influences and the wedding vows of Richard Grosvenor 3rd. That multiplied sigh, bouncing off the sounding board of all those sentimentalists, was as fine a tribute to Mrs. (Olive Higgins) Prouty, to director King Vidor, and to Mr. Goldwyn's roster of players as any one had the right to expect.

Of its star, Nugent expounded:

Miss Stanwyck's portrayal is as courageous as it is fine. Ignoring the flattery of makeup man and camera, she plays Stella as Mrs. Prouty drew her—coarse, cheap, common, given to sleazy dresses, to undulations in her walk, to fatty degeneration of the profile. And yet magnificent as a mother.

The Academy of Motion Picture Arts and Sciences gave Oscar nominations to Barbara Stanwyck (as Best Actress) and Anne Shirley (as Best Supporting Actress). Neither lady won in 1937.

Barbara Stanwyck in Stella Dallas.

Barbara Stanwyck in Stella Dallas.

Anne Shirley, Barbara Stanwyck and John Boles in
Stella Dallas.

49 DEAD END (1937)

Directed by William Wyler; screenplay, Lillian Hellman; based on the play by Sidney Kingsley; music, Alfred Newman; photographer, Gregg Toland; editor, Daniel Mandell; assistant director, Eddie Bernoudy; special effects, James Basevi; art director, Richard Day; costumes, Omar Kiam. Running time, 93 minutes. Released by United Artists. Premiere: Rivoli Theater, New York, 8/24/37

THE CAST:

Drina Gordon, Sylvia Sidney; *Dave Connell,* Joel McCrea; *Baby Face Martin,* Humphrey Bogart; *Kay Burton,* Wendy Barrie; *Francey,* Claire Trevor; *Hunk,* Allen Jenkins; *Mrs. Martin,* Marjorie Main*; *Tommy Gordon,* Billy Halop*; *Dippy,* Huntz Hall*; *Angel,* Bobby Jordan*; *T.B.,* Gabriel Dell*; *Spit,* Leo Gorcey#; *Milty,* Bernard Punsley*; *Philip Griswold,* Charles Peck; *Mr. Griswold,* Minor Watson; *Officer Mulligan,* James Burke; *Doorman,* Ward Bond; *Mrs. Connell,* Elizabeth Risdon; *Mrs. Fenner,* Esther Dale; *Mr. Pascagli,* George Humbert; *Governess,* Marcelle Corday; *Whitey,* Charles Halton; *Intern,* Donald Barry; *Detective Harry,* Thomas Jackson; *Detective,* G. Pat Collins; *Coroner,* Walter Soderling; *Policemen,* Alan Bridge and Wade Boteler; and Bob Homans, Bill Pagwell, Jerry Cooper, Kate Ann Lujan, Gertrude Valerie, Tom Ricketts, Charlotte Treadway, Maude Lambert, Bud Geary, Sidney Kilbrick, Frank Shields, Esther Howard, Lucille Browne, Earl Askam, Mona Monet, Gilbert Clayton.
* in original Broadway production
# in original production, but in another role

The extraordinary success of Warner Bros. in the field of Thirties social gangster films did not go unappreciated at the Goldwyn Studios. Goldwyn was determined to prove that he had no peers in *any* film genre, and *Dead End* was to be his example. Goldwyn, with his wife Frances and William Wyler, dropped into the Belasco Theatre in New York to see the long-running Sidney Kingsley play, bought the rights the following day for something in excess of $165,000, and sailed for Europe after engaging Lillian Hellman to adapt the play to the screen for Wyler to direct.

Wyler had hoped to make *Dead End* in New York, but Goldwyn's fiat was that his own backlot was good enough and Richard Day, his ace designer, could duplicate a New York slum that would be better (worse?) than the original. Later, as Wyler confessed, he was stunned when Goldwyn turned up to complain that the squalor Wyler and Day had created for their East River street set was too dirty! The Day set was a complex of seedy tenements and shops, a tank-corner of the polluted East River, and the back entrance of a luxury Sutton Place apartment that abuts the neighborhood. Gregg Toland's memorable photography, with his relentlessly probing camera searching out every corner of the set, added an elasticity to the physical dimensions to the basic single set, through which Wyler's cast smoothly moves. (Both Richard Day and Gregg Toland received Academy Award nominations for *Dead End.*)

Goldwyn's own stock company, augmented by Sylvia Sidney (on loan from Walter Wanger), Humphrey Bogart (borrowed from Warner Bros.), and Marjorie Main and The Dead End Kids, recruited from Broadway to recreate their stage roles, peopled the screen version of *Dead End.* The ads billed Sylvia Sidney alone, below the title, with Joel McCrea and Humphrey Bogart sharing the next line in slightly smaller type, and Claire Trevor and Allen Jenkins under them in the next smaller size. During the film's reissue several years later, Bogart was accorded sole above-the-title status, befitting both his Forties stardom and his exceptional performance as Baby Face Martin, the killer who returns to the old neighborhood in search of his youth and dies a gangster's death (Joseph Downing had the role on Broadway).

In a part quite similar to her Rose Maurrant of *Street Scene,* Sylvia Sidney plays Drina Gordon (on stage, Elspeth Eric enacted the role) as the archetypal, dewy-eyed poor girl who walks a picket line for a wage high enough to enable her to move out of the slums with her reformatory-bound brother. Drina's earnest struggle to leave the neighborhood is in conflict with her love for out-of-work architect Dave Connell, who dreams of someday rebuilding the slums while harboring a passionate desire to get out. Dave, meanwhile, is infatuated with Kay Burton, a gangster's mistress kept in the luxury apartment overlooking the East River dead end street.

Interwoven with these loves and hopes are the frustrations and disillusionment mirrored in the faces of the neighborhood hoodlums, who canonize murderer Baby Face Martin and his henchman, Hunk, when the two "slink" home where Baby Face hopes to see his hate-filled mother and his old girlfriend turned prostitute, Francey.

Lillian Hellman's intelligent screenplay differed only slightly from the Sidney Kingsley original. Dave Connell is no longer a bitter, crippled artist as he was on stage, where Theodore Newton played the part as "Gimpty." In the film, Dave is given heroic stature, which allows him, rather than the G-men, to kill Baby Face. Kay Burton becomes indefinite in outline because kept women were not yet in the cinema mainstream in the Thirties, and as *Variety* put it, "only wives lived with gents in films." And Francey's stage syphilis was never even mentioned in the screen adaptation, which only alludes to the fact that Baby Face is rather disheartened that his girl had not waited.

"Producer Samuel 'The Touch' Goldwyn," said *Time Magazine,*

was smart enough to import the Geddes-Kingsley gang en masse, the whole dirty, ruthless, gay, heroic, sadistic crew of them . . . the not unhappy ending of the screen version of *Dead End* is no less valid than that of the stage original (and) should strike even the most critical cinemagoers as art rather than artifice.

In his review in *The New York Times,* John T. McManus felt that the film "deserves a place among the important motion pictures of 1937 for its stout and well-presented reiteration of the social protest that was the theme of the original." (The film, however, failed to be listed among *The Times'* Top Ten.) Critic McManus thought that "*Dead End* has been brought smoothly and forcefully to the screen by an admirable cast . . . (and) curtain calls are in order for all the principals with as many as they'll answer to for the youngsters."

The *Newsweek* critic observed:

As confidently as Nelson at Trafalgar expected every Englishman to do his duty, film folk expect a Samuel Goldwyn production to exhibit the kind of excellence they have labeled "the Goldwyn touch." To the last detail of its production, *Dead End* bears that imprint.

Howard Barnes' critique in the *New York Herald-Tribune* mentioned that "(it) had been transferred to the screen as expertly and effectively as one might have expected . . . although the plot has been made more taut and unified, it remains a piece of clever rapportage rather than a dramatically distinguished offering."

Barnes also noted that "William Wyler has explored every corner and alley of a dead end square to give the narrative movement and excitement in his direction, and Samuel Goldwyn has endowed the film with his customary generous production." Of the acting, Barnes said:

Much of the power (of the film) derives from the splendid portrayal by Humphrey Bogart, who creates a sinister human figure against a sinister background . . . (and) Marjorie Main is fine as the bitter mother of Baby Face who greets his perilous return to see her by slapping him across the face.

Variety's critic found *Dead End*

a perfect technical job of reproducing the action of the play. What Goldwyn hasn't done is to enhance the message of the play by letting loose the full power of the screen as a form of art expression different from the drama . . . there is no inventiveness or imaginative use of the cinema to develop the theme further or wham it as hard as the play.

Variety also observed: "Miss Sidney is excellent, one of the best things she has done in months . . . Bogart plays with complete understanding of the character . . . Marjorie Main whines her lines . . . (and) William Wyler's direction is faultless."

Dead End received four Academy Award nominations: Best Picture, Best Supporting Actress (Claire Trevor), and the previously mentioned honors to Messrs. Toland and Day. The film, though, failed to win in any of the categories. As a sort of "trailer" to *Dead End* to whet appetites, Goldwyn allowed a half-hour radio adaptation to be broadcast (Hollywood Hotel, CBS 8/20/37) four days before the picture's New York premiere. In the cast: Bogart, McCrea and Andrea Leeds.

Humphrey Bogart and Allen Jenkins in Dead End.

Sylvia Sidney and Joel McCrea in Dead End.

Wendy Barrie, Gabriel Dell (on ground), Huntz Hall, Bobby Jordan, Leo Gorcey, Bernard Punsley and Billy Halop in Dead End.

Marjorie Main and Humphrey Bogart in Dead End.

50 THE HURRICANE (1937)

Directed by John Ford and Stuart Heisler; screenplay, Dudley Nichols and Oliver H.P. Garrett; based on the novel by Charles Nordhoff and James Norman Hall; music, Alfred Newman; photographer, Bert Glennon; editor, Lloyd Nosler; hurricane sequence directed by James Basevi; location photographers, Archie Stout and Paul Eagler; art directors, Richard Day and Alexander Golitzen; costumes, Omar Kiam. Running time, 110 minutes. Released by United Artists. Premiere, Astor Theater, New York, 11/9/37

THE CAST:

Marama, Dorothy Lamour; *Terengi*, Jon Hall; *Germaine de Laage*, Mary Astor; *Father Paul*, C. Aubrey Smith; *Doctor Kersaint*, Thomas Mitchell; *Governor Eugene de Laage*, Raymond Massey; *Warden*, John Carradine; *Captain Nagle*, Jerome Cowan; *Chief Mehevi*, Al Kikume; *Tita*, Kuulei De Clercq; *Mako*, Layne Tom Jr.; *Hitia*, Mamo Clark; *Aral*, Movita Castenada; *Reri*, Reri; *Tavi*, Francis Kaai; *Mata*, Pauline Steele; *Mama Rua*, Flora Hayes; *Marunga*, Mary Shaw; *Judge*, Spencer Charters; *Guard Captain*, Roger Drake; *Girl on Ship*, Inez Courtney; *Stuntman*, Paul Stader.

Goldwyn's constant efforts to outdo the best the screen had to offer surpassed themselves in his South Seas spectacular based on the novel by Charles Nordhoff and James Norman Hall, the authors of *Mutiny on the Bounty*. The perspicacious producer had been introduced to the story in galley form in late 1935, snapped up the rights to the property, issued press releases about his exciting acquisition that he had assigned Howard Hawks to direct, and sent cameraman Archie Stout and Stout's assistant, Paul Eagler, to the vicinity of Tahiti for background footage.

When Goldwyn and Hawks had their blowup during the filming of *Come and Get It,* with Hawks finally walking out, Goldwyn turned to John Ford, who previously had directed Goldwyn's *Arrowsmith.* At about the same time, James Basevi, the special effects genius who had created the locust plague for *The Good Earth* and the earthquake for *San Francisco,* was borrowed from MGM (probably in one of Louis B. Mayer's weak moments since he once had vowed never to loan his talent to Goldwyn). From Paramount, Goldwyn borrowed Dorothy Lamour, a $75-a-week stock player with only four film credits, but sarong-filling figure, in exchange for the services of Joel McCrea (whom DeMille had wanted for *Union Pacific*). McCrea originally had been assigned the role of the native Terangi by Goldwyn, but got off the film by the daring action of convincing John Ford he was all wrong for the part and then standing aside while Ford battled Goldwyn for a new leading man. According to *Time Magazine,* Jon Hall was picked by John Ford, who had spotted the actor at the Hollywood Playhouse. Hall, a cousin of the coauthor of the novel, had a few earlier film acting jobs under his real name Charles Locher, and subsequently went on to minor fame as Universal chief wartime leading man in a series of Arabian Nights fantasies opposite Maria Montez.

Working with a script by his favorite scenarist Dudley Nichols, Ford and his associate Stuart Heisler, guided his cast through the idyllic romance-cum-savage melodrama plot, in which primitive man finds himself in conflict with the world's civilizing forces. The story, before the big blow at the climax, then drifts leisurely into a Polynesian variation of "Les Miserables" with Jon Hall as Valjean in a sarong and Raymond Massey as Javert as a martinet governor. All pales, however, before James Basevi's savage storm. Goldwyn gave him a budget of $400,000 to stage the twenty minute sequence, which *Time Magazine* described as "a technically superb combination of miniatures, authentic storm shots, tank shots made with wind machines, all blended with bursts of inhuman music as savage as the piping of damnation." Most critics agreed that Goldwyn got his money's worth from Basevi and that the storm that highlights the film and tears the island apart was (and still is) unmatched on the screen.

The Hurricane is the story of Terangi, a handsome young native on the island of Manakoora, who becomes the uncomprehending victim of the white man's justice. Recently married to Marama, he is working as first mate on a ship owned by Captain Nagle, who warns him away from trouble during a layover on Tahiti. Terangi becomes involved in a barroom brawl, however, and is sentenced to six months in jail for breaking a bully's jaw. Deprived unjustly of the freedom he craves, Terangi escapes from his prison repeatedly and receives a longer sentence each time he is recaptured, and a simple six month stretch is expanded to a fifteen year term, which De Laage, the authoritarian governor of Manakoora, refuses to commute, turning a deaf ear to pleas by his wife, the local priest and the island's native chief. Terangi's final escape attempt, during which he kills a guard, leads him on a 600 mile, open water journey in an outrigger, reaching Manakoora and his wife and baby just as hurricane winds begin buffeting the island. The ramrod governor, swearing to recapture Terangi, refuses to be put off by the high winds, in spite of his wife's pleadings, and when she finds herself nearly washed away while trying to reach the safety of the local church, Terangi rescues her and lashes her to a tree as the full fury of the cataclysmic storm lets loose.

When the hurricane subsides, Terangi frees Madame De Laage and then gathers up Marama and their child and heads for another haven. The governor, still on Terangi's trail, spots the natives in their outrigger, but is deterred from his pursuit when his wife begs for their freedom.

The heart-stopping storm held critics spellbound, but the plot left something to be desired. Particularly suspect was John Ford's act allowing Mary Astor, as Madame De Laage, to survive the hurricane with her dress pressed and pleated and her hair neatly waved. Comment also was made of the fact that Jon Hall managed all of his escapes and a 600 mile ocean voyage clean-shaven. Otherwise, as Howard Barnes observed,

The Hurricane has as terrifying a climax as has yet been devised by the screen. In a brilliant piece of film spectacle, one is caught up in the sheer fury of the elements . . . (but it) is so aggressively a show that it falls somewhat short of being a really distinguished motion picture.

Barnes wrote about the acting:

Jon Hall gives a splendid performance, making up for his lack of experience by a definite understanding of the part. Dorothy Lamour fails almost completely to persuade you that she is Polynesian, but there are excellent portrayals of the white inhabitants of the island to bolster the acting of the show.

The Herald Tribune critic also felt that "John Ford has staged it with imagination and power, while Mr. Nichols and Mr. Ford have tried to link the earlier sections of the photoplay to its ending without great success."

Newsweek wrote:

In return for his money, Samuel Goldwyn got a regulation South Seas idyl—and a high wind, the like of which has never blasted and thundered across the screen . . . despite the Goldwyn expedition that sailed to the South Seas to film authentic backgrounds, an aura of the studio hangs over the coral islands and flower-decked natives. Jon Hall strips to the waist effectively as the Tarzanlike Terangi, and Dorothy Lamour disports herself attractively in a sarong. But neither player is called on to do much more than that in the way of a Polynesian impersonation.

Variety referred to The Hurricane as "a production masterpiece from Samuel Goldwyn," noting that "(it) will go down in film history as one of the most impressive things captured on the screen . . . the adaptation is masterful with the dialogue having both charm and force." The paper then called Hall "outstanding," and decided that "Miss Lamour fits her native role excellently . . . Massey plays capitally and forcefully . . . Mary Astor plays the governor's wife suitably enough through not impressively," and then concluded that Thomas Mitchell, providing comedy relief, walks off with the film.

In the view of The New York Times' Frank Nugent: "The hurricane, magnificent as it is, devours only fifteen or so minutes of The Hurricane, and there are long minutes earlier when the footage is merely being nibbled away." His final words, after praising James Basevi's work, were that the film was "one of the most thrilling spectacles the screen has provided this year. That hurricane is a whopper." The critic for Literary Digest reported:

The fabulous Mr. Goldwyn has done it again. Sharpen up your superlatives to greet The Hurricane, bigger, noisier, stormier, wilder than even Sam Goldwyn's previous flights into the incredible . . . the picture is literally a howling success.

Unfortunately, the Basevi special effects were not properly honored if only by the fact that the Academy of Motion Picture Arts and Sciences did not begin awarding efforts in this category until 1939. However, not overlooked was Thomas Moulton who accepted his Oscar for the Sound Department of the Goldwyn Studios. The Hurricane also received two other Academy Award nominations: Best Supporting Actor (Thomas Mitchell) and Best Musical Score (Alfred Newman). Newman's theme music from *The Hurricane*, "The Moon of Manakoora," sweeping romantically through the film, has become the standard whereby all scores for South Seas screenfare are judged. The tune, though, actually was used earlier as part of his score for *Dodsworth* and can be heard during the ocean cruise when Walter Huston first meets Mary Astor.

Jon Hall and Dorothy Lamour in The Hurricane.

Raymond Massey, Mary Astor and Jerome Cowan in The Hurricane.

Jon Hall, Mary Astor and Thomas Mitchell in The Hurricane.

C. Aubrey Smith and Mary Astor in The Hurricane.

51 THE GOLDWYN FOLLIES (1938)

Directed by George Marshall (and H.C. Potter, unbilled); original screenplay, Ben Hecht; additional comedy sequences, Sam Perrin and Arthur Phillips; music director, Alfred Newman; photographer, Gregg Toland; editor, Sherman Todd; assistant director, Eddie Bernoudy; choreographer, George Balanchine; ballet music, Vernon Duke; art director, Richard Day; costumes, Omar Kiam. Running time, 115 minutes. Technicolor. Released by United Artists. Premiere Rivoli Theater, New York, 2/20/38

THE CAST:
Oliver Merlin, Adolphe Menjou; *Themselves*, The Ritz Brothers; *Themselves*, Edgar Bergen and Charlie McCarthy; *Olga Samara*, Vera Zorina; *Danny Beecher*, Kenny Baker; *Hazel Dawes*, Andrea Leeds (singing dubbed by Virginia Verrill); *Leona Jerome*, Helen Jepson; *Michael Day*, Phil Baker; *Glory Wood*, Ella Logan; *A. Basil Crane, Jr.*, Bobby Clark; *Director Lawrence*, Jerome Cowan; *Ada*, Nydia Westman; *Alfredo* (in "La Traviata"), Charles Kullman; *Assistant Director*, Frank Shields; *Theater Manager*, Joseph Crehan; *Igor* (in "The Forgotten Dance"), Roland Drew; *Prop Man*, Frank Mills; *Westinghouse*, Walter Sande; *Auditioning Singer*, Alan Ladd; *The Goldwyn Girls*, Vivian Coe (Vivian Austin), Marjorie Deane, Betty Douglas, Ann Graham, Jane Hamilton, Lynne Berkeley, Judith Ford, Evelyn Terry, Gloria Youngblood; and The American Ballet of the Metropolitan Opera under George Balanchine.

Musical numbers: (performed by)
Romeo and Juliet Ballet (danced by Goldwyn Girls, American Ballet, Vera Zorina, William Dollar)
"Here Pussy, Pussy" (Ritz Brothers)
"Love Walked In" (Kenny Baker)
Reprise: "Love Walked In" (Kenny Baker)
La Traviata Arias:
  Libiam Nei Lieti Calici (Charles Kullmann, Helen Jepson, chorus)
  Sempre Libera (Helen Jepson, Charles Kullmann)
Reprise: "Love Walked In" (Kenny Baker, Andrea Leeds)
"I Was Doing All Right" (Ella Logan)
"Love Is Here To Stay" (Kenny Baker)
"La Serenata" (Helen Jepson)

"Spring Again" (Kenny Baker)
Water Nymph Ballet (danced by American Ballet, Vera Zorina, William Dollar)
"Serenade to a Fish" (Ritz Brothers)
Reprise: "Spring Again" (Kenny Baker)
"I Love To Rhyme" (Phil Baker, Charlie McCarthy, Edgar Bergen)
Finale: "Love Walked In" (Kenny Baker, Helen Jepson, Andrea Leeds)

"Love Walked In," "Love Is Here To Stay," "I Was Doing All Right" and "I Love to Rhyme" by George and Ira Gershwin
"Spring Again" by Kurt Weill and Ira Gershwin
"Here Pussy, Pussy" by Ray Golden and Sid Kuller

In the years since first teaming with Ziegfeld on the making of *Whoopee!*, Goldwyn harbored a vision of producing annual screen spectaculars that would be to film what the Ziegfeld Follies were to the stage. Announcements regularly appeared in the trade press concerning these extravaganzas that invariably were postponed. By the middle Thirties, names of writers who were reportedly working on the Goldwyn project began to be mentioned: a New York newspaper man named Harry Selby, scenarist Harry J. Green, author Alice Duer Miller in collaboration with Bert Kalmar and Harry Ruby, then Kalmar and Ruby with Harry J. Green, followed by Dorothy Parker and her husband Alan Campbell, and Anita Loos and her husband John Emerson. All made contributions to the manuscript, for which Goldwyn reportedly shelled out $125,000 before tearing it up. At one point in 1937, the original idea had been expanded to encompass international talent, and Goldwyn brought his lavish plan to French director, René Clair, hoping for a favorable response to the oft-quoted Goldwynism: "How do you love it?" Clair's apparent lack of enthusiasm failed to deter Goldwyn, who already had engaged George and Ira Gershwin to compose the score, Vernon Duke to provide ballet music, and an illustrious cast from the varied arts (stage, screen, vaudeville, radio, opera and the ballet).

George Gershwin had completed only four songs when he was fatally stricken with a brain tumor and died on 11 July 1937. Vernon Duke completed the score, with Ira Gershwin supplying all the lyrics. Ben Hecht became the scenarist of record and received sole writing billing, and George Marshall was assigned directing chores (with unbilled help from H.C. Potter).

Goldwyn poured two million dollars into this ambitious opulent spectacular—his first all-Technicolor film (*Whoopee!* had been shot in the two-color process), which emerged as a two hour star-laden potpourri of specialty numbers tied together with a bland storyline about a young girl (Andrea Leeds) who acts as inspiration for a film impresario (Adolphe Menjou) while falling in love with a hamburger slinger (Kenny Baker). Greatly disappointing was the waste of such diverse talent as Vera Zorina, the German ballerina making her screen debut and dancing to the choreography of her husband, George Balanchine; the zany Ritz Brothers, whose daffy tune, "Here Pussy Pussy," is among the film's best remembered routines; radio's Edgar Bergen and Charlie McCarthy, plus Phil Baker; musical comedy stars Bobby Clark and Ella Logan; the Metropolitan Opera's Helen Jepson and Charles Kullmann, performing arias from "La Traviata;" the Met's American Ballet Company; and even the 1938 Goldwyn Girls.

Studded with nineteen production numbers, *The Goldwyn Follies,* minus Ben Hecht's banal storyline, might well have been the inspiration for Ed Sullivan's television variety show a decade later. Zorina's water nymph dance, in which the lovely ballerina dazzlingly attired in a skintight gold tunic, rises from the bottom of a fountain, contrasts with the introduction of the subsequent Gershwin standard, "Love Walked In," by Kenny Baker while tossing hamburgers in the air (he sang the song four times in the picture, but it miraculously survived!). The Ritz Brothers' distinctive "Serenade To a Fish" and Ella Logan's delightful "I Was Doing All Right" are juxtaposed with portions of the Romeo and Juliet Ballet, danced by Zorina, William Dollar, the American Ballet and the Goldwyn Girls. "La Serenata" of coloratura Helen Jepson comes within minutes of "I Love To Rhyme" by Bergen and McCarthy and Phil Baker.

The critics awarded Goldwyn accolades for intent, but carped on content. *The New York Times'* Frank Nugent wrote:

Since it bears the Goldwyn trademark, it goes without saying that it is a superior hodgepodge, peopled almost exclusively by superior specialists . . . but none of it, good or bad, has been brought into a semblance of continuity. We are always hearing about faces on the cutting room floor; this is one time when the script wound up there. On the evidence, it appears that Mr. Goldwyn tossed the story out to make room for the cast, and what's left of the Hecht plot reduces Andrea Leeds and Adolphe Menjou to the status of tourist guides during the filming of a Hollywood musical.

Said *Time Magazine:*

The specialties displayed in *The Goldwyn Follies* are sometimes brilliant, sometimes dull, always expensive . . . net result—a choppy extravaganza with many features to suit all tastes and not enough of any of them to suit anybody's.

Variety pointed out that the film

is an advance glimpse at next Sunday's amusement section from any metropolitan newspaper. The mixture, in brilliant hues of Technicolor, turns out to be a lavish production in which certain individual performances and ensembles erase the memory of some dull moments.

The Howard Barnes review (accompanied by Miss Leeds' photo) observed:

Samuel Goldwyn has shot the works in *The Goldwyn Follies.* For it he has assembled a motley throng of "names" and has presented the turns for which they are celebrated in an opulent and brightly tinted extravaganza . . . it would almost appear as though Mr. Goldwyn had tried to see just how much could be crammed into that hybrid form known as the screen musical.

Barnes concluded that "Mr. Goldwyn's *Follies* is a big, beautiful and rather ponderous show . . . notably lacking in humor."

The *Newsweek* critic had this view:

If the *Follies* falls short of its ambitions mark, it is because George Marshall, the director, has had to cram too many personalities and their not always successful routines into the film's two hours. Like Santa Claus, Goldwyn wanted to bring something for everyone's stocking.

At Oscar time in 1938, Alfred Newman's musical score and Richard Day's art and set design received nominations. Incredibly, neither Gershwin's "Love Walked In" nor his "Love Is Here To Stay," both introduced in the film, were included among the ten nominated movie songs, although the title song to Goldwyn's *The Cowboy and the Lady* was.

Harry Ritz and Vera Zorina in The Goldwyn Follies.

Kenny Baker, Andrea Leeds and Adolphe Menjou in
The Goldwyn Follies.

Bobby Clark, Charlie McCarthy and Edgar Bergen in
The Goldwyn Follies.

52 THE ADVENTURES
OF MARCO POLO (1938)

Directed by Archie Mayo (and John Ford uncredited)*; screenplay, Robert E. Sherwood; based on a story by Captain Norman A. Pogson; music director, Alfred Newman; music, Hugo Friedhofer; photographers, Rudolph Maté and Archie Stout; editor, Fred Allen; assistant director, Walter Mayo; special effects, James Basevi; art director, Richard Day; costumes, Omar Kiam. Running time, 100 minutes. Filmed in Sepia. Released by United Artists. Premiere: Radio City Music Hall, New York, 4/7/38

* director John Cromwell also worked on the film for several days

THE CAST:

Marco Polo, Gary Cooper; *Princess Kukachin*, Sigrid Gurie; *Ahmed*, Basil Rathbone; *Kublai Khan*, George Barbier; *Binguccio*, Ernest Truex; *Nazama*, Binnie Barnes; *Kaidu*, Alan Hale; *Chen Tsu*, H.B. Warner; *Persian Ambassador*, Ferdinand Gottschalk; *Chamberlain*, Robert Grieg; *Nicolo Polo*, Henry Kolker; *Visahka*, Lotus Liu; *Bayan*, Stanley Fields; *Toctai*, Harold Huber; *Nazama's Maid*, Lana Turner; *Maffeo Polo*, Hale Hamilton; *Giuseppe*, Reginald Barlow; *Chen Tsu's Son*, Eugene Hoo; *Chen Tsu's Daughter*, Helen Quan; *Chen Tsu's Mother*, Mrs. Ng; *Chen Tsu's Wife*, Soo Yong; *Mongol Guard*, Ward Bond; *Tartar Warrior*, James Leong; *Ahmed's Aide*, Dick Alexander; *Messenger*, Jason Robards; *Venetian Businessmen*, Granville Bates and Theodore von Eltz; *Court Girls*, Gloria Youngblood, Diana Moncardo, Mia Schioka, Dora Young; and Diane Toy, Henry Kerua, Greta Granstedt, Harry Cording, Dick Rich, Joe Woody, Leo Fielding.

In a two page ad in the anniversary issue of *Variety*, Goldwyn prefaced his announcements of his upcoming releases by spotlighting Gary Cooper with the qualifications: "Under exclusive contract to Samuel Goldwyn, the World's No. 1 Box office Star." The producer then went on to herald two new Cooper films, the first being

The Adventures of Marco Polo. Goldwyn had planned this historical adventure shortly after acquiring a story about the thirteenth century traveler from N.A. Pogson (Captain Norman A. Pogson of the British Army). After obtaining a light-hearted screenplay from Pulitzer Prizewinner Robert E. Sherwood, Goldwyn set about assembling a cast of 5000 to be headed by Gary Cooper as the famed Venetian merchant/explorer. The Goldwyn scouts then came up with a Norwegian beauty named Sigrid Gurie who, Goldwyn decreed, would be his next great discovery. When filming began in June of 1937, John Carradine and Veree Teasdale were among the players in the costume epic, as were Alan Hale, Ernest Truex, H.B. Warner (in an extension of the role he had just completed in *Lost Horizon*), several members of Goldwyn's stock company, and a very young Lana Turner. Carradine was soon replaced by Basil Rathbone, as Kublai Khan's conniving minister, and Veree Teasdale by Binnie Barnes, impersonating the haughty wife of the chief barbarian. John Cromwell was the first of a series of directors, but he left after the first five days of shooting. William Wyler was beckoned, but flatly refused the assignment, and Archie Mayo, who was to have worked on *The Goldwyn Follies* was shifted to this project. John Ford has admitted working briefly on *Marco Polo*, doing several action scenes, including a blizzard sequence and the episode of Marco crossing the Himalayas.

Goldwyn, during this time, was said (by *Time Magazine*) to have been interested in signing Marshal Chang Hsueh-Tiang, the kidnapper of Chiang Kai-Shek, to lead Kublai Khan's screen hordes. Returning to the production front, Goldwyn soon began disagreeing with John Cromwell's serious approach and placed himself more in tune with Archie Mayo's action/spectacular concept, which found our hero, as per legend, reluctantly leaving the lovely ladies of Venice to conduct business for his father in Pekin at the court of Kublai Khan. There he becomes involved with the Khan's daughter, protecting her from the evil designs of Ahmed the Saracen, and from an unhappy marriage to the Persian king to whom she had been promised. Gaining the confidence of the Khan, Marco is sent to the rebel camp of Kaidu, the barbarian warrior who has been theatening the Khan. While parrying with Kaidu's grasping wife, Marco manages to save the warrior's life, and asks in return that Kaidu place his rebel army at Marco's disposal to help save Khan's throne from the treacherous Ahmed.

Cooper's Marco Polo is still Cooper and no more farfetched than the impersonations by Rory Calhoun and Horst Buchholz of Marco in the 1960s. *Variety* observed: "Cooper fits the character to the apex of his six feet two," while Howard Barnes felt that "Cooper does all he can to create a character and a series of moods, but he has little opportunity for more than posturing until the slam bang finish."

Time Magazine commented that "This grotesquely cast *Marco Polo* skips like a cockleshell over the surface of Marco's famed Munchausenish travel tale and comes at length to a cockleshell's finale." The *Time* critic then noted:

Producer Goldwyn's Polo finds enough career for any Venetian in naive, unkissed Princess Kukachin with her wide-set eyes, parted, quivering lips, and two-story hairdo. *Marco Polo* will be remembered for introducing the girl Gary Cooper taught to kiss in one four minute cinema lesson.

Newsweek's similar thumbs-down notice mentioned that

unfortunately Robert E. Sherwood's fictional account of the thirteenth century salesman's adventures is worthy neither of its actors' talents nor its producer's infinite capacity for taking pains and spending money . . . (the film) combines the opera-bouffe unreality of Gilbert and Sullivan's *The Mikado*—minus the humor—with the elementary melodramachinations of a Hollywood horse opera.

The magazine's critic concluded with the word that "it is one of the producer's most elaborate productions, and a disappointing case of touch and go with the famous Goldwyn touch."

The Frank Nugent review in *The New York Times*, accompanied by a photo of Sigrid Gurie (by then, already acknowledged to have hailed from Brooklyn, despite the ad catchline "discovered by Samuel Goldwyn in Norway"), *Marco Polo* was described as "a nice enough picture . . . amiably make-believe, rich in the outlandish pageantry Hollywood loves to manufacture, facilely narrated and enjoyably played . . . and the production has the usual smooth Goldwyn finish."

Howard Barnes, meanwhile, found that "Robert E. Sherwood has not only fashioned a trite costume adventure romance rather than an intriguing chunk of history, but has neglected to brighten the work with the sort of fine dialogue that he knows how to write." Barnes also said that "Archie Mayo has staged the show to make individual sequences jump out at you with their flavor, suspense and action, but he has failed to integrate the production into an entertaining whole."

The *Illustrated London News* reviewed *Marco Polo* with these words: "Incredible and splendid, this superproduction permits no subtleties of acting. Mr. Gary Cooper, striding through it with his customary ease, preserves his invincible sincerity against heavy odds." The reviewer for *The New York Sun* though, said summarily; "In spite of its elaborate settings and the presence of Gary Cooper, *The Adventures of Marco Polo* never quite lives up to its promises."

Despite the vast amount of publicity expended on her, Sigrid Gurie never again worked in a Goldwyn film. She drifted along in exotic roles through the Forties and ended her film career working in Grade-B spy thrillers. By contrast, Lana Turner, who received virtually no publicity while laboring on *Marco Polo*, skyrocketed to stardom shortly afterwards under the tutelage of Louis B. Mayer, and when the film was reissued several years later, was accorded costar billing with Cooper despite the fact that they have no scenes together and she has only a few lines of dialogue in her extremely small role.

Sigrid Gurie and Gary Cooper in The Adventures of Marco Polo.

Alan Hale, Gary Cooper and Ernest Truex in The Adventures of Marco Polo.

Sigrid Gurie and Gary Cooper in The Adventures of Marco Polo.

53 THE COWBOY AND THE LADY (1938)

Directed by H.C. Potter; screenplay, S.N. Behrman and Sonya Levien; based on a story by Leo McCarey and Frank R. Adams; music director, Alfred Newman; songs "The Cowboy and the Lady" and "Er-ru-ti-tu-ti" by Lionel Newman, Arthur Quenzer and L. Wolfe Gilbert; photographer, Gregg Toland; editor, Sherman Todd; assistant director, Eddie Bernoudy; art director, Richard Day; costumes, Omar Kiam. Running time, 91 minutes. Released by United Artists. Premiere: Radio City Music Hall, New York, 11/24/38

THE CAST:
Stretch Willoughby, Gary Cooper; *Mary Smith*, Merle Oberon; *Katie Callahan*, Patsy Kelly; *Sugar*, Walter Brennan; *Buzz*, Fuzzy Knight; *Elly*, Mabel Todd; *Judge Horace Smith*, Henry Kolker; *Uncle Hannibal Smith*, Harry Davenport; *Ma Hawkins*, Emma Dunn; *Ames*, Walter Walker; *Henderson*, Berton Churchill; *Chester Dillon*, Charles Richman; *Captain*, Fredrik Vogeding; *Valet*, Arthur Hoyt; *Old Woman*, Mabel Collcord; *Rodeo Riders*, Billy Wayne, Ernie Adams, Russ Powell, Jack Baxley, Johnny Judd.

In the wake of *Woman Chases Man*, the problems involved with bringing *The Cowboy and the Lady* (neé *The Lady and the Cowboy*) to the screen, comprise Goldwyn's second crusade. Humorously chronicled by Garson Kanin, a lengthy tale is spun about how Goldwyn, anxious to find something for Gary Cooper and Merle Oberon while they were drawing their generous salaries, paid Leo McCarey $50,000 for a fanciful yarn he had concocted extemporaneously at a meeting of Goldwyn's senior staff. After turning over to Goldwyn a story outline, McCarey refused to direct the screenplay, which, like *The Goldwyn Follies*, went through the hands of writing talents and teams including Anita Loos and John Emerson, Dorothy Parker and Alan Campbell, and in

the end, S.N. Behrman and Sonya Levien. (The other writers were Frederick Lonsdale, Howard Estabrook, Robert Ardrey, Eddie Moran, Frank Ryan, Gene Fowler, Robert Riskin, and Richard Connell.) Following the McCarey refusal of directorial chores, Goldwyn cajoled William Wyler into joining the project, while withdrawing the previous press releases that the Cooper-Oberon team would be appearing in a Technicolor production for Goldwyn called *You Can Be Beautiful,* announced as late as mid-May of 1937.

Filming of *The Cowboy and the lady* (the title of which, Goldwyn soon learned, was owned by Paramount Pictures and had to be purchased, further escalating costs) began on 15 June 1938 with Wyler directing. Goldwyn replaced him on the 18th for being too slow, and brought in H.C. Potter, who previously had guided Merle Oberon through *Beloved Enemy*. The breezy comedy, that tells of a poor little rich girl, the bored daughter of a presidential candidate, who elopes with a Montana cowpoke, began production amiably enough, but lost several cast members along the way, and finally lost director Potter himself, who had a previous commitment at RKO to do the Astaire-Rogers movie, *The Story of Vernon and Irene Castle*, and turned the director's chair over to Stuart Heisler for the final scenes and retakes. The second male lead in the film had been David Niven, playing a member of the British diplomatic corps. He disappeared in the final cut (although he still is billed third on original stills from the film). Thomas Mitchell, cast as Merle Oberon's politically ambitious father, was replaced early in the filming by Henry Kolker. Benita Hume, Ronald Colman's wife, had been signed to play Merle Oberon's stepmother in the production, but her character was eliminated during one of the continual rewritings and she is not seen in the final print. Goldwyn's original, modest (for him) budget of approximately $600,000, ultimately tripled, but the producer, true to tradition, never stinted in his values.

The Cowboy and the Lady follows the adventures of Mary Smith, the fun-loving daughter of a stuffy Judge who is running for President. When she and her uncle Hannibal innocently become involved in a gambling raid, the Judge whisks them off to Florida, where Mary, out of boredom, persuades her maid Katie and her cook Elly to take her along on a blind date with three cowpokes appearing in a local rodeo. Mary's date, Stretch Willoughby, is captivated by the girl who claims that she is supporting four sisters and a drunken father. Maintaining her masquerade as her own maid, Mary entertains Stretch and his friends at a kitchen party at the Smith mansion, and impulsively accepts his equally impulsive marriage proposal, agreeing to a shipboard wedding enroute to Galveston. When she later displays a distaste for rodeo life, Stretch sends her back to the mansion in Florida with the understanding that she will join him ultimately in his Montana ranch.

When the secret marriage is discovered by Judge Smith's aides, plans for the boss' presidential nomination are hastened and an annulment is proposed for Mary. Puzzled by a telegram that Mary will be delayed, Stretch rushes to the Smith mansion, arriving in the midst of a gala dinner party. Finally learning the truth about Mary's prolonged masquerade, Stretch refuses to abide by the curiosity of the guests and delivers a stinging speech to them before departing. Unwilling to see his niece heartbroken, Uncle Hannibal explains to his brother how his political ambitions are standing between Mary and happiness. The Judge graciously withdraws from the presidential race and accompanies his daughter to Montana and her cowpoke husband.

Cooper and Brennan played sidekicks for the first time in *The Cowboy and the Lady.* It was the second of their seven films together (Brennan previously had had a small role in *The Wedding Night,* in which Cooper had starred). In its review of the film, *Time Magazine* listed the sixteen authors involved and then admitted that:

Critics found it notable chiefly (1) because, as might have been expected, its story, of which the title is an adequate synopsis, appears to be a composite photograph of innumerable other pictures on the same theme, and (2) because, as might not have been expected, it is first-rate entertainment.

Time concluded, however: "Typical product of producer Goldwyn's battery of authors: Gary Cooper and Merle Oberon kissing."

The *Newsweek* critic thought that

the story born of delay, wrangling and a literary assemblyline comes to the screen as a thoroughly enjoyable comedy . . . despite its titular implications, the Goldwyn film lingers longer at Palm Beach than it does on the Montana range and even goes to sea for the runaway marriage. Subsequent complications and conclusions offer little in the way of surprise, engagingly resolved by the stars and their supporting cast.

While *Variety* wrote simply that "the lead is tailormade for Cooper, who gets everything possible out of the role provided," Howard Barnes noted in his review in The *New York Herald Tribune*:

If ever there was a film title which summed up a show succinctly, this is it . . . it seems to me that a moth-eaten tale has received a good deal more than it deserves in this offering The direction is deft and there is a physical production which is as unstinting and as pretentious as one might expect from Samuel Goldwyn. The catch is that the story is so banal that all atempts to make it seem significant or intriguing are to no avail . . . the staging of H.C. Potter is glibly resourceful, but it scarcely succeeds in making dull material seem delightful.

Writing the critique in *The New York Times,* B.R. Crisler said:

The picture still seems to be in need of a final revision to bring it either more nearly into conformity or more ludicrously into nonconformity, with life as it is lived outside of movie studios . . . in spite of four authors, each presumably with a highly developed sense of humor, it just isn't funny enough to justify the very queer picture of American politics and society it presents.

Critic Crisler told his readers that

even Mr. Cooper, the picture's greatest asset, has his moments of diminishing returns when he seems to be quoting himself, or when, utterly forsaken by the authors and the director, he looks about helplessly, like a ghost who wonders if he isn't haunting the wrong house.

The Cowboy and the Lady garnered Oscar nominations in three categories: Best Original Score (Alfred Newman), Best Song (the title tune by Lionel Newman, Arthur Quenzer and L. Wolfe Gilbert) and Best Sound (Thomas Moulton). Mr. Moulton accepted his second consecutive Academy Award, again in behalf of the Samuel Goldwyn Sound Department.

Merle Oberon and Gary Cooper in The Cowboy and the Lady.

Gary Cooper and Merle Oberon in The Cowboy and the Lady.

Patsy Kelly, Gary Cooper, Mabel Todd, Fuzzy Knight, Walter Brennan and Merle Oberon in The Cowboy and the Lady.

54 WUTHERING HEIGHTS (1939)

Directed by William Wyler; screenplay, Ben Hecht and Charles MacArthur; based on the novel by Emily Bronte; music, Alfred Newman; photographer, Gregg Toland; editor, Daniel Mandell; assistant director, Walter Mayo; art director, James Basevi; costumes, Omar Kiam. Running time, 103 minutes. Released by United Artists. Premiere: Rivoli Theater, New York, 4/13/39

THE CAST:

Cathy Earnshaw, Merle Oberon; *Heathcliff*, Laurence Olivier; *Edgar Linton*, David Niven; *Ellen Dean*, Flora Robson; *Dr. Kenneth*, Donald Crisp; *Isabella Linton*, Geraldine Fitzgerald; *Hindley*, Hugh Williams; *Joseph*, Leo G. Carroll; *Mr. Earnshaw*, Cecil Kellaway; *Judge Linton*, Cecil Humphreys; *Lockwood*, Miles Mander; *Cathy as a Child*, Serita Wooton; *Heathcliff as a child*, Rex Downing; *Hindley as a Child*, Douglas Scott; *Harpsichordist (Frau Johann)*, Mme. Alice Ahlers; *Butler (Robert)*, Romaine Callendar; *Miss Hudkins*, Helena Grant; and Susanne Leach, Tommy Martin, Schuyler Standish, Diane Williams, Frank Benson, Harold Entwistle, Philip Winter, William Stelling, Vernon Downing, Eric Wilton, Major Sam Harris.

The saga of how *Wuthering Heights* came to be made, Goldwyn's greatest film of the Thirties and one of the all-time favorite romantic movies, is another story of wheedling, persuasion, cajoling, off-camera battles—all the classic elements associated with the best of the Goldwyn movies. Primarily it was through the insistence of William Wyler that Goldwyn reluctantly agreed to film this literary masterpiece. Wyler had been made aware by Sylvia Sidney during the filming of *Dead End* that Walter Wanger had had a script written for her and Charles Boyer of the 1850 novel by Emily Bronte. Ben Hecht and Charles MacArthur had fashioned a magnificent screenplay, preserving most of the original Bronte dialogue while simplifying the complicated plot, elimi-

nating the undertones of incest and dispensing with the book's entire second generation. Regardless, Miss Sydney confided to Wyler: "It's not right for me and I'm not going to do it, although Wanger doesn't know that yet, and if you ask me, neither is it right for Boyer."

Wyler managed to get a copy of the script before Goldwyn, who turned it down with the complaint: "I don't like stories with people dying in the end. It's a tragedy." Wyler then used the ploy of suggesting that Jack Warner was interested in it for Bette Davis, about which time Goldwyn began suspecting that it might be a perfect vehicle for Merle Oberon, whose contract he then held. The information, in early 1938, that Goldwyn had acquired the Ben Hecht-Charles MacArthur screenplay caused the London *Times* to editorialize:

A minor sensation has been caused by the announcement the Hollywood film version of "Wuthering Heights" is to be called *Wuthering Heights* . . . The decision [was] made by no less a person than Mr. Sam Goldwyn, a legendary figure who has a fine autocratic way with the English language and chronology and things like that . . . Still, the title is not everything, and its retention does not—witness among many others the conspicuous case of *Bengal Lancer*—at all imply that the film will be even remotely identifiable with the book.

Goldwyn first was convinced by Wyler that an all-British cast was mandatory for *Wuthering Heights,* and then uncharacteristically, allowed Wyler the vital task of casting the film itself—aside, of course, from Merle Oberon and Goldwyn's other contract "Britisher," David Niven. It had been Ben Hecht who suggested Laurence Olivier for the role of Heathcliff, and Wyler, who had seen the actor several times on the stage, but was not everly familiar with his film work, soon had fixed on

Olivier as ideal, overcoming reservations that the actor might seem too polished and handsome for the early scenes as the gypsy stable boy. Several unsuccessful attempts to interest Olivier in the role though, began to frustrate Wyler, and seemingly no amount of Goldwyn money could dispel Olivier's bitter memories of his initial brush with American filmmaking several years earlier. Wyler then tested Robert Newton for the Heathcliff role, but these rushes failed to please Goldwyn.

Wyler again sailed for London with hopes this time of convincing Vivien Leigh, then living discreetly with Olivier, that Olivier must play Heathcliff. The actor, it turned out, actually had been intrigued with the role, but was reluctant to leave Miss Leigh behind in London. Wyler's solution: to have Goldwyn give her the role of Isabella. The part of Cathy, Wyler told her, was out of the question, since Goldwyn was making *Wuthering Heights* solely as a picture for Merle Oberon. Although Vivien Leigh insisted that it was either Cathy or nothing, Wyler tried to appease her with the apocryphal response: "Look, Vivien, you're not known in the States, and you may become a big star, but for the first role in an American film, you'll never do better than Isabella in *Wuthering Heights*." Several months later, David O. Selznick cast her as Scarlett O'Hara.

Reassured by his good friend, Ralph Richardson, that a Goldwyn picture could not hurt his career, Olivier reluctantly sailed for the United States in November, returned to Hollywood against his better judgement, found himself immediately at odds with Wyler as well as Goldwyn, and was miserable during the entire time *Wuthering Heights* was filming. He was said to be particularly resentful that Wyler was channeling all of his directional concern on Merle Oberon, and Olivier soon found himself losing patience not only with Wyler, but with his costar (with whom he had made *The Divorce of Lady X* the previous year). His style of acting, too, failed to enthuse Goldwyn, whose brutally frank comments about threatening to close down the picture if something was not done about Olivier further unnerved the actor. Goldwyn had begun to have nagging suspicions that in Olivier he was not getting value for his money, despite Wyler's assurances that the actor was the best leading man available. Olivier, surprisingly, agreed with Goldwyn about the interpretation he (Olivier) was presenting, realizing that he had not evolved a film-acting technique, and as weeks went on, he found not only a considerable change taking place in his acting, but also, slowly, an increased sympathy for Wyler's theories. (Olivier and Wyler worked together once again on *Carrie* in 1952.)

For *Wuthering Heights,* Goldwyn had sent a camera crew to film the Yorkshire Moors that would then be matched and duplicated at Chatsworth in Ventura County, a bleak stretch some forty miles north of Hollywood. And for the filming itself, he had Merle Oberon's well-manicured hands intentionally chapped and roughened by the makeup department, and, because he did not like her in Regency dresses, Goldwyn had Hecht and MacArthur (and supposedly John Huston) switch the period forty years from 1801 to 1841. When filming was completed, Goldwyn—still upset about making a movie in which his star dies at the end—had a final scene shot (disclaimed by William Wyler), in which the ghosts of Cathy and Heathcliffe are reunited on Peniston Crag, where in life the two had spent so many happy hours.

Wuthering Heights (Goldwyn-style), tells the story in flashback—related by Flora Robson to Miles Mander—of the effect a gypsy boy had on the Earnshaw family when brought to live with them from the streets of Liverpool. Young Hindley hates and resents the intruder, and takes every occasion to humiliate the "gypsy scum," while his sister, Cathy, finds her newly adopted brother Heathcliff, a congenial companion, playing with him on the moors or in their make-believe castle under Peniston Crag. Their happiness comes to a sudden end though, with the death of Mr. Earnshaw, and Hindley, the new master of Wuthering Heights, turns Heathcliff out of the house and makes him a stable boy.

As Cathy and Heathcliff grow older, their childhood affection ripens into love, and while Hindley stays in the house, drinking himself into a daily stupor, the two young lovers roam the moors. Cathy urges Heathcliff to run away from Hindley's cruel tyranny, but Heathcliff loves her too much to leave. One day when an elaborate ball is in progress at the home of the wealthy Lintons nearby, Cathy is bitten by a dog. The Lintons, concerned, treat Heathcliff like a villain and he runs away vowing never to return. Cathy remains as a guest and is introduced to another way of life—gay, charming and polite. She encourages the young and polished Edgar Linton to call on her at Wuthering Heights and a deep friendship develops. Still, though, she is in love with the stable boy, even though he stubbornly refuses to better himself, but after a particularly violent quarrel between the two, Heathcliff, unobserved, overhears Cathy tell the Earnshaw housekeeper, Ellen Dean, that she is considering Edgar's proposal of marriage. Heathcliff rushes from the house in a raging blizzard, and Cathy follows on her horse, but is thrown in the storm. She is found by Edgar the next morning, dangerously ill with pneumonia.

Convalescing at the Linton home, Cathy is made to forget Heathcliff by Edgar's constant attentions. She finally consents to marry Edgar, and for two years they live in peace. Heathcliff's sudden reappearance, returning from South America rich and successful, reawakens old feelings deep in Cathy's soul. Acquiring Wuthering Heights by buying up the drunken Hindley's debts and obligations, Heathcliff learns that Cathy has married and proceeds to avenge himself on her and Edgar by paying attention to Edgar's sister, Isabella. Cathy tries to warn her sister-in-law of Heathcliff's vengeful motive, but Isabella accuses her of being jealous and simply wanting Heathcliff for herself. Instead, Cathy goes to Heathcliff to beg him to give up his plan of revenge, but he remains implacable and shortly afterwards marries Isabella. The new Mrs. Heathcliff soon discovers that Cathy was right. Her husband makes her life miserable by coldly refusing the love she desires. When she hears that Cathy is dying, she is almost glad, hoping that then Heathcliff will turn at last to her. But when Heathcliff learns the news, he rushes to the Lintons and pushes his way to Cathy's room. Dying, Cathy admits that Heathcliff was always the only man she had ever loved. She dies then, as Edgar enters with the doctor, and Heathcliff warns them "Leave her alone—she's mine!," making an impassioned plea to the dead Cathy to haunt him always.

As Ellen finishes her story to Lockwood, a neighbor arrives. He swears that he has seen Heathcliff walking the moors with a woman. The three go to the "castle" under Peniston Crag, and there they find Heathcliff, smiling in death, with his arms thrown wide as if in an embrace.

"It has been brought to the screen with great courage and skill. It is at once a fine film and a masterly translation of a literary classic," Howard Barnes raved in the *New York Herald Tribune*.

There is shrewd showmanship in this Samuel Goldwyn production, but it is also marked by a rare integrity. In a brilliant and balanced collaboration, scenarists, director, cast and technicians have succeeded in holding the film to a straight, tragic line. It is a moving and notable motion picture in its own right and it is also a challenging example of how effective an honest treatment can be . . . The result is a distinguished and engrossing screen tragedy.

Frank S. Nugent wrote in *The New York Times*:

After a long recess, Samuel Goldwyn has returned to serious screen business again . . . It is Goldwyn at his best. William Wyler has directed it magnificently, surcharging even his lighter moments with an atmosphere of suspense and foreboding, keeping his horror-shadowed narrative moving at a steadily accelerating pace, building absorbingly to its tragic climax. It is, unquestionably, one of the most distinguished pictures of the year, one of the finest ever produced by Mr. Goldwyn, and one you should decide to see.

An offbeat review of *Wuthering Heights,* though, was printed in *Variety,* which called the film "more of an artistic success for the carriage trade (and) is heavy fare throughout . . . stark tragedy is vividly etched (but) the tempo is at a slow pace, and it's rather dull material for general audiences."

Wuthering Heights, originally scheduled to premiere at Radio City Music Hall, was switched at the last moment, for reasons unexplained, to the Rivoli. Nevertheless, it opened to great acclaim, made an international star of Laurence Olivier, and was chosen Best Picture of 1939 by the New York Film Critics (over *Gone with the Wind*). The film received eight Academy Award nominations: Best Picture, Best Director, Best Actor, Best Supporting Actress (Geraldine Fitzgerald), Best Screenplay, Best Original Score, Best Cinematography, Best Art/Set Decoration. Only Gregg Toland won an Oscar for his superlative photography.

Despite the reviews and the awards, *Wuthering Heights* was a box office disappointment, and it took several re-issues for Goldwyn even to make his money back. (Following his 1950 re-release of the film, Goldwyn finally realized a small profit.)

In addition to Goldwyn's *Wuthering Heights* (he once interrupted a newsman who had begun: "When Wyler made *Wuthering Heights* . . ." and noted: "*I* made *Wuthering Heights*; Wyler only directed it!"), the Emily Bronte classic has been the source of four other film versions to date and many television plays. A 1920 adaptation, made in Great Britain by A.V. Bramble, starred Milton Rosmer and Anne Trevor as Heathcliff and Cathy. Following the definitive Goldwyn production, Luis Bunuel directed a Mexican version, *Cumbres Borrascosas,* in 1953. The costars were Jorge Mistral and Irasema Dilian. Two years later an Egyptian production, entitled *El Gharib,* established itself as a cinema oddity in an Arabic adaptation of one of the English-speaking world's literary treasures. And in 1970, a second British version was produced by Robert Fuest, starring Timothy Dalton and Anna Calder-Marshall. This adaptation found Cathy dying in childbirth and Heathcliff murdered by Hindley.

Wuthering Heights has emerged as the Goldwyn movie most frequently adapted to television, with at least seven different productions staged. Among the various Heathcliff's have been Charlton Heston, Richard Burton, Richard Boone and Tom Tryon. The most notable TV staging was the one in 1958, which David Susskind produced for DuPont Show of the Week. Richard Burton and Rosemary Harris were the ill-starred lovers, under Daniel Petrie's direction from James Costigan's adaptation. Four years later, BBC presented its own production with Keith Michell, Claire Bloom and David McCallum as Heathcliff, Cathy and Edgar. Peter Sasdy was the director.

Laurence Olivier and Merle Oberon in Wuthering Heights.

Laurence Olivier and Merle Oberon in Wuthering Heights.

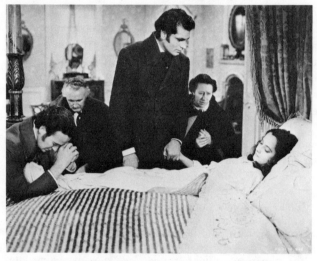

David Niven, Donald Crisp, Laurence Olivier, Flora Robson and Merle Oberon in Wuthering Heights.

Laurence Olivier and Geraldine Fitzgerald in Wuthering Heights.

Laurence Olivier and Merle Oberon in Wuthering Heights.

55 THEY SHALL HAVE MUSIC (1939)

Directed by Archie Mayo; associate producer, Robert Riskin; screenplay, Irmgard von Cube and John Howard Larson*; based on the adaptation by Robert Presnell and Anthony Veiller of the novel by Charles L. Clifford; music director, Alfred Newman; photographer, Gregg Toland; editor, Sherman Todd; assistant director, Walter Mayo; art director, James Basevi. Running time, 101 minutes. Released by United Artists. Premiere: Rivoli Theater, New York, 7/25/39. (Reissued in 1945 as *Ragged Angels.*)
* sometimes credited to Jo Swerling

THE CAST:

Himself, Jascha Heifetz; *Peter McCarthy,* Joel McCrea; *Ann Lawson,* Andrea Leeds; *Professor Lawson,* Walter Brennan; *Frankie,* Gene Reynolds; *Dominick,* Terry Kilburn; *Mr. Flower,* Porter Hall; *Willie,* Tommy Kelly; *Fever Jones,* Chuck Stubbs; *Rocks Mulligan,* Walter Tetley; *Betty,* Jacqueline Nash (Gale Sherwood); *Susie,* Mary Ruth; *Ed Miller,* Arthur Hohl; *Jane Miller,* Marjorie Main; *Heifetz's Manager,* Paul Harvey; *Menken,* John St. Polis; *Davis,* Alex Schonberg; *Mr. Morgan,* Frank Jaquet; *Mr. Wallace,* Perry Ivins; *Inspector Johnson,* Paul Stanton; *Heifetz's Butler,* Charles Coleman; *Pianist,* Dolly Loehr (Diana Lynn); and Dorothy Christie, Alan Edwards, John Kelly, Marjorie Wood, Emory Parnell, Arthur Aylsworth, John Hamilton, Roger Imhof, J. Farrell MacDonald, Wade Boteler, James Flavin, Emmett Vogan, Virginia Brissac, Effie Anderson, Stanley Blystone, Wyndham Standing, Jessie Arnold, Lee Phelps, Ethan Laidlaw, and the Peter Meremblum California Junior Symphony Orchestra.

Goldwyn's foremost contribution to cinema was the monumental effort he exerted to bring culture to the masses—either despite or because of his own limited formal education. His screen versions of literary classics (*Arrowsmith, Nana, Dodsworth, Wuthering Heights*) and important plays (*Street Scene, The Children's Hour* [*These Three*], *Dead End,* and later, *The Little Foxes*) demonstrated his courage in taking financial risks at the box office. So, too, did his projects involving serious music,

beginning in 1938 with *The Goldwyn Follies,* tempering Verdi and Tchaikovsky with Gershwin and Vernon Duke, and ending two decades later with *Porgy and Bess.* Between these two came the movie that was to be known simply as "that Heifetz film," although wags were fond of repeating *New York Post* critic Archer Winston's terse description: "The Dead End Kids in Music School".

In his supreme position in the industry, Goldwyn long had been a major patron of the arts and was on intimate terms with the towering figures in the various creative fields. One such giant was Jascha Heifetz, the internationally renowned violinist, who allowed himself to be coaxed by Goldwyn (circa 1937) into appearing before the motion picture camera. Goldwyn's widely publicized coup led to a barrage of nagging questions, not the least being "What will Heifetz do?" Two years would elapse before Goldwyn could supply an answer, for the producer apparently had not the faintest idea, when inveigling a "yes" from the maestro, how to spotlight Heifetz in a movie.

During this time span, however, Goldwyn managed to inspire two of his writing staff, Irmgard von Cube (subsequently credited with the "original story") and John Howard Larson (listed on screen as author of the scenario), to whip up a four-handkerchief screen tale that would at once touch the moviegoers' hearts and caress their ears. What emerged was a sentimental drama of a dedicated music teacher, striving to keep solvent his school for encouraging and developing the artistic talents of socially deprived children, one of whom, a prospective juvenile delinquent, discovers his latent musical appreciation aroused when finding a stray ticket to Carnegie Hall on the sidewalk, he hears the glorious tones of Jascha Heifetz.

While the Goldwyn writers were forging a script at

their typewriters though, Heifetz was becoming increasingly impatient, and because of endless delays in the film schedule, had been forced to juggle his countless concert dates. Unable to hold off the violinist any longer, Goldwyn brought him to Hollywood despite the absence of a completed script, and under the guidance of Archie Mayo (who previously was to have directed *The Goldwyn Follies*), Heifetz spent four weeks filming and recording his music (five solo numbers), for which Goldwyn paid him $70,000.

A Goldwyn-approved script was finally delivered to the set in the fall of 1938, and cameras began to roll on the production that *Variety* reported to be first *Untitled Jascha Heifetz Picture* and several weeks later, *The Restless Age* with Adolphe Menjou, Sigrid Gurie and Joel McCrea, costarring with Heifetz. Walter Brennan replaced Menjou as the kindly old teacher who gives free music lessons to underprivileged kids; Joel McCrea and Margot Stevenson (soon replaced by Andrea Leeds) were in for romantic interest; and several *Dead End* types, led by Gene Reynolds (who grew up to become the producer of TV's M*A*S*H), took roles as the slum kids who become interested in music. Another of the youngsters in the film was a talented young pianist, Dolly Leohr, who offered a sparkling version of Chopin's "Minute Waltz." She later found fame as Diana Lynn. So, too, did Gale Sherwood who in the 1950s became Nelson Eddy's nightclub partner, Here, under her real name, Jacqueline Nash, she displayed extraordinary range singing arias from several operas.

Not long after production commenced, the project was retitled *Angels Make Music,* then *Music School,* and finally *They Shall Have Music.* (Several years after its initial release, the film became known as *Ragged Angels*—and Heifetz's participation was deemphasized.)

Goldwyn learned, in mid-production, that Heifetz would again be needed for a few vital scenes, including one at the climax, with juvenile orchestra (portrayed admirably by the Peter Meremblum California Junior Symphony Orchestra). Heifetz was implored to try to rearrange his own schedule and, for an additional $50,000, came back to Hollywood. While Archie Mayo was working with the stars in the dramatic scenes, William Wyler was called in to film the concert finale with Heifetz, as well as the playing of Saint-Saens' "Rondo Capricioso," Tchaikovsky's "Melodie," the Dinicu-Heifetz "Hora staccato," and the last movement of Mendelssohn's "Concerto in E-minor."

The plot of *They Shall Have Music* revolves around a young juvenile delinquent, on his way to reform school, who stumbles into a settlement-type music institution about to go under, and with the help of some youth-gang pals, persuades Jascha Heifetz (given sole billing above the title) to help keep the center alive by giving a concert there. "A song for the millions who are hungry for great music," the Goldwyn ad campaign boasted, "it sings the poignant story of a boy, a girl and a dog . . . of kids with dirty face and hungry hearts!" Realizing, of course, that serious music offers a rather specialized appeal, Goldwyn had an alternate campaign prepared for what *Variety* has termed "the yahoo trade." In these ads, instead of a huge close-up of Heifetz with his violin tucked under his chin, a photo of an angry woman brandishing a rolling pin was substituted, along with these exclamatory statements:

> See the battle of the century . . . fifty fighting mothers who showed the cops that Al Capone was a sissy compared to them! See an entire city thrown into turmoil when a $75,000 Stradivarius was stolen! See the latest production by Hollywood's master showman, Samuel Goldwyn, that surpasses the thrills of *The Hurricane,* the drama of *Dead End,* the emotions of *Stella Dallas!*

And while the aforementioned irate mother was screaming: "No cop, no sheriff, no hard-boiled truckdriver is strong enough to get by us! Bring on your tear gas! Our kids will play tonight . . . or else!," dignified Jascha Heifetz was nowhere to be found on the ads and his name was cleverly hidden near the bottom—after those of his fellow stars.

The reviewer for *Variety* wrote that the film is "a natural for the musically minded" and a "combination of excellent script and highlight direction by Archio Mayo lifts the picture's entertaining factors beyond its restrictive appeal. Mayo's direction is zestful and human, and still dramatically tempoed." The *Variety* appraisal of Heifetz' film debut:

> (He) is restrained from attempting a lengthy acting portrayal in his initial screen appearance and he makes no pretense of being an actor, but when he faces the camera to start a number, his confidence in control of his instrument is easily discernible.

The critic for *Time Magazine* called the film

> a triumphant answer to the current Hollywood theory that it is impossible to make a good movie about a great musical celebrity . . . (and) takes Heifetz and his fame for granted, and never catches him with a movie queen instead of a Stradivarius in his arms.

In the *New York Herald Tribune,* Howard Barnes observed that

> (it is) a notable event in the screen's wooing of a rival muse. Samuel Goldwyn's production does an intriguing job of examining musical education in this country . . . (but) I think that a better plot could have been devised than that which you will find in *They Shall Have Music.*

Barnes concluded:

Even with Archie Mayo's excellent direction, the Heifetz film leaves a good deal to be desired as straight entertainment . . . a conventional motion picture plot seems pretty silly support for what would have been an extraordinary musical document without it,

The New York Times notice by critic B.R. Crisler was yanked after the paper's first edition and replaced by a less astringent review by Bosley Crowther, the then third-string film critic. The Crisler critique, ordered withdrawn personally by publisher Arthur Sulzberger (who had attended the film's premiere with his close friend, Jascha Heifetz), said that

In the case of *They Shall Have Music*, which marks the screen debut of Jascha Heifetz, and has been announced as Opus I in the musical works of Mr. Samuel Goldwyn, the temptation is to write about the music—which is, of course, superb—and to skip lightly over the movie with some graceful side remark, such as "All is not Goldwyn that glistens" . . . while emphasizing one's delights with (the music), should one go on to mention casually that the dramatic accompaniment is purely synthetic? When one can obtain such music for the price of a movie admission, would it not be rude to insist that the characters are even more fictitious than the foreword would lead one to believe?

In its place in later editions could be found a more rev-

erent Crowther appraisal, commenting that "Mr. Heifetz plays the violin, that's all. He plays it rapturously and with surpassing brilliance—such a quality and abundance of magnificent fiddling as has never before been heard from a screen." With more temperence, Crowther then noted:

It is a sort of story which is known as a "tear-jerker"—a direct assault upon the soft spots in all doting parents and elder folk. It is made more so by music, and will probobly be very popular. A good cast of actors supports Mr. Heifetz, who is woefully deficient in the few brief excursions he makes in that department—just enough to keep the story together.

Heifetz' subsequent screen appearances were limited to non-acting roles in musical films such as *Carnegie Hall* and *Of Men and Music*. And for *They Shall Have Music*, Alfred Newman received an Academy Award nomination for his scoring. He also was nominated in the same category that year for his work on *The Hunchback of Notre Dame*, for which Goldwyn had lent him to RKO, and for the best original score for both Goldwyn's *Wuthering Heights* and Zanuck's *The Rains Came*, the latter on loan to 20th Century-Fox where Newman was to become music director following his departure from the Goldwyn Studios.

Stanley Blystone, Jascha Heifetz and Paul Harvey in They Shall Have Music.

Walter Brennan, Andrea Leeds and Joel McCrea in
They Shall Have Music.

Jascha Heifetz, Peter Meremblum and Walter Brennan
in They Shall Have Music.

56 THE REAL GLORY (1939)

Directed by Henry Hathaway; associate producer, Robert Riskin; screenplay, Robert R. Presnell and Jo Swerling; based on the novel by Charles L. Clifford; music, Alfred Newman; photographer, Rudolph Maté; editor, Daniel Mandell; assistant director, Eddie Bernoudy; art director, James Basevi; costumes, Jeanne Beakhurst. Running time, 96 minutes. Released by United Artists. Premiere: Rivoli Theater, New York, 9/15/39

THE CAST:

Dr. Bill Canavan, Gary Cooper; *Lt. McCool*, David Niven; *Linda Hartley*, Andrea Leeds; *Capt. Steve Hartley*, Reginald Owen; *Lt. Swede Larson*, Broderick Crawford; *Mabel Manning*, Kay Johnson; *Capt. George Manning*, Russell Hicks; *Col. Hatch*, Roy Gordon; *Miguel*, Benny Inocencio; *Datu*, Vladimir Sokoloff; *Lt. Yabo*, Rudy Robles; *General*, Henry Kolker; *Alipang*, Tetsu Komai; *Mrs. Yabo*, Elvira Rios; *Top Sergeant*, Luke 'Chan; *Army Captain*, Elmo Lincoln; *Moro Priest*, John Villasin; and Charles Stevens, Karen Sorrell, Soledad Jimenez, Lucio Villegas, Nick Shaid, Kam Tong, Martin Wilkins, Bob Naihe, Satini Puailoa, George Kaluno, Caiyu Ambol, Kalu Sonkur Sr.

The Real Glory represents an atypical Goldwyn production—one of the very few action films to come from the famed moviemaker's studios. To direct this rip-roaring tale based on the 1906 Philippine uprising against the Moros, Goldwyn latched onto Henry Hathaway, on his way to a staff job at 20th Century-Fox after completing a lengthy stay at Paramount. Goldwyn already had cast Gary Cooper in the leading role which, under Hathaway's direction, the actor easily turned into a tour-de-force. This was Hathaway's third consecutive Cooper film, following *The Lives of a Bengal Lancer* and *Peter Ibbetson*.

Goldwyn's stress on both action and entertainment in *The Real Glory* did not quite overshadow the elements of the film which, in the minds of several knowledgable critics of the day, smacked of jingoism and stirred on a

minor scale the type of controversy with which Goldwyn later was faced when he made *The North Star*. In fact, several scenes of *The Real Glory* that hinted at glorification of American militarism and of the military itself were deleted at the request of Philippine President Manuel Quezon. And because of the film's flag-waving, a scheduled reissue of it in 1942, under the title *A Yank in the Philippines,* was shelved as being too controversial by the war department (the Philippine Moros had since become our wartime allies).

Strictly as entertainment, *The Real Glory* is a ripsnorter that finds stalwart Gary Cooper defending the fort against Moros catapulting from trees over a stockade, fighting a cholera epidemic, slogging through a trap-filled jungle, fending off a bloodcurdling Moro attack, and saving the tiny American garrison and the local village from a raging flood. There is also time, of course, to romance the daughter of his commanding officer.

Goldwyn's $2 million epic resulted from a screenplay of Charles L. Clifford's novel, worked on in 1938 by Charles Bennett and in 1939 by Gene Fowler, with credit finally being shared by Robert R. Presnell and Jo Swerling. "Always outnumbered . . . never outfought!" was the tag line used to sell the film, which Goldwyn's advertising department called on the ads, "One of the most stirring dramas of love and courage ever brought to the screen!"

Its plot concerns the situation created when the American forces evacuate the Philippines, leaving a small cadre of officers to train the independence-minded natives while helping them fight off forays by the hostile Moros. Dr. Bill Canavan, along with Lieutenants McCool and Larson, professional soldiers of fortune, manage to keep the beleagured white settlement calm under its martinet commander, Captain George Manning. In the days before Manning is to leave for the States, his wife arrives with Linda Hartley, the daughter of Manning's executive officer. At a party at the officers' club, Manning is hacked to death by one of the local terrorists as his wife watches in horror, and Captain Hartley immediately assumes command. Hartley, trying to keep secret his increasing blindness, attempts to rally the officers behind him, but his continuing vacillation allows Canavan more latitude to pursue his own humanitarian work among the natives, and vie with debonair Lieutenant McCool for Linda Hartley's attentions.

When Canavan disobeys orders by taking Miguel, a Moro youngster he has befriended, into the hills to reconnoiter the hostile tribes and witnesses the mystic rites that are to preface a holy war, he is placed under arrest. Meanwhile, the Moros dam the stream, which is the compound's water supply. When a cholera epidemic breaks out, Canavan is released, and with the help of Linda, sets about to put down the eqidemic. Once the disease is curbed, Canavan goes out after Captain Hartley and his men to blow up the dam, as Hartley's blindness finally overcomes him. Canavan succeeds in his mission and rides the raging waters back to the fort, now under siege by the Moros. Following a pitched battle, Canavan and Hartley's men are victorious, and the doctor proposes to Linda, asking her to return with him to Oklahoma where he plans to practice medicine.

In its view of the film, *Life Magazine* noted: "The picture is less a personal triumph for Gary Cooper than for the professional stunt men, headless dummies and repaint experts." *Time* referred to the movie as "The Philippine 'Birth of a Nation,'" and called *The Real Glory* "one of the finest action pictures since Cooper and director Hathaway once before pooled their talents in *Lives of a Bengal Lancer.*"

Frank Nugent's decision, in *The New York Times,* was that

it's a good story, false or true, and it has been made into a whopping adventure film with more action, suspense and melodrama than even a juramentado could shake his bolo at . . . Henry Hathaway directs with all the bugles blowing, the drums rolling and a tall man like Gary Cooper on a parapet heaving sticks of dynamite down on the attackers.

In agreement was Howard Barnes, who said:

Gary Cooper has had some fat roles in his time, but none to compare with that in *The Real Glory* . . . he does a first rate job with the assignment. Aided by some cunningly melodramatic suspense in Henry Hathaway's direction, he makes *The Real Glory* an exciting variation on the old "here come the Marines" formula . . . essentially, it is a cowboy and Indian show, with Cooper ideally suited to his part.

Critic Barnes wrapped up his review by noting: "A Goldwyn production is always handsome and this is no exception. It may be more Wild West showmanship than a faithful historical reconstruction, but it is fun most of the time."

With the conclusion of *The Real Glory,* Samuel Goldwyn lost another leading lady with the departure of Andrea Leeds from the fold. She had done four Goldwyn films and had turned down a role in at least one other, and like those before her who owed their film careers (or resurrection of same) to Goldwyn—Ronald Colman excepted—she left the screen when her star began to sputter after only two further roles.

Broderick Crawford, Andrea Leeds, Gary Cooper and David Niven in The Real Glory.

Gary Cooper and David Niven in The Real Glory.

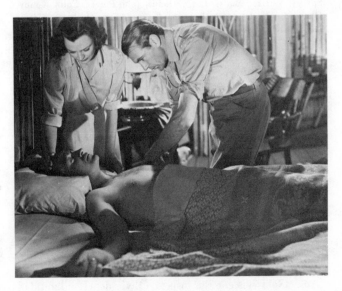

Andrea Leeds and Gary Cooper tend to David Niven in
The Real Glory.

57 RAFFLES (1939)

Directed by Sam Wood; screenplay by John van Druten and Sidney Howard; based on the novel *The Amateur Cracksman* by E.W. Hornung; music, Victor Young; photographer, Gregg Toland; editor, Sherman Todd; assistant director, Walter Mayo; art director, James Basevi; costumes, Travis Banton. Running time, 71 minutes. Released by United Artists. Premiere: Roxy Theater, New York, 1/12/40

THE CAST:
A.J. Raffles, David Niven; *Gwen Manders,* Olivia de Havilland; *Lady Kitty Melrose,* Dame May Whitty; *Mackenzie,* Dudley Digges; *Bunny Manders,* Douglas Walton; *Lord George Melrose,* Lionel Pape; *Barraclough,* E.E. Clive; *Harry Crawshay,* Peter Godfrey; *Maud Holden,* Margaret Seddon; *Bingham,* Gilbert Emery; *Wilson,* Hilda Plowright; *Butler,* Vesey O'Davoren; *Footman,* George Cathrey; *Merton,* Keith Hitchcock; *Umpire,* Forrester Harvey; *Cabbie,* James Finlayson; *School Mistress,* Elspeth Dudgeon; and Eric Wilton, George Atkinson, Frank Baker, Charles Coleman, Olaf Hytten, Douglas Gordon, David Thursby, Charles Irwin, John Graham Spacey, Wilfred Lucas, Larry Dodds, John Power, Colin Kenny, David Clyde, Leyland Hodgson, Harry Allen, Herbert Clifton, George Kirby, Gibson Gowland.

In 1939, Goldwyn decided to remake *Raffles* with his new version of Ronald Colman in the person of David Niven, who would be performing in his first starring role. Goldwyn asked John Van Druten (in the Goldwyn tradition of hiring eminent authors to churn out scenarios) to update the original Sidney Howard screenplay that had served Ronald Colman so well, nine years earlier. Then Goldwyn brought in none less than F. Scott Fitzgerald to "punch up" Van Druten's work, while at the same time, he (Goldwyn) went on a talent borrowing spree for the project. From MGM, he obtained the services of Sam Wood to direct (and with *Raffles,* Wood came into his own as a major craftsman), and from Warner Bros., Goldwyn got the loan of Olivia de Havilland (in

exchange for the services of his favorite "pawn," Joel McCrea). Before he could proceed with his plans for stardom for Niven, he was obliged to come to new contract terms with the already journeyman English actor. While negotiating with Niven's agent, Leland Hayward though, Goldwyn made certain that Niven was made aware of another young actor who was having publicity shots made in *Raffles* costumes; Dana Andrews (discovered by Goldwyn in 1937 at the Pasedena Playhouse and put under contract at $150 weekly without receiving a role for nearly three years!).

The new version of *Raffles* emerges as a virtual scene-for-scene updating of the earlier Goldwyn comedy/thriller. For relevancy, in one instance, Inspector Mackenzie and his Scotland Yard associate, Bingham, are shown watching A.J. Raffles in a televised cricket match (certainly one of the very early glimpses of television being viewed as an entertainment medium in films). Raffles, himself, is played with the roguish flippancy in which David Niven has come to excel, rather than with the debonair, man-about-town charm with which Ronald Colman had approached his game of one-upmanship with Inspector Mackenzie. The game, of course, remains the same: Raffles, relishing the chase by pulling off art thefts and then returning the ill-gotten gains to Scotland Yard through offbeat intermediaries, decides to help a debt-ridden school chum by wangling an invitation to the weekend soireé being sponsored by the latter's wealthy uncle and aunt, and then making off with the old lady's emerald necklace. The plan is to have his friend redeem the stolen jewelry for the reward that must certainly be offered. Raffles though, runs into a petty thief who also has an eye, as well as a light finger on the emeralds.

While deftly portraying the celebrated cricketer/second-story man with his keenly developed *joie de vivre,*

Niven is hard-pressed to keep *Raffles* from being stolen completely by Dudley Digges, as the candy-munching Inspector Mackenzie, and Dame May Whitty, in another of her delightful dowager impersonations. Olivia de Havilland (whose photo, rather than Niven's, accompanied the Howard Barnes review in the *New York Herald Tribune*), playing the lady who hopes to reform Raffles, is decorative in what obviously was a rest period following the frantic schedules she was obliged to observe during the recently completed filming of *Gone with the Wind*. *GWTW* also had taken its toll on director Sam Wood, who worked almost simultaneously on *Raffles*, forcing him finally to hand over the reins of the Goldwyn picture to, according to David Niven, "a gentle and helpful Willie Wyler," who directed the final few scenes.

The ads for *Raffles* ingeniously worked in plugs for four other Goldwyn films, announcing, in all the modesty the professionals in the studio's advertising department could muster: "SAMUEL GOLDWYN—producer of the prizewinning picture, *Wuthering Heights*—presents RAFFLES." And below the title, ahead of the names of the stars: "Another fiction masterpiece filmed by the man who made *Hurricane, Stella Dallas* and *The Real Glory!*"

Reviewing the new *Raffles*, Frank Nugent wrote in *The New York Times*:

(It) goes its way blithely and entertainingly and never once betrays its age by creaking at the plot joints. Put that down primarily to Mr. Niven's credit. His Raffles is one of the nicest tributes to burglary we have seen in many a year. The calling cards he leaves in looted safes, the little notes and tokens he sends to the Yard always are respectful in tone, unmarred by the bravado that has seemed the greatest weakness of Professor Moriarty and the Cisco Kid . . . Mr. Niven makes the game worth playing and the film worth seeing. Nothing outstanding, of course, but pleasant while it lasts, which isn't too long.

Time Magazine figured that:

Directed by Sam Wood with a creepy feeling for suspense, the present *Raffles* outdoes all predecessors by containing not only its burglarious namesakes, but (in Dudley Digges and Dame May Whitty) two of the most accomplished scene-stealers ever brought together in one picture.

And Howard Barnes said:

With his usual insistence upon what might roughly be termed quality, the producer has seen to it that this resurrection of a former success has been given expert ministrations . . . (the cast members) interpret leading roles artfully, while Sam Wood has staged the offering meticulously. In spite of these virtues, I would call the photoplay definitely old hat. As a matter of fact, the very care which has been lavished on the film calls attention to its dated subject matter . . . the new version is a tedious screen drama, dissipating what suspense and excitement are inherent in the subject matter in the mannered gestures of drawing room comedy and plot cliches which used to be part of Scotland Yard melodramas nearly a decade ago.

In *Variety's* opinion, "the present version lacks the sparkle and good humor of the original with Colman . . . Niven is adequate as Raffles, with Dudley Digges providing interesting, amusing and important characterization as the inspector." The paper then noted that

Raffles has been given Class A production values throughout (and) has moments of interest and suspense, but overall is able to generate only slight reaction for a familiar yarn. Too many copies have been struck off from the original in the past decade to provide sponteneity and sustain interest.

In his autobiography, Niven noted: "We finished shooting on 1 September (1939). The picture looked good and Goldwyn was delighted. My contract was munificent. Goldwyn's plans for me were most exciting and all this had happened in less than four years." On 3 September Britain declared war on Germany, and Niven returned to England to rejoin the army, serving for the next six years. He remained, for the duration, under contract to Goldwyn, but would star, after the war, in only two further Goldwyn films.

Raffles itself was to have marked the end of Goldwyn's association with United Artists. In May 1939 he had begun a court fight against Alexander Korda, Mary Pickford, Douglas Fairbanks and Charles Chaplin (he had resented having to share profits with the latter three who had become relatively inactive), asking that they either free him of partnership or sell him complete control of United Artists. Goldwyn already had concluded an agreement to release his future films, beginning with *The Westerner*, through Warner Bros. The court test, though, went against Goldwyn, and United Artists took legal action to prevent the distribution of Goldwyn films by other studios.

Goldwyn's plea to his United Artists partners to "include me out" finally was settled in February 1941, with the company buying back his stock for $300,000, approximately half of what Goldwyn then claimed it was worth.

Olivia de Havilland and David Niven in Raffles.

Dame May Whitty, Olivia de Havilland, David Niven and Lionel Pape in Raffles.

David Niven in Raffles.

Peter Godfrey and David Niven in Raffles.

58 THE WESTERNER (1940)

Directed by William Wyler; screenplay by Jo Swerling and Niven Busch; based on a story by Stuart N. Lake; music, Dmitri Tiomkin; photographer, Gregg Toland; editor, Daniel Mandell; assistant director, Walter Mayo; art director, James Basevi; costumes, Irene Saltern. Running time, 99 minutes. Released by United Artists. Premiere: Fort Worth, Texas, 9/19/40. New York premiere: Radio City Music Hall, 10/24/40

THE CAST:
Cole Hardin, Gary Cooper; *Judge Roy Bean*, Walter Brennan; *Jane–Ellen Mathews*, Doris Davenport; *Caliphet Mathews*, Fred Stone; *Chickenfoot*, Paul Hurst; *Southeast*, Chill Wills; *Lily Langtry*, Lilian Bond; *Mort Burrow*, Charles Halton; *Shad Wilkins*, Trevor Bardette; *Langtry's Maid*, Connie Leon; *Langtry's Manager*, Charles Coleman; *Ticket Man*, Lew Kelly; *Sheriff at Fort Davis*, Stanley Andrews; *Wade Harper*, Forrest Tucker*; *King Evans*, Tom Tyler; *Mr. Dixon*, Arthur Aylsworth; *Teresita*, Lupita Tovar; *Juan Gomez*, Julian Rivero; *Bart Cobble*, Dana Andrews*; *Eph Stringer*, Roger Gray; *Bantry*, Jack Pennick; *Bean's Henchmen*, Bill Steele, Blackjack Ward, Jim Corey, Buck Moulton, Ted Wells, Joe De La Cruz, Frank Cordell; *Homesteaders*, Philip Connor, Capt. C.E. Anderson, Art Mix, William Gillis, Buck Connor, Dan Borzage, Speed Hanson, Gertrude Bennett, Miriam Sherwin, Helen Foster, Arrabella Rousseau; and Heinie Conklin, Hank Bell, Lucien Littlefield, Corbet Morris, Phil Tead, Bill Bauman, Henry Roquemore.
* in screen debut

Several elements combined to make *The Westerner* one of the screen's classic studies of the American frontier. First, naturally, was the prestige of the Goldwyn name (this was the producer's second and last western). Then there was the articulate direction of William Wyler, working on *his* second (feature-length) western—he had made twenty-seven silent two and five-reelers for Universal in the 1920s and later directed the epic *The Big Country*. Gregg Toland's creative photography provided another facet, and most importantly, the matchless interacting between Gary Cooper and Walter Brennan lent the film its final boost to cinema permanency. Why *The Westerner,* fine as it is, has lasted is open to speculation. Curiously actionless, the movie wavers between being a character study of Judge Roy Bean; the tale of a saddle tramp drifting through the Old West; the classic conflict between homesteaders and cattlemen; and the traditional oater filled, as Bosley Crowther described it, "with spectacular crop-burnings and squatter oustings."

Cooper himself had to be convinced by Wyler that his part in the film might not be the greatest, but the point of the story was that the strange (and light-hearted) comradeship between the laconic cowpoke and the ruthless judge affected all that surrounded them. Admitting that the film belonged to Walter Brennan, as the feisty old judge who dispensed his unique brand of law from behind the bar of his saloon in Vinegaroon, Texas in the early 1880s, Cooper said: "I couldn't figure for the life of me why they needed me for this picture. I had a very minor part that didn't require any special effort. All the character had to do was exchange a few shots with the judge in the dramatic moment of the film." What the modest Cooper did not say was that Goldwyn needed him to carry the film as a "name" as not only the foremost action star of the day, but also the highest paid actor in America (and the nation's top taxpayer in 1939-40).

Scenarists Jo Swerling and Niven Busch, using an original story by Stuart N. Lake, played rather loosely with the judge's biography, up to and including the apocryphal gunfight at the climax when the judge bites the dust. (In the version of the Judge Roy Bean legend that starred Paul Newman thirty-two years later, Bean dies a semi-hero, never having met Lily Langtry, the lady he was said to have idolized.) Surrounding the real-life figures of Roy Bean and Lily Langtry were the fictional characters who make up the good guys and the bad guys in *The Westerner*. Into their midst comes Cole Hardin, a fictitious drifter accused of horse thieving and sentenced to hang by Judge Bean. While the "jury" was deliberating though, Cole had discovered Bean's idolatry of Lily Langtry, the famed English actress. When Cole confides to Bean that he knows Lily well, the judge arranges to have the stranger paroled so that he can obtain a lock of Lily's hair.

The two strike up a shaky friendship, and Cole becomes a sort of mediator between the homesteaders, led by Caliphet Mathews, and Bean's cattlemen, after convincing the judge to declare peace between the factions. Falling in love with Caliphet's daughter, Jane-Ellen, Cole finally declares himself on the side of the settlers, and Bean prepares to have him arrested once again, when he remembers the lock of hair Cole had promised to obtain. When Cole finally turns over the prize—a tress cut from Jane-Ellen's head—he discovers that all bets are off as, a few nights later, Bean's men start burning the settlers' crops and homes and kill Jane-Ellen's father. Cole goes gunning for the judge and learns that Bean has gone to nearby Fort Davis to see Lily Langtry, buying out the entire theater. Seated in the front row of the empty house as the curtain goes up, following Lily's overture, Bean is stunned to find Cole facing him with both guns drawn. The two former friends shoot it out in the gaslit theater, with Cole carrying the mortally wounded Bean to "Jersey Lily" for one glimpse before he dies.

In real life, Judge Roy Bean, who had named his Texas town after Lily Langtry, saw her only once, during her stopover at San Antonio in the midst of her American tour in the spring of 1888. Bean died, presumably in bed in 1903, well into his eighties, several months before the actress journeyed to Langtry, Texas, as just another tourist intrigued by the legend of Judge Roy Bean.

For the role of Jane-Ellen, William Wyler had tried to cajole Goldwyn into signing his (Wyler's) actress wife, Margaret Tallichet. Instead, Goldwyn forced on him an ex-Goldwyn Girl, Doris Davenport, who had been elevated in midpicture to ingenue status in Eddie Cantor's *Kid Millions*. (She then did several showgirl parts, changed her name to Doris Jordon to become an RKO starlet, and was rediscovered after testing—as did Wyler's wife—for the Scarlett O'Hara role in *Gone with the Wind*.) Appalled that "she couldn't act for beans," Wyler grudgingly accepted the Goldwyn dictum that Doris Davenport was to be Jane-Ellen. The actress subsequently made just one more film, *Behind the News*, a Republic programmer.

The Westerner also introduced to the screen two other Goldwyn discoveries: twenty-nine year old Dana Andrews (who had been drawing a salary from Goldwyn for nearly three years), and Forrest Tucker, then twenty-five. Andrews was to become, during the war years, one of the screen's few available leading men, alternating assignments between Goldwyn and Darryl F. Zanuck.

Virtually every critic who reviewed *The Westerner* singled out the performance given by Walter Brennan as the judge, for which he became the first actor ever to win three Academy Awards (for supporting performances). John Beaufort wrote in the *Christian Science Monitor*:

Notwithstanding an excellent performance by Gary Cooper, *The Westerner* is Walter Brennan's picture . . . (although) Mr. Cooper's Hardin is excellently done in this actor's easy, laconic style. Mr. Cooper is an economical player who can accomplish much with a flicker of an expression.

Life Magazine observed:

In *The Westerner*, Samuel Goldwyn had perfect material for another pretentious epic of the West. Instead, he produced something much rarer and much harder: a real character study that may go down in movie history as a comedy classic. Expertly acted by Walter Brennan, Bean is a paradoxical renegade, big-hearted and cruel, weak and indomitable.

Bosley Crowther noted that

The Westerner might have been a bang-up, dandy film. We are sorry to say it isn't . . . (although) there are things about it that are excellent. Mr. Brennan is one of them. His clean-cut characterization of the leather-skinned but sentimental judge is one of the finest exhibits of acting seen on the screen in some time. And Mr. Cooper, too, is up to his usual standard of understated perfection.

Crowther's New York colleague, Howard Barnes, also had several reservations about the film.

Samuel Goldwyn has lavished his usual high production polish on *The Westerner*, but it hasn't resulted in a particularly entertaining show. Screen horse opera needs action more than atmosphere to be effective . . . Its chief distinction is the presence of Gary Cooper in the title role. Even he has a hard time with a continuity which only flares fitfully with excitement or suspense.

Barnes then said: "It is probably the fault of the narrative that *The Westerner* is only sporadically entertaining. At the same time, William Wyler hasn't helped matters appreciably in his staging."

In its view of Wyler's work, *The Hollywood Reporter* wrote: "Wyler's direction is forceful and salty. He has his principals do one remarkable thing never before seen, but often looked for by this reviewer—they stop to reload their weapons after the chambers have been emptied in an exchange of shots."

Following completion of *The Westerner*, which, finally, *was* Goldwyn's last movie to be released through United Artists, the producer brought in Alfred Newman to completely rewite the Dmitri Tiomkin score (although Newman contractually could not accept screen credit). This delayed the film's release from February to September of 1940. At Oscar time, in addition to the Best Supporting Actor award accepted by Brennan, James Basevi received a nomination for his Art/Set Decoration and Stuart Lake was nominated for his Original Story.

Walter Brennan and Gary Cooper in The Westerner.

Gary Cooper, Forrest Tucker, Doris Davenport and Fred Stone in The Westerner.

Gary Cooper, Doris Davenport and Walter Brennan in
The Westerner.

Walter Brennan, Gary Cooper and Lilian Bond in The
Westerner.

59 THE LITTLE FOXES (1941)

Directed by William Wyler; screenplay, Lillian Hellman; based on her play; additional dialogue by Dorothy Parker, Alan Campbell and Arthur Kober; music, Meredith Willson; photographer, Gregg Toland; editor, Daniel Mandell; assistant director, William Tummel; art director, Stephen Goosson; costumes, Orry-Kelly. Running time, 116 minutes. Released by RKO Pictures. Premiere: Radio City Music Hall, New York, 8/21/41

THE CAST:
Regina Hubbard Giddens, Bette Davis; *Horace Giddens,* Herbert Marshall; *Alexandra Giddens,* Teresa Wright#; *David Hewitt,* Richard Carlson; *Birdie Hubbard,* Patricia Collinge*; *Leo Hubbard,* Dan Duryea*#; *Ben Hubbard,* Charles Dingle*; *Oscar Hubbard,* Carl Benton Reid*; *Cal,* John Marriott*; *Addie,* Jessica Grayson; *William Marshall,* Russell Hicks; *Sam Manders,* Lucien Littlefield; *Lucy Hewitt,* Virginia Brissac; *Julia,* Terry Nibert; *Simon,* Charles R. Moore; *Hotel Manager,* Alan Bridge; and Kenny Washington, Henry "Hot Shot" Thomas, Lew Kelly, Hooper Atchley, Henry Roquemore.
in screen debut
* in original Broadway production

"I always cast my pictures, got the script polished to perfection, then hired the director," Goldwyn once said. "I'd give him one month to make any suggestions he wanted, and then we'd go to work." Except, seemingly, when the director was William Wyler, whose ongoing battles with Goldwyn resulted, interestingly, in films of even higher quality than Goldwyn himself was accustomed to producing.

In this case, it was *The Little Foxes,* that ranks next to Goldwyn's later *The Best Years of Our Lives* (also directed by Wyler) for perfection. Its filming followed the now established crisis pattern that somehow resulted in excellence. Not, of course, because the property was wanting. In addition to the almost daily producer/director clashes were those between director and leading lady, despite Bette Davis' contention that Wyler was her favorite director (previously they had worked together on *Jezebel* and *The Letter*).

Goldwyn had bought the screen rights to Lillian Hellman's 1939 Broadway hit, and then paid the author to do the screen adaptation. Meanwhile, he began casting the film, borrowing Bette Davis from Warner Bros. in exchange for Gary Cooper's services (on loan, Cooper did *Meet John Doe* and *Sergeant York*). According to Miss Davis, "Goldwyn ten years before had wailed at the sight of my test and refused to hire me at three hundred a week. Now he paid me $385,000 to star in *The Little Foxes.*" The actress has noted: "Like Harry Cohn, Mr. Goldwyn has always been willing to pay for the artists he wanted, and Mr. Warner, on my steely request, gave me Warners' share of the deal." To star opposite Miss Davis, Goldwyn hired Herbert Marshall, her leading man the previous year in William Wyler's *The Letter.* Next, he assigned his newest discovery, Teresa Wright, whom he had spotted on Broadway in *Life with Father* and had brought to Hollywood, to play Regina Giddens' daughter, Alexandra. The role of her love interest (not in the stage version) was given to Richard Carlson, and the remainder of the cast was composed primarily of those who had created the roles originally on Broadway—Patricia Collinge, Dan Duryea, Carl Benton Reid, Charles Dingle and John Marriott.

What then happened to Lillian Hellman's screenplay becomes somewhat fuzzy. Although she receives official screen credit, there also appears a qualifying credit line: "Additional scenes and dialogue by Arthur Kober, Dorothy Parker and Alan Campbell." Kober was Miss Hellman's former husband, whose work on the script (apparently post-Hellman) was augmented, before Goldwyn approved the final draft, by Dorothy Parker and her husband, Alan Campbell. Miss Parker had originally suggested the play's title to Miss Hellman, adapting it from *Song of Solomon*, 2:15—"Take us the foxes, the little foxes, that spoil the vines . . . for our vines have tender grapes."

In her autobiography, Bette Davis described, with some regret, working on *The Little Foxes* with Wyler.

We fought bitterly. I had been forced to see Tallulah Bankhead's performance on Broadway. I had not wanted to. A great admirer of hers, I wanted in no way to be influenced by her work. It was Willie's intention that I give a different interpretation of the part. I insisted that Tallulah had played it the only way it could be played. Miss Hellman's Regina was written with such definition that it could be played only one way. Our quarrels were endless. I was too young-looking for the forty year old woman and, since the ladies of Regina's day had rice-powered their faces, I covered mine with calcimine in order to look older. This Willie disagreed with. In fact, I ended up feeling I had given one of the worst performances of my life. This saddened me since Regina was a great part, and pleasing Willie Wyler was of such importance always to me. It took courage to play her the way I did, in the face of such opposition.

Miss Davis finally admitted: "The filming was torture, the film a smashing sucess both critically and popularly. But Willie and I never worked together again. It is too bad."

Miss Davis, befitting her stardom, and William Wyler, befitting his, were given the very best by Goldwyn. Handsome Orry-Kelly period costumes for her; photographer Gregg Toland, just back from shooting *Citizen Kane,* for him—it was their fifth film together, and cut by Daniel Mandell, working with Wyler for the eighth time.

Set in the South at the turn of the century, *The Little Foxes* concerns the rapacious Hubbard family (seen again at an earlier age in a later Hellman play, *Another Part of the Forest*). Approached by her brothers Ben and Oscar, Regina Hubbard Giddens sees in their business proposition a chance to make a killing. They simply need $75,000 to add to their own equal investments to set up a cotton mill to take advantage of readily available cheap labor. Intrigued by the idea, Regina arranges for a dinner party to size up William Marshall, the Northern financier who is instituting the planned business move. Regina then decides to send her daughter Alexandra, to Baltimore to bring back her banker husband Horace, from a sanatarium where he has been recovering from a heart attack. Arriving home, Horace is badgered ceaselessly by the impatient Regina, but remains firm in his refusal to give her the financing for the sweatshop venture. When Regina is unsuccessful in getting the money, Ben and Oscar, unable to wait any longer for the money, induce Oscar's son Leo, who works in the family bank, to steal enough negotiable bonds from Horace's strongbox to put

up the necessary capital. Regina immediately suspects the theft and decides to blackmail Ben and Oscar into giving her a share of the new business, but Horace thwarts her by claiming he gave Leo the securities as an interest-free loan.

Furious because Horace will not expose Leo, Regina abuses her husband until he suffers a coronary seizure and must beg her for his heart stimulant. She then sits motionless while Horace struggles to climb the stairs to get the medicine that might avert his death. Only after he collapses does she call for help from the servants. A short time later, standing by his deathbed, Regina coldy defies him to make a last minute accusation, but Horace uses his ebbing strength to comfort Alexandra and urge her to get away from her scheming mother and to marry David Hewitt, the young newspaper editor, before the family can push her into a wedding with her hateful cousin Leo.

With Horace now out of the way, Regina once again begins blackmailing her brothers, this time asking for two-thirds of the business in exchange for her silence about Leo's theft. Alexandra overhears the threats and realizes her mother's viciousness. In a final confrontation, she denounces her mother, saying she can no longer live in the same house with the woman who murdered her father, and runs into the rainy night to David, who has been waiting outside to comfort her. Regina watches them from an upstairs window, in full possession of the power and wealth she schemed and killed to achieve—but now unloved and unwanted by anyone.

Several of the Wyler-staged, Toland-photographed scenes have gained deserved reputations as cinema classics. The most famous is the one wherein Horace has his fatal attack. The focus remains on Regina in the foreground as her husband drops his heart simulant and then, being rebuffed in his pleas for help, struggles to get upstairs himself and collapses on the stairs. As the camera stays on Regina, sitting expressionless, Horace is seen, out-of-focus, or simply heard stumbling around in his attempt to save himself. "Toland and I discussed having him in focus," Wyler has said.

Gregg said, "I can have him sharp, or both of them sharp." I said no, because I wanted audiences to feel they were seeing something they were not supposed to see. Seeing the husband in the background made you squint, but what you *were* seeing was her face.

The New York Times has best captured critical opinion in its classic one-liner in its listings whenever *The Little Foxes* turns up on television: "Bette superlative, the others merely excellent." Matching the actress' towering performance were Patricia Collinge's Birdie, Oscar's dipsomaniacal wife; Herbert Marshall's doomed Horace; Dan Duryea's weak-willed, larcenous Leo, Teresa Wright's naive daughter—and on down the line. "The praise of perfection has a sameness about it," observed cinema historian Richard Griffith, "and culling reviews and comments on *The Little Foxes* is monotonous work."

John McCarten wrote in *The New Yorker*:

This industry, The Industry will survive, I begin to think (as) it delivers us *The Little Foxes* . . . One perceives throughout this whole film an assured judgement and good sense which alleviate the sordid plottings and miserable, sad story, and make of it a major screen achievement, one aided by the artistry and sense also of the cast.

Howard Barnes, in his critique in the *New York Herald Tribune,* found: "A fine play has become far finer as a film in the case of *The Little Foxes*. The language of the screen has never proved more eloquent, moving and dramatic . . . Here is an outstanding motion picture." Barnes concluded: "All of *The Little Foxes* is of a piece, from Wyler's direction to Gregg Toland's superlative camera work. The screen has every right to be proud today of something approaching a master work."

In *Variety*:

Samuel Goldwyn's film rates among the best to come out of Hollywood in recent years—a film as great in prestige as it will be at the box office. From the starring Bette Davis down the line to the bit roles, the acting is well-nigh flawless. (She) is again living up to a superb stage performance, and, thanks to the latitude afforded by the camera, even surpassing it. Miss Wright is a newcomer to the screen and is magnificent in a very difficult part as the daughter. A less talented actress in her place could have ruined the picture. Ditto, Miss Collinge, whose performance is memorable.

Newsweek's comment:

The simplest approach to the consideration of Samuel Goldwyn's production is to say that *The Little Foxes* is a superb job of reshaping a successful play for the screen, and one of the finest films to come out of Hollywood in many years . . . Too much credit cannot be given the fine cast Goldwyn has assembled. Only a few of the important players are familiar to film-goers (and) one of the notable contributions of the film is the mass screen debut of six Broadway actors. Topping them all is Teresa Wright (who) turns in a sensitive performances that shares honors with Bette Davis' Regina Giddens.

Bosley Crowther observed:

(It) has now been translated to the screen with all its original viciousness intact and with such extra-added virulence as the relentless camera of director William Wyler and the tensile acting of Bette Davis could impart (and) under the trademark of Samuel Goldwyn, *The Little Foxes* leaps to the front as the most bitingly sinister picture of the year and as one of the most cruelly realistic character studies yet shown on the screen.

(Crowther, however, failed to include the film among his Ten Best at year's end.)

The Little Foxes, Goldwyn's first under his new distribution deal with RKO Pictures, received eight Academy Award nominations: Best Director, Best Actress, Best Supporting Actress (Patricia Collinge), Best Supporting Actress (Teresa Wright), Best Original Screenplay, Best Scoring of a Dramatic Picture, Best Editing, Best Art/Set Design (Stephen Gooson and Howard Bristol).

Teresa Wright stayed on with Goldwyn to become his number one leading lady of the Forties, although, curiously, she made only three further Goldwyn films. Dan Duryea appeared in two other Goldwyn movies *Ball of Fire* and *Pride of the Yankees* before embarking on a lengthy screen career of cinema villainy. He acted the role of Oscar Hubbard, Leo's father, in the film version of *Another Part of the Forest* in 1948.

A footnote to *The Little Foxes*: In April 1967, Lillian Hellman unsuccessfully sued Samuel Goldwyn and CBS, attempting to bar the television showing of the film, charging that her original contract with Goldwyn had prohibited airing of the complete motion picture.

Charles Dingle, Patricia Collinge, Carl Benton Reid and Bette Davis in The Little Foxes.

Herbert Marshall, Teresa Wright and Bette Davis in
The Little Foxes.

Richard Carlson and Teresa Wright in The Little Foxes.

60 BALL OF FIRE (1941)

Directed by Howard Hawks; screenplay, Charles Brackett and Billy Wilder; based on the story *From A to Z* by Thomas Monroe and Billy Wilder; music director, Alfred Newman; song "Drum Boogie" by Gene Krupa and Roy Eldridge; photographer, Gregg Toland; editor, Daniel Mandell; assistant director, William Tummel; art director, Perry Ferguson; Costumes, Edith Head. Running time, 111 minutes. Released by RKO Pictures. Premiere: Radio City Music Hall, New York, 1/16/42

THE CAST:
Professor Bertram Potts, Gary Cooper; *Sugarpuss O'Shea,* Barbara Stanwyck (singing dubbed by Martha Tilton); *Professor Gurkakoff,* Oscar Homolka; *Joe Lilac,* Dana Andrews; *Duke Pastrami,* Dan Duryea; *Professor Jerome,* Henry Travers; *Professor Magenbruch,* S.Z. Sakall; *Professor Robinson,* Tully Marshall; *Professor Quintana,* Leonid Kinskey; *Professor Oddly,* Richard Haydn*; *Professor Peagram,* Aubrey Mather; *Garbage Man,* Allen Jenkins; *Asthma Anderson,* Ralph Peters; *Miss Bragg,* Kathleen Howard; *Miss Totten,* Mary Field; *Larson,* Charles Lane; *McNeary,* Charles Arnt; *Cook,* Elisha Cook Jr.; *"Horseface",* Alan Rhein; *"Pinstripe",* Eddie Foster; *"Benny the Creep",* Will Lee; *Justice of the Peace,* Aldrich Bowker; *District Attorney,* Addison Richards; Gene Krupa and his Orchestra; and Pat West, Kenneth Howell, Tommy Ryan, Tim Ryan, Otto Hoffman, Ed Mundy, Geraldine Fissette, June Horne, Ethelreda Leopold, Walter Shumway, George Barton, Lee Phelps, Merrilee Lannon, Lorraine Miller, Francis Sayles, Pat Flaherty
* in screen debut

In contrast to the first problem-plagued bout with the screwball comedy genre in his *Woman Chases Man,* Goldwyn's second (and final) encounter in *Ball of Fire* must have been an exhilarating experience. Certainly for the moviegoer, it provided more satisfying entertainment. Among the reasons: the director, the script, the cast, the overall production.

Billy Wilder, who coauthored both the original tale and the screenplay, has said:

The story was an original called From *A to Z,* written in German by me in Paris sometime before I ever came to Hollywood. The late Thomas Monroe helped me Americanize it. We then sold it to Mr. Goldwyn when he was looking for a vehicle for Gary Cooper.

Goldwyn paid Wilder and Monroe $7500 for the story and promised another $2500 if the movie became a hit. (The movie did and Goldwyn did). Ginger Rogers had been Goldwyn's choice for the lead opposite Cooper, but having just won her Academy Award for *Kitty Foyle,* the actress turned down Goldwyn claiming that the role of a honky tonk dancer was beneath her. The producer, stung, turned to Barbara Stanwyck, who had just co-starred with Cooper in *Meet John Doe,* the first of the two Warner Bros. films, for which, Goldwyn had made his leading actor's services available.

Working with his longtime (1938–1950) collaborator, Charles Brackett, Wilder turned out a witty screenplay that has been called both an Americanized *Pygmalion* and *Snow White and the Seven Dwarfs* in reverse, dealing with seven scholarly professors who have spent nine monastic years laboring on a new encyclopedia. One, Professor Bertram Potts, is assigned the word "slang" when the committee reaches S and his academic investigations, together with some assistance from the pursuing police, place him face-to-face with a stripper, Sugarpuss O'Shea, he previously had met during a rare sojurn into the city's night life. Because of her involvement with gangster Joe Lilac, Sugarpuss decides the time has come to go into hiding and accepts Potts' invitation to look him up when she is in the neighborhood. At the professors' hallowed brownstone, she easily inveigles from the erudite group an invitation to move in so that they may study her "slang." Her presence soon upsets the stodgy lives of the stuffy scholars, their formidable housekeeper and their regulated, unimaginative existence, but the owlish seven begin to loosen up to Sugarpuss' brash charm and nightly conga lessons. Even Potts finds himself captivated by the attractive guest as she imparts her endless knowledge of slang.

When she is reluctantly obliged to leave, at the urging of Lilac's henchmen, because of her pending marriage to their boss (played by a curiously miscast Dana Andrews in one of his few "hood" roles), she suddenly realizes that she has fallen in love with Potts who, with his literary companions, already has volunteered to drive her to New Jersey. There, the professors think, Sugarpuss is planning to visit her father, but they soon find themselves Joe Lilac's prisoners—at least until after Sugarpuss' wedding. Potts and his cohorts conspire to delay the ceremony and manage to capture the gang just as the police arrive. Sugarpuss and Potts are now able to pursue their own happiness together.

In addition to the delightful performances by the stars as well as Goldwyn's large cast of stock players, *Ball of Fire* (filmed under the unimaginative title *The Professor and the Burlesque Queen,* which ranks in originality with *The Cowboy and the Lady*) was blessed with the brisk direction of Howard Hawks, working on the last of his trio of screwball comedies of the era (*Bringing Up Baby* and *His Girl Friday* lingered as memories of the immediate past); the sparkling photography of Gregg Toland, particularly in the manner it caressed the leading lady; and the sprightly, Oscar-nominated score of Alfred Newman, on loan from 20th Century-Fox to work for his old boss one final time.

The *Time Magazine* critic, in his kind words for *Ball of Fire,* commented that

(it) is saturated with some of the juiciest, wackiest, solid American slang ever recorded on celluloid. The plot is not as fresh as its idea, but the picture will do until its producer, Sam Goldwyn, wins his own lifelong race with the English language.

The reviewer then remarked: "Actor Cooper plays his Mr. Dodds role with the authority of long familiarity, and Miss Stanwyck, once Ruby Stevens of Brooklyn, is equally at home in hers."

Bosley Crowther observed that "(Goldwyn) has produced a picture which deliberately kicks around the language in a manner so colorful and lively that you can almost sense his tongue stuck in his cheek." He called the film a "wholly ingratiating lark," and said of the acting:

Mr. Cooper in the role of a literal encyclopedist working on an analysis of current American slang is just Mr. Deeds with a lot of book-learning. And Miss Stanwyck as the flashy nightclub singer who becomes his fruitful source is strictly the Lady Eve with the same old apples to sell . . . (but) he gives a homespun performance such as only he can give (and she) is plenty yum-yum—meaning scorchy—in her worldly temptress role.

Crowther's summation:

Howard Hawks has kept the whole thing moving at accelerated pace for nigh two hours. That is an awfully long time to drag out a single-note plot, but, oddly enough, it works. Mr. Goldwyn has turned out a very nice comedy, indeed, and old Geoffrey Chaucer must be gulping rather limply at the bottom of his well.

The *New York Herald Tribune's* Howard Barnes was less enthusiastic, feeling that

Ball of Fire fails to live up to its title only because a thin idea has been stretched well up to the breaking point . . . (and) is in no sense a distinguished film, but it has a comical central idea and enough production finish to make it a highly satisfactory entertainment.

In his judgement of the stars:

Gary Cooper would scarcely have been my choice for a research student (but) he is extremely engaging and persuasive as the shy professor . . . (and) Miss Stanwyck is better than she has been since *The Lady Eve.* She has little range as an actress, but she can still do superbly the act which made her famous in the stage's *Burlesque.*

Ball of Fire earned four Academy Award nominations: Best Actress, Best Original Story, Best Scoring of a Dramatic Picture and Best Sound Recording (Thomas Moulton's name was on the nomination). For Barbara Stanwyck, the nomination was especially gratifying. It was her second (of four), again for a Goldwyn picture as *Stella Dallas* had been, and once again for a role in which she had not been Goldwyn's first choice.

Goldwyn's remake of *Ball of Fire* seven years later as *A Song Is Born,* also directed by Hawks, was nearly a scene-for-scene translation altered slightly for the talents of his then starring team, Danny Kaye and Virginia Mayo, plus the inclusion of several swinging jam sessions with the top big band names of the day.

Ralph Peters, Gary Cooper, Barbara Stanwyck and Dan Duryea in Ball of Fire.

Barbara Stanwyck and Gary Cooper in Ball of Fire.

Gary Cooper, Barbara Stanwyck, S.Z Sakall, Tully Marshall, Henry Travers, Leonid Kinskey, Aubrey Mather and Oscar Homolka in Ball of Fire.

61 THE PRIDE OF THE YANKEES (1942)

Directed by Sam Wood; screenplay, Jo Swerling and Herman J. Mankiewicz; based on a story by Paul Gallico; music, Leigh Harline; photographer, Rudolph Maté; editor, Daniel Mandell; assistant director, John Sherwood; art director, Perry Ferguson; special effects, Jack Cosgrove; production design, William Cameron Menzies; costumes, René Hubert. Running time, 129 minutes. Released by RKO Pictures. Premiere; Astor Theater, New York, 7/15/42

THE CAST:

Lou Gehrig, Gary Cooper; *Eleanor Gehrig,* Teresa Wright; *Sam Blake,* Walter Brennan; *Hank Hanneman,* Dan Duryea; Babe Ruth, Himself; *Mom Gehrig,* Elsa Janssen; *Pop Gehrig,* Ludwig Stossel; *Myra,* Virginia Gilmore; Bill Dickey, Himself; *Miller Huggins,* Ernie Adams; *Mr. Twitchell,* Pierre Watkin; *Joe McCarthy,* Harry Harvey; *Coach,* Addison Richards; Robert W. Meusel, Himself; Mark Koenig, Himself; Bill Stern, Himself; *Van Tuyl,* Hardie Albright; *Clinic Doctor,* Edward Fielding; *Mayor of New Rochelle,* George Lessey; *Doctor in Gehrig Home,* Vaughan Glaser; *Lou Gehrig as a Boy,* Douglas Croft; *Laddie,* Rip Russell; *Third Base Coach,* Frank Faylen; *Hammond,* Jack Shea; *Wally Pip,* George McDonald; *Billy,* Gene Collins; *Billy at seventeen,* David Holt; *Fiorello La Guardia,* David Manley; *Colletti,* Max Willenz; *Sasha,* Jimmy Valentine; *Sasha's Mother,* Anita Bolster; *Murphy,* Robert Winkler; *Mr. Larsen,* Spencer Charters; *Mrs. Fabini,* Rosina Galli; *Joe Fabini,* Billy Roy; *Mrs. Robert,* Sarah Padden; *Tessie,* Janet Chapman; *Mrs. Worthington,* Eva Dennison; *Mr. Worthington,* Montague Shaw; *Ed Burrow,* Jack Stewart; *Christy Mathewson,* Fay Thomas; *Specialty Dancers,* Veloz and Yolanda; Ray Noble and his Orchestra; and Bernard Zanville (Dane Clark), Tom Neal, Jack Arnold (Vinton Haworth), John Kellogg, Lorna Dunn, Emory Parnell, Dorothy Vaughan, Patsy O'Byrne, Matt McHugh, William Chaney, Pat Flaherty, Mary Gordon, Francis Sayles.

In his only biographical film, Goldwyn turned out a stirring, uplifting wartime tribute to one of baseball's greatest figures, Lou Gehrig. When word was trumpeted that Goldwyn was preparing his production, a number of baseball fanatics among the acting ranks (Dennis Morgan, Eddie Albert, George Tobias, William Gargan, et al.) offered to play the role simply for the glory, and director William Wellman, also an enthusiast of America's favorite outdoor sport, was said to have asked to work on the film. Goldwyn, though, could see only one man as Gehrig—the all-American actor, Gary Cooper, who turned in a splendid, multi-faceted performance as the ballplayer who had died the previous year at the age of thirty-seven.

To costar with Cooper (in his final Goldwyn picture), Teresa Wright was elevated to leading lady status and offered a sensitive portrayal of the Chicago baseball devotee who became Mrs. Lou Gehrig. Walter Brennan was assigned the role of the fictional sportswriter friend, a character based on Gehrig's close friend, Fred Fletcher, the fishing columnist for the *New York Daily News.* Goldwyn's choice to direct was amiable Sam Wood, who had not given him any trouble during the filming of *Raffles* (and was subsequently asked by Cooper, as a free-lance star, to direct him in three other films). Wood delivered a touching, inspiring movie that focused less on Gehrig's prowess on the baseball field and more on his private life, depicting the utter simplicity and modesty of the man and the tender devotion that he, his wife and his parents had for each other.

For the baseball sequences, Cooper, a righthander, was taught to throw and bunt left-handed and, in many cases, he was seen wearing a Yankees uniform with the numbers reversed so that, when the film was processed also in reverse, he would appear to be a southpaw as Lou Gehrig had been. Another point on which Goldwyn was adamant: the theme music. A stickler for detail, Goldwyn paid Irving Berlin $15,000 for synchronization rights for the composer's evergreen, *Always,* solely because it had been the real-life theme of Lou and Eleanor Gehrig's romance.

The movie's memorable highlight remains the remarkable recreation of the scene in Yankee Stadium on 4 July 1939 when Lou Gehrig, a victim of the rare, paralytic, amytropic multiple sclerosis, gave his heart-tugging farewell speech, after having appeared in an astounding 2,130 consecutive games as the New York Yankees' "Iron Man."

As pictured in the Jo Swerling-Herman J. Mankiewicz screenplay, fashioned from Paul Gallico's original story, Gehrig, as a youngster, dreams of becoming a big league ballplayer, although his devoted parents would like to see him take up engineering. His mother works as a cook at Columbia University to see her son through high school and into Columbia, where he becomes a star athlete. Gehrig is spotted by sportswriter Sam Blake, who recommends him to the New York Yankees. The athlete though, refuses to change his decision to become an engineer until he learns that his mother requires a costly operation. Confronted with hospital bills, Gehrig accepts the Yankees' offer and is sent to the team's Hartford club to gain experience.

Gehrig's mother believes her son to be furthering his studies at Harvard and discovers the truth from an item on the sports page after he has been brought up by the Yankees in June 1925. Heartbroken at first, she becomes reconciled and develops into a rabid baseball fan. In his first game with the team in Chicago, Gehrig meets and falls immediately in love with an attractive spectator, Eleanor Twitchell, who teases him for awkwardly tripping over a pile of bats. Following the Yankees' win in the World Series that year, Gehrig returns to Chicago to propose to Eleanor.

Through the years, Gehrig rises to become one of baseball's greatest heroes, never missing a game. Gloom overtakes the Gehrigs though, when he goes into a slump during spring training in 1939, and when the doctors inform him that he has a rare neurological disease and has but a few years left to live, he resigns from the team in midseason. He tries to keep the truth from Eleanor, but she learns the news and helps the Yankees stage "Lou Gehrig Appreciation Day" whereat a vast crowd assembles to bid the star farewell. "Some people say I've had a bad break," Gehrig tells them tearfully, "but today I consider myself the luckiest man on the face of the earth."

Critic Howard Barnes called the movie

a triumphant and moving screen biography . . . the portrayal of Gehrig by Gary Cooper gives it heroic dimensions, and with Samuel Goldwyn's meticulous production and Sam Wood's cunning staging, *The Pride of the Yankees* is every inch a memorable show.

Barnes felt that

on the surface, the film is singularly lacking in dynamic dramatic appeal, but it has overtones which are fascinating and irresistible . . . (and) it packs an emotional jolt which makes for a stunning entertainment . . . Mr. Cooper is as splendid as one might have expected him to be, but Teresa Wright is not far behind him in her radiant and sympathetic characterization as Mrs. Gehrig.

The *New York World-Telegram's* Alton Cook felt that "Mr. Cooper has seldom been better than he is as Gehrig. His performance grows, as the character grows, from the shy, gawky undergraduate to modest, unassuming hero of millions." In the Bosley Crowther review in *The New York Times* were these observations:

In a simple, tender, meticulous and explicitly narrative film, Mr. Goldwyn and his associates have told the story with sincere and lingering affection . . . it is, without being pretentious, a real saga of American life—homey, humorous, sentimental and composed in patient detail.

Variety said that "Samuel Goldwyn has produced a stirring epitaph . . . (and) Gary Cooper blends neatly into a hero's role. Gehrig is depicted for what he was, a quiet, plodding personality who strived for and achieved perfection in his profession. Cooper amplifies via his own shy screen personality." The paper's critic concluded: "Every acting job in the film is superb."

And this from *Time Magazine:*

The picture tells, with taste and distinction, the model story of his model life in the special world of professional ballplayers. It's a typical U.S. success story, and Gary Cooper plays it with likeable restraint—by being his shy, loping, American self. The best part of *The Pride of the Yankees* is its Grade-A love story.

The Pride of the Yankees received ten Academy Award nominations: Best Picture, Best Actor, Best Actress, Best Original Story, Best Cinematography, Best Scoring of a Dramatic Picture (Leigh Harline), Best Art/Set Decoration (Perry Ferguson), Best Editing, Best Sound Recording, Best Special Effects. Only Daniel Mandell won for his exacting editing. With her Oscar nomination as Best Actress, Teresa Wright gained the unique distinction of being nominated in two different categories for two different roles in the same year. (She won that year for her supporting performance in *Mrs. Miniver.*) She would not appear in another Goldwyn film though, until 1946, despite being named to the cast of several in the producer's frequent press releases.

Teresa Wright and Gary Cooper in The Pride of the Yankees.

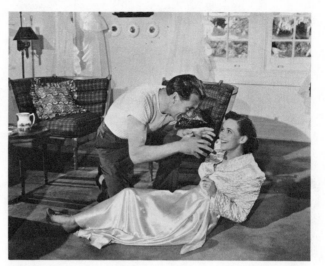

Gary Cooper and Teresa Wright in The Pride of the Yankees.

Gary Cooper in The Pride of the Yankees.

62 THEY GOT ME COVERED (1943)

Directed by David Butler; screenplay, Harry Kurnitz; based on a story by Leonard Q. Ross and Leonard Spigelgass; music, Leigh Harline; song *Palsy Walsy* by Harold Arlen and Johnny Mercer; photographer, Rudolph Maté; editor, Daniel Mandell; assistant director, John Sherwood; art director, Perry Ferguson; costumes, Adrian. Running time, 96 minutes. Released by RKO Pictures. Premiere: Radio City Music Hall, New York, 3/4/43

THE CAST:
Robert Kittredge, Bob Hope; *Christina Hill*, Dorothy Lamour; *Otto Fauscheim*, Otto Preminger; *Baldamacco*, Eduardo Cianelli; *Gloria, "The Glow Girl"*, Marion Martin; *Little Old Man*, Donald Meek; *Margo Vanescu*, Lenore Aubert; *Sally*, Phyllis Ruth; *Norman Mason*, Donald MacBride; *Mildred Smith*, Bettye Avery; *Helen*, Mary Treen; *Lucille*, Margaret Hayes; *Laura*, Mary Byrne; *Nichimuro*, Philip Ahn; *Holtz*, William Yetter; *Faber*, Henry Guttman; *Gypsy Woman*, Florence Bates; *Hotel Manager*, Walter Catlett; *Gregory Vanescu*, John Abbott; *Red*, Frank Sully; *Gross*, Wolfgang Zilzer; *Testori*, Nino Pipitone; *Mussolini*, Joe Devlin; *Hawara*, Kam tong; *Smith*, George Chandler; *Office Boy*, Stanley Clements; *Joe McGirk*, Don Brodie; *Delivery Boy*, Arnold Stang; *Laundry Man*, Willie Fung; *Katrina*, Greta Meyer; and Walter Sonderling, Lyle·Latell, John Mather, Etta Mc Daniel, Ray Turner, Ralph Dunn, Stanley Price, Hugh Prosser, Gil Perkins, John Sinclair, Lane Chandler, Dick Keane, Edward Gargan, Charles Legneur, Anne O'Neal, Hans Schumm, Lou Lubin, Shimen Ruskin, Ferike Boros, Peggy Lynn.

They Got Me Covered was the first of Goldwyn's morale-boosting, entertaining wartime (and postwar) comedies that distinguished his output of the Forties from that of the Thirties, when he had concentrated on romantic dramas with occasional relief from Eddie Cantor. In this decade, Goldwyn would rely on Bob Hope, Paramount's foremost comedian, and Danny Kaye, whom Goldwyn would turn into an overnight movie sensation, to carry the public and the boys overseas to hours of light-hearted (and occasionally light-headed) abandon.

Goldwyn somehow enticed Hope away from his busy schedule on the Paramount lot and at military bases throughout the world to star, along with his (Hope's) "Road" pal, Dorothy Lamour, in an espionage farce set in Washington. David Butler, who had previously directed the Hope-Lamour team (with friend) in *Road to Morocco,* was engaged to lead the pair through this gag-loaded hodgepodge of sabotage nonsense, tailored to suit Hope's particular brand of humor by writer Harry Kurnitz. The film, Hope's first to open at Radio City Music Hall, captured the national attitude by typifying the entertainment that drew filmgoers to the box offices during the darkest days of World War II.

Hope's brash clowning provided some semblance of reason to the picture's convoluted plot, starting with his recall from Moscow as foreign correspondent for Amalgamated News after botching the biggest story of his career and mistaking marching troops of the German invasion of Russia for a parade. Fired by his boss, Norman Mason, newsman Robert Kittredge goes to Washington to drop in on his old girlfriend, Christina Hill, who manages the Amalgamated News bureau there. While trying to rekindle their on-again, off-again romance, Kittredge is visited by a Roumanian agent, Gregory Vanescu, who offers to sell him some valuable information about a spy ring operating in Washington. Realizing this story might win him back his old job, Kittredge wangles $5000 from Christina, but Vanescu is scared off by a pair of enemy agents before he can talk. Later though, the Roumanian manages to get word to Kittredge to send a stenographer to a secret hideout for the valuable data, and Christina has her roommate, Sally, undertake the assignment. After getting the information, however, Sally is kidnapped by the agents who had been trailing Vanescu.

Learning that Kittredge is on their trail, Otto Fauscheim and his associates, Baldamacco and Nichimuro, scheme to discredit the newsman and make him a national laughing stock. Through a lady calling herself Margo Vanescu, they succeed in drugging Kittredge. When he wakes up, he finds himself in Niagara Falls, married to Gloria the Glow Girl, a blonde stripper. Panicky, Kittredge rushes back to Washington where only Christina believes his story, aware that he detests blondes. Gloria, though, soon learns the true reasons for her hasty marriage to Kittredge, but before she can clear his name, she is murdered. From clues found in her room, however, Kittredge traces the spies to a Washington beauty salon, which he enters disguised as a woman after letting Christina know his whereabouts. She turns up as a customer and stumbles onto the fact that the salon is a front for enemy agents. While Kittredge is frantically trying to hold off the spies, Christina phones the F.B.I., with help arriving in time to assist in breaking the spy ring.

Hope, of course, manages to work in his familiar battery of topical jokes and asides to his audience, plus the usual amount of Crosby gags, including one wherein Crosby is heard crooning his perennial *Where the Blue of the Night Meets the Gold of the Day* whenever Hope opens his cigarette case.

Bosley Crowther called the film "another of those pleasantly wacky Bob Hope farces," and then admitted "The business by now is as routine as is Bob's attitude . . . anyhow *They Got Me Covered* doesn't quite measure up in plot or speed to some of Hope's previous excursions into melodramatic farces." Crowther noted finally: "It is Bob who makes the picture—he and his great big gags. So long as he has them, he's covered, no matter how slight the story is."

Howard Barnes commented that

this slapstick spy show is essentially a Bob Hope special. If you delight in his double-takes, puns and pantomime, you are likely to agree with me that this Samuel Goldwyn production is a comparatively beguiling melodramatic farce. If the comedian's familiar antics leave you cold, skip it. Even with the smart Goldwyn ministrations, *They Got Me Covered* could scarcely be called a substantial screen comedy . . . (but) it's Bob Hope's picture, and it is definitely a Hope tour-de-force.

In the opinion of *Variety,*

Samuel Goldwyn has taken a top comic, a top comedy writer and a top comedy director and distilled them into a farce of the broadest stripe. Sometimes it takes and sometimes it doesn't but *They Got Me Covered* as a whole is disappointing in light of past Goldwyniana and the talent that went into it.

The paper's critic felt that

No asset to the film is the quality of much of the acting, particularly that of Miss Lamour, whose flat delivery of her comparatively numerous lines makes Hope have to work twice as hard to sell his gags . . . director David Butler succeeded in keeping the film moving, although it is sometimes a battle against the episodic construction of the situation gags.

Time Magazine raved: "*They Got Me Covered* is Bob Hope at par. The film is almost 100% good, rich Hope, uncomplicated by music, choruses or rival gagsters . . . (and) the girls merely serve as feeders (as) the Young Master takes charge of nearly every scene." *Newsweek,* on the other hand, felt that

They Got Me Covered will be welcomed by Hope's fans, but it falls short of the comedian's best. Other things being equal, it should have been a top-rank film for he has a shrewd and meticulous producer in Samuel Goldwyn and his director is David Butler. The letdown apparently was in the writing department . . . (and) Hope's comic genius springs enternal with only intermittent leverage from a script that strains for the irresponsible idiocy of his recent vehicles. Of even less help is the casting of Dorothy Lamour in a role that requires the erstwhile "Aloma of the South Seas" to talk a lot more than usual and wear twice as much— a self-defeating enterprise whatever way you look at it.

The film, whose title was inspired by Hope's pamphlet biography, of which he reportedly gave away or sold more than three million copies, made a bundle for Goldwyn—and half again as much when it was reissued in 1950 on a double bill with *Up In Arms.*

Dorothy Lamour and Bob Hope in They Got Me Covered.

Lenore Aubert and Bob Hope in They Got Me Covered.

Eduardo Ciannelli and Bob Hope in They Got Me Covered.

63 THE NORTH STAR (1943)

Directed by Lewis Milestone; associate producer, William Cameron Menzies; original screenplay, Lillian Hellman; music, Aaron Copland; songs "Song of the Guerrillas" and "No Village Like Mine" by Aaron Copland and Ira Gershwin; choreographer, David Lichine; photographer, James Wong Howe; editor, Daniel Mandell; assistant director, Sam Nelson; art director, Perry Ferguson. Running time, 106 minutes. Released by RKO Pictures. Premiere: Victoria and Palace Theaters, New York, 11/4/43 (Reissued in 1957 as *Armored Attack*)

THE CAST:
Marina, Anne Baxter; *Kolya,* Dana Andrews; *Dr. Pavel Kurin,* Walter Huston; *Karp,* Walter Brennan; *Sophia,* Ann Harding; *Claudia,* Jane Withers; *Damian,* Farley Granger*; *Dr. Otto von Harden,* Erich von Stroheim; *Rodion,* Dean Jagger; *Grisha,* Eric Roberts; *Boris,* Carl Benton Reid; *Nadya,* Ruth Nelson; *Anna,* Esther Dale; *Olga Kurin,* Ann Carter; *Iakin,* Paul Guilfoyle; *Dr. Max Richter,* Martin Kosleck; *German Captain,* Tonio Selwart; *German Lieutenant,* Peter Pohlenz; *Russian Gunner,* Gene O'Donnell; *Russian Pilot,* Robert Lowery; *Petrov,* Frank Wilcox; *Petya,* Charles Bates; *Specialty Dancers,* Tommy Hall, Ronn Marvin, George Vale, Jack Vlaskin, William Sabbot, Clair Freeman, Eric Braunsteiner, Tamata Laub, Marie Vlaskin, Inna Gest; and George Lynn, Minna Phillips, Edmund Cobb, Bill Walker, Clarence Straight, Jerry Mickelsen, Martin Faust, Grace Cunard, Jack Perrin, Al Ferguson, Emma Dunn, John Judd, Sarah Padden, Teddy Infuhr, Lynn Winthrop (Ruth Brennan), Ferdinand Schumann-Heink, Ray Teal, Crane Whitley, Harry Strang, Lane Chandler, Florence Auer, Constant Franke.
* in screen debut

Here was the extraordinary film that was Samuel Goldwyn's dramatic contribution to the industry's war effort and one of the era's most controversial morale boosters. From an original Lillian Hellman screenplay, it expounded the bravery of the Soviet people by focusing on a collective farm village (the film's title) on the Bessarabian border as it comes under the German blitz in June of 1941. Goldwyn had hoped to become the first producer to pay screen tribute to the valor of our Russian allies, but he was beaten to the box office by a few months by Jack Warner, who turned former Ambassador Joseph E. Davies' book, *Mission to Moscow,* into a motion picture.

Determined to enlighten America about the true life of the Russian people at war, and responding to FDR's call (James Roosevelt, the President's son, was at this time President of Samuel Goldwyn Studios) for a Hollywood effort to portray the courageous exploits of one of our wartime partners, Goldwyn had Miss Hellman write a patriotic scenario about "our side's" fortitude under fire. To the producer, this would not be a nationalistic picture, since no Russian accents would be used. Rather, it would be a study of everyman's struggle for freedom. William Wyler was to direct it and Gregg Toland was to photograph it. Wyler, though, entered the army after completing *Mrs. Miniver,* and Goldwyn instead assigned Lewis Milestone, whose reputation had been established more than a decade earlier with the pacifistic *All Quiet on the Western Front,* as director of this production which, if not pro-war, at least would glorify bravery. To photograph *The North Star,* Goldwyn recruited James Wong Howe, and then proceeded to convince Aaron Copland to write one of his rare film scores for the project.

To people his Russian village, Goldwyn went to his roster of contract players, more or less. Teresa Wright was assigned the role of Marina, the young peasant girl, but she fell ill and was replaced by Anne Baxter (whom Goldwyn borrowed from Darryl F. Zanuck). Her love interest, Damian, would be played by Farley Granger, then an eighteen-year-old novice whom Goldwyn found through a newspaper advertisement. Dana Andrews was given his first (Goldwyn) starring role as a Russian pilot, and Walter Brennan was cast as a philosophical farmer.

The other leads went outside the Goldwyn troupe to Walter Huston and Ann Harding, who, ironically, were to be seen as Ambassador and Mrs. Joseph E. Davies in *Mission to Moscow*. Child star Jane Withers played one of her first grown-up roles as another peasant girl, and Erich von Stroheim, the screen's foremost portrayer of German officers, was chosen for the part of a doctor among the invading troops, a humanitarian who was "just following orders."

The realistic battle sequences in *The North Star* served to buffer much of the static ideological speechmaking (considered in many quarters to be nothing more than Communist propaganda). Wartime brutalities were rather graphic for that period in film history—one of the best remembered scenes is that of Ann Harding, her arms and legs broken by the Germans seeking information about guerrilla activities among the villagers, painfully crawling home across the town square—and many moviegoers recoiled at the pathetic screams of the (off-camera) children being bled for plasma for the invading soldiers.

The early part of the film (approximately thirty-five minutes) offers a colorful depiction of the village of The North Star, its people and their peaceful ways—complete with Slavonic dances by David Lichine and rousing songs by Aaron Copland and Ira Gershwin. This idyllic setting serves to accentuate the inevitable brutalities of the Nazi invasion and the villagers' heroic fight for survival, during which, guerrilla actions and ideological exchanges (primarily between Walter Huston and Eric von Stroheim) alternate footage.

The story line follows a somewhat familiar path: After a village feast celebrating a prosperous farming season and the close of the school term, young lovers Marina and Damian are joined by Damian's pilot brother Kolya, and their school chums, Claudia and her brother Grisha, on a walking trip to nearby Kiev for their first look at a large city. Footsore after a day of walking, they welcome a lift from Karp, the elderly leader of a wagon-train bound for Kiev. The group's merriment is interrupted by a sudden attack by Nazi planes, and Kolya's quick thinking saves the lives of the few in Karp's wagon. Back at the village where the planes have done severe damage, Marina's father, Rodion, organizes the villagers and takes the able-bodied men into the hills to fight as guerrillas, leaving the women and children behind to destroy their crops and homes before the onslaught.

On the race back to the village in Karp's wagon, Kolya and his group come across an abandoned arms shipment destined for the guerrillas, but lying in a truck put out of commission by enemy planes. Piling the arms into the wagon, Kolya instructs the others to get the guns to the fighters while he rejoins his squadron, later to lose his life in a suicide drive into a formation of German tanks and guns. While the group now led by Damian moves into the hills, Pavel Kurin the elderly village doctor, directs the burning operation in the village, but the invaders are able to extinguish the flames. The Germans quickly overtake the town and then start inquiring about the guerrillas. Rodion's wife Sophia, is tortured by the Nazis for refusing to disclose her husband's whereabouts. Then the children are rounded up, and under the supervision of Otto von Harden, the doctor in the occupying Nazi regiment, are bled for their plasma. When one is killed, Dr. Kurin goes to the guerrilla camp and rouses the fighters to an immediate attack. Then he returns to face von Harden, who confesses that he hates the Nazis and does not enjoy bleeding little children, but as an isolated individual obviously cannot do much about the situation. Kurin retorts that people who despise the Nazis and still serve them are worse than the Nazis themselves, then shoots von Harden as the guerrilla attack begins. Claudia is killed and Damian is blinded, but the enemy is destroyed and the remaining villagers head west, determined to defend their country.

Of *The North Star,* Goldwyn himself wrote (in 1943) that

> in telling the story of the Russian people, we can't help but feel that we are telling the story of a people who think and act as do Americans. Both are peace-loving; both love their lands. The pioneering in Russia, as its vast resources were opened to development by the people, resembles closely the development of our own West.

Over the years, however, critics have argued Goldwyn's intentions, some calling the film pro-Bolshevik, others pro-Nazi. *The North Star,* in the final analysis, must be viewed in the context of the prevailing political and social atmosphere.

Lillian Hellman, a veteran of Goldwyn artistic battles, found herself walking a familiar road with *The North Star.* Following the film's premiere, the author discussed at length in *The New York Times* her difficulties with Goldwyn and director Milestone. She had submitted a completed script before Christmas of 1942 and had been assured she would be consulted on any changes. Shortly thereafter, as she noted,

> I received from Mr. Milestone the first fifty pages of the script with "suggested changes" and whole pages of dialogue written by him in a sort of Gregory Ratoff patois, which I was asked to touch up as best I could.

In May, at the screening of a rough cut of the film, Miss Hellman found that, among other changes, her festival scene, envisioned as quiet and gentle, had been realized as "an extended opera bouffe peopled not by peasants, real and live, but by musical comedy characters without a care in the world." Other expository scenes had been altered, shortened, resequenced, or just eliminated, and the film's intended meaning was radically different from what she had written, and she insisted on creating a new ending that would at least conform to the film's altered shape. The author's final (recently written) words on the subject: "It was a big-time, sentimental, badly directed, badly acted mess."

Critical approval of *The North Star* was expected because of the film's importance in 1943. Howard Barnes was the most enthusiastic, writing in The *New York Herald Tribune*:

It is an eminently sincere and sometimes brilliant account of the Nazi invasion of the U.S.S.R. Lillian Hellman has composed an original script with eloquence and passion, and Lewis Milestone has used his directorial skill to give the production depth and meaning . . . Walter Huston does a superb job as the Soviet doctor and Ann Harding is better, I think, than she has ever been as the tragic mother.

Barnes thought:

There is brilliant direction and acting in *The North Star*. It has obviously been written from the heart. Even though it is hopped up with Hollywood showmanship, it is likely to be a challenging slug for our side and the post-war world in which we are certain to be involved.

Bosley Crowther called Goldwyn's film

lyric and savage . . . a heroic picture, the force of which is weakened only by the fact that in it Mr. Goldwyn and Mr. Milestone have too freely mixed theatrical forms. *The North Star* has so much that is moving and triumphant that its sometime departures from reality may be generally overlooked.

Time viewed *The North Star* as

a cinemilestone for four reasons: (1) the first major attempt by the U.S. to present Russia's war with the Nazis as heroic defense by the people of their homes, (2) the first attempt to draw the vast struggle by focusing on the resistance of one village, (3) the most successful attempt to show a sickening German atrocity in credible terms, and (4) the most successful attempt to show the decisive role which Russian guerrillas have played in defeating the Germans . . . No other Hollywood film has done the job quite so well.

The most bitter denunciations of *The North Star* came from the Hearst-controlled papers, although the initial run of the *New York Sunday Mirror* following the film's premiere contained a highly complimentary review. The presses were halted though, after the first million or so copies had been printed, and on orders from the top, a new critique was substituted, describing Goldwyn's epic as pure Bolshevist propaganda. The review went on to consider that the entire project might well have been bankrolled by Josef Stalin himself. Similar savage attacks were launched throughout the Hearst syndicate.

It is about *The North Star* that one of the memorable Goldwynisms supposedly was uttered: "I don't care if we don't make a dime with this picture, as long as every man, woman and child in America sees it." Whether this $3 million production ever made that dime for Goldwyn is doubtful, but the controversy and subsequent advertising and publicity problems notwithstanding, *The North Star* earned six Oscar nominations: Best Original Screenplay, Best Cinematography, Best Scoring of a Dramatic Picture, Best Art/Set Decoration, Best Special Effects (Clarence Slifer and R.O. Binger), and Best Sound (Thomas T. Moulton).

The North Star and the other two important pro-Russian films of the era, Warner Bros.' *Mission to Moscow* and MGM's *Song of Russia,* today rank as cinematic curios. Only *The North Star* actually exists via television—and then, only barely. The film, one of the very few by Goldwyn, was acquired by NTA and reissued theatrically in 1957 in a drastically reedited version, under the title, *Armored Attack!* NTA, going over the film frame by frame, hacked twenty-two minutes out of it, turned it into an action picture with a Soviet background, eliminated every mention of "comrade," added stock footage from the Hungarian uprising of 1956, and inserted a narration warning of the menace in the East following the defeat of Nazism. As one of the NTA spokesmen said: "The only thing we couldn't take out was Dana Andrews running around in a damn Soviet uniform." *Armored Attack!* is seen this way on television and in no way illustrates the famous Goldwyn touch that has become part of cinema history.

Anne Baxter and Farley Granger in The North Star.

Carl Benton Reid and Ann Harding in The North Star.

*Dana Andrews, Walter Brennan, Farley Granger, Jane
Withers and Anne Baxter in* The North Star.

64 UP IN ARMS (1944)

Directed by Elliott Nugent; associate producer, Don Hartman; screenplay, Don Hartman, Allan Boretz and Robert Pirosh; based on the play *The Nervous Wreck* by Owen Davis; music director, Louis Forbes; score, Ray Heindorf; songs, Ted Koehler and Harold Arlen, except "Melody in 4-F" and "Manic-Depressive Pictures Presents" by Sylvia Fine and Max Liebman; dances staged by Danny Dare; photographer, Ray Rennahan; editors, Daniel Mandell and James Newcom; assistant director, Louis Germonprez; art directors, Perry Ferguson and Stuart Chaney; technical advisors, Lt. Richard Day and Lt. Eunice C. Hatchitt. Running time, 105 minutes. Technicolor. Released by RKO Pictures. Premiere: Radio City Music Hall, 3/2/44

THE CAST:

Danny Weems, Danny Kaye; *Virginia Merrill*, Dinah Shore; *Joe Nelson*, Dana Andrews; *Mary Morgan*, Constance Dowling; *Colonel Ashley*, Louis Calhern; *Blackie*, George Mathews; *Butterball*, Benny Baker; *Info Jones*, Elisha Cook, Jr.; *Sergeant Gelsey*, Lyle Talbot; *Major Brook*, Walter Catlett; *Ashley's Aide*, George Meeker; *Mrs. Willoughby*, Margaret Dumont; *Captain*, Richard Powers (Tom Keene); *Singer at Dock*, Donald Dickson; *Mr. Higginbotham*, Charles Arnt; *Dr. Freyheisen*, Charles Halton; *Dr. Weavermacher*, Harry Hayden; *Dr. Campbell*, Charles D. Brown; *Dr. Jones*, Maurice Cass; *Master of Ceremonies*, Tom Dugan; *Sourfaced Waiter*, Sig Arno; *Head Waiter*, Fred Essler; *Sherwood*, Edward Earle; *Interrogator*, Leonard Strong; *Bandmaster*, Rudolph Friml, Jr.; *The Goldwyn Girls*, Betty Alexander, Gale Amber, Gloria Anderson, Jan Bryant, Alma Carroll, Joan Chaffee, Linda Christian, Virginia Cruzon, Helen Darling, Myrna Dell, Dorothy Gardner, Inna Gest, Renee Godfrey, Ellen Hall, June Harris, Eloise Hart, Mary Ann Hyde, June Lang, Rosalyn Lee, Florence Lundeen, Mickey Maloy, Virginia Mayo, Dorothy Merritt, Lorraine Miller, Mary Moore, Kay Morley, Diana Mumby, Lee Nugent, Dorothy Patrick, Shelby Payne, Helen Talbot, Ruth Valmy, Ricki Van Dusen, Alice Wallace, Virginia Wicks, Audrey Young; and William Davidson, Larry Steers, Eddie Waller, Oliver Prickett (Blake), Matt McHugh, Pete Cusanelli, Maryon Adair, Herbert Evans, Stanley Gilbert, John Hamilton, Isabel Withers, Hans Schumm, Eddie Kane, Frank O'Connor Anne O'Neal, Virginia Farmer, Bill Hunter, George McKay, George Magrill, James Harrison, Lillian Randolph, Peter Chong, Bruce Wong, Benson Fong, George T. Lee, Knox Manning.

Dancers: Maxine Armour, Bonnie Barlowe, Karen Knight, Audrey Korn, Helen McAllister, Marjorie Raymond, Joet Robinson, Eleanor Shaw, June Wayne, Barbara Williams.

Musical numbers: (performed by)
"Manic-Depressive Pictures Presents" *The Lobby Number* (Danny Kaye)
"Now I Know" (Dinah Shore)
"All Out for Freedom" (Donald Dickson, men's chorus, Goldwyn Girls)
Reprise: "All Out for Freedom" (Donald Dickson)
"Tess' Torch Song" (Dinah Shore)
"Melody in F" (Danny Kaye)
"Jive Number" (Danny Kaye, Dinah Shore, Goldwyn Girls)
Reprise: "Jive Number" (Danny Kaye, Dinah Shore)
Reprise: "All Out for Freedom" (Danny Kaye, Dinah Shore, cast)

Among Goldwyn's greatest achievements during the Forties was the instant screen stardom he offered to Danny Kaye in Kaye's first feature-length film, *Up In Arms*, which Goldwyn had had revamped from his first Eddie Cantor success, *Whoopee!* (While totally different from one another, each film used as its source Owen Davis' 1925 play, *The Nervous Wreck*.) Frank Quinn, critic for the *New York Daily Mirror*, announced enthusiastically that "not since Greta Garbo made her cinematic bow has there been anything so terrific as the inimitable Danny." Quinn found Kaye "one of the most naturally exhilarating and spontaneous personalities in film history. 'Phenomenal' is the true appraisal of Danny's devastating debut."

Kaye had established himself with his individual brand of comedy, glib mimicry and matchless patter songs through long years on the road, first on the Borscht circuit, then in vaudeville and on into variety shows. In 1937 and 1938, he made a series of two-reel screen comedies for Educational Pictures, shot in Astoria, New York, by Art Miller (with then unknowns like Imogene Coca and June Allyson, among others). Kaye was spotted by producer Max Liebman who put the comic in his *Straw Hat Revue* on Broadway in 1939, performing several sophisticated satires written by Sylvia Fine who would soon become Mrs. Kaye. On the basis of his initial Broadway success, Kaye was offered an MGM contract at $3000 a week, turning it down in favor of appearing with Gertrude Lawrence and Victor Mature in *Lady in the Dark,* and stopping the show nightly with his specialty number, "Tchaikovsky." Then he signed for the lead in Cole Porter's *Let's Face It* in late 1941, and obtained Porter's permission to include in the score the hilarious "Melody in F," written for him by Sylvia Fine and Max Liebman. When not appearing on Broadway, Kaye could be found entertaining in smart clubs both in Chicago and New York, such as La Martinique (where, in 1940, he was convulsing the high-rollers for $250 a week). It was at Billy Rose's Diamond Horseshoe where Goldwyn found Danny Kaye in 1943, offered him star billing at $150,000 per film, and signed him to a five-picture contract. In his wisdom, Goldwyn had Kaye's red hair dyed blonde for his debut movie, but Kaye balked at the suggestion of plastic surgery to alter his nose (a problem Goldwyn finally solved by makeup and camera angles).

Danny Kaye created a sensation as a wacky hypochondriac who takes a job as an elevator operator in a medical building to be near his doctors, and is finally drafted with his roommate and their respective girlfriends. Two Kaye specialty numbers were worked into the film: his trademarked scat song, "Melody in F," reprised from *Let's Face It,* and the hilarious satire on motion picture extravaganzas, "Manic-Depressive Pictures Presents" (familiarly known as the "Theatre Lobby Number"), both written by Sylvia Fine and Max Liebman.

As a one-man laboratory of imaginary maladies, Danny Weems finds himself classified *1A* and inducted with his pal, Joe Nelson. Danny does not quite know how to break the news to the girl he loves, Mary Morgan, who happens to be in love with Joe. Mary joins the WACS with her friend, Virginia Merrill, whose eye has been on Danny for some time. Having completed their training, the boys are sent to an embarkation point for transport to the South Pacific, and the girls manage to sneak away from their nurses regiment to bid Danny and Joe goodbye. Because of Danny's bungling, Virginia and Mary find themselves aboard the troopship as it pulls out, and while Virginia can explain her presence as an army nurse, Mary technically is a stowaway, and Danny's efforts to keep her from being discovered by his commanding officer,

Colonel Ashley, keeps the ship in a constant state of pandemonium. Eventually though, her presence becomes known, and Danny gallantly takes the blame, knowing he will be tossed in the brig. When the ship arrives at its Pacific destination, Danny is confined in a guardhouse at the edge of camp, only to be captured during a Japanese raid. Through a series of bluffs however, he manages to outwit his captors, and leading twenty captured soldiers, he returns to camp to be acclaimed as a hero.

Amid all this (and his two specialty numbers) is a score by Ted Koehler and Harold Arlen, giving Dinah Shore several solo spots—including the Oscar-nominated song, "Now I Know"—among the ten production extravaganzas. In addition, Goldwyn has tripled his usual ensemble of Goldwyn Girls including Virginia Mayo (who subsequently would be elevated to Kaye's permanent leading lady during his Goldwyn stay), keeping their shapely frames somewhat hidden in army khakis for much of the footage until an elaborate dream sequence when the girls are allowed flimsy negligees while emerging, incredibly, from the tops of trees.

"Expertly showcasing the comedic talents of Danny Kaye in his first starrer," *Variety* reported,

> *Up In Arms* is a filmusical that's expensively mounted in the best Goldwyn tradition of elaborateness. Kaye is definitely star material. Another newcomer, Constance Dowling, is both an eyeful and talented in a straight acting part and should also go far in picture . . . Elliott Nugent capably handled the directing . . . and Goldwyn spent plenty of coin on the production, but it should all roll back along with plenty of profit.

In her three and a half star review in the New York *Daily News,* Kate Cameron wrote, simply: "One realizes that Danny Kaye belongs in the ranks of the great comic specialists of our day."

Time called the film "easy, handsome, unabashed," and noted:

> It was a fantastic idea to festoon a completely unreal version of World War Two around Danny Kaye . . . (and) barring a few lapses of taste, it is fun to watch and food to look at. The heart, liver and lights of this cinemusical is Kaye (whose) mimicry, patter and general daftness are as deft as a surgeon's incision.

And the *London Evening Standard* said this of the film's star: "He is a comedian who is really original . . . he has such a wide range in the art of entertainment and his mimicry is witty, his slapstick resounding."
Critic Howard Barnes agreed, saying:

> The chief distinction of *Up In Arms* is that it brings Danny Kaye's talents to the screen. He is superbly funny in the dither and double-talk ditties that made him famous on the stage, although too often his clown-

ing is buried in an extravagant and pretentious musical melange which is in questionable taste at the moment . . . The sheer opulence of the offering will undoubtedly enchant most filmgoers as Samuel Goldwyn, a stickler for high-class pictorial spectacle, has shot the works (and) Elliott Nugent has staged the show briskly and handsomely. *Up In Arms* is a resplendent travesty, produced with more trimmings than taste.

Bosley Crowther, commenting on Kaye, confided:

Now that he has perfected his explosive humor to such a degree that people begin to disintegrate the moment he walks upon a stage, Samuel Goldwyn has arranged a conjunction of Mr. Kaye and the screen. It stands to reason that millions of persons are immediately imperiled thereby, for every one of Mr. Kaye's perfections—and a few of his imperfections—are generously repeated in *Up In Arms* . . . of course, Mr. Goldwyn has dressed his picture in bright Technicolor finery and put aboard his troopship some Army nurses who would make malaria a rare privilege . . . if only the story were better—hey, what else do we want with Danny Kaye!

Goldwyn staged his premiere of *Up In Arms* at Radio City Music Hall in early 1944, but later mounted a more elaborate showing in a rented dance hall near Reno, Nevada, next to the railroad tracks, to point up his continuing opposition to the "monopolistic practices" inherent in motion picture exhibition. For years he had waged a futile battle to force theatre owners and the various motion picture circuits to pay him a percentage of his pictures' grosses, rather than continuing the standard practice of allowing them to show his product on the customary flat rental basis. For his well-publicized showing of *Up In Arms* Goldwyn turned up to drive the last spike that fastened the 400th chair to the floor of the El Patio Ballroom, as a Hollywood contingent led by Mary Pickford watched.

Dana Andrews, Danny Kaye and Dinah Shore in Up In Arms.

Danny Kaye and Dinah Shore with The Goldwyn Girls in Up In Arms. *Virginia Mayo is the blonde at top center.*

Louis Calhern, Danny Kaye and Constance Dowling in Up In Arms.

235

65 THE PRINCESS AND THE PIRATE (1944)

Directed by David Butler; associate producer, Don Hartman; screenplay, Don Hartman, Melville Shavelson and Everett Freeman; based on the adaptation by Allen Boretz and Curtis Kenyon of a story by Sy Bartlett; music, David Rose; song, "(How Would You Like To) Kiss Me in the Moonlight" by Jimmy McHugh and Harold Adamson; photographers, Victor Milner and William Snyder; editor, Daniel Mandell; art director, Ernst Fegte. Running time. 95 minutes. Technicolor. Released by RKO Pictures. Premiere: Cincinnati, Omaha and Kansas City, 11/7/44. New York premiere: Astor Theater, 2/9/45

THE CAST:

Sylvester Crosby, Bob Hope; *Margaret Warbrook,* Virginia Mayo (singing dubbed by Louanne Hogan); *Featherhead,* Walter Brennan; *Governor La Roche,* Walter Slezak; *The Hook,* Victor McLaglen; *Pedro,* Marc Lawrence; *"Bucket of Blood" Proprietor,* Hugo Haas; *"Boar's Head Inn" Landlady,* Maude Eburne; *Don Jose,* Adia Kuznetzoff; *Mr. Pelly,* Brandon Hurst; *Alonzo,* Tom Kennedy; *Captain of "Mary Ann",* Stanley Andrews; *The King,* Robert Warwick; *Lieutenant,* Tom Tyler; and *The Goldwyn Girls,* Lillian Molieri, Loretta Daye, Betty Ruth Caldwell, Betty Thurston, Pat Farrell, Kay Morley, Betty Alexander, Ruth Valmy, Alma Carroll; and Ralph Dunn, Bert Roach, Francis Ford, Ray Teal, Mike Mazurki, James Flavin, Edwin Stanley, Weldon Heyburn, Edward Peil, Bill Hunter, Crane Whitley, Alan Bridge, Al Hill, Dick Rich, Frank Moran, Jack Carr, Oscar 'Dutch' Hendrian, Colin Kenny, Stewart Garner, Art Miles, Vic Christy, Robert Hale, Constantine Romanoff, Helen Thurston, Ernie Adams, Sammy Stein, Ted Billings, Rondo Hatton.

Promising Bob Hope a musical extravaganza developed from a swashbuckling farce, embellished with a more substantial plot than *They Got Me Covered,* plus magnificent Technicolor, a fresh and lissome leading lady, and eight delectable new Goldwyn Girls to ogle, Goldwyn

was able to lure Paramount's superstar funnyman away from his home lot for the second (and last) time during the eighteen year Hope reign as Adolph Zukor's house comic. And with David Butler again directing, Goldwyn lavished on his star and the appreciative audiences a sumptuous, brightly colored burlesque which, in production values, outdid anything Hope was ever offered by Paramount. "The great Goldwyn," wrote Howard Barnes in his review of the film,

> has dressed a wacky plot in such pretentious garb that the Hope quips are sometimes smothered in investiture . . . (and) one has to settle for the babes and the big, beautiful production to be quite happy with *The Princess and the Pirate.*

As Hope's costar, Goldwyn assigned Virginia Mayo, the only Goldwyn Girl whom Goldwyn himself would turn into a star. She had been a chorus girl in Eddie Cantor's *Banjo Eyes* (the Broadway musical version of *Three Men on a Horse* that Cantor at last was able to do) in 1941, and was dancing at Billy Rose's Diamond Horseshoe in late 1942 when Samuel Goldwyn, there, ironically, to see Danny Kaye, spotted her and put her under contract as a Goldwyn Girl. She was to appear in Kaye's first Goldwyn film and costar with him in his remaining four under his initial five picture contract. (Between *Up In Arms* and stardom in *The Princess and the Pirate,* Goldwyn allowed Virginia Mayo to accept small roles elsewhere, and she appeared briefly in two Betty Grable musicals, *Sweet Rosie O'Grady* and *Pin-Up Girl,* and in larger roles in a minor RKO musical, *Seven Days Ashore,* and in the pseudo-biographical *Jack London,* where she met and later married the leading man, Michael O'Shea.)

Mayo, an eyeful in Technicolor, proved a refreshing foil for Hope who amid his unceasing barrage of jokes, finds himself an eighteenth century vaudevillian (and a coward for all seasons) aboard a packet ship, *Mary Ann,* egotistically passing himself off as Sylvester the Great. Among his fellow passengers is Margaret Warbrook, who is really a princess, fleeing incognito to the West Indies to avoid an undesirable marriage arranged by her father the King. A band of cutthroats, led by the infamous Hook, boards the *Mary Ann* and abducts Margaret. To avoid walking the fatal plank, Sylvester disguises himself as a toothless old Gypsy hag, and is taken along. On Hook's brigantine, one of the buccaneers, Featherhead, offers to help Sylvester and Margaret escape if they will deliver a treasure map stolen from Hook to his (Featherhead's) brother at the pirate stronghold of Casa Rouge.

At Casa Rouge, however, the pair fails to locate the elusive brother, and to get money to live, Sylvester and Margaret obtain jobs as entertainers at the Bucket of Blood Tavern (on the same bill with Ye Goldwyn Girls, as the sign by the door advertises). The tough house proves quite a challenge for Sylvester who is driven from the stage by a barrage of fruit. Margaret, however, is somewhat more acceptable to the leering audience, among whom is the island's governor, La Roche, who recognizes her and has her kidnapped in hopes of extracting a generous ransom from the King. Sylvester, too, is tossed into prison on the assumption that Margaret's father will pay handsomely for the privilege of hanging this accomplice. When Hook and his blackguards turn up at Casa Rouge, determined to learn the whereabouts of the stolen map, Featherhead seeks out Sylvester, and during Hook's assault on the Governor's fortress, knocks out Sylvester before the map can be destroyed and tattoos it on the vaudevillian's chest. Then, in the confusion of the attack, Featherhead once again helps Sylvester escape with Margaret, and believing that Hook has been killed, Sylvester returns, disguised as the pirate chief, and takes command of Hook's ship. When Hook himself returns to the ship, the two "captains" alternately appear at the wheel and give contradictory orders to the confused, but obedient crew. Hook finally comprehends the situation and has Sylvester tossed into irons until he can devise a fiendish torture. The doomed Sylvester is finally saved by the timely arrival of one of the King's ships, the pirates are subdued, the governor is arrested, and Margaret is allowed to marry the man of her choice. Sylvester prepares to embrace her as she walks past him and throws her arms around one of the King's sailors, Bing Crosby. With an incredulous look, Sylvester insists: "I work my brains out for nine reels and some bit player from Paramount comes over and steals my girl. That's the last picture I'll ever make for Goldwyn."

"Anything called *The Princess and the Pirate* with Bob Hope starred is a tipoff on its frank escapology," commented *Variety*. "This Goldwyn production makes no attempt to be anything else, and Hope plays it that way, all the way . . .(and) from start to finish, he dominates the action with well-timed colloquial nifties."

In the *New York Herald Tribune,* critic Howard Barnes wrote:

If you find Hope as inimitably amusing as ever, you won't care about a gag or two at any point in the proceedings. There are so many of them in this Goldwyn production that they crowd each other out of continuity and demand the anomaly of blackouts in Technicolor . . . Hope is, of course, the be-all and end-all of the show (and David Butler's direction makes the most of him and the decor).

Bosley Crowther accepted *The Princess and the Pirate* for the luxuriant entertainment it was meant to be, noting that

Hope proves to a host of bloody cutthroats that the gag is mightier than the sword (and) proved to the audience that he can literally keep a film alive, even when his retinue of writers rather obviously and languidly despair. For there are moments in this burlesque when it seems that all the authors have run out, leaving Mr. Hope and plot to fumble and bluff as best they can. In those moments, there come looks of blank amazement upon Hope's perpetually youthful face—expressions which one might gather are not feigned for dramatic effect.

Crowther further observed that "Virginia Mayo is quite a pleasant show in her own right . . . (and) there are plenty of handmaidens in scanty costumes sashaying about. Mr. Goldwyn has not spared the doubloons."

Newsweek referred to the film as "strictly escapist entertainment on a typically generous Goldwyn budget of some $2,000,000," and observed that

from start to finish, director David Butler plays this roistering rigamarole for the broadest travesty, and the gags explode with the hit-and-miss ebullience of corn in a popper. Some of the gags are all they should be; others swing telegraphically from the floor to hit only the breeze; all are vastly improved by Hope's presence and his inimitable delivery . . . Miss Mayo is lovely in Technicolor and more than adequate to the film's negligible acting demands.

At year's end, the Academy of Motion Picture Arts and Sciences nominated the Goldwyn swashbuckler in two categories: Best Scoring of a Dramatic Picture (David Rose) and Best Art/Set Design for a Color Film (Ernst Fegte).

Curiously, Goldwyn premiered his film in the Midwest and played it throughout the country before bringing it into New York nearly three full months after its initial engagements. This uncharacteristic move was unique in Goldwyn's distribution history.

Virginia Mayo, Bob Hope and Victor McLaglen in The Princess and the Pirate.

Bob Hope and Virginia Mayo in The Princess and the Pirate.

Bob Hope and Walter Brennan in The Princess and the Pirate.

66 WONDER MAN (1945)

Directed by Bruce Humberstone; screenplay, Don Hartman, Melville Shavelson and Philip Rapp; based on an adaptation by Jack Jevne and Eddie Moran of a story by Arthur Sheekman; music director, Louis Forbes; score, Ray Heindorf; song "So In Love" by Leo Robin and David Rose; specialty numbers, Sylvia Fine; choreographer, John Wray; photographers, Victor Milner and William Snyder; editor, Daniel Mandell; art director, Ernst Fegte. Running time, 98 minutes. Technicolor. Released by RKO Pictures. Premiere. Astor Theater, New York, 6/8/45.

THE CAST:

Buzzy Bellew/Edwin Dingle, Danny Kaye; *Ellen Shanley*, Virginia Mayo; *Midge Mallon*, Vera-Ellen* (singing dubbed by June Hutton); *Monte Rossen*, Donald Woods; *Schmidt*, S.Z. Sakall; *Chimp*, Allen Jenkins; *Torso*, Edward S. Brophy; *Ten-Grand Jackson*, Steve Cochran; *District Attorney R.J. O'Brien*, Otto Kruger; *Assistant District Attorney Grosset*, Richard Lane; *Mrs. Leland Hume*, Natalie Schafer; *Mike (Sailor)*, Huntz Hall; *Girlfriend*, Virginia Gilmore; *Cop in Park*, Edward Gargan; *Mr. Wagonseller*, Grant Mitchell; *Mrs. Schmidt*, Gisela Werbiseck; *Prima Donna*, Alice Mock; *Stenographer*, Mary Field; *Opera Conductor*, Aldo Franchetti; *Stage Manager*, Maurice Cass; *Bus Driver*, James Flavin; *Drunk in Club*, Jack Norton; *Bartender*, Frank Orth; *The Goldwyn Girls*, Ruth Valmy, Margie Stewart, Alma Carroll, Georgia Lange, Karen Gaylord, Mary Moore, Gloria Delson, Deannie Best, Mary Meade, Martha Montgomery, Ellen Hall, Phyllis Forbes, Mary Jane Woods, Katherine (Karin) Booth and Chili Williams; and Al Ruiz, Willard Van Simons, Charles Irwin, Cecil Cunningham, Chester Clute, Eddie Kane, Ray Teal, Leon Belasco, Billy Wayne, Eddie Dunn, Ralph Dunn, Luis Alberni, Roseanne Murray, Eddie Acuff, Harry Depp, John Kelly, Byron Foulger, Sarah Selby, William Newell, James Farley, Frank Melton, Barbara La Rene.

Dancers: Maureen Cunningham, Georganne Smith, Janet Lavis, Dorothy Jean, Betty Marion, Jane Allen, Doris Toddings, Jean Marley, Helen McAllister, Virginia Kepler, Helen McCowan, Carolyn Haney, Charles Teske, Ray Nyles, Walter Pietila, Bob Mascagno, Eddie Cutler, Allen Pinson; *Entertainers*, Grace Johnson, Dorothy Koster, Loretta Daye, Susan Scott, Alice Stansfield, Betty Lane, Mickey Maloy, Alice Kersten; *Opera Singers*, Noel Cravat, Nick Thompson, Nino Pipitone, Baldo Minuti.

* in screen debut

Musical numbers: (performed by:)
"Bali Boogie" (Danny Kaye, Vera-Ellen, Jack Norton, Goldwyn Girls)
"So in Love" (Vera-Ellen, Cecil Cunningham, Goldwyn Girls)
danced by Vera-Ellen and the boys
"Ortchi Chornya" (Danny Kaye)
"Opera Number" (Danny Kaye, Alice Mock)

Delighted with the enthusiastic reception accorded his first Danny Kaye film, Goldwyn concluded that the comedian's rabid audience deserved a double dose of Kaye the second time around and proved, in *Wonder Man*, that two Danny Kayes actually did provide twice the fun. With the expected gloss and style, together with glittering Technicolor, a couple of new screen discoveries and the luscious 1945 display of Goldwyn Girls, the producer in his only film that year served up another grand entertainment to surround his new star. *Wonder Man*, "the work," wrote John McCarten in *The New Yorker*, "of no less than six eager and fertile minds," showcases Kaye as twins in an original, rather elaborate fantasy, into which are incorporated well-established Kaye routines and patter songs (written by Sylvia Fine), as well as his unique double-talk bits and rubber-faced contortions. Danny Kaye appears in virtually every foot of the film. Goldwyn received no complaints from the comedian's legion of fans.

Kaye's frenetic clowning and Goldwyn's expert cast obscure the silliness of the fantastic story in which the star appears as both a brash, carefree nightclub performer and his bleak, scholarly brother whose second home (or perhaps his first) is the public library, because, as he confesses, "I love the smell of leather bindings." The tale revolves around the twins' psychic adventures when the flashy one is killed by gangsters and enters the body of his bookish brother whose quiet life is suddenly complicated to the point of madness. "Within these modest limits," wrote Bosley Crowther in his review, "the tremendously talented young man manages to give an exhibition of most everything he can do, and all of it is amusing."

Easily overshadowing some of the less inspired original ideas written for him in *Wonder Man,* are the two classic Kaye turns that years earlier he had perfected in his club act. First is the side-splitting routine in which Kaye sings "Orchi Tchornya" as a jovial Russian baritone suddenly seized with a sneezing fit. Then there is the memorable, more elaborate "Opera Number" in which he explodes into a crazy operatic parody that finds him, at the climax, wrestling with diva Alice Mock in an insane duet. Manny Farber, critic for *Nation,* observed that

> Kaye manages each of his efforts so that it comes at the best moments, very clear and well, and he's very deft in surprising you with the unexpected, such as repeating a yell even a fifteenth time, or, as in the sneezing act, managing an infinite number of improvisations on a single idea.

To support Kaye in *Wonder Man,* Goldwyn assigned lovely Virginia Mayo (this was the first of her four Goldwyn films as Kaye's leading lady), plus his new discovery, pert dancer Vera-Ellen, who had been a Radio City Music Hall Rockette and a singer with the Ted Lewis band before becoming a featured dancer in such Broadway musicals as Kern and Hammerstein's *Very Warm for May* (1939), Cole Porter's *Panama Hattie* (1940), and Rodgers and Hart's *By Jupiter* (1942). A Goldwyn talent scout spotted her in the 1943 revival of Rodgers and Hart's *A Connecticut Yankee* and gave the nineteen-year-old singer/dancer a contract. Curiously, in her two Goldwyn films—both with Kaye, Mayo, and another Goldwyn discovery, Steve Cochran—her singing was dubbed. In *Wonder Man,* she performed Sylvia Fine's exotic "Bali Boogie" with Kaye (who, as the club performer, plays her fiance) and the Oscar-nominated Leo Robin/David Rose song, "So in Love," in a production number that included (Miss) Cecil Cunningham and the Goldwyn Girls.

Wonder Man's plot: On the eve of his marriage to Midge Mallon, his dancing partner, flamboyant club star Buzzy Ballow is murdered by gangster Ten Grand Jackson's henchmen, Chimp and Torso, to keep him (Buzzy) from talking to the District Attorney about one of Jackson's killings he had witnessed. Shortly after

Buzzy's body has been dumped into a lake in Prospect Park, his scholarly brother, Edwin, whom he had not seen in years, is irresistibly drawn to the site from the local delicatessen where he had gone to obtain a late-night repast for the very rare date he was then entertaining, Ellen Shanley, the pretty librarian with whom he suddenly found himself entranced. At the park, Edwin meets Buzzy's ghost who explains his murder and insists that Edwin avenge the death by delivering to the D.A. the evidence needed to convict Jackson. When the bookish brother refuses, the ghost demonstrates that he can enter Edwin's body and compel him to be uncharacteristically brash. Edwin reluctantly agrees to impersonate Buzzy, and whenever he finds himself in a difficult situation, he is saved by the timely appearance of his ghost twin. Complications arise when Edwin finds himself in a jam with Ellen, with whom he has fallen in love, while trying to hold off Midge, who believes he is Buzzy and expects him to marry her immediately. Then there is Ten Grand Jackson who has mistaken Edwin for Buzzy and orders him killed again.

When Buzzy's ghost becomes drunk while parrying, through Edwin, with Jackson at the club, Edwin finds himself deserted during his crucial interview with District Attorney O'Brien and his assistant, and he is forced to flee from Jackson's henchmen who chase him through the streets of New York and corner him backstage at the Metropolitan Opera House. There, Edwin masquerades as a grand opera baritone, and by singing the story of the gangsters' murders to the D.A., seated out front, succeeds in having Jackson, along with Chimp and Torso, captured. Buzzy's spirit is finally satisfied, allowing Edwin to resume his normal, placid life and marry Ellen, while Midge finally succumbs to the wedding proposals of clubowner Monte Rossen.

As glittering Goldwyn entertainment, *Wonder Man* is unmatched. *Variety* confessed that

> all the finery that Goldwyn could muster has gone into his latest Danny Kaye starrer . . . (which) will more firmly establish the Broadway comedian in the upper picture ranks. It's the type of yarn that enables him to give way to the uninhibitive and distinctive style of comedy that has sent him soaring to stardom . . . Niftily Technicolored and expensive looking all the way, (the film) is all Kaye, and there's no mistaking that without him, it would be decidedly commonplace.

The *Variety* critic admired the ladies, deciding that

> the blonde Virginia Mayo screens like the couple of millions that are indicated to have been spent by Goldwyn on the picture, and Vera-Ellen is a fine young hoofer who can handle lines well, too. Direction by Bruce Humberstone is aimed for broad laughs, and got 'em.

The New Yorker said simply: "Given adequate material, Danny Kaye is one of the most versatile and generally satisfactory comedians on the screen. This he gets in *Wonder Man*."

In his rave review in *The New York Times,* Bosley Crowther disclosed that *Wonder Man* "sneaked like the Twentieth Century Limited into town" and called the film "fantastic—a wholesale, complete and exhaustive demonstration of Mr. Kaye" with "Mr. Kaye—both of him—running away with the show." Crowther's conclusion: "There are stretches of tedium in the middle—Mr. Kaye's writers nodded now and then—but the idea is right for this rare cutup and he whirls it around both of his heads."

Time Magazine wrote:

Wonder Man is a temperate enough description of Danny Kaye in his second full-length movie. Barring Kaye and the pretty hoof-and-mouthing of the flea-sized, dainty screen newcomer, Vera-Ellen, the picture is about as short on drive, sparkle and resourcefulness as a Samuel Goldwyn production can be. But fortunately there is no barring Danny Kaye, a one-man show and, at his frequent best, a howling good one. Besides being a brilliant comic entertainer, Kaye has considerable talent as a straight actor . . . Granted what he

is given to work with—a first-rate idea developed in second gear—Danny Kaye does a beautiful job.

Howard Barnes felt that

a fantastic theme is loaded with laughter (and) Danny Kaye does the loading . . . He makes *Wonder Man* something of a one-man show. For all of Goldwyn's immaculate Technicolor production and a bevy of beauties, the film hangs together on his performance. He is asked to do a great deal more than a star of his stature should be charged with, in keeping a musical fantasy funny and smooth. He never fails the offering . . . (and) make *Wonder Man* a wonder show.

Shortly before the premiere of *Wonder Man* (which, in addition to the Oscar nomination for Best Song, received the Academy Award for Best Special Effects, concocted by photographer John Fulton and sound engineer A.W. Johns), Goldwyn sent forth the news that his next Danny Kaye picture would be *Hans Christian Andersen,* which originally had been planned several years earlier as a vehicle for Gary Cooper (with William Wyler directing from a Jo Swerling script)! The Goldwyn/Kaye *Hans Christian Andersen* would not be realized for another seven years.

Natalie Schaefer, Danny Kaye and Virginia Mayo in Wonder Man.

Virginia Mayo and Danny Kaye in Wonder Man.

Otto Kruger, Danny Kaye and Richard Lane in Wonder Man.

241

67 THE KID FROM BROOKLYN (1946)

Directed by Norman Z. McLeod; screenplay, Don Hartman and Melville Shavelson; based on the screenplay by Grover Jones, Frank Butler and Richard Connell from the play *The Milky Way* by Lynn Root and Harry Clork; music, Carmen Dragon; songs, Jule Styne and Sammy Cahn, except "Pavlova" by Sylvia Fine and Max Liebman; vocal arrangements, Kay Thompson; choreographer, Bernard Pearce; photographer, Gregg Toland; editor, Daniel Mandell; art directors, Perry Ferguson and Stewart Chaney. Running time, 114 minutes. Technicolor. Released by RKO Pictures. Premiere: Astor Theater, New York, 4/18/46

THE CAST:

Burleigh Sullivan, Danny Kaye; *Polly Pringle,* Virginia Mayo (singing dubbed by Dorothy Ellers); *Susie Sullivan,* Vera-Ellen (singing dubbed by Betty Russell); *Gabby Sloan,* Walter Abel; *Ann Westley,* Eva Arden; *Speed MacFarlane,* Steve Cochran; *Spider Schultz,* Lionel Stander; *Mrs. E. Winthrop LeMoyne,* Fay Bainter; *Wilbur Austin,* Clarence Kolb; *Photographer,* Victor Cutler; *Willard,* Charles Cane; *Fight Ring Announcer,* Jerome Cowan; *Announcer,* Don Wilson; *Announcer,* Knox Manning; *Matron,* Kay Thompson; *Master of Ceremonies,* Johnny Downs; *Mr. LeMoyne,* Pierre Watkin; *Killer Kelly,* Frank Riggi; *The Goldwyn Girls,* Karen X. Gaylord, Ruth Valmy, Shirley Ballard, Virginia Belmont, Betty Cargyle, Jean Cronin, Vonne Lester, Diana Mumby, Mary Simpson, Virginia Thorpe, Tyra Vaughn, Kismi Stefan, Betty Alexander, Martha Montgomery, Joyce MacKenzie, Helen Kimball, Jan Bryant, Donna Hamilton; and Robert Strong, Billy Newell, Tom Quinn, Billy Bletcher, Billy Wayne, George Sherwood, George Chandler, Donald Kerr, Jack Roper, Steve Taylor, Al Hill, Jay Eaton, Syd Saylor, Betty Blythe, Ralph Dunn, Eddie Hart, Eric Wilton, Alexander Pollard, Billy Benedict, Mary Forbes, Snub Pollard, Hal K. Dawson, Jack Norton, Billy Nelson, Dulce Day, Jack Gargan Lester Dorr, Jack Cheatham, John Indrisano.

Dancers: Gil Dennis, Bob Gompers, Tony Conde, Danny Drake, Rudolph Andrean, Michael Collins, Rudolph Silva, Kenneth McAndish, Alfred Burke, Robert Forrest; *Acrobatic Dancers,* Jody Black, Mabel Boehlke, Betty Yeaton, Dorothy Clarke, Gertrude Gault, Shirley Sharon; *Dancer* in "Hey, What's Your Name" Number, Jimmy Kelly; *Dancers* in "I Love An Old Fashioned Love Song" Number Eddie Cutler, Harvey Karels and Al Ruiz.

Musical Numbers: (performed by)
"Sunflower Song" *Opening Number* (Goldwyn Girls)
"Hey, What's Your Name?" (Vera-Ellen) *danced by Vera-Ellen, Jimmy Kelly and men*
"You're the Cause of It All" (Virginia Mayo)
"Welcome, Burleigh" (Goldwyn Girls)
"I Love an Old-Fashioned Song" (Virginia Mayo) *danced by Eddie Cutler, Harvey Karels and Al Ruiz*
"Pavlova" (Danny Kaye)

Samuel Goldwyn's first postwar treat for the moviegoers of the world was another lush, tune-filled Danny Kaye extravaganza, *The Kid From Brooklyn,* the most elaborate of the five Goldwyn/Kaye productions. For this one, Goldwyn reached back to the screenplay of the 1936 Harold Lloyd movie, *The Milky Way,* the entertaining saga about the meek milkman who is led to believe that he is a great prizefighter and finds himself middleweight champion of the world. The same basic group of players who supported Kaye in *Wonder Man* again surrounded the star, along with a few additions: Walter Abel, Fay Bainter, and from Danny's popular radio show, Eve Arden (who had appeared with Danny in *Let's Face It*) and Lionel Stander, playing the role he had in the Harold Lloyd version. Other than the later *Hans Christian Andersen,* this film is more of a musical than any of the movies Kaye made for Goldwyn, featuring six songs by

Jule Styne and Sammy Cahn—all performed by Virginia Mayo, Vera-Ellen and the gorgeous Goldwyn Girls (eighteen this time)—and the priceless "Pavlova" number by Kaye, written years earlier by Sylvia Fine and Max Liebman for Danny's act at the Chez Paree in Chicago.

Kaye appears to have been more comfortable following in Harold Lloyd's shoes than in Eddie Cantor's (in the earlier *Up in Arms*), or Gary Cooper's (in the later *A Song is Born*), while personalizing the story to such an extent that he can claim complete ownership. The original source of *The Kid from Brooklyn*, neé *The Milky Way*, was a very short-lived (forty-seven performances) 1934 Broadway play by Lynn Root and Harry Clork that had the same title as the Harold Lloyd cinemazation. The stage cast included Hugh O'Connell as the milkman, Brian Donlevy as the soon-to-be ex-champ, Leo Donnelly as his crooked manager, and Gladys George as the manager's girlfriend—the roles played in the Goldwyn film by Danny Kaye, Steve Cochran, Walter Abel and Eve Arden, respectively.

"It is immediately apparent," concluded *Newsweek's* critic

that Goldwyn spent considerable thought and a lot of money—reportedly $2,000,000—on the job. In addition to Kaye, the price of admission includes the best in Technicolor, a pleasant score, first-rate supporting players, and, of course, the current Goldwyn Girls, any one of whom can supply the body for a story that is sometimes lacking in substance.

In *The Kid from Brooklyn*, Burleigh Sullivan, a mild-mannered milkman whose affection for his lovely girlfriend, club singer Polly Pringle, is matched only by that he has for his horse, stops by the club where his sister Suzie is singing, only to find her being bothered by a couple of drunks. Unknown to Burleigh, one of them is Speed MacFarlane, the middleweight boxing champ, the other is his thick-skulled trainer, Spider Shultz. Inadvertently, Burleigh is drawn into a brawl with them, and in the confusion, Spider knocks out Speed, but the newspapers credit the punch erroneously to Burleigh, much to the chagrin of Speed's manager, Gabby Sloan. Burleigh, at Suzie's urging, goes to Speed's apartment to explain what happened, only to knock him out again—accidentally—just as the reporters burst into the room. In a frantic attempt to make the best of a situation that could cost him a fortune, Gabby hits on the idea to build up Burleigh as a fighter and then match him against Speed in the ring. Burleigh at first declines, until Gabby convinces him that he can make enough money to marry Polly.

The rigorous training, in which Ann Westley, Gabby's wise and wisecracking girl, offers Burleigh some invaluable pointers about his footwork by teaching him to box to the strains of a Viennese waltz, gives the former milkman a modicum of confidence. That is bolstered when he

unwittingly wins a series of fixed fights, causing his head to swell as rapidly as his new-found fame. He has become insufferable though, much to the disgust of both Polly, who finally leaves him, and Suzie, who has fallen in love with Speed. Burleigh's success in the ring causes his former boss, Wilbur Austin, the dairy tycoon, to buy the fighter's contract from Gabby just before the scheduled match between Burleigh and Speed, for the benefit of the milk fund drive being sponsored by Mrs. E. Winthrop LeMoyne.

Polly and Suzie urge Speed to knock out Burleigh to teach him a lesson, but through the stupidity of Spider, Speed is given knockout drops, enabling Burleigh to emerge the victor, marry Polly, accept a partnership in Austin's dairy, and see Suzie marry Speed. Gabby and Spider, meanwhile, secure jobs as milkmen at Burleigh's largess.

Amid all of these proceedings, Danny Kaye takes time out to spar with Fay Bainter and do his memorable satire on Martha Graham and her "Six Crackers." All of which caused *Variety* to suggest that "the Samuel Goldwyn/ Danny Kaye combine has outdone itself in *The Kid from Brooklyn*, topping the two highly successful previous efforts in almost every phase of production." That paper's critic continued:

The film is aimed straight at the belly and laughs, and emerges as a lush mixture of comedy, music and gals, highlighted in beautiful Technicolor and ultra-rich production. The film's accessories are all in conformity with the richness evidenced throughout. Gals wear gowns that should panic the femmes and Goldwyn's sets are something to talk about. Kaye is spotted in almost three-fourths of the picture's sequences, but the audience will be clamoring for more at the fadeout.

Time Magazine was less enthusiastic.

At the picture's start, Danny's nag passes out between the shafts. Danny, who has to pull Sam Goldwyn's rather cumbersome vehicle practically unaided, also works like a horse, He delivers the laughs, but they can't drown out a good deal of creaking, clanking and whiffing. Only the deftest kind of comic manipulation would keep such foolishness fast and light, but deftness is largely lacking.

The upbeat conclusion was that "laughs are a precious commodity these days, and, even in an off-picture, Danny Kaye can furnish more than most people."

Between these two critical extremes lay most of the reviewers' notices. Howard Barnes wrote:

Danny breezes through (the film) to make it an irresistible comedy, (and) those who may have supposed that Kaye was something of a one-man vaudeville act will be surprised to discover that he is a very accomplished actor in his newest film assignment . . . Even with incidental songs and the ubiquitous Goldwyn Girls, the show is smoothly scintillating. It has been adroitly directed by Norman Z. McLeod, while Kaye makes *The Kid from Brooklyn* the sheer delight that it is.

And this from Bosley Crowther:

The widely expanding popularity of the incredible Danny Kaye will reach the flood level, no fooling, when the comic's new Samuel Goldwyn film gets out on the nation's theatre screens. So let this be an unsolemn warning: look out for the inundating wave. For whatever cause the gent has given for delight in his two previous films is repeated with drums in this new musical . . . Mr. Kaye has the best opportunity that he has yet had upon the screen to show his superior talent for broad and beguiling burlesque. And he takes full advantage of it in classically clownish style.

The New York Times critic also felt that

Unhappily, there must come moments when Mr. Kaye is not on the screen and those are the moments this picture perceptibly drags. Mr. Goldwyn has tried to correct this with the not unaccelerated charms of Vera-Ellen and Virginia Mayo and a phalanx of gorgeous Goldwyn Girls . . . In short, the show is uneven, but then, what could you expect? Science and Mr. Goldwyn haven't yet found a balance for Danny Kaye.

John McCarten, writing in *The New Yorker*, said:

The Milky Way is with us once again, and it is still funny stuff, mostly because the milkman involved is Danny Kaye, who is rapidly reaching that happy point where he can do no wrong, his face aglow with innocent madness . . . Although he plainly isn't in need of much assistance, he gets quite a deal of it anyhow, particularly from sprightly Vera-Ellen. Done up in shiny Technicolor, the film is pretty as a posy, and you are herewith urged to take a look at it.

Of the five Goldwyn/Kaye films of the mid-1940s, *The Kid from Brooklyn* not only was the most profitable, grossing, according to *Variety*, $4,000,000, but also was the best all-around collaboration. Neither of the succeeding two had the sumptuous trappings nor the elaborate production numbers, despite the increased production costs of more than $1,000,000 each over that of *The Kid from Brooklyn*. Nor did they have the added sparkle of Vera-Ellen. Goldwyn had his publicity department distribute press handouts to the effect that, following her loanout to 20th Century Fox for *Three Little Girls in Blue*, she would star for him in his version of the Comden and Green Broadway musical, *Billion Dollar Baby*. Vera-Ellen, though, never returned to the Goldwyn Studios, moving instead to MGM where she would dance in two films each with Gene Kelly and Fred Astaire, and end her film career after fourteen movies (including one more, *White Christmas*, with Danny Kaye at Paramount).

Vera-Ellen, Danny Kaye, Lionel Stander and Steve Cochran in The Kid from Brooklyn.

Eve Arden, Steve Cochran, Vera-Ellen, Danny Kaye and Walter Abel in The Kid from Brooklyn.

Virginia Mayo, Danny Kaye and Clarence Kolb in The Kid from Brooklyn.

68 THE BEST YEARS OF OUR LIVES (1946)

Directed by William Wyler; screenplay, Robert E. Sherwood; based on the verse novel *Glory For Me* by MacKinlay Kantor; music director, Emil Newman; score, Hugo Friedhofer; photographer, Gregg Toland; editor, Daniel Mandell; assistant director, Joseph Boyle; art directors, George Jenkins and Perry Ferguson; costumes, Irene Sharaff. Running time, .172 minutes. Released by RKO Pictures. Premiere: Astor Theater, New York, 11/21/46

THE CAST:

Milly Stephenson, Myrna Loy; *Al Stephenson*, Fredric March; *Fred Derry*, Dana Andrews; *Peggy Stephenson*, Teresa Wright; *Marie Derry*, Virginia Mayo; *Wilma Cameron*, Cathy O'Donnell; *Homer Parrish*, Harold Russell; *Butch Engle*, Hoagy Carmichael; *Hortense Derry*, Gladys George; *Cliff Scully*, Steve Cochran; *Mr. Milton*, Ray Collins; *Pat Derry*, Roman Bohnen; *Mrs. Parrish*, Minna Gombell; *Mr. Parrish*, Walter Baldwin; *Mrs. Cameron*, Dorothy Adams; *Mr. Cameron*, Don Beddoe; *Woody Merrill*, Victor Cutler; *Luella Parrish*, Marlene Aames; *Prew*, Charles Halton; *Mr. Mollett*, Ray Teal; *Thorpe*, Howland Chamberlain; *Novak*, Dean White; *Bullard*, Erskine Sanford; *Rob Stephenson*, Michael Hall; *George Gibbons*, Ralph Sanford; and Clancy Cooper, Hal K. Dawson, Amelita Ward, Bert Conway, Blake Edwards, Donald Kerr, Heinie Conklin, Alan Bridge, John Ince, Mary Arden, Billy Newell, Teddy Infuhr, Leo Penn, Pat Flaherty, Tom Dugan, Earle Hodgins, Mickey Roth, Peggy McIntyre, Harry Cheshire, Joyce Compton, James Ames.

In the three decades since its release, much has been written of the film universally regarded as Goldwyn's *chef d'oeuvre,* as well as one of the towering achievements of the American cinema. Because of its undenied status in our cultural heritage, it has been analysed and dissected, reviewed countless times and judged virtually flawless, whether taken in context of the immediate postwar period or reflectively with the benefit of thirty years worth of subsequent history.

Goldwyn's inspiration for this masterwork was said to have come from an issue of *Time,* which his wife, Frances, had brought to his attention. It featured a picture story (7 August 1944) of the return of several injured war veterans. Shortly thereafter, Goldwyn commissioned (for $12,500) MacKinlay Kantor, returning to the United States after many months as a war correspondent in England, to turn his experiences into an original story. Kantor's subsequent blank verse novel, *Glory for Me,* the story of three veterans coming home to face the uncertainties of civilian life, was turned over to Goldwyn the following January, and playwright Robert E. Sherwood was then engaged to develop it into a screenplay—although Goldwyn was obliged to wait nearly a year until Sherwood fulfilled previous stage commitments.

William Wyler, meanwhile, was just completing his wartime service and coming back to Hollywood where he owed Goldwyn one film on his prewar contract. Goldwyn let Wyler choose among various properties—one, a proposed biography of Eisenhower; another, a screen version of Robert Nathan's novel, *The Bishop's Wife.* Wyler, instead, became interested in the project, on which Sherwood then was pushing ahead, and in early 1946, he (Wyler) and Goldwyn began casting the film. From the Goldwyn stock company came Teresa Wright, Dana Andrews, Virginia Mayo and Steve Cochran, together with countless character actors whose performances, individual and ensemble, have sparked so many of Goldwyn's movies. To head the superb cast, Fredric March was enticed back from the Broadway stage for his third (and last) Goldwyn film, and Myrna Loy, who had appeared in brief roles in two movies for Goldwyn early in her career, was approached by Goldwyn personally to accept another brief role—together with, this time, top billing. Two newcomers were hired to round out the cast: Cathy O'Donnell, previously seen fleetingly, billed as Ann Jordan, in Goldwyn's *Wonder Man,* and later to become William Wyler's sister-in-law; and a non-professional, Harold Russell, a double amputee who had lost both hands in a wartime training accident. Russell had acted, as himself, in an Army-made film, *Diary of a Sergeant,* which Wyler, as an Air Force colonel, had seen several years earlier, remembering the ex-paratroop sergeant when casting *The Best Years of Our Lives.* (The Goldwyn film was to be Russell's only professional acting job; he subsequently became National Commander of the AMVETS.)

Filming on *The Best Years* began on 15 April after Sherwood had finished hammering the Kantor novel, running 434 pages, into shape for the screen. On 9 August Wyler called it "a wrap." He had shot 400 reels of film (subsequently edited down to sixteen), and Goldwyn had a $2 million plus investment. Wyler, Goldwyn and Daniel Mandell spent the next two months in the editing room so that Goldwyn might have something to "sneak preview" in mid-October, planning to use audience reactions as a guide to further cutting the two hours and forty minutes of story.

The enthusiastic response given to *The Best Years of Our Lives* at its sneak preview convinced Goldwyn to forego additional editing, and in totally uncharacteristic move, he then arranged a booking at the Hollywood Pantages, in January. Only an astonished Wyler could talk Goldwyn into opening the film earlier, at least for a week's run in Los Angeles to qualify for the Academy Awards. Goldwyn, instead, premiered the movie in New York on reserved seats in late November and still managed a West Coast opening before the deadline for Oscar consideration.

The Best Years of Our Lives follows three veterans who meet for the first time while hitching a plane ride home to Boone City (patterned, reportedly, after Cincinnati): Al Stephenson, a middle-aged infantry sergeant and bank executive in private life; Fred Derry, an Air Force captain and former soda-jerk; and Homer Parrish, a young seaman who had lost both hands in action and wore articulated hooks in their place. At his smart apartment house, Al is greeted by his wife Milly, and discovers that his two children, Peggy and Rob, have matured during his absence, making him feel somewhat awkward and self-conscious by the subtle changes in his family's attitudes toward one another. The war, he will soon find, has changed his outlook both at home and in business,

where he must reconcile himself to the country's new social conscience.

The old frame house, to which Homer returns, finds his parents waiting uncertainly with his next-door girlfriend, Wilma. Shocked silence and a muffled, motherly sob greets the sight of Homer, who feels himself grotesque and the object of embarrassing childhood curiosity by his young sister and her playmates. Worse, he thinks that Wilma, his childhood sweetheart, will go through with their long-planned marriage only out of pity. Fred, meanwhile, comes home to a dreary, rundown shack on the wrong side of the tracks, where he learns from his gin-soaked father and slovenly stepmother that Marie, the girl he had married only a few days before being shipped out, had moved away and taken a job as a nightclub singer.

The story then centers around Al's gradual resumption of his domestic ties and of his work at the bank where he is made vice-president in charge of small loans to veterans; Fred's discouragement over financial difficulties that compelled him to resume work at the drug store he had left before the war; and Homer's attempts to escape from his over-considerate family and his efforts to discourage the deep love Wilma has felt for him, despite his disability, until she convinces him that their love can overcome his misfortune.

The three veterans from disparate backgrounds find their lives entwined within a few days. Al and Milly go for a night on the town, along with Peggy, and end up at Butch's place, where Homer, Butch's nephew, has stopped for a few beers. Fred, having located Marie with her ex-Marine boyfriend, Cliff Scully, learns that she no longer finds him attractive out of uniform and eventually demands a divorce. He, too, happens into Butch's where the three veterans have an early reunion. Al and Fred both get roaring drunk and are helped back to the Stephenson home by Milly and Peggy. Fred, over the next few weeks, finds himself falling in love with Peggy, but Al tries to break up the romance because he does not want his daughter hurt by an involvement with a married man.

At the bank, Al draws the wrath of his superiors by approving a GI loan to a veteran with a shaky credit rating, and is obliged to convince his senior bankers that there is no better investment than providing able-bodied and willing workers with jobs. Fred settles back into harness as a soda jerk in the now chain-controlled drugstore, where he feels that his experience and service qualify him for a more responsible spot. He is taken back on the pretext of being an assistant manager filling in behind the soda counter, until he punches a loud customer who talks scornfully about the worthiness of war. Homer discovers that his disabilities are too much both for him and his family, and is on the point of despair until

Wilma's love becomes apparent to him.

Fred's self-pity takes him to a graveyard of old junked bombers that await the sledgehammer, and he climbs into the nose of a dead B-17 where he relives a few fleeting wartime memories, before one of the workmen orders him down—and offers him a job. Al has accomplished his transition by telling his associates at a welcome-home dinner that did not go off to war and win battles by first demanding collateral from Uncle Sam, as the bankers had wanted him to do with the young farmer who wanted a GI loan. And Homer, having shown his sweetheart what it will mean to endure a man with "hooks," marries Wilma in the film's final scene, with Al and Milly at the wedding, along with Peggy, who sees Fred, the best man, for the first time since their breakup and goes to his side.

Several memorable sequences stand out especially: the touching, wordless scene in which Milly first realizes that Al has come through the front door; the poignant shot of Homer's mother, allowing an uncontrollable wail at the first sight of his mechanical hands; the moving passage when Homer demonstrates to Wilma the fact that he is helpless without his harness as it comes time to prepare himself for bed; the wedding, at which Homer shows his skill at placing the ring on Wilma's finger.

Among the strongest scenes, composed meticulously by Gregg Toland, is the one in Butch's place where we see Fred in a telephone booth at the far end of the room, calling Peggy to tell her that he will not see her again, while Al leans on the piano in the foreground, watching Homer and Butch play "Chopsticks." The shot is constructed with two dramatic centers of interest with a stationary camera.

Variety's Abel Green succinctly summed up the general feelings of the critics in a single line: "Samuel Goldwyn's *The Best Years of Our Lives* is one of the best pictures of our lives." Howard Barnes (without once mentioning Samuel Goldwyn!) wrote:

> The screen unleashes a full measure of its latent power and wonder in *The Best Years of Our Lives*. Rarely have the potentialities of a medium been so dazzlingly disclosed . . . With Wyler's consummate staging of the production, (the film) sets the highest standards of cinematic quality and meets them triumphantly.

Newsweek gave the film "E for Epic" and felt that "Goldwyn and Wyler have outdone themselves. Their current collaboration is one of the finest to come out of Hollywood in a dozen years." And *Time* wrote:

Producer Goldwyn, cheerfully shooting the works as glittery a collection of scripting, directing, acting and technical talents as $3 million could buy, has bought himself a sure-fire hit—with a little to spare . . . it was put together with good taste, honesty, wit—and even a strong suggestion of guts.

The Best Years of Our Lives made virtually all Ten Best lists and is included among Bosley Crowther's collection of the fifty greatest films of all time (at least through 1967). The New York Film Critics voted it Best Picture of the Year and chose Wyler as Best Director. It also won seven Academy Awards (out of eight nominations): Best Picture, Best Director, Best Actor (Fredric March), Best Supporting Actor (Harold Russell), Best Screenplay, Best Scoring, Best Editing. (Only Gordon Sawyer, nominated for Best Sound Recording, failed to win.) In addition, Samuel Goldwyn was given the Irving Thalberg Award and Harold Russell received a special award "for bringing hope and courage to his fellow veterans through his appearance in *The Best Years of Our Lives*." Russell thus became the only actor in film history to receive two Oscars for a single performance. *The Best Years of Our Lives* also received the first British Academy Award as Best Picture, and was given the French Victoire Award.

The film grossed more than $11,000,000 in its initial run and several reissues. Goldwyn brought it back once again in 1954, supported by a brand new, $250,000 ad campaign, in the 1.65 to 1 widescreen ratio, and again it cleaned up at the box office. Four years later, Wyler sued Samuel Goldwyn for backpay he claims was due him for directing the film. Wyler's original contract called for him to receive twenty percent of the profits (Robert Sherwood was to get five percent), and he now claimed Goldwyn owed him $408,356. Goldwyn countered with the assertion that Wyler already had gotten $1,400,000 for *The Best Years of Our Lives,* but nevertheless, settled out of court for an undisclosed sum in 1962.

In 1975, Samuel Goldwyn Productions belatedly entered television, getting together with Lorimar Productions, the outfit responsible for *The Waltons,* and turned out a ninety-minute TV adaptation of *The Best Years of Our Lives.* Entitled *Returning Home,* it starred Dabney Coleman, Tom Selleck and James R. Miller in the roles taken in the original classic by Fredric March, Dana Andrews and Harold Russell, respectively. The "ABC Movie of the Week" presentation, directed by Daniel Petrie, was designed as a pilot film for a projected series.

Myrna Loy and Fredric March in The Best Years of Our Lives.

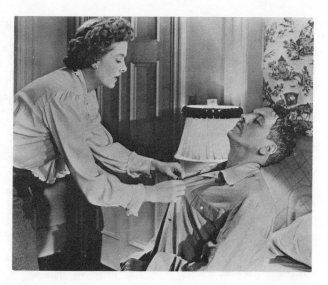

Gladys George, Dana Andrews and Roman Bohnen in
The Best Years of Our Lives.

Teresa Wright and Dana Andrews in The Best Years of Our Lives.

Dana Andrews in The Best Years of Our Lives.

Cathy O'Donnell and Harold Russell in The Best Years of Our Lives.

Fredric March, Teresa Wright and Dana Andrews in The Best Years of Our Lives.

69 THE SECRET LIFE OF WALTER MITTY (1947)

Directed by Norman Z. McLeod; screenplay, Ken Englund and Everett Freeman; based on a story by James Thurber; music director, Emil Newman; score, David Raksin; songs "Anatole of Paris" and "Symphony for Unstrung Tongue" by Sylvia Fine; photographer, Lee Garmes; editor, Monica Underwood; art directors, George Jenkins and Perry Ferguson; costumes, Irene Sharaff; special effects, John Fulton. Running time, 110 minutes. Technicolor. Released by RKO Pictures. Premiere: Woods Theater, Chicago, 8/4/47. New York Premiere: Astor Theater, 8/14/47

THE CAST:
Walter Mitty, Danny Kaye; *Rosalind van Hoorn*, Virginia Mayo; *Dr. Hugo Hollingshead*, Boris Karloff; *Mrs. Mitty*, Fay Bainter; *Gertrude Griswold*, Ann Rutherford; *Bruce Pierce*, Thurston Hall; *Tubby Wadsworth*, Gordon Jones; *Mrs. Griswold*, Florence Bates; *Peter van Hoorn*, Konstantin Shayne; *RAF Colonel*, Reginald Denny; *Hendrick*, Henry Corden; *Mrs. Follinsbee*, Doris Lloyd; *Anatole*, Fritz Feld; *Catl Maasdam*, Frank Reicher; *Van Hoorn Butler (Tyler)*, Milton Parsons; *Wolfman*, George Magrill; *Grimsby*, Joel Friedkin; *Dr. Pritchard–Mitford*, Lumsden Hare; *Dr. Benbow*, Henry Kolker; *Dr. Remington*, John Hamilton; *Dr. Renshaw*, Charles Trowbridge; *Dream Sequence Narrator*, Vincent Pelletier; *The Goldwyn Girls*, Mary Brewer, Betty Cargyle, Sue Casey, Lorraine DeRome, Karen X. Gaylord, Mary Ellen Gleason, Jackie Jordan, Georgia Lane, Michael Mauree, Martha Montgomery, Pat Patrick, Irene Vernon, Lynn Walker; and Harry Harvey, Mary Anne Baird, Jack Gargan, John Tyrell, Bess Flowers, Sam Ash, Harry Depp, Dick Earle, Broderick O'Farrell, Wilbur Mack, Ralph Dunn, Jack Cheatham, Mary Forbes, Pierre Watkin, Ernie Adams, Hank Worden, George Lloyd, Syd Saylor, Billy Bletcher, Eddie Acuff, Wade Crosby, Dorothy Granger, Dorothy Christy, Dick Rush, William Haade, Minerva Urecal, Billy Newell, Paul Newlan, Chris Pin Martin, Sam McDaniel, Betty Blythe, Maude Eburne, George Chandler, Ethan Laidlaw, Moy Ming, Beal Wong.

The Goldwyn decision to star Danny Kaye in a film version of James Thurber's gentle little tale first spun in *The New Yorker* in 1939 was dismaying news to the Thurber cultists—and to Thurber himself, who was said to have commented, when learning that Goldwyn was planning to film his short story, "I'll pay $10,000 to him *not* to touch it!" What had been the unadorned little narrative of a frustrated, middle-aged, hen-pecked husband who escapes from reality in heroic daydreams emerged on the screen as a multicolored Goldwyn spectacular with Mitty alternating his daydreams with real-life thrills as he becomes enmeshed with a gang of jewel thieves, headed by Boris Karloff!

Goldwyn spent $3,000,000 on the spectacle that allowed his number one star to romp through seven different characterizations in his role as Walter Mitty (here a timid mother's boy, working as a proofreader in a pulp fiction publishing house and dreading the moments he must spend with his grasping fianceé). Two more of the classic Danny Kaye routines were conveniently worked into the plot—his amazing patter number "Symphony for Unstrung Tongues" and the elaborate "Anatole of Paris"—but these accounted for the only musical numbers in the film, allowing the newest brigade of Goldwyn Girls only brief screen time in the latter Kaye routine.

The dream sequences showoff Kaye at his best, but they form just a patchwork quilt through which has been woven a rather silly and somewhat conventional light-comedy spy plot. As Mitty, however, Kaye imagines himself a daring sea captain, guiding his ship through a raging typhoon; a swishy French fashion designer

("Anatole of Paris"); a fearless western gunfighter known as "The Perth Amboy Kid;" a Mississippi riverboat gambler staking his fortune to win the hand of a Southern belle; a noted surgeon performing an impossible operation to save a patient's life; and a dashing R.A.F. pilot shooting down dozens of Nazi planes. And in every dream sequence, Virginia Mayo turns up as the heroine, while playing a similar role in the real-life adventures.

These non-Thurber adventures: Walter Mitty, dominated at home by his mother and at the office by his overbearing boss, Bruce Pierce, becomes involved with a mysterious blonde, Rosalind Van Hoorn, when she enlists his aid to escape from a sinister character who is following her. Mitty learns that her uncle was the custodian of a fortune in jewels, and that international thieves are after the gems. As he becomes more enmeshed in her scheme to provide safe-keeping for the jewels, Mitty finds his life increasingly in danger, and when he tries to explain the predicament to his mother and his fiancee, Gertrude Griswold, they begin to suspect him of insanity and steer him to the office of Dr. Hollingshead. The psychiatrist, who actually masterminds the jewel-theft ring, tricks Mitty into believing he had imagined his experiences. Mitty's mother then arranges for his marriage to Gertrude, but at the altar, he discovers in his pocket a memento from Rosalind proving that his adventures with her had been real. Mitty rushes from the church to Rosalind's home, where he manages to capture Hollingshead and his cohorts and rescue her from their clutches.

Thurber himself, upon finding how his story had been corrupted, reportedly was somewhat annoyed, and as specified in *Life Magazine,* was appalled by Kaye's songs in gibberish, the "Dick Tracy plot" and the traditional Goldwyn opulence of production, and supposedly commented "It began to be bad with the first git-gat-gittle. If they'd spent one tenth the money, it would have been ten times as good."

Apparently, the major critics were not dyed-in-the-wool Thurberites, for most had the usual praise that for years they had been showering on both Goldwyn and Kaye. *Time* called *The Secret Life of Walter Mitty*

Danny Kaye's funniest movie . . . as usual, he is really the whole show. His straight patter numbers seem a little less funny as the years go by, but his dream-life parodies of heroism are in every sense out of this world.

Variety felt:

Kaye without a doubt has never been better. He reveals a greater smoothness and polish thespically and a perfection of timing in his slapstick than has ever been evident in the past. The role is perfect for permitting him to run through a gamut of characterizations . . . Norman Z. McLeod's direction keeps the action relatively fast and sharp.

Thomas M. Pryor, reviewing in *The New York Times,* decided that

Even though Danny Kaye's Walter Mitty is not precisely the mousey chap Mr. Thurber wrote about with such delightful and devastating accuracy, he is an agreeable facsimile. It is, in fact, quite unfair to expect Mr. Kaye to become a character for any length of time . . . (and) *The Secret Life of Walter Mitty* clears the way for his versatile talent in many turns. (It) is a big, colorful show and a good one. Perhaps it is just a little too big, for it is difficult to sustain a comedy for close to two hours without a letdown every so often. Much of the flavor of the Thurber character is lost because of the lack of contrast between Walter Mitty's dream world and actual experiences.

The Howard Barnes notice said:

An enchanting fantasy by James Thurber has been given a multitude of Hollywood trimmings in *The Secret Life of Walter Mitty.* It has Danny Kaye in the title role, a group of Goldwyn Girls modeling corsets, fancy color effects, and a great deal of slapstick. Somewhere in the general panoply and excitements, a delightful concept becomes hopelessly befuddled. There is no end of production pomp in (the film), but a fragile fantasy has been blown out of all proportions in its screen translation.

Newsweek agreed, exclaiming:

It is a depressing thought, but the followers of Danny Kaye will probably be entranced by *The Secret Life of Walter Mitty* in spite of the fact that the picture is a complete bastardization of the original, and great, short story by James Thurber . . . For reasons best known to himself Samuel Goldwyn decided that Thurber had not gone far enough in his characterization of Mitty. Granted, the original story had to be expanded in order to make a full-length movie, it was *not* necessary to alter the characters and the plot so completely that only the dream sequences—and not all of them—contain anything of Thurber.

Thurber's Walter Mitty (which *almost* prompted a Goldwyn sequel several years later) was somewhat better served in the charming off-Broadway stage production in 1964 and, while avoiding the use of the Mitty name itself, in the fanciful little TV series, "My World and Welcome To It" in the early 1970s, with William Windom as the Thurberish daydreamer.

Goldwyn originally had announced June Haver as Danny Kaye's leading lady in *Walter Mitty,* but personal problems prevented her from accepting the role. Instead Goldwyn elevated Virginia Mayo to star billing (coequal with Kaye) for the first time, on the strength of the notices she had received for her dramatic work in *The Best Years of Our Lives*—which was the only chance Goldwyn ever gave her to be more than sensational Technicolor decoration for either Bob Hope or Danny Kaye to ogle.

Thurston Hall, Fay Bainter, Danny Kaye and Boris Karloff in The Secret Life of Walter Mitty.

Danny Kaye and Virginia Mayo in The Secret Life of Walter Mitty.

Gordon Jones, Virginia Mayo and Danny Kaye in The Secret Life of Walter Mitty.

Danny Kaye and Virginia Mayo in The Secret Life of Walter Mitty.

70 THE BISHOP'S WIFE (1947)

Directed by Henry Koster; screenplay, Robert E. Sherwood and Leonardo Bercovici; based on the novel by Robert Nathan; music director, Emil Newman; score, Hugo Friedhofer; song "Lost April" by Edgar DeLange, Emil Newman and Herbert Spencer; photographer, Gregg Toland; editor, Monica Collingwood; art directors, George Jenkins and Perry Ferguson; costumes, Irene Sharaff. Running time, 109 minutes. Released by RKO Pictures. Premiere: Astor Theater, New York, 12/9/47.

THE CAST:

Dudley, Cary Grant; *Julia Brougham,* Loretta Young; *Henry Brougham,* David Niven; *Professor Wutheridge,* Monty Woolley; *Sylvester,* James Gleason; *Agnes Hamilton,* Gladys Cooper; *Matilda,* Elsa Lanchester; *Mildred Cassaway,* Sara Haden; *Debby Brougham,* Karolyn Grimes; *Maggenti,* Tito Vuolo; *Mr. Miller,* Regis Toomey; *Mrs. Duffy,* Sarah Edwards; *Miss Trumbull,* Margaret McWade; *Mrs. Ward,* Anne O'Neal; *Mr. Perry,* Ben Erway; *Stevens,* Erville Alderson; *Defense Captain,* Bobby Anderson; *Attack Captain,* Teddy Infuhr; *Michel,* Eugene Borden; *Hatshop Proprietress,* Margaret Wells; The Mitchell Boychoir; and Almira Sessions, Claire DuBrey, Florence Auer, Kitty O'Neill, Isabel Jewell, David Leonard, Dorothy Vaughan, Edgar Dearing, Don Garner, Edythe Elliott, Shirley O'Hara, Joseph J. Greene.

In appreciation of the 1940s boom in cinema angels—from *Here Comes Mr. Jordan* and *The Horn Blows At Midnight* to *Angel on My Shoulder* and *It's A Wonderful Life*—Samuel Goldwyn decided to bestow his cinematic blessings and production elegance on Robert Nathan's fragile angel fable, *The Bishop's Wife,* written two decades earlier. It described how a full-bodied guardian angel answers a young bishop's prayers for guidance and spiritual comfort in the midst of a crisis in his life.

The title role was given to Teresa Wright, who then went through wardrobe fittings, and before production began, learned she was pregnant. ("Goldwyn never forgave me for that," she has admitted.) To replace her, Goldwyn borrowed Loretta Young, as well as Cary Grant, from Dore Schary at RKO and then cast his own, recently demobilized David Niven as the man of the cloth. William Seiter was hired to direct them in the delicate screenplay, in which Robert E. Sherwood and Leonardo Bercovici entwined comedy, drama and fantasy. Somewhere along the way, Goldwyn became disenchanted with the way his production was progressing, and he replaced director Seiter with Henry Koster with instructions to begin again. "There was criticism because I threw away nearly $900,000 worth of my picture and started it all over," Goldwyn was quoted in *Life Magazine.*

I can't help it, that's just the way I make pictures. I threw out three screenplays. I changed directors in the middle. You might say I had some disagreements on this one. One was with Cary Grant. He said, "You want me to be happy, don't you?" I said, "I don't give a damn if you're happy. You are going to be here for only a few weeks and this picture will be out a long time. I would rather you should be unhappy here, and then we can all be happy later."

Cinema historian Edward Connor, in his *Films in Review* article entitled "Angels on the Screen," said that

One might expect a little theological research in the presentation of an angel sent to help an Episcopal bishop, but "Dudley" was the non-theological, Dale Carnegie type, in a Brooks Brothers suit, so dear to the hearts of Hollywood scripters. The dialogue provided (him) was barren of eternal verities but heavy with such platitudes as "you must have faith in yourself," and when he took his leave to return to heaven, he gave the impression he preferred the earthly charms of Loretta Young to the Beatific Vision.

Cary Grant's angel, in fact, is a personable chap whose minor miracles are performed in the manner of a magician's sleight-of-hand routines, and who proceeds not only to give the somewhat bemused and occasionally anxious bishop the guidance requested, but also to patch up his marital problems and, in a delightful side plot, aid a frustrated old professor by inspiring him to write a long-planned book on Roman history.

As Dudley the angel, he immediately ingratiates himself with the family of Henry and Julia Brougham. Henry has been trying desperately to raise money from his rich parishoners to erect a new cathedral and has been finding less and less time for either his wife or his friends of humbler days. And after a particularly frustrating day with Agnes Hamilton, a wealthy, arrogant widow, upon whose contribution the building of the cathedral depended, Henry prays for help. Incredulous at first at the arrival of Dudley, Henry soon becomes convinced of his new guest's heavenly status and agrees to take Dudley on as his new "assistant." With his supernatural powers of insight and his Heavenly touch, Dudley sets about straightening out the Brougham's problems in addition to those of others in the community, bringing a spot of romance back into Julia's life (while hiding the fact that he is an angel) and transforming Mrs. Hamilton into a gracious, generous woman, assuring Henry of the funds for the cathedral. Aware that Julia has formed a fond attachment for Dudley though, Henry's gratitude turns to resentment and jealousy. Dudley accepts this as a sign that Henry's love for his wife has been rekindled, and he leaves the household, erasing from the minds of everyone all memory of him. Henry and Julia are left to discover themselves more in love than ever, as if a miracle had happened to them.

The Bishop's Wife (or, as it was shortly thereafter retitled, *Cary and The Bishop's Wife,* because Grant was concerned that, although he had top billing, he was not one of the title stars, and Goldwyn was convinced that he could attract a wider audience by advertising the film as a romantic comedy rather than one with a religious background) was the Royal Command film in London in 1947, as well as Goldwyn's Christmas gift to the screen world.

"A Yuletide fantasy to gladden filmgoing optimists," was Howard Barnes' decription of *The Bishop's Wife,* before he expressed his reservations.

It still takes considerable credulity to follow the rather obvious entertainment pattern of this Goldwyn production. Robert E. Sherwood has inserted brave and eloquent lines into the proceedings, and they have import as well as dramatic excitement. Unfortunately, they tend to become both repetitious and laggard. . . . Henry Koster has directed it with effective precision but far less imagination than the theme demanded.

The Bishop's Wife is uplifting and entertaining; it is a pity that it is not a more cohesive and commanding motion picture.

The New York Times' Bosley Crowther wrote:

Certainly communion with angels is traditional at Christmas time, which is the season when most of us mortals need angelic reassurance anyhow. So there is nothing especially surprising about the miracle that occurs in *The Bishop's Wife*—except that it is superb. And that is very surprising, in view of the realistic fact that it is a sentimental whimsey of the most delicate and dangerous sort . . . It is as cheerful and repectful an invasion of the realm of conscience that we have seen. And it comes very close to being the most enchanting picture of the year . . . We cannot recommend you to a more delightful and appropriate Christmas show.

(*The Bishop's Wife* made *The New York Times'* Ten Best list.)

Variety was in complete agreement:

It has a warmth and charm that makes believable the fantasy and has been put together with complete understanding by all involved. Samuel Goldwyn's marshalling of cast, director, writers and physical values stamps it with a class touch. Cary Grant is the angel of the piece and has never appeared to greater advantage; Miss Young gives a moving performance; and Niven's cleric character is played straight but his anxieties and jealousy loosen much of the warm humor gracing the plot.

In *Commonweal,* Philip T. Hartung wrote:

After a talky start, director Henry Koster weaves a picture that is at times quite lovely; and in the skating scene it gets as close to poetry as movies ever do. The argument bogs down occasionally and can hardly be considered orthodox. But as a sophisticated Christmas carol, *The Bishop's Wife* comes through nicely and should please adults who like their movies off the beaten track.

Time Magazine spoke for the dissenters:

Adapted from Robert Nathan's 1928 novel, *The Bishop's Wife* is Samuel Goldwyn's and RKO's special Christmas cookie. It is a big, slick production. The only thing it lacks is taste. Some moviegoers may also be distressed by the lack of Christmas spirit in what is apparently the moral of the picture: you can't trust a soul with your wife.

The Bishop's Wife won an Academy Award for Best Sound Recording (Goldwyn Sound Department) plus an Oscar nomination for Best Film Editing (Monica Collingwood).

Cary Grant, David Niven and Loretta Young in The Bishop's Wife.

Loretta Young and Cary Grant in The Bishop's Wife.

Cary Grant, David Niven and Loretta Young in The Bishop's Wife.

71 A SONG IS BORN (1948)

Directed by Howard Hawks; screenplay, Harry Tugend;* based on the story *From A to Z* by Thomas Monroe and Billy Wilder; music directors, Emil Newman and Hugo Friedhofer; songs, Don Raye and Gene DePaul; photographer. Gregg Toland; editor, Daniel Mandell; art directors, George Jenkins and Perry Ferguson; costumes, Irene Sharaff. Running time, 113 minutes. Technicolor. Released by RKO Pictures. Premiere: Astor Theater, New York, 10/19/48

* no screen credit given

THE CAST:

Professor Hobart Frisbee, Danny Kaye; *Honey Swanson,* Virginia Mayo (singing dubbed by Jeri Sullivan); *Professor Magenbruch,* Benny Goodman; *Professor Twingle,* Hugh Herbert; *Tony Crow,* Steve Cochran; *Dr. Elfini,* J. Edward Bromberg; *Professor Gerkikoff,* Felix Bressart; *Professor Traumer,* Ludwig Stossel; *Professor Oddly,* O.Z. Whitehead; *Miss Bragg,* Esther Dale; *Miss Totten,* Mary Field; *Mr. Setter,* Howland Chamberlain; *Joe,* Paul Langton; *Adams,* Sidney Blackmer; *Monte,* Ben Welden; *Ben,* Ben Chasen; *Louis,* Peter Virgo; *District Attorney,* Joseph Crehan; and Tommy Dorsey and his Orchestra, Louis Armstrong and his Orchestra, Lionel Hampton and his Orchestra, Charlie Barnet and his Orchestra, Mel Powell, Louis Bellson, Harry Babasin, Alton Hendrickson, Buck and Bubbles, The Page Cavanaugh Trio, The Golden Gate Quartet, Russo and the Samba Kings; and Norman Getner, Muni Seroff, John Impolito, Will Lee, Barbara Hamilton, Janie New, Alice Wallace, Pat Walker, Lane Chandler, William Haade, Joe Devlin, Jack Gargan, Robert Dudley, Karen X. Gaylord, Irene Vernon, Diana Mumby, Martha Montgomery, Marjorie Jackson, Shirley Ballard, Jill Meredith, Donald Wilmot.

Musical numbers: (performed by)
"A Song Is Born" (Chorus)
"Bach Boogie" (Buck on piano)
"Anitra's Dance" (Buck on piano, Benny Goodman on clarinet)
"Muskrat Ramble" (Mel Powell Septet)
"I'm Getting Sentimental Over You" (Tommy Dorsey and Orchestra)

"Blind Barnabas" (Golden Gate Quartet)
"Redskin Rhumba" (Charlie Barnet and Orchestra)
"The Goldwyn Stomp" (Louis Armstrong with Lionel Hampton and Orchestra)
"Daddy-O" (Virginia Mayo with Page Cavanaugh Trio)
"Stealin' Apples" (Lionel Hampton, Benny Goodman, Mel Powell, Harry Babsin, Alton Hendrickson)
Reprise: "A Song Is Born" (Musicians)
"Mockin' Bird" (Golden Gate Quartet)
Reprise: "A Song Is Born" (Virginia Mayo with Louis Armstrong, Benny Goodman, Tommy Dorsey, Lionel Hampton, Charlie Barnet, Mel Powell, Louis Bellson)
"Longhair Jam Session" (Virginia Mayo the Professors, Bubbles)
"Oh, Genevieve" (Danny Kaye, the Professors)
"Guadeamus Igator" (The Professors)
"Joshua Fit De Battle" (Golden Gate Quartet)
"Anvil Chorus" (Ensemble)
"Flying Home" (Louis Armstrong, Benny Goodman, Tommy Dorsey, Charlie Barnet, Mel Powell)

The Goldwyn remake of *Ball of Fire,* filmed more or less intact by Howard Hawks and virtually the same crew who labored on the original (cameraman Gregg Toland, editor Daniel Mandell, art director Perry Ferguson, et al.), was the last Danny Kaye appearance under his original five picture Goldwyn contract—and it was Virginia Mayo's finale for Goldwyn also. Little was altered in the conversion to *A Song Is Born* other than making the professors musicologists, and unfortunately none of the scintillating routines Kaye's fans had come to expect were included. Nothing by Sylvia Fine was used—only two new songs by Don Raye and Gene De Paul, together with several big band classics. Hawks, directing his only musical, simply reshot his earlier film, this time in Technicolor with Danny Kaye and Virginia Mayo standing in for Gary Cooper and Barbara Stanwyck. Much of the joy of the new version lies in the scenes between Kaye and the passel of great jazz musicians—Benny Goodman (acting as well as playing), Tommy Dorsey, Charlie Barnet, Louis Armstrong, Lionel Hampton, Mel Powell, Buck and Bubbles, etc.—whose welcome appearances are rather extraneous to the plot itself.

Danny is asked to play fairly straight, keeping his madcap self under wraps, as Professor Hobart Frisbee, who, with his somber cohorts (among them: Benny Goodman!), is studying the evolution of jazz, and in an after-hours spot, comes across singer Honey Swanson, swinging through "Daddy-O" with the Page Cavanaugh Trio (in the earlier version, a dubbed Barbara Stanwyck was doing "Drum Boogie" with Gene Krupa's Band).

The story then simply follows the original as written by Billy Wilder and Thomas Monroe in the new (unbilled) screenplay by Harry Tugend—the club singer hides out from the district attorney and her gangster boyfriend in the monastic Totten Foundation where a group of professors are writing a history of music. Into the proceedings come Tommy Dorsey and his Orchestra doing "I'm Getting Sentimental Over You;" Charlie Barnet and his Band performing "Redskin Rhumba;" Lionel Hampton, Benny Goodman and Mel Powell jamming "Stealin Apples;" the Golden Gate Quartet singing "Mockin' Bird;" Louis Armstrong, with Goodman, Dorsey and Barnet in a driving "Flying Home," and more.

Robert Hatch, film critic for *New Republic,* bemoaned that

A Song Is Born is a framework for displaying the skills of a number of great jazz musicians (and) successfully obscures these talents. The musicians do not perform enough, nor do they perform at the top of their abilities. They look as though they found the whole performance embarrassing, and they are right. . . . I suspect that anti-Goldwyn mutterings in jive circles may in the end mount up to a movement.

Of the stars, Hatch said: "Danny Kaye contributes the kind of goggling humor that Harold Lloyd a good many years ago wisely decided he had run into the ground; Virginia Mayo contibutes her natural endowments, which are considerable."

Time Magazine was similarly downbeat in its appraisal:

A Song Is Born may not be entirely satisfactory to either hepcats or squares . . . (it) is designed as a starring vehicle for Danny Kaye, but is almost drowned out in the blare. When the plot is serving only as a link between jam sessions, it is useful and quietly inoffensive. When it brims over into outlandish mugga-juggery about gangsters, a torch singer and a crew of antiquated musicologists, the yarn gets in the way of

the hot licks, and the plottiness dooms Kaye to the role of master of ceremonies.

Said Otis L. Guernsey Jr., in the *New York Herald Tribune*:

In order to keep the Danny Kaye pot boiling, Samuel Goldwyn has reached into the files . . . (he) and Hawks have put on a slick, gaudy display, but they do not quite justify the story's reappearance. With his hands tied in a nearly straight role, and having no one to play to, Danny Kaye has merely hidden his light under a secondhand bushel . . . (and) the film is left straining archly at whimsies.

From *Newsweek* came:

Encouraged by Samuel Goldwyn, Danny Kaye forgets himself in *A Song Is Born,* and no one will regret the lapse more than his fans. What Kaye forgot, specifically, is that he is a hilariously funny man with fine frenzy and a gibbering lyric . . . (and) there is too little spontaneous comedy in the screenplay to compensate for the loss. With Kaye languishing under wraps, this inexplicably twice-told tale proves an ill-advised experiment all around.

Bosley Crowther explained that

Danny Kaye's admirers, than whom there are none more intense, are likely to strain their eyes looking for their boy in *A Song Is Born.* For the Danny who ambles through this picture is but a shade of the scintillant comedian whom the screen fans have come to love. Indeed, he is something of a specter amid a hodge-podge of animated acts, and, to make it thoroughly depressing, he doesn't sing one song . . . The picture as a whole, which is done in color—we don't know why, reflects the tedium resulting from the restriction of Mr. Kaye.

Even *Variety* printed a review that was a step or two below the usual enthusiasm reserved for Goldwyn's classy films. While admitting that "with a star-studded cast plus the usual lush mountings given by Goldwyn to the Kaye films, there's no question that (it) will chalk up hefty grosses," *Variety* felt that

The film represents a slight letdown from his previous efforts, largely because Kaye does none of the special songs usually penned for him by Sylvia Fine. The revised situation gives Goldwyn a chance to toss into the film the name maestros and vaudeville acts whose work, for a change, is neatly integrated into the script, and when Kaye is working with them, the picture is standout entertainment. The rest of the cast follows the comic's fine thesping under Hawks' capable touch for comedy.

By the time *A Song Is Born* had gone into release, Danny Kaye had played his first memorable engagement at the London Palladium, easily capturing the town. He then dismayed Goldwyn with the information that he would not be re-signing with the man who had made him a star, but instead had accepted an offer from Jack Warner. The second blow came when Goldwyn then learned that Virginia Mayo, too, had signed with Warner Bros., where she was to star in a half dozen musicals and a similar number of costume dramas, with an occasional straight, contemporary role thrown in (i.e., Cagney's *White Heat*).

Danny Kaye with J. Edward Bromberg, Hugh Herbert, Benny Goodman, O.Z. Whitehead, Ludwig Stossel and Felix Bressart in A Song Is Born.

Virginia Mayo and Danny Kaye in A Song Is Born.

Danny Kaye with Buck, Benny Goodman, Tommy Dorsey, Charlie Barnet, Louis Armstrong and Lionel Hampton in A Song Is Born.

72 ENCHANTMENT (1949)

Directed by Irving Reis; screenplay, John Patrick; based on the novel *Take Three Tenses* by Rumer Godden; music director, Emil Newman; score, Hugo Friedhofer; song, Don Raye and Gene DePaul; photographer, Gregg Toland; editor, Daniel Mandell; art director, George Jenkins; costumes, Mary Wills. Running time, 102 minutes. Released by RKO Pictures. Premiere: Astor Theater, New York, 12/25/48

THE CAST:

Gen. Sir Roland Dane, David Niven; *Lark Ingoldsby,* Teresa Wright; *Grizel Dane,* Evelyn Keyes; *Pax Masterson,* Farley Granger; *Selina Dane,* Jayne Meadows; *Proutie,* Leo G. Carroll; *Pelham Dane,* Philip Friend; *Marchese Del Laudi,* Shepperd Strudwick; *General Fitzgerald,* Henry Stephenson; *The Eye,* Colin Keith-Johnston; *Lark as a child,* Gigi Perreau; *Rollo as a child,* Peter Miles; *Selina as a child,* Sherlee Collier; *Pelham as a child,* Warwick Gregson; *Mrs. Sampson,* Marjorie Rhodes; *Uncle Bunny,* Edmond Breon; *Willoughby,* Gerald Oliver Smith; *Jeweler,* Melville Cooper; *RAF Officer,* Gaylord (Steve) Pendleton; *Lance Corporal,* Dennis McCarthy; *Air Raid Warden,* Matthew Boulton; *Corporal,* Robin Hughes; *Narrator,* William Johnstone.

Following his series of Bob Hope and Danny Kaye comedies and musical confections, Goldwyn decided that the moviegoing public was once again ready for a good cry. *Enchantment,* with the unmatched, and probably unmatchable, Goldwyn panache, immediately brings to mind the opulent romantic dramas that had been marked by the Goldwyn stamp during the Thirties, and it was— as *Time Magazine* noted—"a tear-squeezer." Goldwyn's advertising department boasted in its ad-copy line "just about the most wonderful love story ever filmed" of this poignant tale of two generations of lovers in parallel romances, shown in alternating sequences past and present to give the impression that the two love stories

are being resolved at the same time in the same London town house.

Artfully staged by Irving Reis, cleverly adapted by John Patrick, stunningly photographed by Gregg Toland (this was his last film), and movingly enacted by David Niven and Teresa Wright in particular, *Enchantment* is a faithful cinemazation of the Rumer Godden story that had been published first in *Ladies' Home Journal* as *A Fugue in Time,* and in novel form was entitled *Take Three Tenses.* As immaculately produced soap opera as well as a sentimental period piece, with Goldwyn hovering, unseen, over every frame. *Enchantment* remains as a '40s reminder of what "a Goldwyn picture" is all about.

The film opens in wartime London and centers around General Sir Roland Dane, an elderly gentleman who has lived a lonely life haunted by memories of the past. Into his home at 99 Wiltshire Place comes Grizel Dane, an American ambulance driver who is his brother Pelham's granddaughter, together with Pax Masterson, a Canadian flyer. To them, Sir Roland recalls his earlier days when he lived in the same house along with Pelham, their older sister Selina, and their father's ward Lark, who had been brought to live with them when they all were children. Spinsterish Selina always had resented Lark, whose transformation into a beautiful woman turned Selina's resentment to hatred. Roland, then an improvident young rogue had fallen deeply in love with Lark, but had as a rival for her affections an Italian nobleman, Marchese Del Laudi. Roland, though, finally convinced Lark to wait for him while he completed his officer training, but the jealous Selina, fearing that Lark would take her place as the head of the household, cunningly separates the two lovers with a monstrous lie (telling Lark that Roland has gone off to Africa with his regiment for five years), and Roland returns home to discover that Lark has run off with the Marchese.

Back in the present, Roland senses that a romance has developed between Grizel and Pax, and then stumbles onto the fact that Pax is Lark's nephew and has been turned down by Grizel on the eve of his departure for the frontlines. Remembering his own grief, Roland urges Grizel to join Pax while there is still time, and she locates the flyer during an air raid. As they embrace in the midst of a bombardment, one of the bombs shatters the Dane mansion, killing old general.

Time Magazine said: "David Niven and Teresa Wright steal the show so completely that in the end it becomes a plea for the past tense, on almost any terms." *Newsweek* felt:

As it stands—deliberate in peace and artfully contrived as an emotional holiday—*Enchantment* is genuinely moving on its own terms and produced by Samuel Goldwyn with a careful good taste that should disarm the critics of lachryma-and-old lace. Backed by Irving Reis' direction and the late Gregg Toland's fluid photography, an excellent cast strengthens the film's claim to romantic plausibility. Miss Wright, one of the screen's finest, glows as the Cinderella who captivated three men, and Niven does a fine job bridging the years, with a special bow going to seven-year-old Gigi Perreau for a tremendously appealing impersonation of a very small Lark.

Bosley Crowther admitted: "In the light of this joyful season . . . it would be a disgraceful misanthrope who would whip out a verbal pocket-torch and try to expose imperfections in (it) . . . this is certainly a picture which beats the drum loudly for love." *The New York Times* reviewer also judged that

David Niven is full of bounce as the young guardsman of the Victorian romance, in studied contrast to his maundering melancholia as the same fellow in his old, nostalgic days. And Teresa Wright plays the young lady of his youthful romance and his living dreams with that breathless, bright-eyed rapture which she so remarkably commands.

His conclusion: "For all we know, it may very well be 'just about the most wonderful love story ever filmed.'

That is a matter of fine opinion. We are pleased, however, to note that the ads don't call it '*the* most wonderful.' They merely say it is 'just about.' "

In the New York *Herald Tribune*, Howard Barnes wrote:

There is fine performing with David Niven and Teresa Wright carrying the chief burden of a somwhat cumbersome plot. The production is as immaculate as one might have expected from the Goldwyn Studios, with brilliant reconstructions of English life in various decades. Irving Reis has directed it painstakingly, winding up with a terrific sequence of London in the blitz. *Enchantment* has breadth and some of the quality of the title, but it lacks screen power and cohesion . . . There is charm and proficiency in *Enchantment,* but little real enchantment.

Enchantment marked the end of Niven's career as a Goldwyn star. With his return from the war, Niven had worked on a series of films on loanout from Goldwyn, including lengthy assignments before and after *Enchantment* in exhaustive Alexander Korda costume dramas, *Bonnie Prince Charlie* and *The Elusive Pimpernel.* When Niven reluctantly asked to be released from the remaining two years of his contract, he was astonished when Goldwyn told him: "You're free as soon as you hit the street." Teresa Wright also concluded her stay with Goldwyn in *Enchantment.* Her Goldwyn career had been plagued by illnesses and unrealized projects, and following *Enchantment,* she was to have had the title role in *Roseanna McCoy* opposite Farley Granger, but another illness forced her out of the project and she never again worked for Goldwyn.

On the other hand, *Enchantment* began what has been termed Goldwyn's "Farley Granger epoch." Granger had made his debut in Goldwyn's *The North Star* in 1943, but his option had been dropped when he joined the army. After the war, he got himself flashy killer roles in Nicholas Ray's *They Live By Night* and Hitchcock's *Rope,* leading Samuel Goldwyn to express renewed interest in him and sign him to a five year contract. Following *Enchantment,* Granger had leading roles in five of the subsequent six Goldwyn films.

David Niven, Teresa Wright and Jayne Meadows in Enchantment.

Farley Granger and Evelyn Keyes in Enchantment.

Teresa Wright and Jayne Meadows in Enchantment.

Jayne Meadows and David Niven in Enchantment.

David Niven in Enchantment.

73 ROSEANNA McCOY (1949)

Directed by Irving Reis; screenplay, John Collier; based on the novel by Alberta Hannum; music director, Emil Newman; score, David Buttolph; song "Roseanna" by Frank Loesser; photographer, Lee Garmes; editor, Daniel Mandell; art director, George Jenkins. Running time, 100 minutes. Released by RKO Pictures. Premiere: Charleston, West Virginia, 8/17/49. New York premiere: Capitol Theater, 10/12/49

THE CAST:
Johnse Hatfield, Farley Granger; *Roseanna McCoy,* Joan Evans*; *"Devil Anse" Hatfield,* Charles Bickford; *Old Randall McCoy,* Raymond Massey; *Mounts Hatfield,* Richard Basehart; *Allifair McCoy,* Gigi Perreau; *Sarie McCoy,* Aline MacMahon; *Tolbert McCoy,* Marshall Thompson; *Phamer McCoy,* Lloyd Gough; *Little Randall McCoy,* Peter Miles; *Thad Wilkins,* Arthur Franz; *Ellison Hatfield,* Frank Ferguson; *Bess McCoy,* Elisabeth Fraser; *Levisa Hatfield,* Hope Emerson; *Abel Hatfield,* Dan White; *Grandma Sykes,* Mabel Paige; *Cousin Zinny,* Almira Sessions; *Cap Hatfield,* William Mauch; *Medicine Seller,* Alan Bridge; *Dance Caller,* Sherman Saunders; *Strong Man,* Bert Goodrich; *Joe McCoy,* Pat Flaherty; and Ray Hyke, Ethan Laidlaw, Jerry Anderson, Donald Gordon, Cliff Clark, Hank Mann, John "Skins" Miller, Lester Dorr, Dawn Hudson, Corinne Van Lissel, Ida Moore, Myra Marsh, Ruth Sanderson, Guy Wilkerson, Gertrude V. Hoffman, Al Kunde, Chuck Hamilton, James Kirkwood, Robert O'Neill, Rory Mallinson, Pat Walshe.
* in screen debut

For the Goldwynites accustomed to the producer's high-style romantic dramas and lavish musicals, *Roseanna McCoy* offered a curious departure. Goldwyn had moved into practically virgin (by Hollywood standards) territory with his decision to delve into American folklore for a cinematic view of the legendary Hatfield-McCoy feud in the Blue Ridge Mountains of the 1880s. Combining his desire to recreate an authentic picture of early American superstitions and ignorances, while correcting cruel distortions and satirizations of several generations and erasing the stereotypes created by hillbilly comic strips, Goldwyn had scenarist John Collier weave historical facts throughout the framework of the Alberta Hannum novel he was adapting, setting the famous feud against a background of young love. Unfortunately, the handicaps produced by the years of stereotypes and caricatures proved to be insurmountable, despite the handsome recreation of the exciting era and the work of the fine cast Goldwyn had recruited from the veteran ranks. The result: a Romeo and Juliet story transplanted to the banks of the Big Sandy River on the West Virginia/Kentucky border. Since *Roseanna McCoy,* in Goldwyn's wisdom, focused on young romance—interpreted by Farley Granger, with the boyish charm that had made him a teenaged idol in the Van Johnson mold, and newcomer Joan Evans, a fourteen-year-old beauty Goldwyn's scouts had discovered in an exclusive girls' school in New York—little opportunity was left for full-bodied character development allowing the elders of both clans to remain merely shadowy figures. (One reason for Goldwyn's decision to spotlight Granger and Evans undoubtedly had been the success in 1947 of MGM's *The Romance of Rosy Ridge,* a backwoods melodrama wherein Van Johnson costarred with then newcomer Janet Leigh.) Most critics applauded Samuel Goldwyn not only for his good intentions with the film, but also for his latest discovery, Joan Evans, who, *Newsweek* proclaimed, "handles the part of an older girl in love with the insight and confidence of a veteran." The role, it seems, was to have been played by Teresa Wright until Goldwyn decided to terminate her contract following *Enchantment,* charging that she had been "uncooperative" in publicizing his pictures.

Joan Evans—the last in the long string of Goldwyn's "personal" discoveries—was a ninth-grader at the Birch-Wathen School in Manhattan and the daughter of playwright Dale Eunson, who had written *Guest in the House,* and magazine writer Katherine Albert. Together the Eunson/Albert team wrote such films as *How to Marry a Millionaire, The Star, Gidget Goes to Rome,* and the autobiographical *All Mine to Give* (which had been dramatised on television in the Fifties as *The Day They Gave Babies Away,* with Joan Evans narrating). Goldwyn's hopes to make Miss Evans a major star were crushed though, despite the fact that he poured much of his publicity efforts behind her. She made only three Goldwyn films—each with Farley Granger.

In the film version of the Hatfield-McCoy saga, Roseanna, the belle of the McCoy clan, and her hot-tempered lover, Johnse, are given credit for ending the feud rather than the blame for igniting it, and in the words of *Newsweek,* "love is credited with greater power than squirrel rifles." Despite the long-standing, but dormant hatred between both families, Roseanna and Johnse are attracted to one another when they first meet at a country fair. She tries to forget him, but when he comes to her one night, she lets him carry her off to his family's mountain home on the other side of the Big Sandy River. Johnse's father objects to their marriage, but his mother does what she can to make the girl comfortable, while the defiant Johnse goes in search of a preacher. During Johnse's absence, his deranged brother, Mounts, attempts to attack Roseanna, but is foiled by the arrival of old "Devil Anse," who, for the sake of peace in his own family, arranges for Roseanna to be returned safely to her folks, where she tries to explain her deep love, and thus avert a blood feud between the clans. Her father is unhappy about the match, but is finally convinced that he must accept the couple. Before Johnse can come for his bride, however, Mounts Hatfield precipitates a fight between some of the Hatfields and McCoys wherein Roseanna's little brother, Randall, is seriously wounded, and the old feud breaks out in all its fury.

Convinced that Johnse was not responsible for the new outbreak in hostilities, Roseanna makes her way to his side, and they decide to escape the family hatred together. As they ride along the river into the direct line of fire, both sides silence their guns, and there is a suggestion at the fadeout that their love has ended the feud.

Time Magazine found that:

Though far too romantic to be real McCoy, *Roseanna* is a moderately entertaining movie that successfully avoids the bearded cliches of most hillbilly fiction and sticks to a safe middle ground between authenticated history and conservative Hollywood tradition. Highlight of the picture is Miss Evans, whose natural, unadorned charm gives an appealing, homespun finish to the slick production.

Thomas M. Pryor wrote in *The New York Times:*

There is much feudin', fussin' and lovin' in this pictorially handsome recreation of the fabulous enmity between the Hatfields and the McCoys, but the characters lack the stature of true persons . . . *Roseanna McCoy,* as adapted by John Collier, does not have as much heart or narrative integrity as did the Alberta Hannum novel on which the film is based . . . However, Mr. Goldwyn appears to have a rich find in the fledgling Miss Evans, and Irving Reis has directed her in a performance that demands considerable emotional display.

In his critique in the *New York Herald Tribune,* Otis L. Guernsey Jr. saw the film as "a melange of whining bullets fiddle music at a fair, a whippoorwill call in the watches of the night, and bare shoulders and wistful features outlined by the technique of half-lighting" and noted that

the accent of John Collier's script is on love rather than murder, and Irving Reis' direction sometimes allows the melodrama to get out of hand. There are just enough active scenes in the show to keep it cooking, but it is a lukewarm Kentucky brew . . . Romeo and Juliet in homespun, with a happy ending.

Guernsey's opinion of the performances:

Miss Evans displays a definite screen personality in her first appearance, but she is not consistently equal to the extravagance of passion required here. Richard Basehart does one good turn as a crazed killer and then slips like the rest into overstatement and whisker-twirling. In general, the actors are victims of the stylized treatment and squirrel-rifle dialogue in which the script is written.

Cue Magazine, like others, referred to the Romeo and Juliet quality of the tale and concluded that "although *Roseanna McCoy* is a far cry from Shakespeare's classic, its story is literate, dramatic, excellently acted, and, in brief, good solid entertainment." Similarly upbeat was the *Variety* notice:

Samuel Goldwyn has fashioned a fresh and strikingly dramatic film in *Roseanna McCoy,* a tender yarn unfolding to a smashing climax against a backwoods setting of love and violence . . . a first-rate screenplay by John Collier has imaginatively tailored the historical facts for a tightly knit cinematic framework, literate without being literal, somber and poetic, yet honestly human. The cast standout is Goldwyn's latest discovery, Joan Evans, (who) brings to her natural physical assets the charm of an unsophisticated yet easy manner. Farley Granger contrasts well with a tense and muscular performance.

Newsweek viewed:

. . . the film is generally faithful to Kentucky history.

And despite a good deal of routine melodrama, it has moments of being rather impressive in its homespun honesty. At best it is a straightforward portrait of a people who have more often been caricatured Dogpatch style for their jug and gun-toting propensities than taken seriously.

Roseanna McCoy was the second consecutive Goldwyn association between director Irving Reis and several actors he had guided through *Enchantment*: Farley Granger and talented youngsters Gigi Perreau and her brother Peter Miles. Except for the substitution of photographer Lee Garmes for the late Gregg Toland, the production staff of the two films basically was the same.

The Hatfield/McCoy legend popped up cinematically as a ninety-minute television movie, based on the same material (though uncredited) used by Goldwyn, and shifted slightly to focus not on the burning teenaged love affair between Roseanna and Johnse but on the respective clans, headed by Jack Palance as Old Devil Anse Hatfield and Steve Forrest as Randall McCoy. Virginia Baker (Palance's real-life wife) and Joan Caulfield portrayed the matriarchs of the feuding families. *The Hatfields and the McCoys,* as the film was cleverly titled, was directed in late 1974 by Clyde Ware, who also coauthored it.

Raymond Massey and Charles Bickford in Roseanna McCoy.

Farley Granger and Joan Evans in Roseanna McCoy.

Raymond Massey and Aline MacMahon in Roseanna McCoy.

Ethan Laidlaw, Frank Ferguson, Farley Granger and
Richard Basehart in Roseanna McCoy.

74 MY FOOLISH HEART (1949)

Directed by Mark Robson; screenplay, Julius J. and Philip G. Epstein; based on the short story *Uncle Wiggily in Connecticut* by J.D. Salinger; music director, Emil Newman; score, Victor Young; title song by Victor Young and Ned Washington; photographer, Lee Garmes; editor, Daniel Mandell; art director, Richard Day; costumes, Edith Head. Running time, 98 minutes. Released by RKO Pictures. Premiere: United Artists and Four Star Theaters, Los Angeles, 12/25/49. New York premiere: Radio City Music Hall, 1/19/50

THE CAST:
Walt Dreiser, Dana Andrews; *Eloise Winters,* Susan Hayward; *Lew Wengler,* Kent Smith; *Mary Jane,* Lois Wheeler; *Martha Winters,* Jessie Royce Landis; *Henry Winters,* Robert Keith; *Ramona,* Gigi Perreau; *Miriam Ball,* Karin Booth; *Miriam's Escort,* Tod Karns; *Sergeant Lucey,* Philip Pine; *Night Club Singer,* Martha Mears; *Dean Whiting,* Edna Holland; *Usher,* Jerry Paris; *Grace,* Marietta Canty; *Red Cross Receptionist,* Barbara Woodell; *Mrs. Crandell,* Regina Wallace; *Waiter,* Marcel de la Brosse; and Phyllis Coates, Bud Stark, Ed Peil Sr., Kerry O'Day, Ray Hyke, Billy Lord, Tom Gibson, Bob Strong, Kay Marlow, Sam Ash

Goldwyn's final film of the Forties was in the grand manner that had distinguished so many of his "women's pictures"—a true, four-handkerchief weeper, highlighted by a smashing, Oscar-nominated performance by Susan Hayward, and outstanding direction by Mark Robson in the first of his three Goldwyn productions (all with Dana Andrews as leading man and Robert Keith in tangy supporting characterizations). For his romantic drama, Goldwyn dipped into the works of J.D. Salinger and came up with the writer's wry tale, *Uncle Wiggily in Connecticut,* a short story that first appeared in *The New Yorker* and today is still read in the Salinger collection, *Nine Stories.* Goldwyn assigned the writing project to Julius J. and Philip G. Epstein, the screenwriting twins

who, while under contract to Warner Bros. in the Forties, wrote *Casablanca, Mr. Skeffington* and other memorable dramas, as well as comedies like *The Male Animal, The Man Who Came To Dinner* and *Arsenic and Old Lace.* Freres Epstein, wrote *Variety,* produced "a script that is honest and loaded with dialogue that is alive"—and provided a tour-de-force effort for Miss Hayward that she eagerly embraced (despite Goldwyn's house loyalty to Dana Andrews by giving him top billing). Goldwyn provided extra insurance by commissioning Paramount's staff composer, Victor Young, to write a sentimental score based on a single theme that, with words by Ned Washington, went on to become a pop music classic and was generally acknowledged the first title tune that helped sell a movie. (The song garnered the second of the film's two Academy Award nominations.)

A tearful marital crisis envelops the body of the film, and broaches the crucial problem of what to do with a failed marriage, in which the wife is a dipsomaniac and the husband wants a divorce as well as the child who, he is unaware, is not really his. Eloise Winters is, at twenty-eight, an "afternoon tippler," married unhappily to Lew Wengler, a former Army officer who had been her college roommate's fiance and whom Eloise had tricked into marrying. Furious when Lew asks for a divorce, she is about to disclose that their daughter Ramona is not his child, but Mary Jane, the girl from whom she had stolen Lew and whom Lew now wants to marry, persuades her to keep her secret. As she packs up to leave, an old evening gown awakens memories in Eloise. She recalls a New York hotel in 1941 where, dejected by catty remarks about her ordinary gown at a party, she had her spirits lifted by a good-looking, dinner-jacketed, party-crasher, Walt Drieser. He had communicated

269

with her several days later, and she sneaked out of the New York City college she was attending to keep a rendezvous with him.

A month later, he had been drafted, and they made the most of one of his overnight passes, ending the evening with a kiss in the dormitory elevator, where the shocked dean had found them and had Eloise expelled. Her parents come in from Boise, Idaho, to meet Walt, who ingratiates himself to Mr. Winters, a sympathetic hardware storeowner. Eloise had planned to leave with her folks, but her understanding father, knowing she would be unhappy, had permitted her to stay in New York to be near Walt's camp. Shortly after the attack on Pearl Harbor, Walt is ordered overseas after a seven-day leave, which he spends with Eloise in a last whirl of excitement—and Eloise becomes pregnant. Aware of her condition, she keeps the news from Walt, unwilling to force him into marrying her. Shattered when she learns that Walt has been killed in a training accident, Eloise then receives a letter from him, written just before his death, asking her to marry him. To shake Eloise out of her melancholy, Mary Jane, her college friend, had taken her to a dance where she was introduced to Lew Wengler, whom she decided would be a good father for her unborn child, and although she did not love him, had accepted his marriage proposal to hide her shame.

As her thoughts return to the present, Eloise realizes she had been cruel not only to Lew but to her daughter. She agrees to his divorce request and promises to give up Ramona. Lew, however, decides that a child's place is with its mother, even though the mother is on her way to becoming an alcoholic.

"*My Foolish Heart* is the kind of movie that gives women a good cry and men a bad time," wrote *Time*.

In its dry-eyed moments, this damp fable is brightened by some well-written patches of wryly amusing dialogue. The whole picture wears an air of quality, thanks to Samuel Goldwyn's handsome production and a group of sincere performances, directed by Mark Robson . . . The film's makers seem to have shot two different endings, and then decided to give the heartstrings an extra wrench by using them both.

Newsweek said:

The skillful handling of a romantic drama makes it a superior film of general adult appeal . . . a film that relies heavily on the persuasiveness of its actors, and the entire cast is first rate . . . From the complex and delicately staged by-play of a scene of attempted seduction to the plane crash that kills Andrews, the star-crossed history of a wartime romance is both credible and moving. These sequences form the emotional core of the film, and director Robson has made them real and valid enough to carry the rest, including a high-minded if somewhat doubtful happy ending.

In *Variety's* opinion,

My Foolish Heart ranks among the better romantic films. Deft and sure in wringing the utmost from a sound story by winning performances and socko direction, it can't miss . . . (and) Samuel Goldwyn's production supervision is another example of his instinctive good taste in bringing to the screen fundamental emotions in real-life style.

The journal made note of the acting this way:

Miss Hayward too often hasn't had the opportunity to portray an honest, dramatic character. She does in this, and her performance is a gem, displaying a positive talent for capturing reality . . . (and) there is a wow of a performance by Robert Keith as (her) father. He certainly rates additional meaty roles.

(Goldwyn had enticed Keith back to the screen following several years on Broadway playing Doc in *Mister Roberts*. Although his screen career dated back to the early Thirties, Keith had only a handful of previous movie roles. Today he is best remembered simply as the father of television and screen actor Brian Keith.)

John McCarten, critic for *The New Yorker*, spoke for the dissenters in his review:

My Foolish Heart offers us Susan Hayward as a star-crossed matron given to belting the bottle and indulging in cynical chatter . . . (and) is full of soap-opera cliches, and it's hard to believe that it was wrung out of a short story by J.D. Salinger that appeared in this austere magazine a couple of years ago. The scriptwriters have certainly done Mr. Salinger wrong.

Bosley Crowther advised his readers in *The New York Times*:

This picture describes in glistening detail the dewy raptures of a wartime romance and the constant despairs of a young lady who finds herself with child and her unwed lover killed . . . it must be said that Mr. Goldwyn hasn't done an indifferent job so far as putting together a production with style and devices is concerned. His picture is handsomely located in an assortment of New Yorkish sets, and the smooth tricks by which he strokes the tear glands are strictly and dutifully Grade A.

Mr. Crowther's compatriate in film criticism, Otis L. Guernsey, observed:

There are, according to production information, 102 two-shots of Susan Hayward and Dana Andrews in *My Foolish Heart*. This number is a solid clue to the sort of love story which has been produced by Samuel Goldwyn. What might be taken as a typical, ill-fated wartime romance is recorded here in a style which is full of conversational detail without character detail, full of sorrow and stars' faces, but largely devoid of the imaginative human touch . . . Director Robson manages to touch up a scene here and there into something more than a recital of feelings, but there is no sustained emotion and no crescendo, (and) *My Foolish Heart* never quite reaches out its hand to touch the object of its scrutiny.

Dana Andrews and Susan Hayward in My Foolish Heart.

Robert Keith and Susan Hayward in My Foolish Heart.

Kent Smith and Susan Hayward in My Foolish Heart.

75 OUR VERY OWN (1950)

Directed by David Miller; screenplay, F. Hugh Herbert; based on his story; music, Victor Young; photographer, Lee Garmes; editor, Sherman Todd; art director, Richard Day; costumes, Mary Wills. Running time, 93 minutes. Released by RKO Pictures. Premiere: Victoria Theater, New York, 7/27/50

THE CAST:
Gail, Ann Blyth; *Chuck,* Farley Granger; *Joan,* Joan Evans; *Lois Macaulay,* Jane Wyatt; *Gert Lynch,* Ann Dvorak; *Fred Macaulay,* Donald Cook; *Penny,* Natalie Wood; *Frank,* Gus Schilling; *Zaza,* Phyllis Kirk;* *Violet,* Jessie Grayson; *Bert,* Martin Milner; *Gwendolyn,* Rita Hamilton; *Jim Lynch,* Ray Teal; *Boy,* Harold Lloyd Jr.*
* in screen debut

During the postwar years, Goldwyn had been turning his attention more increasingly to sentimental screen fare and as he moved into the 1950s, he chose to concentrate, it seems, on films glorifying American suburbia and the value of family life—so stunningly realized earlier in *The Best Years of Our Lives.* With typical Goldwyn panache, *Our Very Own,* the first of these stunningly appointed, well-scrubbed views of middle-class America between the wars, was spectacularly advertised as being "all heart" and aimed at the young moviegoers—with a stand-up likeness of heart-throb Farley Granger in swimming trunks caught in a romantic clinch with Ann Blyth on a lonely beach. (This advertising ploy was similar to the one used the previous year for *Roseanna McCoy,* in which Granger is shown about to sink his teeth into the bare shoulder of Joan Evans.)

Goldwyn used as the focal point of his production an original story by F. Hugh Herbert (who had written such teenage larks as *Kiss and Tell, Margie* and *A Kiss for Corliss*), describing the mental and emotional confusions of an eighteen-year-old girl who, on the eve of her high school graduation, discovers that she is an adopted child, and told in true "junior miss" style. To direct this comedy/drama, Goldwyn selected David Miller, late of the last Marx Brothers movie, *Love Happy,* and to people it, he augmented the standard Goldwyn roster with top-billed Ann Blyth, borrowed from Universal-International, Jane Wyatt (in her pre-"Father Knows Best" days), a preteen Natalie Wood, and veteran Ann Dvorak, nearing the end of a long film career.

Goldwyn's film poses the difficult question about whether an adopted child should be informed of his or her status in the family—and then veers off toward the romantic entanglements of its pubescent leads. Knotty problems such as who is taking whom to the senior prom, together with a little tenderness on the porch swing and a bit of playful sand-throwing at the beach, take precedence over more realistic confrontations like parental neglect in sensibly discussing the adoption with the girl, or allowing her to learn the identity of her true mother, a slattern from the other side of the tracks. Instead, it is all strictly mom, pop, three daughters, a television set, two cars, and a little white house in a little white town in California, lovingly photographed by Lee Garmes and romantically scored by Victor Young.

For as far back as she could remember, Gail Macaulay has been the contented oldest sister of a typical American family, happy and secure at home, in love with Chuck, a neighborhood lad who works in the local TV appliance shop. Her younger sister, Joan, has been making her jealous by playing up to Chuck during his daily visits, causing, finally, an angry, claw-baring showdown between the two girls following a party Gail had thrown in their parents' living room. Joan first had been slapped down for wearing Gail's party dress without permission and then had been seen precociously encouraging Chuck while dancing with him. The two sisters have words, and Joan, in a fit of envy, lets slip the guarded piece of news that Gail is an adopted child. Stunned, Gail has the information confirmed by her "parents," and sinks into deep depression.

Discovering the whereabouts of Gert Lynch, her real mother, Gail has her wealthy girlfriend, Zaza, also the daughter of a broken home, drive her to the rundown apartment building where the Lynch's live. There Gail has a disillusioning reunion with Mrs. Lynch, fortuitously involved in a beer and poker session when her daughter comes to call for the first time. Gail is shocked by Gert Lynch's harsh words and is told never to come back. Sulking far into the night at Zaza's home, Gail reluctantly agrees to see Chuck, who gives her a second verbal going-over, and she decides at last to stick by the Macauley's who, after all, have always given her the best of everything. And at her graduation, Gail incorporates into her valedictory speech the truths she has discovered about familial love and the worth of a good home.

Robert Hatch wrote in *The New Republic*:

One of the nicest things that can happen to a child, Samuel Goldwyn tells us, is to raised at home. Since this picture invariably identifies this wholesome institution as The American Home, Goldwyn may believe it to be unique to this country . . . the ironical thing about the Macaulay family of *Our Very Own* is that if it constitutes the typical American family, Hollywood made it that way. They talk in movie formulas, dress in movie clothes, and are prepared to tear each other's throats out for the favors of Farley Granger, who has been reduced in this picture from an actor to a movie star. There is no substance to these people, no integrity and no tradition, and the only reason they escape the fool killer is that F. Hugh Herbert wrote the scripts and provided it with a happy ending.

In *The New Yorker*, John McCarten said:

For at least a quarter of *Our Very Own*, Mr. Samuel Goldwyn subjects us to his idea—the Goldwyn Touch—of how the American middle-class lives . . . As photographed by Lee Garmes, the young lovers of *Our Very Own* nuzzle up to each other handsomely on land and sea, but it's hard to take their amours seriously, as the young lady in the case has yet to graduate from high school and the young gentleman has yet to progress in the world beyond the point of putting up TV aerials.

Time was equally as harsh, noting:

Our Very Own, coming out four-square in favor of the U.S. Home and Family, sets up what might be the most piercing din of twanging heartstrings since *Stella Dallas*. In telling the story of the Macaulays, producer Samuel Goldwyn has spared nothing to make them

typical of Hollywood: a home out of *House Beautiful,* two cars, a servant and elegant wardrobes . . . The movie is as slick, sugary and shallow as cake icing.

Time felt, though, that "the best thing in the picture is the anguish and suspense of the sequence in which the girl goes to the wrong side of the tracks to see her mother for the first time . . . Veteran Ann Dvorak gives a touching performance."

And *Newsweek* observed that

despite David Miller's able direction, and effective performances by the youngsters involved, *Our Very Own* is too pat to be as convincing as it should be. In producing this family epic, Goldwyn's idea apparently was to glorify the resounding brightness of the typically upper-bracket American home.

In Otis Guernsey's opinion,

Typical is the only word for the atmosphere of Mr. Goldwyn's latest entertainment . . . carefully designed for those who like to watch a knotty family problem drawn out to the last detail of emotional action and reaction. It documents a way of life that surely must excite the envy of audiences outside this unfortunate nation (and) is as wholesome as breakfast food and American as ice cream and cake. It offers its customers exactly what they want to see, and it should overwhelm them with reassurance.

His colleague on the critical beat, Bosley Crowther, called *Our Very Own*

a clearly machine-made comedy-drama . . . If Mr. Herbert and Mr. Goldwyn had been sincere in their desires to consider the problems of adoption in a sensible and realistic way, they would have gone into several matters that are not even touched upon . . . Adoption deserves clarification with something better than farcical laughs and corny sobs.

More upbeat was *Variety's* review:

Our Very Own does a good job of depicting the spirit of the teenager and the value of family life. It does it all rather obviously with quite a number of tried and true tricks, but end results are dramatics that manage to capture considerable flavor of the adolescent age and parental problems, Samuel Goldwyn's production touch has supplied the script with a physical background that never overglosses characters or plot, and director David Miller is reasonably sure in handling the dramatics. The film is a series of high spots of good trouping, climaxing in a finale that will wring sniffles from the femmes and throat-clearing from the males.

Our Very Own emerged as popular screen fare during the summer of 1950 and marked the high point of Farley Granger's status as a darling of the day's teenyboppers. In it, Phyllis Kirk made her screen debut, as did, in a bit part, Harold Lloyd Jr., and a very young Martin Milner made an early screen appearance as Joan Evans' gawky boyfriend. At Oscar time, *Our Very Own* was cited with a nomination for Best Sound Recording (Goldwyn Sound Department).

Farley Granger and Ann Blyth in Our Very Own.

Joan Evans, Farley Granger and Ann Blyth in Our Very Own.

Ann Dvorak and Jane Wyatt in Our Very Own.

76 EDGE OF DOOM (1950)

Directed by Mark Robson; screenplay, Philip Yordan; based on the novel by Leo Brady; music director, Emil Newman; score, Hugo Friedhofer; photographer, Harry Stradling; editor, Daniel Mandell; art director, Richard Day; costumes, Mary Wills. Running time, 99 minutes. Released by RKO Pictures. Premiere: Astor Theater, New York, 8/3/50

THE CAST:

Father Roth, Dana Andrews; *Martin Lynn*, Farley Granger; *Rita Conroy*, Joan Evans; *Mandel*, Robert Keith; *Craig*, Paul Stewart; *Julie*, Mala Powers; *Irene*, Adele Jergens; *Father Kirkman*, Harold Vermilyea; *First Detective*, John Ridgely; *Second Detective*, Douglas Fowley; *Mrs. Pearson*, Mabel Paige; *J.T. Murray*, Howland Chamberlain; *Mr. Swanson*, Houseley Stevenson Sr.; *Mrs. Lally*, Jean Innes; *Mrs. Moore*, Ellen Corby; *Ned Moore*, Ray Teal; *Mary Jane Glennon*, Mary Field; *Mrs. Dennis*, Virginia Brissac; *Mrs. Lynn*, Frances Morris

The Goldwyn Touch, from a publicity standpoint, was best demonstrated in the summer of 1950 when he premiered on Broadway his somber drama, *Edge of Doom,* one week after the opening next door of *Our Very Own.* By installing the two films in adjoining theaters he not only heralded his name and product(s) on the block-long billboard above the side-by-side Astor and Victoria Theaters in Times Square, but also provided maximum exposure with six marquee sides emblazoned with the Goldwyn name, as well as those of Farley Granger and Joan Evans, his two most exploitable talents—both of whom were in each film, although in *Edge of Doom,* they had no scenes together.

Edge of Doom is atypical of Goldwyn's work—a grim, relentless study of an emotionally wrought young man who kills a priest after being rebuffed in his plans for a lavish funeral for his mother. Taken from the novel by Leo Brady, a professor at Catholic University (Goldwyn had paid $150,000 for the rights to the book), it was hammered into a screenplay by Philip Yordan, the author of *Anna Lucasta,* and filmed in just thirty-eight days by director Mark Robson and Goldwyn's "stock" company headed by Dana Andrews. The Yordan screenplay mixes psychological overtones with religious generalities—revolt against poverty intertwined with questions about the moral precepts of the Church. The resulting film garnered scathing comments from the critics, exemplified by Otis Guernsey, who wrote in the *New York Herald-Tribune*:

> *Edge of Doom* is a decadent piece of moviemaking which panders to the box office with sensationalism poorly disguised in social and religious comment . . . merely a gloomy murder story tricked up with a few solemn words.

Stung by the barrage of negative notices, which were confirmed by a personally ordered poll at the Astor Theater, Goldwyn decreed that a new prologue and epilogue be attached to the film, along with some voice-over commentary by Dana Andrews—a highly unusual occurrence for a movie that not only had just premiered in the spotlight of tremendous publicity (some paid, some free), but also was still running. Ben Hecht was rushed in to write the new dialogue and Charles Vidor was pulled off preproduction work on Goldwyn's *Hans Christain Andersen* to film the new footage, which changed the story of a pathological killer obsessed with his mother's funeral, to the success story of a priest in winning a misguided young man back to the faith. (This additional footage was not seen during the film's premiere engagement, nor was it reflected in any of the New York or national magazine reviews.)

Edge of Doom tells of Martin Lynn, a delivery man for a small florist shop, who harbors an overweaning love for his mother and undying hatred for the church that failed to absolve his dissolute father who had committed suicide a few years earlier. When Mrs. Lynn dies, Martin becomes obsessed with the idea that she rates a big funeral even though he has not the money to pay for it. Desperately, he urges the local priest, Father Kirkman, who previously had refused to help his father, to keep his mother from "just being shoveled into the ground." Embittered when the testy priest unsympathetically turns him down, Martin kills him with a silver crucifix. In his panicky flight, Martin comes across a theater (showing, ironically, *Our Very Own* starring Farley Granger), which has just been robbed by Craig, a petty hood who lives with his moll, Irene, in the flat below Martin's. By his terrorized actions, Martin becomes a suspect in the theft and is taken to police headquarters for questioning. There, Detective Mandel begins to suspect he may be connected with the killing of Father Kirkman, but he is cleared when a woman who had witnessed a figure leaving the church at the time of the killing erroneously identifies Craig as the murderer.

In the meantime, Father Roth, the slain priest's assistant, has begun his own investigation, along with Rita Conroy, Father Kirkman's pretty niece, and begins to feel that the tortured youth, Martin Lynn, may know more than he is telling. Martin's girlfriend, Julie, tries to help her distraught beau, who finds himself hounded by detectives and rebuffed by the local mortician, and finally convinces him to go to the funeral parlor where his mother awaits burial. There he meets the understanding Father Roth, and then breaks down, admits his guilt and asks forgiveness. In the added prologue and epilogue, Father Roth, who has inherited the poor parish, relates the story to his young assistant, explaining how faith is part of the human soul—giving the church the final word.

Missing on the screen were the many pages of the Leo Brady novel that delved into Martin Lynn's neurotic state of mind, and the character of Father Kirkman was only sketchily developed, as was that of the priest's niece who, like Martin, also had turned from the church through her determination to marry a divorced man.

"This depressingly long-drawn-out story," wrote *Newsweek,*

gives Farley Granger another chance to play virtually the same role he handled with a great deal of sensitivity in *They Live by Night* several years earlier. But this time, Granger's equally knowing performance ends up second best in competition with a morose and often maladroit script . . . Under the thoroughly capable direction of Mark Robson, (the cast) and especially Mala Powers as Granger's neglected girlfriend perform with homey simplicity. But Granger's plight is

painted in too lugubrious a monotone to have either the social significance or poignancy it ought to have.

Time noted that, in contrast to the book's exemplary study,

on the screen, the story becomes a second-rate melodrama with a wispy religious motif . . . Director Robson's accent on gloom, the script's blurry counterfeit of the novel's hero, and actor Granger's lack of depth and force all combine to produce an effect which is neither dramatic nor provocative, but merely overwhelmingly monotonous.

In *The New Republic,* this was the gist of James R. Newman's critical comments:

Hollywood's genius for stifling talent and rewarding incompetence has seldom been demonstrated more brilliantly than in *Edge of Doom,* another of the industry's pretentious attempts to produce drama from abnormal psychology. The hero . . . is played by Farley Granger, whose acting consists of clenching his fists at his sides, standing rigidly in a bath of artificial sweat while the camera and light men work their magic, and once in a while burying his little face in his hands.

John McCarten, critic for *The New Yorker,* admitted:

This is a pretty weird little item, but (it) does have in its favor a cast that goes about its strange business with an inexplicable will . . . although (Farley Granger) certainly makes the boy a tiresome fellow to have around.

Thomas M. Pryor, in *The New York Times,* called the film

a somber study of a tortured victim of frustration, spun out with rising and falling impact . . . (it) follows a rather conventional melodramatic course and depends for its excitement on physical forces, such as the staging of the manhunt and Martin's desperate efforts to escape detection. Mark Robson's direction gives flashes of high tension to the film . . . (but) there is a deliberateness about the action which gives *Edge of Doom* the appearance of having been contrived.

Championing the thumbs-down cause was Otis Guernsey:

The molten misery poured from Samuel Goldwyn's *Edge of Doom* misses an intelligent dramatic mold and flows all over the place. Director Robson gives it a certain style, which the material is not able to match. Shallowly conceived and inadequately acted, it is a muddled, morbid interlude of specious hysteria . . . Farley Granger is not up to the task of sustaining a whole picture with studied monomania (and) does not seethe but is limited to varying degrees of unhappiness in a monotonous performance.

The most upbeat review came from *Variety*:

It has been made with all of Samuel Goldwyn's usual attention to detail, played to the hilt by a good cast, and directed with impact by Mark Robson . . . Farley Granger stands out as the boy; Dana Andrews scores as the young priest; Robert Keith is excellent as the detective; Paul Stewart makes his petty thief character topnotch.

Following her role in *Edge of Doom,* Joan Evans left the Goldwyn fold, never having lived up to her earlier promise of his extensive publicity, and added only a handful of other screen credits during the Fifties before settling into domesticity.

Farley Granger and Mala Powers in Edge of Doom.

Robert Keith, Joan Evans and Dana Andrews in Edge of Doom.

Farley Granger and Dana Andrews in Edge of Doom.

77 I WANT YOU (1951)

Directed by Mark Robson; screenplay, Irwin Shaw; based on stories in New Yorker Magazine by Edward Newhouse; music, Leigh Harline; photographer, Harry Stradling; editor, Daniel Mandell; assistant director, Ivan Volkman; art director, Richard Day; costumes, Mary Wills. Running time, 102 minutes. Released by RKO Pictures. Premiere: Criterion Theater, New York, 12/23/51

THE CAST:
Martin Greer, Dana Andrews; *Nancy Greer,* Dorothy McGuire; *Jack Greer,* Farley Granger; *Carrie Turner,* Peggy Dow; *Thomas Greer,* Robert Keith; *Sarah Greer,* Mildred Dunnock; *Judge Jonathan Turner,* Ray Collins; *George Kress Jr.,* Martin Milner; *Harvey Landrum,* Jim Backus; *Celia Turner,* Marjorie Crossland; *George Kress Sr.,* Walter Baldwin; *Ned Iverson,* Walter Sande; *Gladys,* Peggy Maley; *Anne Greer,* Jerrilyn Flannery; *Tony Greer,* Erik Nielsen; *Gloria,* Ann Robin; *Caroline Krupka,* Carol Savage; *Train Porter,* James Adamson; *Art Stacey,* Harry Lauter; *Bartender,* Frank Sully; and Robert Johnson, David McMahon, Jimmy Ogg, Melodi Lowell, Jean Andren, Charles Marsh, Don Hayden, Lee Turnbull, Paul Smith, Rolland Morris, Al Murphy, Dee Carroll, Ralph Brooks.

Goldwyn's second—and final—fifties cinematic valentine to contemporary Americana, blending cheers, tears and a large serving of patriotism, was the occasion, it seems in retrospect, for one final gathering of the producer's stock company, together with Dorothy McGuire, borrowed for the event from David O. Selznick. *I Want You* was to be, Goldwyn had envisioned, his personal Korean War movie, staged somewhat less ambitiously than *The Best Years of Our Lives,* but with as much pride. Based on stories by Edward Newhouse that had been published in *The New Yorker* and molded into a screenplay by Irwin Shaw, *I Want You* follows a typical American family as the impact of the Korean War makes itself felt, and tells of two brothers, the women they love, and various kinfolk in a time when Uncle Sam again sends out his call to arms. The film, which borrowed both its message and its title from the legendary recruiting poster, was directed by Mark Robson (his third time out for Goldwyn), who managed to keep the Shaw script, which wavered on the brink of bathos, from slipping into soap opera. Robson was unable, however, to imbue any immediacy into the somewhat sterile proceedings, nor fire his actors into performances of any import, except for a single, telling scene toward the climax, in which Mildred Dunnock (as the mother) denounces Robert Keith (the father) for his jingoistic stances and tall-tale telling of imagined heroics, and in a grand gesture, tears his World War One trophies from the living room mantel.

"It's a pretty lugubrious story that Samuel Goldwyn has his people trying to tell," reported critic Bosley Crowther.

It is a story of average Americans resisting the necessity of facing up to another war and then finally standing still for it because it is the patriotic thing to do. And because it is plainly lugubrious and open to questions by some skeptics here and there, Mr. Goldwyn and his people are trying to sell it on terms of sentiment and romance . . . With all due regard for Mr. Goldwyn and the facile pen of Mr. Shaw, it must be said that the quality of their persuasion does not match the intensity of their concern . . . (and) Mr. Robson, who directed the effort, might have been dressing a window for a department store.

I Want You begins in the summer of 1950. Martin Greer, a World War Two veteran, lives with his wife Nancy and their two small children and runs the family construction business with his father. His younger brother, Jack, has recently joined the firm after gradu-

279

ating from high school, and is looking forward to the return of his girlfriend, Carrie, who has been away at college. Jack and Carrie are in love and pay little heed to the fact that her father, Judge Turner, has frowned on their adolescent romance. At the outbreak of war in Korea, Jack receives his draft notice, and despite a plea from their mother, Martin cannot bring himself to write a letter declaring his brother essential to the business, particularly since he had just refused a similar request from George Kress, one of his oldest employees, on behalf of George Jr.

When the draft board, on which Judge Turner is a member, rules that Jack's old knee injury is no longer cause for exemption, Jack bitterly accuses the judge for using the decision as an excuse to break up his romance with Carrie, and when Carrie turns down his suggestion that they elope immediately, his resentment leads to a childish rift between them. Further dissension is caused when Jack's sister-in-law, Nancy, berates him for his petulant attitude. Reluctantly, Jack accepts his draft notice, and after seeing him off to camp, his mother returns home and tears from the walls the souvenirs collected by her husband as mementoes of service in World War One, revealing that she knew for all their years of marriage that he had been nothing more than a general's orderly, not the hero he long had pretended to be, and seeing her son off to war made her unable to look at them again.

Martin, meanwhile, throws himself more deeply into his business until he receives a visit from his old C.O., Harvey Landrum, who tells Martin that he had just reenlisted and suggests that Martin himself seriously consider joining up again to help in the nation's program of building defense airstrips. Martin puts off his decision until word arrives that George Kress, Jr., the boy for whom he had refused to request a deferment, had been killed in action. After a long struggle with his conscience, Martin tells Nancy that he has decided to reenlist, shortly after his brother Jack's post-basic leave. Jack, changed by boot camp, had returned with a more mature attitude, and with Judge Turner's blessings, had married Carrie, and now both Nancy and Carrie were resigned to waiting for peace and the return of their men.

Variety viewed *I Want You* as "prestige filmmaking" and compared it to *The Best Years of Our Lives,* noting that

the new film is of fine calibre, productionwise. The performances are uniformly in top groove, each character coming through as believably as the folks next door . . . but the completeness and socko humorous and

dramatic quality that so distinguished the original is lacking (and) the film is devoid of any real dramatic highpoints. Interesting as it is, and put together in good taste, *I Want You* never really gets off the ground.

Time Magazine said:

The picture shows the impact of the Korean War on a movie-typical U.S. middle-class family and concludes tearfully that home ties must yield to the tug of patriotic duty. Producer Samuel Goldwyn coats this sternly real subject with a shiny glaze of sentimentality . . . (and) most of the time, *I Want You* uses its characters as puppets in an object lesson, moving too dutifully through their paces to command belief.

Similarly unenthusiastic was *Newsweek's* critic, who commented that

unfortunately the screenplay offers a collection of "typical American" characters, and they appear in a "typical American" small-city setting which has all the exaggerated realism of a painting by Norman Rockwell. Throughout the film, the American scene is demeaned by being made a stereotype, and Samuel Goldwyn's latest effort suffers irremediably by it.

Otis L. Guernsey, Jr., in his review in the *New York Herald Tribune,* thought that *I Want You* "is too fat, too sentimental and has too glossy a coat of paint on its problems to rank as a decisive movie interpretation of the modern era." In his critique, he went on:

Though Shaw's dialogue carefully avoids platitudinous expressions in neat pieces of screen writing, his script as a whole leaves one with the feeling that the American grain runs deeper and the fiber is tougher than has been indicated here . . . All of the actors, except Farley Granger, who must play an earnest and resentful youth, have been directed by Mark Robson into an off-handed, restrained style of performing which, along with Shaw's dialogue, keeps the picture's feet on the ground.

With *I Want You,* Dana Andrews concluded his Goldwyn contract (he had worked in eight films) as well as the one with 20th Century-Fox (Goldwyn had sold half of Andrews' contract to Darryl F. Zanuck shortly after *The Westerner* in 1940). *I Want You* was cited at Oscar time in only one category: Best Sound Recording (Gordon Sawyer named on behalf of the Goldwyn Sound Department). It was the second of three consecutive Academy Award nominations in that category. And, for nostalgia, the Oscar-nominated "My Foolish Heart," the title song from Goldwyn's 1949 success, was incorporated into the score written by Leigh Harline.

Robert Keith and Farley Granger in I Want You.

Dana Andrews and Dorothy McGuire in I Want You.

Mildred Dunnock, Farley Granger, Dorothy McGuire, Dana Andrews and Robert Keith in I Want You.

Walter Baldwin, Jim Backus and Dana Andrews in I Want You.

78 HANS CHRISTIAN ANDERSEN (1952)

Directed by Charles Vidor; screenplay, Moss Hart; based on a story by Myles Connolly; music director, Walter Scharf; score, Frank Loesser; choreographer, Roland Petit; photographer, Harry Stradling; editor, Daniel Mandell; art directors, Richard Day and Antoni Clavé; costumes, Clavé, Mary Wills and Mme. Karinska. Running time, 120 minutes. Technicolor. Released by RKO Pictures. Premiere: Criterion and Paris Theaters, New York, 11/25/52

THE CAST:

Hans Christian Andersen, Danny Kaye; *Niels,* Farley Granger; *Doro,* Jeanmaire; *Peter,* Joey Walsh; *Otto,* Philip Tonge; *The Hussar* in "Ice Skating Ballet", Eric Bruhn; *The Prince* in "The Little Mermaid", Roland Petit; *Schoolmaster,* John Brown; *Burgomeister,* John Qualen; *Celine,* Jeanne LaFayette; *Stage Doorman,* Robert Malcolm; *Farmer,* George Chandler; *First Gendarme,* Fred Kelsey; *Second Gendarme,* Gil Perkins; *Lars,* Peter Votrian; *The Princess* in "The Little Mermaid", Betty Uitti; *Sea Witch* in "The Little Mermaid", Jack Klaus.

Musical numbers: (performed by)
Overture *Orchestra*
"The King's New Clothes" (Danny Kaye and children)
"Inchworm" (Danny Kaye and children)
"I'm Hans Christian Andersen" (Danny Kaye)
"Wonderful Copenhagen" (Ray Linn, sailors, chorus, Danny Kaye, Joey Walsh)
Reprise: "I'm Hans Christian Andersen" (Danny Kaye)
"Thumbelina" (Danny Kaye)
Ice Skating Ballet (Dancers, Eric Bruhn, Jeanmaire)
Dream Fantasy (Farley Granger, Jeanmaire, Danny Kaye)
"The Ugly Duckling" (Danny Kaye, Peter Votrian)
"Anywhere I Wander" (sung by Danny Kaye) *danced by Jeanmaire*
Reprise: "I'm Hans Christian Andersen" (Danny Kaye)
Wedding Fantasy *danced by Jeanmaire, Danny Kaye and dancers,* (sung by chorus)
"No Two People" (Jeanmaire, Danny Kaye and chorus)

"The Little Mermaid" Ballet *danced by ballerinas, Jeanmaire, Roland Petit, male dancers, Betty Uitti, Jack Klaus*
Finale: "The Ugly Duckling" (Danny Kaye)
     "Wonderful Copenhagen" (Danny Kaye)
     "The King's New Clothes" (Danny Kaye and children)
     "Thumbelina" (Danny Kaye, children, chorus, John Brown, John Qualen)
     "I'm Hans Christian Andersen" (Chorus)

Goldwyn's long-cherished dream of producing a fairy tale about one of the world's most famous fairy tale tellers reached fruition in the Technicolor spectacular, on which was lavished more than $4,000,000. *Hans Christian Andersen* had been an oft-postponed Goldwyn project for nearly fifteen years and once had been announced as a starring vehicle for Gary Cooper (under William Wyler's direction). Goldwyn had had his efficient publicity department spread the word when Danny Kaye was a Goldwyn star that Kaye would soon begin filming it—in the mid-forties. Finally, after amassing sixteen complete screenplays, for which he paid a small fortune Goldwyn felt Hans Christian Andersen's time had come, and with a story by Myles Connolly and a screenplay by Moss Hart, he (Goldwyn) spun an elaborate musical tale which visualized Andersen as a happy village cobbler from Odense who makes children laugh, to the chagrin of the local schoolmaster facing empty classrooms.

Goldwyn's over-generous pocketbook allowed for a $400,000 ballet sequence (which runs seventeen minutes), a grand salary of $175,000 to lure Danny Kaye back to the fold as the star, a fifteen-song score by Frank Loesser (only eight were used), even $14,000 on shoes alone! Moira Shearer, the British ballerina who had starred in the screen version of Hans Christian Andersen's *The Red Shoes,* was signed to costar with Kaye and Farley Granger (who would play her husband). Her pregnancy, though, forced Goldwyn to seek a last-minute replacement, which he found in Renee Jeanmaire (here using only her last name), the petite French ballerina from the Ballet de Paris—and wife of Roland Petit, who choreographed Goldwyn's film and danced the role of The Prince in "The Little Mermaid" ballet extravaganza. Filming under Charles Vidor began on 21 January 1952 and proceeded for 109 days, ending on 26 May. Cutting the elaborate film was completed in time for a Thanksgiving Day dual world premiere at two Manhattan theatres.

"There is so much spread across the screen in this expensive show that one hardly knows where to begin a description of it," Otis L. Guernsey wrote in the *New York Herald Tribune.* "The film demonstrates the sheer hypnotic power of the musical kaleidoscope technique . . . This *Hans Christian Andersen* is a victory mainly of production technique, a bona fide Goldwyn dazzler."

Goldwyn never meant his expensive, brightly hued bauble to be a screen biography, and admitted such in the opening credits "disclaimer"—but the Danish people themselves failed to be appeased by Goldwyn's forthright admissions and were appalled at the Goldwynesque portrait of their national hero, who, unlike the man portrayed on the screen, *was* a trained shoemaker of foster parents, but gave up the trade to move on to serious literature and a considerable amount of broadening travel.

Goldwyn and his millions notwithstanding, *Hans Christian Andersen* rested on Danny Kaye's shoulders, and with the exception of the lengthy ballet interlude, Kaye was asked to be on camera ceaselessly—in his most subdued manner. Critical opinion remains divided about this crucial casting, but *Time* felt that

> For all this movie magnificence, the film's most genuinely affecting moments are in Kaye's performance in the title role. Looking a little like a Danish Walter Mitty, (he) forgoes his familiar scat type of clowning to give a gentle, appealing and restrained characterization.

On the other hand, this came from Hollis Alpert in *Saturday Review*:

> Kaye . . . has been kept under such restraint that his performance has all the zest of a glass of beer gone flat. Without any clowning to do, Danny Kaye is simply not very interesting, and it's hard to get worked up over his encounter with a ballet dancer in Copenhagen and his rather foolish mooning over her.

In the Goldwyn production, Hans Christian Andersen is a local cobbler who tells delightful stories with which he enchants the children of Odense, and causes the town fathers to ask him to leave. With his apprentice, Peter, Hans decides to try his fortune—at cobbling—in Copenhagen, where he immediately gets himself in trouble with the law for unwittingly breaking a town ordinance. Peter, meanwhile, has evaded the police, and hiding at the Royal Theater, he overhears that the prima ballerina is in desperate need of a cobbler. Peter come forth and offers Hans' services, if he can be bailed out of jail. Hans is brought to the theater to make a special pair of slippers for the star, and immediately falls in love with her, not suspecting that she is happily married to the ballet director, Niels, though they frequently and publicly quarrel. Witnessing one of these marital squabbles, Hans tries to intercede, but is banished from rehearsals for his effort.

That night, Hans writes to the ballerina—a love letter disguised as a fairy tale about "The Little Mermaid" who discovers she has sought love from the wrong man. Through a series of accidents, it falls into the ballerina's hands, and she sees it not as a love letter, but as a wonderful ballet theme. When Hans learns, through Peter, that the ballerina has the letter, he rushes to tell her of his great love, only to learn that the ballet has left on tour, and he can do nothing but moon over the ballerina.

Waiting for the ballerina's return, Hans sets up shop in Copenhagen, and is soon up to his old tricks of telling tall tales to starry-eyed children. One of the stories is "The Ugly Duckling," told to comfort a little lad with a bald head. The boy's father, a newspaper publisher, prints the story and Hans becomes famous, Meanwhile, the ballet returned from its tour, with its opening night featuring "The Little Mermaid." When Hans over-insistently demands that he present a special pair of slippers to the ballerina, he is unceremoniously locked in a closet by her preoccupied, exasperated husband. Unable to see his ballet, Hans nevertheless can hear the music and his imagination conjures up the scenes. The following morning, the ballerina, wondering why Hans had not attended the opening, learns that her husband had locked him up. Sending for Hans, the ballerina realizes that he is in love with her, and in a touching scene, she enlightens Hans as to the real situation. Hans decides to return to Odense with Peter, and there is greeted as a celebrity and everyone—including the grumpy old schoolmaster—listens enchanted to his stories.

"A charming fairy tale," *Variety* reported,

> done with the taste expected of a Goldwyn production . . . Danny Kaye, setting aside his usual antic drolleries and comedy airs, does a very fine job of the title role, sympathetically projecting the Andersen spirit and philosophy . . . The lavish budget allotment given the picture by Goldwyn is evident throughout.

Newsweek chimed in calling it

chiefly a tribute to the producer's acknowledged good taste and his willingness to spend money to achieve it . . . (and) both Goldwyn and director Charles Vidor have conjured up a gay and lovely never-never land for the holiday season; fortunately, they also had the good sense to give Frank Loesser a free hand in making his exciting score an integral part of the narration.

Bosley Crowther felt that "Samuel Goldwyn's familiar reputation as a maker of quality films, full of exquisite production and painstaking craftsmanship, should receive further elevation from his handsome *Hans Christian Andersen.*" Crowther was less enthusiastic about some parts of the whole.

Quite simply, Mr. Hart has not created a character for Mr. Kaye to play, let alone a credible reflection of the famous Danish teller of tales. His Hans Christian Andersen is lumpish, humorless and wan. No wonder Mr. Kaye is unable to stoke up magnetism in the role. However, he does bravely manage to make merry with Mr. Loesser's songs and convey something of a jovial spirit of a musical fairy tale.

Goldwyn's *Hans Christian Andersen* grossed $6,000,-000, according to *Variety,* making it the third highest grossing Goldwyn film (after *The Best Years of Our Lives* and *Guys and Dolls*). It received Oscar nominations in six categories: Best Song ("Thumbelina"), Best scoring of a Musical Film, Best Art/Set Design for a Color Film, Best Cinematography, Best Costume Design

(Clavé, Mary Wills, Mme. Karinska), Best Sound Recording (Gordon Sawyer). *Hans Christian Andersen* failed to win any Academy Awards. Twenty-two years later, the Goldwyn production was the basis of a London stage musical starring Tommy Steele in the title role. The Frank Loesser songs written for, but not used in, Goldwyn's film were reinstated, along with the popular "No Two People," "The Ugly Duckling," "Inchworm," "Thumbelina," "Wonderful Wonderful Copenhagen," "Anywhere I Wander," "The King's New Clothes," and the title song, all being introduced and popularized by Danny Kaye.

Hans Christian Andersen marked the end of the continuous thirty-year output of Goldwyn films. After making seventy-eight films—one or two, and sometimes three, a year—Goldwyn decided to cut back, producing only two more, both lavish spectaculars, in the succeeding seven years. None of the Goldwyn "stars" were kept under contract, with Farley Granger the last departure. Danny Kaye moved on to Paramount Pictures, Jeanmaire made only one further film in America (Crosby's new version of *Anthing Goes*), and young Joey Walsh, then fourteen, left films after appearing in Stanley Kramer's *The Juggler* the following year. He reemerged in the late 1960s as an actor in *Anzio* and in 1974 as writer and coproducer (with Robert Altman) of Altman's *California Split*. For his adult career, he is known as Joseph Walsh.

Danny Kaye and friend in Hans Christian Andersen.

Jeanmaire and Farley Granger in Hans Christian Andersen.

Danny Kaye and children in Hans Christian Andersen.

Danny Kaye and children in Hans Christian Andersen.

79 GUYS AND DOLLS (1955)

Directed by Joseph L. Mankiewicz; screenplay, Joseph L. Mankiewicz; based on the musical play by Jo Swerling and Abe Burrows; adapted from the short story *The Idylls of Sarah Brown* by Damon Runyon; music director, Jay Blackton; score, Frank Loesser; choreographer, Michael Kidd; photographer, Harry Stradling; editor, Daniel Mandell; costumes, Irene Sharaff. Running time, 158 minutes. CinemaScope and Eastman Color. Released by Metro-Goldwyn-Mayer. Premiere: Capitol Theater, New York, 11/3/55

THE CAST:

Sky Masterson, Marlon Brando; *Sarah Brown*, Jean Simmons; *Nathan Detroit*, Frank Sinatra; *Miss Adelaide*, Vivian Blaine*; *Lt. Brannigan*, Robert Keith; *Nicely-Nicely Johnson*, Stubby Kaye*; *Big Jule*, B.S. Pully*; *Benny Southstreet*, Johnny Silver*; *Harry the Horse*, Sheldon Leonard; *Rusty Charlie*, Dan Dayton; *Society Max*, George E. Stone; *Arvide Abernathy*, Regis Toomey; *General Cartwright*, Kathryn Givney; *Laverne*, Veda Ann Borg; *Agatha*, Mary Alan Hokanson; *Angie the Ox*, Joe McTurk; *Calvin*, Kay Kuter; *Liverlips Louis*, Johnny Indrisano; *Mission Member*, Stapleton Kent; *The Champ*, Matt Murphy; *Cuban Singer*, Renee Renor; *Havana Waiter*, Julian Rivero; *The 1955 Goldwyn Girls*, Larri Thomas, Jann Darlyn, June Kirby, Madelyn Darrow, Barbara Brent; and Harry Wilson, Earle Hodgins, Harry Tyler, Major Sam Harris, Franklyn Farnum, Frank Richards.
* in original Broadway production

Musical numbers: (performed by:)
Overture: "Guys and Dolls"/"A Woman in Love" (chorus)
"Fugue for Tin Horns" (Frank Sinatra, Johnny Silver and Dan Dayton)
"Follow the Fold" (Jean Simmons, Kay Kuter and group)
"The Oldest Established" (Frank Sinatra, Johnny Silver, Stubby Kaye and ensemble)
"I'll Know" (Jean Simmons and Marlon Brando)
"Pet Me, Poppa" (Vivian Blaine)
"Adelaide's Lament" (Vivian Blaine)
Reprise: "Follow the Fold" (Marlon Brando and Jean Simmons)
"Guys and Dolls" (Frank Sinatra, Johnny Silver, Stubby Kaye)
"Adelaide" (Frank Sinatra)

"A Woman in Love"
   (1) (Ruben De Fuentes)
   (2) (Vocal trio with guitars)
   (3) *Instrumental Small Combo*
   (4) (Renee Renor)
   (5) (Jean Simmons and Marlon Brando)
"If I Were a Bell" (Jean Simmons and Marlon Brando)
Reprise: "A Woman in Love" (Jean Simmons and Marlon Brando)
"Take Back Your Mink" (Vivian Blaine and The Hot Box Girls)
Reprise: "Adelaide's Lament" (Vivian Blaine)
"The Crap Game Dance" *Dance ensemble*
"Lucky Be a Lady" (Marlon Brando and ensemble)
"Sue Me" (Vivian Blaine and Frank Sinatra)
"Sit Down, You're Rockin' the Boat" (Stubby Kaye and ensemble; Kathryn Givney, Mary Alan Hokanson, Jean Simmons)
"Follow the Fold" (Kathryn Givney and gamblers)
Finale: "Guys and Dolls" (Stubby Kaye and ensemble)

After a three-year lapse, the Goldwyn name once more lit up the screen with a lavish, star-studded, multicolored musical extravaganza, blessed with the legendary "touch." In typical Goldwyn style, he had shelled out $1,000,000 to Broadway producers Feuer and Martin (to that time, the highest price paid for any screen property), and then allocated another $4.5 million for the budget. The sweeping Goldwyn gestures continued, when he astounded Hollywood by hiring not only director Joseph L. Mankiewicz, who never before (nor since) handled a musical subject, but also Marlon Brando and Jean Simmons, with no previous musical experience, as two of the four leads. Even Goldwyn's selection of Frank Sinatra to play Nathan Detroit raised an eyebrow or two in tinsel-land, considering the acclaim that had greeted Sam Levene on Broadway in the role that he rightly called his own. Goldwyn also let out the word that Betty Grable was to play Adelaide, but the part finally went, rightfully, to Vivian Blaine, who had created it in the original stage version (which ran on Broadway for 1200 performances).

Frank Loesser was then called upon to add three new songs to his original score (ten from the original show were used, "A Bushel and a Peck" and "I've Never Been in love Before" were dropped, and "Pet Me, Poppa," "A Woman in Love" and "Adelaide" were added), and Michael Kidd was brought in to restage his original choreography, especially his "Luck Be a Lady" production number, combined with "The Crap Game Dance" in an elaborately appointed sewer. Joseph L. Mankiewicz, meanwhile, had revamped both plot and characters to the screen, managing to cling to the plotline, which Jo Swerling and Abe Burrows had crafted for the stage from Damon Runyon's unique literary world.

Guys and Dolls basically is the story of two romances— one between Sky Masterson, the high-rolling gambler, and Sarah Brown, the young lady in charge of the Broadway branch of the Save-a-Soul mission; the other between Nathan Detroit, proprietor of the oldest established permanent floating crap game, and Miss Adelaide, the brassy blonde who heads the floor show in a joint called the Hot Box and "the well-known fiancee" of Nathan to whom she has been more or less engaged for fourteen years. Nathan, needing money to rent a suitable suite (or backroom, garage or sewer) for his floating crap game, bets Sky $1,000 he cannot make it to Havana inside twenty-four hours with a mission doll named Sarah. Sky, accustomed to dolls "wit' nice teeth and no last names" puts a proposition to Sarah: in return for her company, he promises to deliver twelve of "the devil's first-string troops" to her prayer meeting come Saturday night. Sarah takes him up on the deal, but Sky, yielding to a soft impulse brought on by love, gallantly denies that he succeeded, blowing the wager with Nathan and finally picking up his marker from Sarah by bringing to her mission twelve of his pals—including such underworld denizens as Nicely-Nicely Johnson, Big Jule, Benny Southstreet, Harry the Horse, Rusty Charlie, Society Max and Angie the Ox. This gesture puts Sky "in real good" with Sarah, and everything works out satisfactorily, with a double wedding being performed at high noon in Times Square.

The new singing team of Brando and Simmons (heard on an extended-play 45 rpm record in lieu of a regular soundtrack recording, made unavailable due to Sinatra's contractual commitments) pleasantly surprised the doubters who had expected the worst: they duetted on "I'll Know," "If I Were A Bell" and the new "A Woman in Love," introduced in a lengthy Havana sequence, while Brando himself soloed on "Luck Be A Lady." Sinatra enthusiasts were dismayed by his meager amount of vocalizing. His one solo number was "Adelaide," while he duetted with Vivian Blaine in "Sue Me" and did some ensemble work with Stubby Kaye and Johnny Silver (recruited, along with B.S. Pully, from the original Broadway company) and Dan Dayton.

Stephen Sondheim, who reviewed *Guys and Dolls* in *Films in Review,* felt:

The two major flaws in [the film] are Oliver Smith's sets and Frank Sinatra's performance. Samuel Goldwyn, Joseph Mankiewicz and Mr. Smith apparently couldn't make up their minds whether the scenery should be realistic or stylized. As a result, they have the disadvantages of both, and these disadvantages work against the very special nature of Runyonesque story-telling . . . Sinatra ambles through his role as though he were about to laugh at the jokes in the script (and) sings on pitch, but colorlessly—Sam Levene sang off-pitch, but acted while he sang. Sinatra's lackadaisical performance, his careless and left-handed attempt at characterization, not only harm the picture immeasurably, but indicate an alarming lack of professionality.

Sondheim observed, though, that

Brando . . . acts with personality and conviction and sings pleasantly; Jean Simmons is surprisingly appealing as Sarah Brown, a part with almost no potential . . . both could give lessons to most of the more polished voices in Hollywood on how to *act* a lyric. The real hero of the picture is Stubby Kaye (who) does more to create the atmosphere of Runyon's New York than all the scenery lumped together.

Time called *Guys and Dolls* "a Sam-dandy of a picture show, a 158-minute blur of unmitigated energy, and one of the year's best musicals." Then its critic lost his enthusiasm, saying:

Faithful in detail, the picture is false to the original in its feeling. The Broadway production was as intimate as a hotfoot; the Goldwyn movie takes a blowtorch full of Eastman color and stereophonic sound to get the same reaction . . . (but) as a whole, the show is strong enough to carry its weak parts.

Newsweek wrote:

People will probably go to this very expensive movie simply to watch Marlon Brando dance and to hear him sing. They will learn that at times he has a provocative husk to his voice; as a dancer, he executes only a few simple ballroom steps. Also of interest is the steady evolution of the onetime quavery-voiced Ophelia, Jean Simmons, into a girl of normal impulses . . . The most resounding message of the movie, though, is that even the most expensive talent can go flat in the presence of $1,000,000.

Hollis Alpert, in *Saturday Review,* acclaimed *Guys and Dolls* as "one of the great ones," noting:

I am not quite sure whether it is the Goldwyn touch or the Mankiewicz stamp that has been put on [the film], but of one thing I'm certain: the two should collaborate more often. As it turns out, Mr. Goldwyn distinguished himself all along the line in his casting, but he had a stroke of luck in getting Joseph L. Mankiewicz to do the screenplay and directing. Or was it pure and simple canniness?

(Curiously, critic Alpert then erroneously credited Michael *Todd*, rather than Michael *Kidd*, with the staging and choreography!)

In the *New York Herald Tribune,* William K. Zinsser raved:

The biggest news is this: Goldwyn gambles and wins! It's more than "a probable twelve to seven" that *Guys and Dolls* will be one of the most popular movies ever made. The film retains the purity of the Broadway musical (and) Joseph L. Mankiewicz, writer and director of the movie, has kept most of the funny lines and added some of his own.

Critic Zinsser's opinion of the acting:

Brando and Sinatra look too young for their roles as veteran gamblers . . . but this is quibbling. Miss Sim-mons and Miss Blaine are irresistible and the other actors are duly Runyonesque, and Mankiewicz has caught the tenderness that lies unsuspected beneath their striped coats, pointed lapels and black shirts. *Guys and Dolls* is a superior musical.

Bosley Crowther determined:

Samuel Goldwyn was playing an odds-on favorite when he plunked $5,000,000 to make a film of *Guys and Dolls* (and) the gamble this time has paid off richly. *Guys and Dolls* romped across the finish line in its premiere well in front, where it rightly belongs. Under the guidance of director Mankiewicz . . . this musical comedy classic gets a great ride all the way.

Crowther included the film in the "second ten" of his year-end "Ten Best" list.

To cover his bet, Goldwyn arranged for *Guys and Dolls* to get story breaks in every major consumer magazine as well as *Life* and *Time* covers. The gamble paid off at slightly less than 2 to 1. *Guys and Dolls* has grossed $8,000,000, placing it second among Goldwyn's all-time money-makers. At the Oscar sweepstakes, though, it received only three nominations: Best Art/Set Design (color picture); Best Costume Design; Best Color Cinematography.

Marlon Brando, Jean Simmons, Frank Sinatra and Vivian Blaine in Guys and Dolls.

Frank Sinatra and Vivian Blaine in Guys and Dolls.

Jean Simmons and Marlon Brando in Guys and Dolls.

Jean Simmons and Marlon Brando in Guys and Dolls.

80 PORGY AND BESS (1959)

Directed by Otto Preminger; screenplay, N. Richard Nash; based on the musical play *Porgy and Bess* by DuBose Heyward and George and Ira Gerswhin; the novel by DuBose Heyward, and the play *Porgy* by DeBose and Dorothy Heyward; music director, Andre Previn; associate music director, Ken Darby; choreographer, Hermes Pan; photographer, Leon Shamroy; editor, Daniel Mandell; art directors, Serge Krizman and Joseph Wright; costumes, Irene Sharaff. Running time, 146 plus intermission. Todd-AO and Technicolor. Released by Columbia Pictures. Premiere: Warner Theater, New York, 6/24/59

THE CAST:

Porgy, Sidney Poitier (singing dubbed by Robert McFerrin); *Bess,* Dorothy Dandridge (singing dubbed by Adele Addison); *Sporting Life,* Sammy Davis Jr.; *Maria,* Pearl Bailey; *Crown,* Brock Peters; *Clara,* Diahann Carroll (singing dubbed by Loulie Jean Norman); *Serena,* Ruth Attaway (singing dubbed by Inez Matthews); *Jake,* Leslie Scott; *Peter,* Clarence Muse; *Annie,* Everdinne Wilson; *Robbins,* Joel Fluellen; *Mingo,* Earl Jackson; *Nelson,* Moses LaMarr; *Lily,* Margaret Hairston; *Jim,* Ivan Dixon; *Scipio,* Antoine Durousseau; *Strawberry Woman,* Helen Thigpen; *Elderly Man,* Vince Townsend Jr.; *Undertaker,* William Walker; *Frazier,* Roy Glenn; *Coroner,* Maurice Manson; *Detective,* Claude Akins.

Musical numbers: (sung by:)
Overture (Andre Previn and Orchestra)
"Summertime" (Diahann Carroll and chorus)
"Crap Game" (Joel Fluellen, Diahann Carroll and chorus)
"A Woman Is a Sometime Thing" (Leslie Scott, Earl Jackson, Sammy Davis Jr., Diahann Carroll and chorus)
"Honey Man's Call" (Clarence Muse)
"They Pass By Singing" (Sidney Poitier)
"Yo' Mammy's Gone" (Earl Jackson)
"Oh Little Stars" (Sidney Poitier)
"Gone, Gone, Gone" (Leslie Scott and chorus)
"Porgy's Prayer" (Sidney Poitier)
"My Man's Gone Now" (Ruth Attaway and chorus)
"The Train Is At the Station" (Dorothy Dandridge and chorus)
"I Got Plenty O' Nuttin'" (Sidney Poitier and chorus)

"Bess, You Is My Woman Now" (Sidney Poitier and Dorothy Dandridge)
"Oh, I Can't Sit Down" (Pearl Bailey, Sammy Davis Jr. and chorus)
"I Ain't Got No Shame" (Chorus)
"It Ain't Necessarily So" (Sammy Davis Jr. and chorus)
Reprise: "I Ain't Got No Shame" (Chorus)
"What You Want Wid Bess?" (Dorothy Dandridge and Brock Peters)
"It Take a Long Pull To Get There" (Leslie Scott and men)
"De Police Put Me In" (Clarence Muse)
"Time and Time Again" (Ruth Attaway)
"Strawberry Woman's Call" (Helen Thigpen)
"Crab Man's Call" (Vince Townsend Jr.)
"I Loves You, Porgy" (Dorothy Dandridge and Sidney Poitier)
"Oh, De Lawd Shake de Heaven" (Chorus)
Reprise: "Summertime" (Diahann Carroll and chorus)
"Dere's Somebody Knockin' At de Do'" (Earl Jackson and chorus)
"A Red-Headed Woman" (Brock Peters)
"Clara, Don't You Be Downhearted" (Chorus)
Reprise: "Summertime" (Dorothy Dandridge)
"There's A Boat Dat's Leavin' Soon For New York" (Sammy Davis Jr.)
"Good Mornin' Sistuh" (Chorus)
"Bess, Oh Where's My Bess?" (Sidney Poitier)
Finale: "I'm On My Way" (Sidney Poitier and chorus)

At age seventy-five, Samuel Goldwyn, the last of the pioneer-moguls, with the passing of his long-ago partner, Cecil B. DeMille, made his final picture. The project: a stupendous cinemazation of *Porgy and Bess,* on which Goldwyn would lavish both money and care (as usual), survive crises (as usual), and have the ultimate word (as usual). To direct such a production, long conceded by the industry to Goldwyn as the only man capable of doing justice to this undertaking, he engaged Rouben Mamoulian, who had staged both the original Broadway version of DuBose and Dorothy Heyward's dramatic play, *Porgy,* in October 1927 and the first musical version of *Porgy and Bess* by DuBose Heyward and George and Ira Gershwin eight years later.

For the male lead in his film extravaganza, Goldwyn determined that a strong, "name" black actor was essential. The only black "star" at the time was Harry Belafonte, who was then on the verge of placing his film acting career in limbo. Belafonte declined Goldwyn's invitation to play Porgy. Goldwyn was then made aware of Sidney Poitier, an intense, dynamic young actor who, on the basis of his recently completed, but as yet unseen role in *The Defiant Ones,* was on the threshold of stardom. Goldwyn sent out the word; Poitier heard it. Then, supposedly on the advice of the black community's various pressure groups, many of which considered the characters and denizens of Catfish Row as written in the 1925 novel derogatory to the race, Poitier suddenly asked to be released from his commitment. Goldwyn honored the request, but remained undaunted in his plans to film what he considered the greatest of all American musicals.

By early summer of 1958, the search for another black actor of Poitier's intensity, power and stature (in the non-physical sense, considering the character of the crippled Porgy) had proved fruitless. Goldwyn once again summoned Poitier, and with director Mamoulian at his side, pressured the actor into reconsidering the role. Following a lengthy session, in which the cajoling Goldwyn used all of his formidable persuasive powers to overcome Poitier's reservations, and according to *Life* Magazine, promised the actor a film that would always be identified with him during what Goldwyn envisioned as a long, illustrious career, an enthused and totally flattered Poitier leaped to his feet and gushed: "I will come to you completely pure, virginal and unprejudiced."

Poitier himself said, in a 1959 *Films and Filming* interview,

> Other roles may come and go, but I expect the role of Porgy to stay with me for a lifetime. Ten years from now, somebody will call out "Porgy" and I'll stand up and salute and say "Yes Sir" . . . so whatever enthusiasm I put into forthcoming parts—and believe me, I try to give all my ability and energy to all of them— I still feel that Porgy is the one I may be considered by. I couldn't be happier if it turns out that way.

Goldwyn's next problem: a Bess for Porgy. Dorothy Dandridge, frequent costar of Harry Belafonte, was Hollywood's ranking black leading lady and really the only actress Goldwyn considered, even if her Bess was to be a conception remarkably similar to that of her previous role in *Carmen Jones.* With Porgy and Bess both cast, Goldwyn was faced with the decision of singing voices for his acting leads, Miss Dandridge was a nightclub singer, but lacked an operatic range, and she had

been dubbed in *Carmen Jones.* Poitier, with no musical training at all, was at even more of a disadvantage. Robert McFerrin was engaged to sing the role of Porgy off-camera and Adele Addison would thus sing Bess. The production's other two leads were less difficult to cast, and because of the distinctive styles of the two, both Pearl Bailey as Maria and Sammy Davis Jr. as Sporting Life (Davis had actively campaigned for the role) were allowed to do their own singing. Goldwyn had attempted to get Cab Calloway for Sporting Life, the role he had played in the lavish U.S. State Department-sponsored tour of *Porgy and Bess* in the mid-fifties, but Calloway was unavailable (although he is featured on the soundtrack recording from the Goldwyn film, replacing Sammy Davis Jr. because of contractual commitments). The role of the vicious Crown was given to Brock Peters (who did his own singing), while singer Diahann Carroll, as Clara, was dubbed by Loulie Jean Norman.

2 July 1958 was set as the starting date for the production. Hours before the cameras were to begin rolling, the entire Catfish Row set and the complete *Porgy and Bess* wardrobe went up in flames at a loss of $2.5 million. Goldwyn immediately issued instructions to replace everything. Twenty-five days later, he discharged Rouben Mamoulian as director of the film, paying him his full $75,000 salary and writing it off simply as a difference of conceptual interpretation. Otto Preminger, who had replaced Mamoulian on *Laura* in 1944, was installed by Goldwyn in the director's chair. Previously Preminger had worked with Dorothy Dandridge, Pearl Bailey, Brock Peters and Diahann Carroll in *Carmen Jones.*

The Mamoulian dismissal sparked a minor confrontation between the Screen Directors' Guild and Samuel Goldwyn. The Guild was finally obliged to make a decision, particularly as to which director would receive screen credit. Mamoulian already had worked on *Porgy and Bess* for eight months, handling all of the prerecording and the singing, but since he had not actually shot a foot of film because of casting problems and the fire, the Guild decided against his receiving credit on the final print.

Despite the somewhat stagey mounting by Preminger and the fact that both of the leads appear too well scrubbed and a shade too urbane to have been festering in Catfish Row, *Porgy and Bess* offers a fitting hallmark to the Goldwyn career and received enthusiastic notices, aside from the observations that the legendary American folk opera had become in 1959 "Samuel Goldwyn's *Porgy and Bess*" just as, four years earlier, the delightful Damon Runyon musical had emerged on the screen as "Samuel Goldwyn's *Guys and Dolls.*"

Sammy Davis Jr. strutted Sporting Life and made him the venal figure DuBose Heyward had meant him to be, despite some unintentional "50s shuckin' and jivin," and Pearl Bailey managed to sublimate Pearl Bailey and become for the occasion Maria, the cookshop woman, whose personality alone could light up Catfish Row. The murderous Crown was truly malevolent in the hands of Brock Peters, both in the killing of Robbins and the rape of Bess, and his stunning singing voice matched his exceptional performance. The hurricane sequence swept across the Todd-AO screen as forcefully as did the climactic scene in Goldwyn's *The Hurricane* more than two decades earlier.

In short, every penny of the original $5,000,000 (plus the extra $1.5 million on which Goldwyn gambled when deciding that nothing less than the expansive Todd-AO process would do this production justice) lavished on *Porgy and Bess* showed. With advertising and promotion expenses, the break-even gross was placed at $15,000,000, with all profits earmarked for Goldwyn's various foundation charities. To date, *Porgy and Bess* has not recouped its original costs and does not appear on *Variety's* annual chart of "All-Time Box Office Champs," those films grossing more than $4,000,000.

While *Time* complained of the film's "cinematic monotony" and felt that "Otto Preminger had directed most of it as though it were a Bayreuth production of *Gotterdammerung*," most critics praised Goldwyn for creating such superior entertainment if not for simply bringing the memorable Gershwin score to the screen. Bosley Crowther found *Porgy and Bess*

a truly magnificent motion picture and more than a credit to the original and oft-revived folk opera . . . a stunning, exciting and moving film, packed with human emotions and cheerful and mournful melodies. It bids fair to be as much of a classic on the screen as it is on the stage.

(*The New York Times* listed it among the Ten Best Films of 1959.)

Walter Lowe, writing in *The Christian Science Monitor,* said:

Let it be to the credit of Samuel Goldwyn, to whom the motion picture screen already owes a good deal, that he has filmed *Porgy and Bess* without trying to make it something that it is not. Let it be to his credit too that he managed to create a film that is in impeccable taste and that neatly sidesteps some of the more obvious pitfalls of perpetuating racial stereotypes.

In the *New York Herald Tribune,* Paul V. Beckley praised Goldwyn for "a rich and devoted filming," and commented that "the work deserves the respect as one of the most ambitious and, frankly, one of the finest cinematic versions of an opera, and even its flaws ought to be seen in the light of the serious magnitude of the task its makers have set themselves."

Variety reviewed:

The two big come-on names here are Gershwin and Goldwyn. A classic has received the high-gloss treatment and should find plenty of admirers . . . Time alone can report whether the screening of the folk opera adds up to a selective appeal or a universal-appeal feature. The end result may fall between.

Porgy and Bess won three Academy Awards: Best Scoring of a Musical Picture (Andre Previn and Ken Darby), Best Costume Design (Irene Sharaff), Best Sound Recording (Gordon Sawyer).

Maurice Manson, Sammy Davis Jr., Claude Akins, Dorothy Dandridge and Sidney Poitier in Porgy and Bess.

Sidney Poitier, Dorothy Dandridge and Pearl Bailey in
Porgy and Bess.

Dorothy Dandridge and Sidney Poitier in Porgy and Bess.

Sammy Davis as Sportin' Life in Porgy and Bess.

PART 3
A Gallery of Goldwyn Stars

Goldwyn Star Gallery (following name, is number of Goldwyn films in which acted)

Ronald Colman (18)

Vilma Banky (7)

Eddie Cantor (6)

Miriam Hopkins (4)

Anna Sten (3)

Joel McCrea (7)

Fredric March (3)

Merle Oberon (5)

David Niven (9)

Gary Cooper (8)

Sigrid Gurie (1)

Andrea Leeds (4)

Walter Brennan (10)

Dana Andrews (8)

Teresa Wright (4)

Farley Granger (7)

Danny Kaye (6)

Joan Evans (3)

Virginia Mayo (7)

APPENDIX:
THE GOLDWYN CRAFTSMEN

Samuel Goldwyn

George Fitzmaurice (directed 11)

William Wyler (directed 8)

George Barnes (photographed 17)

Gregg Toland (photographed 37)

Viola Lawrence (edited 7)

Sherman A. Todd (edited 9)

Daniel Mandell (edited 27)

Alfred Newman (scored, conducted or arranged 36)

The peerless team of William Wyler and Gregg Toland (on the set of Wuthering Heights*).*

RADIO VERSIONS OF
SAMUEL GOLDWYN FILMS

Lux Radio Theatre (CBS)

"The Dark Angel" (6/22/36) with Merle Oberon, Herbert Marshall

"Tonight or Never" (1/25/37) with Jeanette MacDonald, Melvyn Douglas

"Dodsworth" (4/12/37) with Walter Huston, Nan Sunderland

"Dodsworth" (10/4/37) with Walter Huston, Nan Sunderland

"Stella Dallas" (10/11/37) with Barbara Stanwyck, John Boles, Anne Shirley

"Arrowsmith" (10/25/37) with Spencer Tracy, Fay Wray

"Come and Get It" (11/15/37) with Edward Arnold, Anne Shirley

"These Three" (12/6/37) with Barbara Stanwyck, Errol Flynn, Mary Astor

"Beloved Enemy" (12/27/37) with Madeleine Carroll, Brian Aherne

"Wuthering Heights" (9/18/39) with Barbara Stanwyck, Brian Aherne, Ida Lupino

"The Westerner" (9/23/40) with Gary Cooper, Walter Brennan, Doris Davenport

"Wuthering Heights" (11/4/40) with Ida Lupino, Basil Rathbone

"The Cowboy and the Lady" (1/20/41) with Gene Autry, Merle Oberon

"Ball of Fire" (6/1/42) with Barbara Stanwyck, Fred MacMurray

"The Pride of the Yankees" (10/4/43) with Gary Cooper, Virginia Bruce, Edgar Buchanan

"Wonder Man" (3/25/45) with Danny Kaye, Virginia Mayo

"The Bishop's Wife" (12/19/49) with Tyrone Power, Jane Greer, David Niven

"My Foolish Heart" (8/28/50) with Dana Andrews, Susan Hayward

"Our Very Own" (6/11/51) with Farley Granger, Diana Lynn, Joan Evans

"The Bishop's Wife" (5/11/53) with Cary Grant, Phyllis Thaxter

"Our Very Own" (10/5/53) with Robert Wagner, Terry Moore, Joan Evans

"Wuthering Heights" (9/14/54) with Merle Oberon, Cameron Mitchell

Screen Guild Theatre (CBS)

"Come and Get It" (3/15/42) with Edward Arnold, Walter Brennan, Laraine Day

"Ball of Fire" (11/30/42) with Paulette Goddard, Kay Kyser

"Dodsworth" (2/1/43) with Bette Davis, Walter Huston, Nan Sunderland

"They Got Me Covered" (2/15/43) with Bob Hope, Dorothy Lamour

"The North Star" (1/3/44) with Anne Baxter, Farley Granger, Walter Huston, Ann Harding, Jane Withers

"The Dark Angel" (5/8/44) with Merle Oberon, Ronald Colman

"The Nervous Wreck" ("Whoopee!") (8/14/44) with Edward Everett Horton, Mary Astor

"The Princess and the Pirate" (3/26/45) with Bob Hope, Virginia Mayo

"The Little Foxes" (8/6/45) with Bette Davis, Teresa Wright, Otto Kruger, Charles Dingle

"Wuthering Heights" (2/25/46) with Merle Oberon, Cornel Wilde, Reed Hadley

"The Cowboy and the Lady" (4/29/46) with Olivia de Havilland, Gregory Peck, Patsy Moran

"Barbary Coast" (6/24/46) with Mary Astor, Charles Bickford

"Arrowsmith" (9/16/46) with Gregory Peck, Barbara Britton, Jean Hersholt

"The Best Years of Our Lives" (5/19/47) with Dana Andrews, Virginia Mayo, Warren William, Cathy O'Donnell, John Beal

"The Secret Life of Walter Mitty" (10/3/47) with Danny Kaye, Virginia Mayo

"The Bishop's Wife" (3/1/48) with Cary Grant, Loretta Young, David Niven

"The Best Years of Our Lives" (11/24/48) with Myrna Loy, Fredric March, Teresa Wright

"Enchantment" (3/34/49) with David Niven, Teresa Wright, Jayne Meadows

"The Cowboy and the Lady" (4/20/50) with Ginger Rogers, Macdonald Carey

The Campbell Playhouse (CBS)

"Arrowsmith" (2/3/39) with Helen Hayes, Orson Welles

"The Hurricane" (11/5/39) with Mary Astor

"Dodsworth" (11/26/39) with Walter Huston, Fay Bainter, Nan Sunderland

"Come and Get It" (12/31/39) with Frances Dee

"The Nervous Wreck" ("Whoopee!") (4/4/40) with Eddie Cantor

"Tarnish" (6/6/40) with Margaret Lindsay, Donald Briggs

Louella Parsons' Hollywood Hotel (CBS)

"Dead End" (8/20/37) with Joel McCrea, Andrea Leeds, Humphrey Bogart

Philip Morris Playhouse (CBS)

"The Little Foxes" (10/10/41) with Tallulah Bankhead

"Wuthering Heights" (10/17/41) with Sylvia Sidney, Raymond Massey
"Ball of Fire" (10/2/42) with Barbara Stanwyck, Gary Cooper

Textron Theatre (CBS)
"Arrowsmith" (11/16/44) with Helen Hayes, Myron McCormick
"Arrowsmith" (10/6/45) with Helen Hayes, Dean Jagger
"Wuthering Heights" (11/24/45) with Helen Hayes, Martin Gabel

Hollywood Players (CBS)
"Pride of the Yankees" (9/24/46) with Joseph Cotten

The Star and the Story (CBS)
"The Pride of the Yankees" (2/13/44) with Walter Pidgeon, Teresa Wright
"Wuthering Heights" (3/5/44) with Walter Pidgeon, Merle Oberon
"Arrowsmith" (7/2/44) with Walter Pidgeon, Ruth Warrick, Otto Kruger

Matinee Theater (CBS)
"Wuthering Heights" (10/22/44) with Victor Jory

Stories America Loves (CBS)
"Dodsworth" (12/8/41–1/9/42) (serialized version of the film)

This Is Hollywood (CBS)
"The Best Years of Our Lives" (3/15/47) with George Brent, Dana Andrews, Harold Russell, Cathy O'Donnell
"The Kid from Brooklyn" (3/22/47) with Danny Kaye, Virginia Mayo

Studio One (CBS)
"Dodsworth" (5/27/47) with Santos Ortega, Anne Burr, Everett Sloane
"Wuthering Heights" (9/30/47) with Fletcher Markel, Miriam Wolfe, Anne Burr
"Dodsworth" (2/3/48) with Walter Huston, Anne Burr

Screen Director's Playhouse (NBC)
"The Best Years of Our Lives" (4/17/48) with Dana Andrews
"Pride of the Yankees" (9/30/48) with Gary Cooper, Frank Lovejoy
"Wuthering Heights" (8/9/51) with Dorothy McGuire, James Mason, Pamela Kellino
"Raffles" (9/14/51) with Douglas Fairbanks, Jr.
"Enchantment" (1/24/52) with Joseph Cotten, Mala Powers

Ford Theatre (CBS)
"Wuthering Heights" (4/1/49) with Montgomery Clift, Joan Lorring

Theatre Guild on the Air (NBC)
"Dead End" (2/24/46) with Richard Conte, Joan Tetzel, Alan Baxter
"Dodsworth" (10/6/46) with Walter Huston, Jessie Royce Landis
"The Little Foxes" (1/4/48) with Agnes Moorehead, Thomas Mitchell, Zachary Scott
"Street Scene" (12/11/49) with Richard Conte, Diana Lynn, Shirley Booth
"The Milky Way" ("The Kid from Brooklyn") (3/26/50) with Danny Kaye, Shirley Booth
"Arrowsmith" (12/16/51) with Tyrone Power, Loretta Young

TELEVISION ADAPTATIONS OF SAMUEL GOLDWYN FILMS

"Wuthering Heights" with John Baragray, Louisa Horton, Ethel Griffies and Vaughan Taylor. Kraft Television Theater, NBC, 11/24/48
"Arrowsmith" with Van Heflin and June Dayton. Robert Montgomery Presents, NBC, 10/9/50
"Dodsworth" with Ruth Chatterton and Walter Abel. Prudential Family Playhouse, CBS, 10/24/50
"Wuthering Heights" with Charlton Heston and Mary Sinclair. Studio One, CBS, 10/30/50
"The Bishop's Wife" with Martha Scott, Richard Derr and Philip Bourneuf. Robert Montgomery Presents, NBC, 4/23/51
"Wuthering Heights" with William Prince and Meg Mundy. Broadway Television Theater, 4/6/53
"Arrowsmith" with Richard Kelly, June Dayton, Joseph Wiseman, Biff McGuire and James Broderick. Kraft Television Theater, ABC, 5/6/54
"Cynara" with E.G. Marshall, Ruth Matteson, Murray Matheson, Joanne Woodward (as Doris), Barbara Barrie and Patricia Englund. Pond Theater, ABC, 5/12/55
"Wuthering Heights" with Richard Boone, Peggy Webber and Sean McClory. NBC Matinee Theater, NBC, 11/30/55
"Arrowsmith" with Grant Williams and Meg Randall. NBC Matinee Theater, NBC, 12/5/55
"Dodsworth" with Fredric March, Claire Trevor (Emmy performance) and Geraldine Fitzgerald. Producers' Showcase, NBC, 4/30/56
"The Little Foxes" with Greer Garson, Franchot Tone, Sidney Blackmer, E.G. Marshall and Eileen Heckart. Hallmark Hall of Fame, NBC, 12/16/56
"Wuthering Heights" with Tom Tryon, Barbara Rush

and Sean McClory. NBC Matinee Theater, NBC, 4/8/57 (first color adaptation of a Goldwyn film)

"Wuthering Heights" with Richard Burton, Rosemary Harris, Denholm Elliott, Cathleen Nesbitt and Patty Duke. DuPont Show of the Month, CBS, 5/9/58

"Arrowsmith" with Farley Granger, Diane Baker, Oscar Homolka, Francis Lederer, Ivan Dixon and Ellen McRae (later Burstyn). DuPont Show of the Month, CBS, 1/17/60

"Wuthering Heights" with Keith Michell, Claire Bloom and David McCallum. (British) 1962

"Nana" with Katherine Scofield. (British) 1973

"Returning Home" ("The Best Years of Our Lives") with Dabney Coleman, Tom Selleck, James R. Miller, Whitney Blake, Joan Goodfellow, Sherry Jackson and Laurie Walters. ABC Movie of the Week, ABC, 4/29/75

Samuel Goldwyn

INDEX

(Italicized numbers refer to photographs)